POKER PIONEER

The Autobiography of

Tom McEvoy

World Champion & Hall of Famer

Written by Tom McEvoy and Brad Smith

ISBN: 979-8-9900878-0-4 (Paperback Edition)
ISBN: 979-8-9900878-2-8 (Hardcover Edition)
ISBN: 979-8-9900878-1-1 (Ebook Edition)

Library of Congress Control Number: 2024907766

Front cover design concept by Axel Von Kaenel
Front cover photo by Pamela Shandel
Back cover photo by Clark McCarrell Photography
Interior design by Integrative Ink

To my grandchildren, Marissa and Chayse.
I hope you are as proud of your grandpa as I am of you both.

And to my children, my siblings, and their spouses.
My love for you all is boundless.

TOM McEVOY: POKER PIONEER

- ♦ First to win WSOP Main Event via winning a satellite tournament.

- ♣ First to publicly play poker against a computer—and win.

- ♥ First to write instructional books on poker tournament strategy.

- ♠ Among the first, in 1985, to advocate to the WSOP against top-heavy tournament payouts and for paying more players.

- ♦ Among the first, in 1988, to advocate to the WSOP to pause tournament play after 12 hours and resume the next day.

- ♣ One of the principal leaders in the poker tournament no-smoking petition drive.

- ♥ First to run a smoke-free poker tournament in Las Vegas.

- ♠ First Main Event champion hired to run the WSOP (then fired the day before it started).

- ♦ First official online pro host of PokerStars.

- ♣ Won the first and only WSOP Champion of Champions Binion Cup, topping the field of 20 former Main Event champions.

- ♥ Played with, and beat, the best players of his time on the planet.

- ♠ Authored or coauthored 14 poker strategy books.

Tom to me is a legend of the game. He definitely did a lot in his time to advance poker and make it better for all of us.
—*Matt Savage, Executive Tour Director of the World Poker Tour*

Tom approached poker much more like a business and viewed the game more in an academic way.
—*Jack Binion*

Tom has perfect honor, ethics, and morals. And that's important. Not every champion in our world is pure. Tom has earned my respect.
—*Phil Hellmuth*

One of the things he did for everybody probably saved my life. He was one of the main forces against smoking in the poker room.
—*T. J. Cloutier*

Tom has always been a gentleman, at the poker table and outside, win or lose. His reputation in the poker world is definitely impeccable.
—*Mori Eskandani, President of PokerGO*

CONTENTS

PROLOGUE

Tom McEvoy is a poker pioneer. Without his influence, the game as we enjoy it today wouldn't be the same.

Five decades ago, he moved his family of five across the country to replace his career in accounting with a career as a professional poker player, way before it was cool or even acceptable. His own parents kept their eldest son's new taboo line of work a secret for years.

At the time, Tom viewed poker differently than most. He didn't have a gambling bug; he had a poker passion. His goal wasn't to become a riverboat gambler; it was to support his family doing what he loved. In 1979, that was a unique perspective. And to virtually everyone he knew in his home state of Michigan, Tom was deranged. But he persisted.

In pursuing his goal, he discovered two things about poker that were relatively new and exciting—Texas Hold'em and poker tournaments—and he practiced and honed his skills in both like he was working on a master's degree. Except there was no poker university, no established curriculum. So, he studied hard on the only felt-topped school of poker available—the tournaments of Las Vegas, Reno, Gardena, and Atlantic City.

Then, against the wishes of his peers, he shared the strategies and lessons he had learned in the graduate school of hard knocks:

what the bruises of defeats and the elations of victories had taught him. He literally wrote the first successful books on tournament poker and helped educate an entire generation.

Over his 50-year poker adventure, Tom has won the WSOP Main Event, led the drive to end smoking in poker rooms, and earned over $3 million. He has known and successfully competed with most of the top poker pros who, alongside him, have been enshrined in the Poker Hall of Fame. Twenty-six years after becoming World Champion, he won the first and only Binion Cup, besting a field of the 20 living World Series of Poker Main Event winners.

It's often been noted that in the early days of tournament poker, the fields were smaller. The fields are always smaller when you are breaking new ground. Wouldn't you like to know more about what those early days, the players, and the poker culture were like?

Now you can.

FOREWORD

by Phil Hellmuth

High Honor and "Health Points"

To my man Tom McEvoy, who has maintained the highest honor and integrity for 40 years in the poker world: Tom, we all thank you for those extra "Health Points!" Folks, the vast majority of those in our poker world do not know this: We all owe a debt of gratitude to the Poker Hall of Famer Tom McEvoy for leading the charge (along with Kasey Castle and Paul Ladanyi) on eliminating smoking at the tables. For those interested in more information, Google "The Smoking Petition Tom McEvoy." Folks, I am old enough to remember the days when I sat down at the poker table with "chain smokers" (I still remember who the chain smokers were!), who smoked one cigarette after another for hours on end. I paid close attention to whether I was sitting downwind of the steady stream of nasty-smelling secondhand smoke, doh! If I was downwind, then I would lean forward or back in my chair to avoid the brunt of the foul-smelling stream!

I first met Tom in 1986, and we hit it off immediately. Before I met Tom, I knew two things about him: Tom was a World Champion of Poker and Tom had an impeccable reputation! Of course, that was rare! I mean, there was only one World Champion of Poker crowned per year, and not everyone in the poker world owns that kind of perfect reputation. I quickly found out that in addition to his high ethics and honor, Tom was a super-nice guy who was kind to everyone and treated everybody with respect. One thing that we had in common is that we were both from the Midwest. Generally speaking, in my experience, I have found Midwesterners to be very nice people, and Tom was no exception. Back then, Tom was "New School," and of course, now, in 2024, Tom is "Old School."

What else can I say about Tom? 1) He has perfect honor and ethics (which he is proud of and sets a great example for all poker players); 2) he has won four WSOP (World Series of Poker) bracelets; 3) he is a World Champion of Poker; 4) he is in the Poker Hall of Fame; and 5) he is beloved in the poker world. This list above alone is remarkable! Oh, how about this: Tom has authored and coauthored 14 excellent books (four with T. J. Cloutier) on how to play poker. Tom's book are:

- *How to Win at Poker Tournaments (1985)*
- *Tournament Poker (1995)*
- *No-Limit and Pot-Limit Hold'em (1997)*
- *Championship Stud: 7-Card Stud, Stud 8 or Better, Razz (1998)*
- *Championship Omaha : Omaha High-Low, Omaha High and Pot-Limit Omaha (1999)*
- *Championship Hold'em (2000)*
- *Beat Texas Hold'em ((2002)*
- *The Championship Table: At the World Series of Poker (2003)*
- *Championship Satellite Strategy (2003)*
- *No-Limit Texas Hold'em: The New Players Guide to Winning Poker's Biggest Game (2004)*

- *Championship Tournament Poker (2004)*
- *How to Win No-Limit Hold'em Tournaments (2005)*
- *Win Your Way into Big Money Hold'em Tournaments (2005)*
- *107 Hold'em Tournament Hands (2011)*

Folks, here's one little-known fact about our boy Tom McEvoy. Tom destroyed—shot them up with an actual gun in the desert—many of his trophies! I am looking forward to reading about that story. And I am looking forward to learning about how Tom came from Grand Rapids, Michigan, and then conquered the poker world in 1983 by winning two WSOP Bracelets, including the Main Event! I look forward to reading along with you about Tom's ups and downs over 40-plus years as a professional poker player. Must have been one hell of a ride!

—*Phil Hellmuth*

PREFACE

by Marcia McEvoy Madden, PhD.

My brother Tom is, well, complicated.

My family—my parents, siblings, and I—have always been pretty protective of my dear brother Tom, and here's why. He's a really good person with a generous heart, but he has very terrible judgment about other people. I'm a licensed psychologist with a doctorate in psychology, and I diagnosed him privately many years ago as having a mild form of Aspergers Syndrome, on the lower autism spectrum. Tom has significant challenges picking up social cues, so in situations that require "street smarts," he is frequently socially awkward and oblivious. He can't correctly evaluate who to trust, and time and time again over the years he has trusted the wrong people. He has systematically been taken advantage of by a whole slew of grifters, opportunists, liars, cheats, and ne'er-do-wells because he does not have good radar about people's true intentions and motivations. He is pretty easily fooled by superficial kindness and fake friendliness.

I would describe Tom as selectively focused. What he lacks in ability to pick up social cues is counterweighted by his ability to easily pick up cues most people miss when playing competitive games like poker or backgammon. He is super bright, and he has amazing focus when he is competing. For example, he is a gifted, agile table tennis player with excellent eye-hand coordination and quick reflexes that require a ton of concentration. When he wants to concentrate, and it is very important to him, he can be laser focused. But in normal interpersonal situations—not so much.

Tom has many true friends who are very loyal to him, who totally understand his idiosyncrasies and love him anyway, like his family. But some of his social and emotional behavior might, if you didn't know him very well, seem rude or inappropriate. For instance, at a party he will often disappear after 30 minutes to take a nap or read a book in another room. And it never occurs to him that that is a strange thing to do. We all just accept him and love him for who he is.

—Marcia McEvoy Madden

Poker is not a matter of life and death.
It's much more important than that.
—Unknown

INTRODUCTION

by Tom McEvoy

Hi, my name is Tom McEvoy. Nice to meet you.

My life has revolved around professional poker—the game itself and the people associated with it—for close to half a century. And just as there are multiple kinds of poker games, there are multiple kinds of poker people. The good, the bad, and the ugly; I have met, known, befriended, and associated with most of the prominent names in poker over the 50 years of my professional career. You are about to read about many of them and glimpse the impact the complex poker community has had on my life.

For me, it's been a wild up-and-down ride. Feast or famine. Big money and bankruptcy. International fame and local obscurity. Ecstatic highs and depressing lows. A topsy-turvey poker life.

I want to tell you something. I never used to think I was a very interesting guy. But when I look back, I've had just a hell of a career and a fascinating life. When you think of all the great poker players, I might not come to your mind. But I have had my fingers in just about every poker pie you can think of—major tournament champion several times over, author or coauthor of 14 poker strategy books, global poker ambassador, card room and major tournament manager, prop player, seminar speaker, teaching instructor, television personality, player advocate, charity event volunteer, and more. And I was good enough at the game to beat the 20 living Main Event World Champions in 2009 to win the first and only Binion's Cup.

You might say I have a Doctorate in Pokerology. I know what I've accomplished—far more than most who play poker seriously. But I've had monumental failures, too. Fame in poker is a very small, limited thing compared to the rest of the world, and it doesn't always lead to material wealth. I'm not a wealthy man, as measured in money. But in terms of family, friends, and health; in poker jargon, I'm running extremely good. I'm comfortable and I really eat well for a guy of relatively modest means. I have a cozy small home that's nicely furnished. I have managed to get along with my ex-wives, ex-girlfriends, and with my three adult kids. And I have the best and most loyal friends and family anybody could ever have.

Call me old-fashioned if you want to. I'm one of those old-fashioned people to whom the truth still matters. So, I want to tell my life story like it was. Most of the stuff that happened to me is fair game. The way I see it, it's a lot more interesting when you tell the truth about the good stuff and the bad stuff. I've never been much of a bullshitter and have always pretty much stuck to the straight and narrow. I'm not going to change now that I'm in my twilight years.

It's often said that life is a journey, not a destination. Well, my journey has been a heck of a ride. It's my life, and welcome to it.

—*Tom McEvoy*
2024

Families are the compass that guides us.
They are the inspiration to reach great heights, and
our comfort when we occasionally falter.

—Brad Henry

CHAPTER 1

The Early Years. How My Family Instilled My Drive to Embark on, and Excel in, a Career in Poker.

I was born November 14, 1944. I had a great childhood, growing up in a Catholic home in Grand Rapids, Michigan, just after World War II. Dad was a veteran, and the GI Bill helped him secure the second house built on the block as the city expanded into the area farmlands. As a kid I used to roam those farms to steal asparagus, which I don't even like, and I usually got caught.

My parents both worked hard, and we never wanted for anything nor missed a meal. Like most guys, I grew up playing the typical sports of the day—baseball, football, basketball—but I never excelled. You could say my middle-class upbringing was typical Americana stuff. But growing up as a McEvoy in Grand Rapids taught me many valuable lessons that helped form the basis for my poker career.

The McEvoy family in Grand Rapids.
Alan, Mom, Marcia, Dad, Steve, and me.

My Dad—the First McEvoy Hall-of-Famer

I am extremely proud of my dad, Sargeant Harry Kirby "Mac" McEvoy Jr., who was born in 1910 and raised in Oak Park, Illinois. A true patriot, he enlisted in the Army at age 31 after the Japanese bombed Pearl Harbor. He was able to opt for the Army Air Corps, which he viewed as a safer way for an "older" guy to serve his country. In the service he discovered he excelled at writing and was stationed stateside in Grand Rapids to write for the Army magazine. He jokingly referred to his "war injury" that occurred when his typewriter fell off the stand and banged up his knee. Later he would write several short stories and even a novel (never published) and several "how-to" books on his hobby. I like to think I inherited my limited writing skills from him. And his sense of humor.

While serving in Grand Rapids, he met Marie Estelle Wright at a dance. The "hot babe" was surrounded by interested GIs, but he summoned the courage to plow his way through the crowd and convince her to bust a move with him. He definitely made a good impression, and about a year later, before he was discharged from the Army, he married my mom on September 25, 1943. I think that made me a Valentine's Day baby. Anyway, it was the first and only marriage for both of them, and they were both 33.

Not long after he was discharged, Dad got a job as a traveling paint salesman for Dutch Boy Paints. His three-state territory took him away many nights, but never for more than a week at a time, and he was home more than he wasn't. He worked that job for almost 30 years, finding comfort in the stability of the income it afforded a married man with four children to raise. I was born in 1944, followed by my brother Steve in 1946, my brother Alan in 1948, and, unexpectedly, my sister Marcia in 1955. Dad had a couple of years of college, Mom none, and they were absolutely determined that all of their children attend and graduate from college. Mission accomplished.

But selling paint wasn't my father's passion. His hobby was making knives, and he was obsessed with every aspect of creating and throwing knives. He used to toil for hours after work in his shop in the basement crafting new throwing knives, many of which he was able to patent, and he developed his own throwing

techniques. Some of his knives were actually used in combat in Vietnam. As his reputation grew, he discovered a great many other enthusiasts and founded the American Knife Throwers' Alliance. He wrote several books on the subject, including *Knife Throwing: A Practical* Guide, which is still considered the most authoritative guide on every aspect of the sport. You can still buy many of his books on knife and tomahawk throwing on Amazon, for which my family still receives royalties to this day. Dad became the first McEvoy Hall-of-Famer when he was inducted into the Cutlery Hall of Fame in 1991. Following in Dad's footsteps was a big part of the reason I was obsessed with getting inducted into the Poker Hall of Fame. I wanted to be recognized like my dad. More on this in Chapter 27.

Dad was not a big risk taker. He was so scared by his vivid memories of growing up during the Depression and what it did to out-of-work families that he was afraid to take a chance on himself. In short, he did not have an ounce of gamble in his system. He started the Tru-Balance Knife Company in 1949 as a hobby/business for fun. But he didn't follow his heart and his passion for his hobby fully until he retired from the paint business, his financial foundation, when he started collecting Social Security at age 62. That's when he embarked on his dream full-time with his knife company, where he found himself making more money than he ever did working for others. He also found more professional happiness and fulfillment in the knife business after he had officially retired from his day job. Dad died in 1993 after enjoying his last 21 years doing what he loved most. This didn't go unnoticed by his eldest son. It was a big factor in my decision not to wait, and to chase my dream at an early age.

My Mom—Bipolar, High-Strung, and Ahead of Her Time

Mom was a trip, and I loved her very much. She approached life with boundless energy and a level of hyperactivity that amazed and inspired me. Mom was a flapper back in the day and never gave up dancing until she was in her late 70s, when she got Alzheimer's and couldn't remember the moves anymore. She was really smart and was the salutatorian of her high school class. She also excelled in the kitchen and was a great cook. I inherited her love of food, but not its preparation. I can burn ice, and without a microwave, I would probably starve.

It was her prowess in the kitchen that led Mom to be among the first to discover Tupperware. She built a business selling the newfangled airtight plastic containers, throwing parties where she presented products to fascinated housewives, and recruited them to join her in her multilevel marketing mission. She worked her business for over 30 years, until she was 78 years old, when only her Alzheimer's could force her to retire. Mom was a dedicated pioneer in a little-known, and not especially respected, profession. Maybe I got part of my desire to be a pro in the then obscure profession of poker from her.

Mom was a super-hyper dynamo that sometimes went off the rails. She yelled and screamed all the time, at everybody, especially at my dad. I don't know how he stood it sometimes, but he did. I inherited a less intense version of her bipolar disorder. I also inherited her stubbornness. She was a fierce lady who got what she wanted and didn't take no for an answer.

Mom was a devout Catholic, and she was the driving force behind the fundraising to eventually build the Parish of the Holy Spirit Church and grade school (that I attended for five years). She prayed the rosary all the time, even when she was driving. That led to several tickets for speeding and erratic driving, so many she once got hauled into court. She tearfully threw herself on the mercy of the court, and the empathetic judge said he wouldn't fine her if she promised not to get another ticket for driving under the influence of praying the rosary. After hearing that verdict, Mom burst into tears. The astonished judge asked why she was so upset. She tearfully admitted she already had gotten another ticket a few days after the one she had just been tried for. Amused but exasperated, the judge let her off.

The funny thing was that when she got pulled over, her first reaction was to let the officer have it at full volume, as she often did with her kids and even her husband. To say it was loud at my house was an understatement. She often let her feelings be known at full volume, but she was fiercely loyal to her family. One time, when I was about 13, Mom got a call from the neighbor, my buddy Jimmy's mom. She was unhappy that I had beaten her son out of his allowance money playing poker and demanded to know what Mom was going to do about it. She didn't hesitate to tell the neighbor that if her son wasn't bright enough not to play poker with me, he probably learned a valuable lesson and got what he deserved, and that while she was not going to have me return the money, she would lay down the law that I was never to play poker for money with Jimmy again. When she hung up, she wiped the smile off my face with a tongue lashing so loud that I swear Jimmy's mom could hear it all the way across the street. Mom didn't shy away from letting her feelings be known. I inherited that, too, just not with all the volume.

My Grandma—My First Poker Coach

Grandma Mary Louise McEvoy was an independent woman long before it was popular, and she had a huge impact on my life. Born in 1882, she lived most of her life where Dad was born in Oak Park, Illinois, a suburb of Chicago. She loved to gamble and drive her stick-shift car. At the ripe young age of 72, she took a tumble and broke her hip . . . at the racetrack betting the horses. But that didn't stop her driving. Well into her 80s, she used to make the three-hour drive east around the southern tip of Lake Michigan to come visit us in Grand Rapids, bringing her own personal card table with her. She would often stay for weeks at a time.

Grandma taught me and my brothers how to play poker. I knew a full house beat a flush before most kids knew their ABCs. I was good at numbers, and the game helped me learn math at a young age. As early as when I was age five, Grandma would set me on her knee and give me a dollar's worth of coins—dimes, nickels, and pennies—and then spend the next few hours winning it back from me. We played all kinds of crazy wild card games. After her racetrack injury, she would sit down on the floor, prop her bum leg up on pillow, and we'd play penny ante (nickel limit) poker for hours. She kept all the money she won back, and I got tired of that, which made me determined to get better at the game. I learned to love the mechanics and strategy of poker and began to hone my skills. The better I got, the longer it took Grandma to win back her money.

Though I couldn't beat my grandmother, I became a shark at an early age, taking first marbles and eventually money from my childhood buddies. By the time I was nine, Grandmother was helping me and my brothers host weekly Saturday poker games with the kids in the neighborhood, where we regularly took their allowances. I'm embarrassed to admit this, but when I was a teenager my friend across the street had a paper route and every week, I'd beat him out of his paper-route money. He couldn't figure out why he was losing every time, but it was because I had been trained by my grandmother. His mom laid down the law that he could no longer play heads-up poker with me, but he begged me to play and swore he wouldn't tell his mom. He loved to play, and he continued to lose to me, but he never ratted me out. We are still friends to this day.

My Siblings—They Got the Brains in the Family

My brothers and sister have led very successful lives—more successful than my own, I must admit. But I'm glad to say we stay in touch often, which goes to show how much love they share for their once wealthy, now poorer poker-pro brother. The feelings are reciprocated, in spades (hearts, diamonds, and clubs, too). I'm very proud of them.

My oldest brother, Steve, was born two years after me in 1946. He was studying to get his master's degree in psychology when Uncle Sam drafted him to serve in Vietnam, where he toiled as a combat medic. Thankfully, he didn't see a lot of combat. He's got a lot of Dad in him, and when he came home, he got into the insurance business. Later, he assisted Dad in the McEvoy family knife company, eventually succeeding our father in the business. He ran the company until the Internet changed the market, and then sold the business in 2017.

Brother Alan came along in 1948. We weren't the closest in age, but I fought with him more than any of my other siblings, maybe because we are so much alike. Alan McEvoy, Ph.D., is Professor of Sociology and Head of the Department of Sociology and Anthropology at Northern Michigan University. He is also an author of several books and articles on the heavy topics of rape, partner violence, child maltreatment, bullying, youth suicide, even gambling addiction. He's a good card player and very competitive because, like me, he was schooled in cards by Grandma McEvoy. He's even played in a few WSOP senior events.

My sister, Marcia McEvoy Madden, joined the family ten years later in 1955. I was pretty much out of the house for her formative years, so I can claim no part of her success. To give you some perspective, she was the flower girl in my first wedding. Marsha earned a Ph.D. in Psychology from the University of Cincinnati, and also went on to coauthor a book and several articles on psychology-related topics with our brother Alan.

So, as you can tell, I grew up with a pretty brainy, competitive bunch.

Me, Steve, Marcia and Alan.

Courage and insanity have a lot in common.
—Tom McEvoy

CHAPTER 2

Boyhood and Bullies. The Young Nerd with Thick Glasses.

Grade school and high school were not the easiest of times for me. Because I was born on November 14, I just barely made the class of 1962. I was one of the youngest in my class, graduating at age 17, when most of my classmates were 18. Had I been born two weeks later, I would have been one of the oldest in the class of 1963. Intellectually I could do the work, but I was immature. Adolescence is bad enough, but the age difference just made it worse. I would have been better off, when I think about it, to have been held back a year.

Growing up, I wasn't exactly large in stature. Admittedly, I was also a bit of an odd duck. I think that gave me an advantage later in my poker career, because I wasn't just like everyone else. We are all unique individuals, but some people conform a little bit more than others, and, well, I was one of those who walked to the tune of his own drummer. So, I was an easy target for bullies. Both boys and girls.

One of the most valuable life lessons I learned in parochial school was that I cannot stand to be bullied and threatened. I was in fourth grade when it was discovered I was nearsighted, and I first got the first of many pairs of coke-bottle glasses, which I would wear until I was 54. No doubt this added to the perception of me as this wimpy little guy people thought they could push around—until they tried. When that happened, I learned another side of me comes out entirely. As you'll see as you accompany me on my life's journey, I have survived some terrifying threats. One person threatened to shoot me. A black belt in karate threatened my life, balling his fist in my face in anger. For some reason I stay reasonably calm in these kinds of situations. Don't ask me why. Courage and insanity are kind of similar.

Please don't think I'm a goody-two-shoes. I'm not. I have a temper, and I lose it sometimes. And I can be a little bit vengeful. You can question my judgment at times, for sure. I've made mistakes and I would do a lot of things differently. But I don't lack for intestinal fortitude. I've been knocked down to the canvas many times, but I always kept getting back up.

I was mercilessly bullied in school. That's part of life. Kids would tease me, and instead of laughing it off and handling it differently, I would get mad. Bullies would get a reaction from me, so they would do it even more. It wasn't just the boys; the girls did it, too. It started in grade school and got worse in my first two years of high school.

I got into a fistfight the day they took our freshman pictures. I was teased for wearing a suitcoat. When I objected, I got a couple of punches in the nose and got blood on my nice clean clothes. I didn't get knocked down though. I learned I could stand up for myself.

Also, as a freshman, in my homeroom I was being picked on cruelly right and left by the guy that was president of our class that year. I was short and this guy was at least a head taller than me. One day, I was walking out of my homeroom with my arms full of books. He was behind me, and he jarred my books loose from my hands, and they scattered all over the floor. We hadn't quite exited the room yet, so the homeroom nun was standing there watching the whole episode. I literally saw red. I turned around and—pow—I hit him right in the face. Right in front of the nun. He did not hit me back. It was a one-punch fight. I got a week's worth of detention. It was worth it, though. He never picked on me again. I wouldn't say we became friends, but he was even nice to me after that. Lesson learned.

I wasn't getting bullied and teased because I was a brainiac. Oh no. I went to West Catholic my first two years of high school, where I was about a C student. I got straight Ds in Latin, fell behind and failed the second semester of geometry, yet managed a few Bs here and there. For my junior and senior years, I changed schools and attended East Catholic. When I started my junior year, I began taking business courses for the first time, and I started making the honor roll.

A nonathlete taking business classes wasn't exactly viewed as studly. In typing class, I beat out all the girls in a contest for a gold medal. I wasn't the fastest typist, just the most accurate. When the teacher announced, "Big upset. McEvoy wins!" the teasing continued, but it became more good-natured. I decided to take a second year of typing. It was a decidedly feminine pursuit—87 girls and three boys. So, as you can imagine, I wasn't overly popular with the ladies. Regardless of the ribbing, I had found my niche. My high school business education allowed me to test out of several courses in accounting, math, and typing at the business school I attended right after high school.

Bullying and teasing be damned, I had developed the courage to take my own path and pursue what made me happy. Later, this would have some questioning my sanity.

Only those who attempt the absurd will achieve the impossible.
—Albert Einstein

CHAPTER 3

My Journey from Grand Rapids to Las Vegas.

I played a little poker in high school with my friends, and a little more in college. I never turned down the opportunity to play in a poker game, because it was in my blood. I won more than I lost, but my poker goal then was more social than financial. This is the point in life where you are thinking about the future, and I wasn't thinking about poker as something I could do for a living.

My first passions. Numbers. And Romance.

Poker had taught me I was good with numbers, and I enjoyed crunching them. So, after two years of excelling (straight As) at high school bookkeeping, I set my sights on accounting as a profession. I was determined to fulfill my parents dream of having a college-graduate son, and my dream of a bachelor's degree in accounting.

After graduating from high school in 1962, I attended a local business college and earned an associate degree in a two-year accounting program. In my last term, I was taking a night class, which was a two-hour course with a much more relaxed atmosphere than day classes, with a break in the middle. That's where I met the future

Mrs. McEvoy, Roberta "Bobbi" Mallory. Bobbi took the initiative to approach me during a night class break, and we got to know each other better. She told me that she had noticed me during the day and thought it might be interesting to get to know me a little better (even though I was very nerdy with thick glasses), but she thought I was kind of cute. One thing led to another. I asked her out, we started dating, and I fell in love with her . . . and vice versa.

This was 1964, and I was in my second year of college at the local business school. My goal was to get my four-year degree, so I went looking for a college that would take my credits. That was Ferris State University, about an hour north of Grand Rapids in Big Rapids, Michigan. During those last two years at Ferris State, I would make the commute home to Grand Rapids almost every weekend to go on dates with Bobbi. Sometimes I'd have the use of a car, sometimes I'd hitchhike. We spent a lot of time together and got to know each other really well.

Once we finished business school, Bobbi started working as an accountant in Grand Rapids. By then it was understood between us that I'd continue on with schooling to get my bachelor's degree, then we would plan our future together. I graduated from college, technically, after the summer term of 1966. That's when I took a three-month extra-credit course as a paid intern with a CPA firm in Grand Rapids. I wanted to be a CPA, and an internship in my field was a good way to pad my resume with some real-life experience. Afterward, I actually got my diploma, a Bachelor of Science degree in accounting, in 1967. During that time, I came to grips with what I thought I wanted to do with the rest of my life. Get an accounting job, get married, and put down roots in Grand Rapids. Bobbi and I got engaged, and after I finished the internship, we got married on June 24, 1967. I was 22 and Bobbi was 24. She told me later she knew if we got married, we would have cute kids, which we did. I married the second girl I'd ever dated.

But it wasn't just Bobbi and accounting that had my attention at Ferris State University. As happens to most collegians, away from home for the first time, my exposure to the world was starting to expand. University life expanded my perspective of a familiar game that would ultimately lead me to Las Vegas.

My second passion: Table tennis. Yep, Ping-Pong.

My folks had a Ping-Pong table in the basement, and my brothers and the neighborhood kids played regularly. By the time high school came along, I could regularly beat all of them—and their friends. So I was no stranger to the sport when I went off to college, and soon discovered there were tables in all the dorms. As incoming students, we dorm residents seemed to gravitate to the tables as a way to socialize and get to know each other. And participate in some friendly competition. I played a lot, traveling from dorm to dorm, challenging and meeting more guys and expanding my circle of friends. The winner stayed on the table, and the most I remember winning was ten games straight.

My roommate for one year was the one guy I couldn't beat on a regular basis. But a year after I was out of college, he had no chance of ever beating me again. That's because Grand Rapids was a hotbed of table tennis activity. There was a table tennis club and a weekday league that I knew about, and I was looking forward to getting home and joining the fun. I knew I couldn't join the club and play in the league until I had graduated from college, which remained my top priority. I returned home to Grand Rapids after college in 1966, started my accounting internship, and immediately got active in the club.

We had a really powerful table tennis club, with some of the best players in the country. For example, we had the guy who was the number-two ranked player in the entire country in our club, Dell

Sweeris. He could beat everybody, always. His wife, Connie, won the national table tennis championship for women in 1971, and was with the group that went to play in China that year as part of the "Ping-Pong Diplomacy" team. They used to play mixed doubles together. She was a short girl, maybe 4' 10", and he was over six feet tall. It was a riot watching them, when she would duck down when he hit a massive drive. By the way, I beat her once, but only once. They are both in the Table Tennis Hall of Fame and the Michigan Sports Hall of Fame.

Even though Dell was a legend in table tennis, nobody, no matter how good, could make a living at table tennis back then, and Dell became a CPA like I originally planned to be. Dell loved the sport, and for years he ran the club, the leagues, and managed tournaments, usually held on weekends. This is where I first learned how tournaments were organized and run. I soaked up the knowledge, and later helped the club host and run tournaments for a few years. Table tennis in Grand Rapids was extremely competitive and very exciting, and I became totally immersed in all aspects of the game. The players were great people, and I became fast and lifelong friends with many of them.

At first, I was a sub in the league. The year after I got back to Grand Rapids, 1967, interest in the sport had grown so much that the club went from one league to two leagues, held on Monday and Thursday nights at a community activity building. The Monday-night league was the big league, where all the best players competed. By then I was a regular in both leagues. As my game improved, I got to be one of the captains in both leagues; only the best players got to be captains.

The more I played, the better I got. One time I beat a world-class player, Danny Seemiller, in a tournament six months before he became the number-one player in the country. He went on to win five U.S. Men's Singles Championships, and also served as the

U.S. Olympic head coach. Danny was a U.S. Table Tennis Hall-of-Famer. He was also a poker player, and played in my home game many times.

In 1976, I went to Philadelphia to play in the national table tennis championships. They had different classes, and I got all the way to the finals in Class C and the semi-finals in Class B. Because of the ranking system they used, I was—briefly—ranked 60th in the country. I credit table tennis as the game that taught me to compete. Really compete. You have to hone your skill because it's a one-on-one game—just you against your opponent both physically and psychologically. I hated to see the end of my table tennis playing days.

I was more or less forced to stop playing because of a change in the rules. I was an unorthodox player because I used an all-wooden bat, or paddle. With my wooden paddle I could block smash hits and send the ball back over the net with a reverse spin. That's the way I beat some top-ranked players, because they couldn't handle the reverse spin, something they rarely encountered. Eventually, they outlawed wood as a striking surface, which took my weapon away, and I basically retired. I figured I would be cannon fodder if I had to play with a different kind of paddle than I'd been using—successfully—for years.

For me, table tennis was much more than just competing at the table. I was heavy into all aspects of table tennis for 20 years. I became a regional tournament director for the United States Table Tennis Association (now called USA Table Tennis) for four or five years, and eventually the national tournament director for two or three years. I was friends with the previous regional tournament director, and I thought I could do a better job than him, which I did. No ego here. I loved the prestigious but unpaid and time-consuming directorship, and I only resigned when I moved to Vegas. Besides managing table tennis events, I also umpired. There are different levels of umpire—local, regional, and national—and I achieved them all. I umpired quite a bit, including the national team tryouts. Then I reached the pinnacle of table tennis officiating, ultimately passing the test to become an International Umpire. This qualified me to umpire at the world championships. But I never did. After I received my certificate, I never umpired a single match the rest of my life.

The direction of my life had changed.

Still, as you'll see, if it wasn't for my table tennis career, I doubt whether I would have ever wound up in Las Vegas.

Working my way out of the corporate world

After college graduation, I got hired on by the local CPA firm where I had interned. I wanted to continue with them, but my financial needs were growing. Not exactly shy, I had the audacity to ask for a raise that was bigger than what they wanted to give me. I had worked for $100 a week and I asked for a salary of $125. By the time they counteroffered $115 a week, I had already answered an ad in the newspaper and interviewed with one of the largest national accounting firms, Ernst and Ernst. They offered me $125 a week and I took it. I worked for them for one tax season. Then they decided they didn't need me anymore, just before I was scheduled to take my CPA certificate exam. So, I never took that exam. In the long run, that was probably a good thing. I was a better accountant than many people I knew in the profession who had passed the exam, and I'm sure I would have passed it. But then my life would have gone down a different path.

Lots of companies need an accountant. Without my certificate and in need of a job, this time I applied at a local business. Over the next six years, I worked for seven companies. I was fired three times and left the other four. One company went out of business, and two companies had had enough of me after a three-month probationary period. I wasn't exactly your typical mild-mannered little accountant. One owner was cheating people out of money. And, for perspective, he had a "big shot" son working for him who used to pop into work in a bathing suit for a few minutes before popping out again. I freaked out on the owner and told the dirty so-and-so that I had plenty on him, and that I was helping to organize a strike against his company. So, he punched me—then fired me. Imagine that!

Yet all during this very "stable" work history, Bobbi and I were very productive. We had invested in a house, two cars, and three cats. But more importantly, we had become the proud parents of three beautiful children. Melanie was born July 19, 1969 (one day before the moon landing), Michael on March 1, 1972 (one day after Leap Year), and Patrick on April 3, 1974.

I got fired from my last corporate accounting job when I was 33, on May 11, 1978. I wasn't surprised—I knew it was coming. The second president I worked for at this company called me into his office and told me, "Tom, we could not have had a better accountant than you." Then he fired me.

This was the longest I had been in one corporate job in my life. I started working for this company at age 28, in 1973. I lived in Grand Rapids, and the company was located in Saugatuck, about a 40-mile commute from my house. The drive wasn't fun in Michigan weather, and I had to work five-and-a-half days a week when I started. The first president I worked for at this company was a rough-and-tumble guy who intimidated most of his employees. Except me. He took a liking to me, and after a year or so he promoted me to office manager. All this made some of my coworkers a tad jealous. The president also liked to go to Vegas and play blackjack, so I bought him a book on how to beat the dealer. I had no problems with this guy whatsoever, and I was disheartened when he retired and moved to (guess where) Las Vegas. About a year after I got fired, I ran into him there, and we had a grand time when he showed me around town.

I was not big on political correctness. I did things that one doesn't do if he wants to continue working. As I said, I had been hired as an accountant and then got promoted to office manager, reporting to the company controller. This guy was only about three years older than me, so I wasn't going any further up the corporate ladder. I was okay with that, and I liked my job. But I think the controller wasn't crazy about the competition. It was a nice promotion, but it eventually helped lead to my downfall.

The clerical staff I now supervised were by and large a bunch of little old ladies that had been entrenched in the company a long time, some for decades. I got along fine with them—until I became their boss. When the company started growing, I was tasked with expanding the clerical staff. I hired two younger women, one who was in her early twenties and the other in her mid-thirties (about my age). They were super-efficient and highly productive, and I began to rely on them more and more. They were better workers than the old-timers, and frankly, I liked them better. As time went on, the senior clerical staff began to resent them, and me. Unwittingly, I had created a staff of disgruntled old ladies. Not good.

My boss, the controller, was, to put this kindly, a "stick-up-the-butt" kind of guy. Very rigid about getting his way, and his concept of the "right" way to do things. For example, he didn't like the fact that I was playing tennis (my other main form of exercise besides table tennis) with a guy from marketing on my lunch hour. The controller asked me to stop, which I did, but then I defied him and started playing again. That ticked him off. That and the fact that I just didn't fit his idea of the corporate or professional mold. I didn't meekly obey, and I didn't conform. I was probably the only Democrat in the company, and this was at the time when Nixon was going through all his nonsense, and I was quick to point out the implications of Watergate.

Understand: I wasn't exactly a people person, and you can see how I had managed to tick off quite a few people in the company. Truth is, I enjoyed working with numbers more than people back then. For example, I had severe allergies and was constantly blowing my nose. I had tissues all over the place, which didn't bother me in the least, but in hindsight was kind of disgusting. I see these things quite clearly now, but at the time the impression I was making didn't fully register. I don't blame anyone for firing me, by the way. They all had their reasons, and when I look back, I knew I could have done some things differently and was at least partly to blame.

But at the time I was busy with a lot on my mind. Like commuting 40 miles to work at least five days a week, helping to raise a family, and playing and helping to manage table tennis leagues two nights a week. On top of all of this, poker was becoming a bigger part of my life, which probably contributed the last straw to my demise at the company.

My real passion. Yep, poker.

After I graduated from college, some of my table tennis buddies invited me to be their guest at the private Polish Falcon's Club in Grand Rapids one Friday night to play in their $2 poker game. I remember thinking if I lose, I probably won't come back, but let's see how it goes. I won $15, which was a good win for the size of the game. The club was a fraternal organization, and of course they had a bar. It was a very social place, and if you participated in their activities you were expected to contribute to the organization's bottom line by buying drinks or snacks. Since I don't drink and play, or drink and drive (I lived about four miles from the club), I was the lone guy who ordered candy bars. I went back to the club several years ago, and they remembered who I was and my candy bars. I enjoyed the atmosphere, the players, and the poker game. The bar legally had to close at 2 a.m., and that's when the game usually broke up.

This Friday night poker game became a regular part of my life, and it was how my thirst for the game really took hold of me. I didn't win every time, nobody does, but I was making a little extra money on a consistent basis. I got to know the guys really well, and together we decided we wanted to play longer than we could Friday nights at the Polish Falcon's Club. So, we started our own home game and upped the ante to $5 dealer's choice. There were three of us that rotated hosting the game. We soon started playing on a regular basis, not every weekend but most weekends. Often the game would last two days, breaking up late on Sunday. Sometimes it would break up sooner, but a lot of times we just kept on playing. This home game lasted for the better part of six years.

When I hosted, it was a family affair. The host got a little rake to pay for food and beverages. My wife, who was a good cook, prepared meals for everybody. When I was elected to the World Series of Poker Hall of Fame, my daughter, Melanie, made a little speech where she talked about those home games. Unbeknownst to me, Bobbi was getting a little annoyed preparing goodies and serving guys with names like Whitey, Petey, and One-Eyed Jack in her basement, so she decided to get in on the action in her own way. She started charging a little fee to the players to use a cot to sleep on if they got tired, and then charged extra for a blanket! Those guys, my friends, never told me about that!

Naturally, I was the biggest winner at these home games. That made me the "go to" guy for credit, and I did get burned sometimes, or had to opt for alternative forms of payment. One guy was a hope-and-a-prayer kind of player that too often played every hand down to the last card, the "river." He owed me so much money, which he couldn't pay, so I had to take it out in trade. He painted my house a bright Kelly green with a shamrock on the white shutters—a little nod to my McEvoy Irish heritage—much to the chagrin of the neighbors. He did a good job, and I got my money's worth, but it was the only way I was going to get anything out of this guy.

Through table tennis I had become friends with some Black guys who also played poker, and I invited them to the game. Remember, Grand Rapids was a very conservative, very Republican town. One of my neighbors had seen these guys going into the house and, a little alarmed, asked me what was going on. When I told him he said, "Tom, I saw all these guys coming in and out of your house, and I didn't think they were relatives!" My Black buddies reciprocated the poker invitation, and sometimes I went down to the Black section of town, where I was the only White guy at the poker table. They were good players, and I didn't do quite as well in that game. I stopped playing there after one guy came in showing off his piece, albeit in a nonthreatening way. That was uncomfortable, and I realized I didn't like the idea of poker players carrying guns. Still don't.

In our home games we played mostly Seven Card Stud, but Hold'em—what's that? Nobody in Grand Rapids had even heard of it until I started making trips to Vegas in 1978, and I introduced the game back home. The players were curious about Hold'em, so I explained it and the rules. We played it some, but not much.

At my house, we played in the basement. This was the early 70s, and smoking was prevalent and almost synonymous with poker. Oh my God, after the weekend game the basement would stink to high heaven for days. I attribute the death of one of my best friends to cigarettes. I have never smoked, but these were the experiences with smoking and especially secondhand smoke that greatly influenced my efforts to ban smoking in the World Series of Poker tournaments. But more on that in Chapter 18.

The home game group was a mixed bag. We had players who were clueless, some that had a little bit of a clue, and a couple who were not terrible. They used to tell me they knew I was the best player they had ever seen, but they continued to play anyway. It was a social group, and it wasn't like we were playing for thousands of dollars. I didn't win every time, but I won way more than anyone else in the game. Even at a $5 betting limit, the winnings could add up. Basically, playing successfully in these home games is where the poker bug really took hold of me.

And this bug was probably what got me fired from my last corporate job. Finally. I was burning the candle on both ends and in the middle with table tennis, job, family, and poker. Frankly, when I got to work on Mondays, I wasn't all that fresh. Sometimes I even forgot to shave. I think this was the straw that broke the camel's back. In retrospect, that was a good thing.

My poker journey heads in a different direction. Yep, West.

Six months before I got fired from my last corporate job, in December of 1977, I went out to Las Vegas to compete in the National Table Tennis Championships at Caesars Palace. I discovered they happened to have a poker room there that featured $5/$10 7-Card Stud. I was attracted to that game like a bear to honey. I couldn't stop, and I was up all night playing poker. Naturally, I didn't do too well in my table tennis matches. But as a poker newcomer, a tourist, playing against guys who were trying to make a living off that game, I won $1,000 in six days. Now, when your annual salary is $18,000 a year, and the president of your company is making about $50,000 a year, it wasn't hard to do the math. I could make what the boss was making doing something fun. And I didn't have to work for anybody.

I vividly remember the flight home from Vegas. I was flush with my poker success, and my mind was filled with wonder. Was I a better poker player than I had previously thought, or was I just lucky? The money wasn't burning a hole in my pocket, it was burning a hole in my brain. I enjoyed the time playing poker immensely, but was that just because I won? Was this a fluke? Could I consistently compete on this level where the stakes were higher? Could there be more here? I resolved to go back to Vegas to find out as soon as I could.

The seed had been planted. I put Vegas on my schedule for my next vacation the following August. I was going to go back and give poker another shot. What I didn't take into account was because this is the hottest month of the year, it is therefore the worst month for poker activity. Thank goodness I got fired on May 11, 1978, so

I went back to Vegas earlier than planned. Joining the ranks of the unemployed just made me more determined than ever to give poker in Vegas another go.

My wife, Bobbi, had never objected to me playing poker because I made money. She knew I was the best player, and the vast majority of the time I brought home extra cash that supplemented the family income. After I got fired, I collected my two-week severance pay, went on unemployment, and told Bobbi that before I started looking for a new job I wanted to go back out to Vegas for a couple of weeks. There was a table tennis tournament in Grand Rapids coming up, and I wanted to use the money I would make running the tournament to go back out to Vegas and play poker. I wanted to test the waters to see if I could enjoy the same poker success I had six months ago. She said go ahead and go.

Although I liked accounting, I had grown sick of working for other people. Being told when I can take a vacation and for how long. When I can do this and when I can do that. I wanted to work for myself! That's common enough, but I didn't have any capital, or a plan. Yet. I had a wife, three kids, a mortgage, and a long list of responsibilities. Now what was I going to do? People get trapped in these situations and never get out. My dad faced this and wouldn't take a chance on himself until he retired and got Social Security. I say, if you love what you're doing, the money will usually come. And even if it doesn't, you'll probably be happier doing something you like. Well, I liked playing poker and I liked making money at poker! If I had been a loser at poker, I wouldn't have pursued it. But it was a fun thing to do, and it provided extra money for me. Consistently.

That first two-week trip back to Las Vegas, I made over $3,000, about two months' worth of my previous salary, so our family income wasn't going to be hurting. Plus, Bobbi was doing a little bit of daycare at our house to make some extra money for the family.

After I got back to Michigan, I ran the table tennis tournament and continued to collect unemployment. Now I could afford to continue to test the poker waters out West. I didn't win every time. Won the second trip, lost the third, etc. But overall, I was ahead.

It was on my first trip back to Vegas after getting fired, in May 1978, that I discovered the World Series of Poker. I literally found it by accident. I stumbled into the Horseshoe, and I saw this big crowd, eight people deep, watching two guys playing poker. I asked what all the fuss was about, and someone told me it was the final table of the World Series of Poker. The two guys playing heads-up were Bobby Baldwin and Crandell Addington. Baldwin would win, and witnessing the event gave me a tremendous rush. I was amazed by the whole thing—it made a big impact on me. We didn't have poker tournaments in Michigan, and I wanted to learn more about this poker tournament thing.

I had seen that the Golden Nugget was hosting Hold'em tournaments, so I decided to try them out. I cashed in the first two tournaments I played in. The buy-in was $110. Tournaments were in their infancy then, and the format was evolving. We were playing with real casino chips—not tournament chips. You played down until 10 percent of the field was left, and then you "won" or kept every chip in front of you. I had the most chips in one, and was a close second in the next one. Hooked me for life. That's when I decided once and for all that poker was what I wanted to do for a living. That meant moving my family West, and figuring out what town had the best poker.

I varied my visits out West to explore the venues and sample the waters. I visited my cousin, Dan, who lived in Long Beach, California, where I could stay for free. Draw poker was legal in nearby Gardena, so he would drive me down there to the card rooms. They also played a new-to-me-poker game—Low-Ball. I wasn't much of a Low-Ball player at first, but I learned. We had to deal our own cards back then because there were no professional dealers. I was becoming more familiar with the poker culture and its signals. For example, when the floor man would say "Well, we're giving you new cards, boys," it was a hint to start pulling a buck out of each pot to give to the floor man. I was learning the way things worked and getting better at Draw poker and eventually even Low-Ball.

California was fine, but I liked Nevada better. I flew back and forth from Michigan to Vegas multiple times for the better part of a year, and I started expanding my trips to about three weeks at a time. I was there on a shoestring budget each trip and the accountant in me knew I didn't have much money but *did* have a mortgage and bills to pay. At one time I had $4,000 of poker profits in my pocket, the most money I had ever had in my life in cash. I thought that was really something special. And I was gaining confidence in my game.

For my Vegas trips, I found a little cheap place to stay downtown for $40 a week. The room only had a little latch on the door so that if you pushed hard enough it would break right off. I shared a bathroom with the occupant of another room. There was no security. If you had anything of value, you wouldn't want to risk leaving it in the room. This hotel was the cheapest place I could find where I could have access to playing poker downtown and to the bus routes to get to the Strip. I don't remember the name and I don't think it's there anymore. It wasn't in the greatest area of downtown, but it was near enough to Fremont Street that I didn't feel like I was going to get mugged at night. I never had any trouble there—none—zero.

The hotel was within easy walking distance of the Horseshoe, which on and off had a poker room, and the Golden Nugget. The Stud games were played on the Strip. Caesars Palace and the MGM Grand featured 7-Card Stud. The Stardust spread Razz, that was their feature, but they also played some Stud and Hold'em. I learned how to play Hold'em at the Stardust and downtown.

Reno was still the other choice for a new home base in Nevada. Reno had colder weather, I knew, but I didn't know how good the poker action was up there. So, I flew up there in December 1978, and boy, it was cold. Plus, to my surprise, I saw they had snow. The poker was okay, but there were more and better games in Vegas. For me it was a no-brainer. The weather wasn't nearly as bad as Michigan, but I wasn't going to move to a cold place again. (On a side note, it was during my short visit to Reno that I met the poker guru David Sklansky at a $15/$30 Limit Hold'em game. It was before he wrote *The Theory of Poker*, but I had purchased and read a couple of the little books he had written on Hold'em and I knew who he was. That started a friendship, not a hang-out-together friendship, but a casual friendship that continued until I found out what a snake he was. I discuss that in Chapter 30.)

Sklansky wasn't the only famous author I met during my early trips to Nevada. At the time, Doyle Brunson had his own publishing company, B & G Publishing, on Industrial Road in Las Vegas, behind the casinos on the Strip. I tracked down the address, and I went there with the intention of spending a hundred bucks buying his brand-new self-published book titled *How I Made a Million Dollars Playing* Poker, which later became his best-selling *Super System*. The guys I was playing poker with in Vegas were raving about it. I was into books on poker and had read every one I could get my hands on, cover to cover, several times. Brunson's and Sklansky's books provided good insight, but the rest just seemed to scratch the surface. Poker literature was wanting, in my opinion, which was one of the reasons I would later author or coauthor several poker books that dug deeper into the game.

I walked into Doyle's place of business on December 1, 1978, and sure enough, there sat the man himself behind his desk. I recognized him immediately, and I went up to him to talk with him and buy the book. I asked him to date and sign it, of course. He signed the same thing to a lot of people, I imagine: "To (your name here). May all your deals be good ones." He is pretty gracious like that. (Even though he didn't want me to be in the Hall of Fame, but that, too, is a story for another chapter.)

After Doyle signed my new book, I remember pointing my finger at him, not in a mean way, and saying, "One of these days, I'm going to be playing at the same table as you. You just wait and see." He just laughed. I'm sure he had heard that a million times. Five years later, we were both at the final table at the Main Event, which I won, and he came in third. I'm sure he'd been challenged like this before, but not too many people have actually pulled it off. I'm the exception that proves the rule that you can dream, and have it come true if you have guts, ambition, and above all, talent. Sorry, sometimes I sprain my shoulder patting myself on the back like that.

Years later, after I'd won the World Series, Doyle told me he remembered me from that first encounter at the store. He said, "I thought you were fresh off the farm." Funny, since I've never been on a farm in my life. Unfortunately, I did sell the book he signed for me because I needed the money. The guy I sold the book to ended up spending time in jail on a drug charge. Sad but true.

I commuted to Las Vegas for a whole year, staying about three weeks at a time. Each session I played was a learning experience, and most were profitable. Then I'd fly back to Grand Rapids and go back on unemployment. It took me a whole year to use up the 26 weeks of unemployment I was entitled to. You couldn't collect if you were out of state, so I had to reapply when I got back home between visits to Vegas. When I was home, I had a lot of time on my hands, and I used it to study poker. I read poker books like Doyle's over and over. After I started studying, I got better. I had no idea how the odds were so stacked against me—I was oblivious to that— I just knew that I was going to learn the games and that I was going to get better. And always in the back of my mind was the memory of what I was leaving behind and did not want to go back to—working for other people in Michigan, where I hated the climate.

Convincing the skeptics. Yep, everybody.

So now, to make my poker dream come true, I first have to deal with the wife and the family. None of them wanted to move to Vegas. I said look, I'm paying the mortgage and living expenses here, and I gotta go out there. I told them I was not going to be happy with my life unless I found out if I could make it as a poker player. I had to try this, and the only way to try it was for me to be in Las Vegas full time. I did not want to break up the family. I did not want to get a divorce, but this is something I had to do. I told them what I wanted to do was sell the house after the school year was over, so there would be no disruption with the kids' schooling, and then move out there. All this went over like a lead balloon.

Bobbi was reluctant, to say the least, and the kids didn't want to leave all of their friends. I remember thinking, how many times are you going to remember your friends when you're that young? The kids were little then, Melanie was nine, Michael was seven, and Patrick was five. My wife's entire family was in Grand Rapids. She knew nobody in Vegas. I knew nobody in Vegas except some of the guys I played poker with. Nevertheless, I repeated that I have to try and do this. I told her if she didn't want to move, I couldn't force her. But I was going to move out there and try to do poker full time, and I wanted the whole family to go with me. If I failed and couldn't make it as a player, I reiterated that all businesses need accountants, and I would find work. It's not like I was not going to support the family. It's just that I wanted to do it by working at poker for myself instead of working for someone else.

Bobbi did not want us to split up, even though we were not getting along the best. In fact, it was kind of a relief getting away from her when I took my trips out west to play poker. I liked being on my own for a while. I had already made up my mind I was not going to live my life wondering "What If?" That's what happens to so many people who might have broken out of the mold and pursued what they thought they were destined for . . . but they weren't willing to take that risk. I was. I knew my dad wasn't able to do that, but I wasn't scarred by the Depression. I'm a bit of a gambler and I'm willing to take more chances.

You have to understand that I'm really not a big gambler. I never was. I'm a poker player. There's a difference, a big difference. Obviously, poker involves luck, so every hand is a gamble. But when you're serious about winning at poker, you don't rely on luck. Rather, you go to war with luck. Luck is uncontrollable and fickle, but skill is always your ally. I felt I had developed enough skills to go out to Vegas and make a living at the poker tables. It takes these poker skills to be able to put yourself in a position to get lucky. It was this combination of sharpened skill and a little luck that led to my win at the World Series of Poker. And that changed everything.

It took her awhile, but Bobbi finally caved in. Very reluctantly. She was a tough sell. When I talked to our parents, it was NO SALE. They asked me if I was out of my mind. Are you crazy? You're going to move to Vegas, try to play poker, and move our grandchildren 2,000 miles away to where we will never see them? They laid the guilt trips on me hot and heavy. I understood, but I was determined.

My dad said, "Every gambler dies with his ass hanging out of his pants." In other words, dies broke. I said, "Dad, you're not playing against the house when you're playing poker. Somebody has to win. They can't all lose. So, some of the players are winning, and I'm not going to be happy unless I try this." My family did everything they could to talk me out of it. They thought I was making the biggest mistake of my life, and they weren't nice about how they felt. I just remember them being very, very upset and completely unsupportive. I'm pretty sure my parents were actually ashamed and embarrassed that their son was seeking his future as a game bird. I had to go against every relative and friend as well as my wife and kids. That's how stubborn I am once I get an idea in my head.

Speaking of friends, the guys I played poker with in Grand Rapids thought I was crazy, too. They knew I was the best player in our poker game, but thought this was a joke, trying to play poker professionally. It was one thing to beat your buddies at home, but going up against the best players in the country? They told me there's a reason they call Las Vegas the "graveyard of hometown poker champions." This was "common knowledge," I knew, but my competitive nature saw that as a challenge.

Despite the opposition, I kept telling everyone who would listen that within five years I would be playing for a world championship (I did it in four). They all told me I was crazy and that I'd be back in Michigan within six months. So, no pressure from the people I knew and loved at all. Right.

The only one who loved the idea was my friend and cousin, Dan, in Long Beach—it would give him more excuses to come to Vegas. Everyone after that, to a person, thought I was out of my mind. Grandma had moved to Florida to be near her daughter, so she was basically out of the picture. She died in 1980, living long enough to see me move to Vegas, but not long enough to see me win the World Series.

Vegas or bust. Yep, my last commute.

So, after Bobbi finally agreed, we moved to Las Vegas in the summer of 1979. We had sold our house and just about everything we owned. I bought a new car, a bright red station wagon, to start the cross-county adventure. Me, my wife, three kids, and four cats. We didn't have much room, so each child was allowed one just one suitcase for clothes and keepsakes. The cats were kept pretty doped up to keep them calm for the long trip and to smuggle them into motels along the way. We rented a small U-Haul trailer and taped a sign on the back that read "Vegas or Bust." After our last meal before leaving, we threw our plates away instead of cleaning and packing them. We couldn't bring everything but took what we could, including one piece of furniture—the octagon-shaped poker table I had played home games on in my basement. Then off we went on our four-day move to Las Vegas.

We were going pretty far out on a limb. There were no cell phones in those days, and communication wasn't easy. I had no phone number and no address, because we didn't know where we were going to live. We figured on staying in a motel for a couple of days once we got there until we could find a place to rent. I didn't have anything prearranged. We would have to deal with it all once we got out there. I had about $5,000 to my name.

A scary thing happened on the trip. We had stopped at a truck stop about a mile off the highway to use the bathroom. After the pee break, the family got in the car, and we started driving back toward the freeway. Several minutes later, I looked in the back seat and I said, "Where's Mike?" He was not in the car. His sister Melanie had said nothing. His brother Patrick had said nothing. They had both assumed he was in the back behind all the luggage. Oh my God. I had not quite reached the entrance to the freeway yet, so I stopped and started backing up, but with the trailer, that wasn't working. I had no choice but to get out and just walk the long way back to the truck stop. About that time, a semi-truck was coming toward us, and the driver stopped. He had Mike. That bighearted trucker had seen my son, figured out what happened, and thought he could catch up with us and find our bright red station wagon, even though it was getting close to twilight. Why is it that the middle child seems to have the most misadventures?

We arrived in Las Vegas around July 4, the hottest time of the year, and also the time Vegas World (now the Strat) was opening. We immediately started looking for a place to rent. We found a condo at 3944 Visby Lane, not too far from the Strip, off Flamingo Road and south a few blocks behind where the Horseshoe (formerly Bally's, and before that, the MGM) is now. That put us close to the poker rooms at MGM and Caesars, and not too long a drive to get downtown. We lived there for four years. My life as a professional poker player had begun.

One old-timer said Grand Rapids Tom is so good at the game
he could win with a hand full of soda biscuits.

— Sports Form, *October 6, 1979,*
article on Tom McEvoy's Tournament
winnings at the Golden Nugget

CHAPTER 4

Leading Up to the 1983 WSOP Main Event.
My First Four Foundation Years in Vegas.

After my arrival in Vegas in July 1979, and after getting the family settled into our condo rental, I started playing. I made money right from the start. My first half year I more than matched my former income as an accountant, and I was my own boss. I was playing poker, on average, six days a week, with my sessions lasting four to five hours. I had come to town with $5,000 in cash and a new car, and I never had to go to work for a paycheck. I made money right off the bat—immediately—at my new job. Poker.

The early years—poker tournaments

For me, there was a new twist on poker that I was really thirsting to absorb: Tournaments. There were no poker tournaments in Grand Rapids, so they were completely new to me. I didn't play tournaments until I wandered into the Golden Nugget in 1978, before I had moved to Vegas. I started my tournament career there by cashing in the first two I ever played. In those days, we played with casino chips (not tournament chips) and the last 10 percent of the field still in got to keep the chips they had accumulated. I finished second—second-most money—in the first one, a $110 freezeout (no re-entries allowed). I actually won—got the most money—in the second one. So I started right out winning tournaments back-to-back. And I kept developing my skills. This was a time when a lot of people didn't know how to play tournaments. I was learning fast and adjusting my strategies and I was getting really good results. We're not talking about fields of thousands of players; we're talking about fields of 40 or 50. Maybe 70 on a good day. Big enough for me to really develop good tournament strategies and skills.

Tournaments hadn't caught on big like they are now. But they did have low-limit buy-in tournaments all over Vegas—mostly Hold'em and some Stud—at various smaller casinos. Almost every day of the week, I'd find some sort of tournament around town to play in. Casinos like the Aladdin, Golden Nugget, Silver City, Jolley Trolley (which became the Golden Eagle for a short time), Bingo Palace, Imperial Palace, Showboat, Maxim, Silver Bird, and Sahara. Playing tournaments in these smaller casinos around town was where I first met a lot of great poker people like future Hall of Famers Johnny Chan, Bill Boyd, Eric Drache, and Jack McClelland. Drache and McClelland cut their teeth as players and poker room managers, and both would later become WSOP tournament directors for a number of years. There were a lot of names you might find familiar gaining tournament experience at these casinos.

Spoiler alert. I'm a packrat and I keep pretty meticulous records. So, I have documentation to back up many of the claims I make in this book. I'll be honest and forthright, and I'll share the good, the bad, and the ugly. Being a poker pro is no bed of roses. But it isn't a boring life.

Of course, cash wins don't make the newspapers (thank goodness). But placing in tournaments did. There were several small publications in Las Vegas that reported on gaming and poker. Every time I cashed in any of these low-limit tournaments, my name made these papers. Smaller publications like the *Sports Form* and the *Las Vegas Sports Book*, and larger newspapers like the *Las Vegas Review-Journal* and the *Las Vegas Sun*. This growing local fame started a habit with me that has continued to this day. Every time I see my name in an article, I put the article in my scrapbook. No ego here, just pride.

It was the poker players who gave me my first nickname, "Grand Rapids Tom." It was inevitable, I guess, since I was from Grand Rapids, and it seemed like every poker player just had to have a moniker. Here's a sample of the kind of writeups I was starting to receive.

> *It pays to visit Las Vegas when you're a cracker jack poker player and can put in some time at the tables. Filling the bill is the player they call "Grand Rapids Tom." He's been visiting Las Vegas for the past two months, and Torrid Tom has been winning poker tournaments all around town and kept his hot hand going at the Golden Nugget by scoring top prize of $600 at the $110 buy-in Hold'em freezeout play. He wins so often and under such varied conditions that he's a walking advertisement for the fact that poker is all skill and not just luck. You'd have to be a top player to win with the consistency shown by the Grand Rapids fellow.*
>
> —Sports Form, *October 6, 1979*

I loved the challenge of poker tournaments. I was developing my own strategies and techniques at a time when you couldn't go get information on the internet or buy books on the subject. From the first time I witnessed the World Series of Poker Main Event being played in 1978, I wanted to be part of it. I knew that to be competitive, you had to have good tournament skills. That was always in the back of my mind as I honed my game.

And it was working. In my first half-year as a Vegas resident, I won five tournaments and finished third once, netting over $4,000. Over the following three years prior to my 1983 World Series victories, I won 13 tournaments, placed second eight times and third ten times, netting over $91,000. I didn't cash in every tournament, but I was averaging about one cash per month.

I was also playing occasional out-of-town tournaments, mainly up in the Reno/Lake Tahoe area, where a tournament circuit of sorts was starting to form. By the early 1980s, Amarillo Slim's Super Bowl of Poker was in full swing. I would drive or fly up to Reno for a few weeks at a time, but mostly I was playing in Vegas.

Amarillo Slim with me in Tahoe.

My first major tournament win was Amarillo Slim's Super Bowl of Poker Limit Hold'em tournament held at Del Webb's Sahara Tahoe in Lake Tahoe in 1982. The buy-in was $1,000, and they had attracted 96 players. The tournament paid the top three spots: 60 percent for first ($57,600); 30 percent for second ($28,800 to Tom Hood) and 10 percent for third ($9,600 to Howard Andrew, aka "Tahoe," who became a good friend). Hood and Andrew planned to chop the tournament (split the top money prize) after they eliminated me, but I had a different plan. I busted out Howard in third place, and he liked to say later that he "launched my poker career." Hood had over 60 percent of the chips when we got heads-up. I was the relative newcomer, and Hood said, "no way" when I asked if he wanted to "save anything or split anything." An hour later I busted him out. I had sold shares of myself going in, so I got to keep about $20,000 of the first-place money. Plus, I left a $2,000 tip, which was pretty hefty back then. At the time, this was the biggest win, the biggest money, and the biggest thrill, of my life. As icing on the cake, my winning hand was almost a straight flush in spades.

For some reason, after this win, the poker/gaming press began referring to me as "Grand Rapids Tom" less and less. My full name was now being used, which I thought was fine. I was a Las Vegan now, and no longer a Grand Rapids guy. Within the poker community, which admittedly wasn't that large, I was growing in stature. To quote one newspaper clipping about me, "No longer was he just a solid poker player. Now he is a great solid player."

By the time I got my big breakthrough by winning the World Series in 1983, I had played less No-Limit Hold'em than practically anybody in the field, but I'd played more *tournament poker* than probably anyone in the field. Tournaments were still a relatively new thing, but as they kept getting more popular, I saw that players were developing better tournament skills. The competition was getting better.

The early years—poker cash games

When I made up my mind to become a professional poker player, I decided I was going to learn how to play all the games. At the beginning I was focusing mainly on $5/$10 7-Card Stud (sometimes a little higher), and I was a regular at Caesers Palace. Sometimes I played at the old MGM Grand (which became Bally's and is now the Horseshoe). They were the only two places that focused on 7-Card Stud. The Stardust casino on the Strip spread an occasional 7-Card Stud game, but their main emphasis was on Limit and Pot-Limit Hold'em, and Razz, so I played down there some. The other casino I frequented was the Golden Nugget, where I played mostly $10/$20 Limit Hold'em.

I became a top-notch Razz player (I won a WSOP bracelet in Razz in 1986) playing at the Stardust, despite the reputation this poker room had for turning a blind eye to all kinds of cheating that was going on. Cheating, from collusion to chip swiping right at the tables, was much more prevalent in those days. A winning cash player had to beat these shenanigans and the rake.

I also played Stud 8 or Better (also known as 7-Card Stud Hi/Lo) to a certain extent, which wasn't my favorite game. (I placed eighth in this game at the WSOP in 1986). The Dunes hosted some Stud 8 or Better cash games. I also played Jacks or Better Draw High (I played in this event at the WSOP a couple of years, but never cashed) and Draw Low Ball. One game I didn't play much of was Deuce to Seven No-Limit Single Draw.

In my early years in Vegas, Omaha was relatively new and gaining momentum. We first started playing Limit, then switched to Pot-Limit in about 1982. Omaha didn't really "come on the scene" until 1984, the first year it became a World Series of Poker bracelet event. (I came in third in that very first Pot-limit Omaha World Series tournament. I put a bad beat on Mike Sexton that 20 years later he was still reminiscing about. I made an aggressive play on him at the final table, got lucky and hit a gut shot, and broke his heart.)

By playing all these games, I made up my mind that Hold'em was going to be my main game. Limit Hold'em and 7-Card Stud were my two strongest games, followed by Razz.

Where I really learned to play Hold'em was at the Golden Nugget downtown. The best Hold'em games in Vegas were there. Back then the game was Limit, not No-Limit. If a casino spread No-Limit back then, it was usually for a select group of players—hardly a place to learn the ropes. I cut my teeth at the Golden Nugget playing their $10/$20 games. The Stardust had smaller Hold'em games—$3/$6 and $5/$10. Eventually they went to $10/$20 also. I played more $10/$20 Limit Hold'em than any other game.

As I said, I played on average about six days a week, taking the occasional day off. I never was a morning person, so mostly I played late afternoons and evenings, and sometimes I played late into the night. I got into this terrible night owl sleep schedule, which I've had for most of my life now. There was no particular pattern to what game I played or what casino I visited. There was a wonderful freedom to playing whatever and wherever I felt like that day. It was my job, and I loved it.

I learned that playing too long wasn't for me. One time, I played Razz for two days straight, and it about did me in. That's a long time to maintain focus and concentration. I thought, alright, this around-the-clock stuff is way too hard on me. It wasn't good for my marriage, either, and at that time, that meant a lot to me.

Expressing my American Dream in a Letter to Mom and Dad

Tuesday, February 12, 1980

Dear Mom & Dad,

It is Tuesday night, and I am a little drained. I just won a big poker tournament for $2,300. Last year I won about $8,700 since the move and a couple of thousand more before that. I am playing better than ever and have become a top-notch Hold'em player. Hold'em is a variation of 7-Card Stud and is very popular in Vegas, although it is not played much back in the Eastern states.

We really need a yard for the kids. Right now, they play quite a bit in a big ditch near our townhouse. I am trying to save up $30,000 so we can buy a house. I figure that I should be able to get a mortgage with a down-payment that large. Anything at all decent will cost between $60,000 and $90,000. Inflation is causing havoc in the prices of homes and the longer we wait the more it will cost. So you see I have a definite goal to shoot for. So far I have $7,000 in the bank, so that is a start.

I thoroughly enjoy what I am doing, and I am proving what I said all along—that I can make it as a professional poker player. I think you still have misconceptions about what I am doing and what I am up against. First of all there are hundreds of professional and semi-professional poker players that live in Las Vegas. Many are working in the casinos and playing in their off hours. Many of them need the stability of a regular job. Some work only to support their gambling habit. Many are married and have families. I must compete every day against other professionals as well as tourists. The very best poker players in the world either live here or visit frequently. The competition is fierce, but if you are good, and I am good, the financial rewards can be great. I have gained a reputation all over town among my colleagues as a good player, and you have seen the write-ups I have sent you.

I have realistic hopes of permanently avoiding ever going back to work for anyone else—unless it is on my own terms. I wonder if you fully realize what I feel inside—being completely independent and on my own. I can come and go as I please, with my time entirely my own. I can always find a poker game day or night seven days a week. I really enjoy what I am doing and don't mind spending the long hours necessary to make a living at it. Bobbi claims I have become a work-a-holic, and she is right. I have been playing seven days each week.

Other good poker players are habitually broke because of other vices and a lack of self-discipline. I have good discipline and an intense desire to win. If I really want something I am willing to make the necessary sacrifices to get it.

I have met hundreds of interesting people, and I feel I have broadened my character and personality. Bobbi has been a great source of strength for me and is used to our new lifestyle. It was very difficult for her at first, but now that we are established, she loves it out here and appreciates the many benefits that this town has to offer. The kids all have lots of new friends and are doing well at school.

Take care for now and Bobbi and the kids send you their love.

Tom

The early years—net poker winnings

Like any good (former) accountant, I kept meticulous records. I made money my first half-year in Las Vegas, but I no longer have those records, nor my income tax returns (yes, I paid taxes on my earnings, though like most people, I may have fudged the numbers a bit). I think the 1979 records got tossed when I lost my second house in my second divorce. But I have my net poker earnings records from 1980 on. Here are the round numbers of the first four years of my poker pro career, 1979 thru 1982.

August to December 1979: Tournament winnings of $4,150

1980: won $29,500
- $5,000 7-Card Stud (Cash: $5/$10 mostly, sometimes $10/$20)
- $14,500 Limit Hold'em (Cash: $10/$20 mostly. Sometimes smaller and sometimes higher)
- $1,000 Razz
- $500 Draw High
- $1,000 7-Card Stud Freezeout Tournaments
- $7,500 Limit Hold'em Freezeout Tournaments

1981: won $44,000
- $11,100 7-Card Stud
- $21,100 Limit Hold'em
- (-$100) Razz
- $1,100 7-Card Stud High-Low Split
- $1,300 7-Card Stud Freezeout Tournaments
- $9,500 Limit Hold'em Freezeout Tournaments

1982: won $48,000
- (-$2,800) 7-Card Stud

- $24,800 Limit Hold'em
- $1,600 Razz
- $2,200 7-Card Stud High-Low Split
- $2,200 7-Card Stud Freezeout Tournaments
- $18,200 Limit Hold'em Freezeout Tournaments
- $800 Razz Freezeout Tournaments
- $1,000 7-Card Stud High-Low Split Freezeout Tournaments

The early years—family life

The first year was a little rough on the kids, having to make so many life adjustments: new schools, new friends, etc. In Michigan, Bobbi was a daycare provider, a certified professional caring for the kids of lots of single moms in our home. So, my kids were used to a house full of extra kids/friends, seven to ten at a time. Now it was just them.

Bobbi was very intelligent, Mensa in fact. With my new venture, she was a bit nervous about finances and the future in general. Who wouldn't be? She figured she needed to get a job with benefits, so shortly after moving to Vegas, she took the Civil Service exam, earned one of the highest scores, and got a full-time job with the Post Office. Not long after that, we got a second car. It was a Pinto, with nothing automatic . . . steering, windows, gear shift . . . very bare bones, so Bobbi could get to work. Like my poker earnings, her earnings were considered the family's money. Together, we started saving for a goal of Bobbi's, which was to buy a house.

For the first three-and-a-half years in Vegas, we rented a two-level condo with three bedrooms and two bathrooms. There was a master bedroom and a smaller bedroom upstairs. We put the boys in the master bedroom, and Melanie in the other bedroom. Both had red shag carpet. There was a separate bathroom upstairs they shared.

Downstairs was carpeted in blue shag, including our bedroom. Being new at the Post Office, Bobbi was working all kinds of hours, with shifts that changed every few months. My hours playing poker were not consistent either, to say the least, so we took the downstairs bedroom so we could come and go and not disturb the kids.

In the beginning, we basically roughed it. My beloved poker table had a cover, and we used it as our dining table, along with two lawn chairs we had brought from Michigan. Shortly after we arrived in Vegas, we celebrated Melanie's tenth birthday, and as part of her celebration, she got to sit at the table in one of the lawn chairs. She remembers that with great pride. Slowly but surely, we added furniture, and the condo became home.

Urban life in the Vegas condo community was completely different for Melanie, Mike, and Pat. The school bus stop was right outside the entrance to the condo complex, so instead of walking a couple of blocks to school like they did in Grand Rapids, each morning they walked to the bus stop to go to school. Because of the odd hours Bobbi and I kept, the kids were alone quite a bit, which wasn't unusual for Vegas back then. The condo community sort of watched out for itself, and we felt the kids were safe. When they were alone, Melanie watched over her brothers, and it wasn't long before she was babysitting other kids in the neighborhood. If one of her parents (or the next-door neighbor) were home, she even babysat a nearby infant. You'd never trust your baby to an eleven-year-old these days. Melanie has always been mature for her age.

Las Vegas wasn't green like Grand Rapids. There was more concrete than dirt. Next to the condo complex were concrete drainage-control ditches built for the storm drain system. They were "secured" by a chain-link fence, but the neighborhood kids knew how to get in. Those ditches became playgrounds. All the kids played in these ditches. My boys would come home with crawdads and scorpions. They staged fights between scorpions and fire ants. Of course, they learned other concrete pastimes like roller skating and skateboarding on the sidewalks between the units.

Yet there were some similarities to the Midwest, like Little League baseball. I was able to use some of my non-nocturnal poker time to help coach my son Michael's Little League team, the Utes. I remember the time with those young guys fondly.

We lived in the condo for the better part of four years. We started out renting with the option to buy. About two years after we moved in there, we opted to buy the place. After we bought the condo, things got complicated. We learned the people we were renting the condo from didn't own it—they didn't have a clear title to it. They had bought it as an investment property, and they were using our payments to make their payments. When we learned about this "little" snafu, I had to hire a lawyer.

After all was said and done, we were able to pay off what we owed on it in full, and that was less than what the folks we were renting it from owed their bank on the property. They ended up having to sign a note to me to pay me off over a two-year period. And they did. When we sold the condo, we didn't make any money on it, just sold it for close to what we had in it. No equity at all.

With Bobbi's job at the Post Office and my poker earnings, we were able to save up enough money for a down payment on a house. I did borrow a little money from Dad to help with the purchase. So, we had the money, and our credit was good enough despite me being in a questionable profession. We bought the house in January or February of 1983, just before the World Series started in April. Nice house in a nice neighborhood on Mountain Valley Road off Tropicana. After Bobbi and I got divorced, I gave her the house, and our son Michael bought it later and lived there for a few years. It was my residence for seven years.

My first house in Las Vegas.

My life changed when the dealer burned and turned too soon.
—Tom McEvoy

CHAPTER 5

Before the Main Event:
My First World Series of Poker Bracelet.

M y World Series of Poker experiences were growing. I played in one event the year after I arrived in Vegas in 1980, the $500 Stud event, and one event in 1981. No cashes. In 1982, I played in five events. I won a satellite for the $5,000 7-Card Stud event in which I made the final table. This event paid the last six players, and I was the "Bubble Boy," meaning I came in seventh. I did one better in the $1,000 7-Card Razz event, where eight players made the money, and I finished in sixth place and cashed for $3,200.

My plan in 1983 was to play in four $1,000 buy-in events: Limit and No-Limit Hold'em, Razz, and Stud Hi-Lo Split. Note that I had to come up with an extra $25 over the buy-in totals because that was the extra charge each player paid as the "entry fee" to cover tournament administration.

Playing in the Main Event was in my dreams, but not on my radar. My plan was to sell shares of myself in these $4,000 events in order to get in. Financially, the Main Event buy-in of $10,000 was well beyond my bankroll, or my ability to attract sponsors with that kind of money.

I had very little No-Limit Hold'em experience, but I had played a lot of Pot-Limit Hold'em, which has some similarities to No-Limit. By this time, I had played in as many tournaments in Las Vegas as I could, and that experience gave me an advantage. Most of these tournaments were Limit Hold'em and 7-Card Stud, and a few were No-Limit Hold'em, but I found the skills needed to win were applicable to multiple poker games. As I played in them, I was actively developing my own system of playing tournament poker, which was uncharted territory. There was no place to turn for insight on the subject—experience was key. My WSOP competition held the advantage in the game of No-Limit Hold'em, but my tournament experience far outpaced theirs.

The 1983 World Series of Poker began the sequence of events on my road to poker history. I played but didn't cash in the Razz and Stud High-Low Split tournaments. Next up was the Limit Hold'em tournament, eleventh of the fourteen WSOP events that year. At 11:00 a.m. on Thursday, May 12, 1983, I began play in the tournament that resulted in a big shot of adrenaline for my poker career. There were 234 players, 20 more than had ever turned out for any WSOP tournament. Fewer than half of them were poker pros.

Back then, the WSOP ran from mid-April to mid-May, and all events except the Main Event were scheduled to be two-day tournaments. The Horseshoe Casino in downtown Las Vegas, home to the World Series of Poker, was bursting at the seams. All the hotel rooms in downtown Las Vegas were booked. Poker was a tiny part of Horseshoe owner Benny Binion's overall casino operations, and the Horseshoe didn't even have its own card room at the time. So, there were poker tables sort of jammed in all throughout the casino. They even temporarily closed a restaurant and put in poker tables, and they took out some slot machines so they could set up a few tables on the main floor.

They didn't have enough room or enough poker tables for this many tournament entrants, so some of the tournament games were played across the street in rival casino card rooms at the Golden Nugget, the Four Queens, and the Fremont. We players even made jokes about "making the final casino." As players busted out at these casinos and a table was broken down, the remaining players were transferred to the Horseshoe and simply carried their chips across Fremont Street with them. My table was at the Horseshoe, and we were surrounded by slot machine players who seemed oblivious to the whole poker thing.

My life changed when the dealer burned the top card (placed it face down on the table) and turned the next card (revealed it face up on the table) too soon.

How many times has a dealer made a mistake that cost a player money? Many times, in my case. The dealers are better now than they used to be, but these kinds of mistakes still happen all the time. To set the stage, I'm playing late on the first day of the two-day tournament. There were 234 entries and they paid nine spots. Only roughly 4 percent of the tournament entrants would get paid. We were up to fairly big limits, about $800 and $1600. The deal came and I had 7 - 7, pocket 7s. I'm up against a guy who has big, suited cards—the A-J of diamonds. The board was paired (not with a 7) when he made a flush on fourth street, the fourth of five "up" or community cards. I didn't put him on that, so I decided to bluff with an aggressive raise, representing that I had made a flush. Since the board was paired, he was a little fearful his nut flush (the best flush possible) might be beat by a full house, so he just called after we got all the extra money in the pot. But the dealer didn't see this final action, and he had already burned and turned the last, or "river" card—before the actual final action.

So, we asked for Eric Drache, the Tournament Manager, to come over. We knew what the rule would be. They would have to take back that river card, shuffle it into the remaining unused cards in the deck, then burn (take the next card off the top and place it face down) a card, and turn (place face up) a new river card. This time the river card was a 7, one of only two cards left in the deck that would save me. I hit a "two-outer" to make a full house on a dealer error. That changed my entire life. Instead of losing this pot as I was supposed to, I won this giant pot, which set the stage to get me to the next day. Day One finished with 44 players, and I was in 13th place with $6,500 in chips, slightly north of my goal of having $6,000. The leader had twice as many chips as I did. In second place was a guy by the name of Johnny Chan, with $11,500 in chips. But I was still alive. I had a big enough stack to get to the final table the next day, with a legitimate shot at being one of the top nine finishers and making at least some money.

That night, I had a conversation with my middle child, Michael. He has a cognitive thing where sometimes he would sense things before they happened. For example, one time he woke in the middle of the night screaming that something had happened to a neighbor, only to find out later the man had passed away that very night, at the very time Michael's nightmare woke him up. So, I asked him if he had any sense of what was going to happen in the tournament. He said that two numbers were popping up in his head, number 1, and number 5. He said he didn't know what they meant. The next day I made the final table. I was in fifth place in chip count and had drawn seat number five. And of course, I later finished number one.

On the final day, I survived a lot of swings, and my chip stack was up and down like an elevator. I got knocked down in chips and came back, over and over. It was gut wrenching. At one point, when we were three-handed, I had less than 20 percent of the chips on the table. The Irishman Donnacha O'Dea had over half the chips, and James Karis, a tough-playing tourist from Pittsburgh, was in second place with the rest of the chips. O'Dea went on a furious rally for a while, running over Karis and me until he lost a few hands and tightened up. Then I went on a rush and beat Karis for a whole series of pots, and beat O'Dea a few times, too. I went from a distant third to first, accumulating 70 percent of the chips after I knocked Karis out of the tournament.

That left Donnacha O'Dea and me heads-up in the finals. In the decisive hand, Lady Luck was on my side again. I got O'Dea all in with J - 2, but he was ahead with Q - 6. The board ran out 7, J, Q, 8, before I spiked a 2 on the river for two pair to win the tournament. He told me later he blamed me for the fact that it cost him 16 years before he finally won a bracelet because he couldn't beat me that day. He was the best-known player in Ireland, an Olympic swimmer, and a drop-dead movie-star-handsome man. My wife, Bobbi, like most of the women watching, drooled over him. Interestingly, he and I had played in the finals of a tournament at the Stardust casino a couple months prior. In that tournament we got down to three players, and I tried to make a deal. He wouldn't do it. I went out third, so he had made the correct decision. Fast forward to the WSOP Limit Hold'em tournament, and this time I didn't suggest a deal. I knew he was a real tough player, and that he didn't like to make deals. Regardless, I just wanted to play him. After I won, I found out what a nice guy he was, and we became, and remain, friends. A week later, he made the final table of the Main Event with me, where he came in sixth.

When asked by the media about the victory afterward, my comment was, "If you had only $3,000 to your name, and had just won $117,000—well, that says it all. I can't believe it. You'll have to excuse me, I'm in space."

I netted $60,000 in this event, and you can read why in Chapter 9, "Let's Make a Deal."

For the World Series of Poker, the one-table satellite to the
Main Event was the acorn that grew into the mighty oak.
                                              —*Tom McEvoy*

CHAPTER 6

♣ ♦ ♥ ♠

Winning a Satellite. My Main Event Prelude.

In 1983, I had only been a full-time Las Vegas poker professional for
four years, plus one year when I commuted from Grand Rapids,
Michigan. So, for this Las Vegas poker grinder, the World Series of
Poker Main Event entry fee of $10,000 was an almost insurmount-
able amount of cash. Still, I wanted to play in it so very badly.

The Limit Hold'em tournament I had just won paid $117,000,
of which I got to keep $60,000. As a $10/$20 poker grinder with
a modest bankroll, $60,000 was the most money I ever had in my
life! Yes, I had the money to enter the Main Event, but I am not an
"easy come, easy go" kind of guy. I wasn't about to put up a sixth,
or $10,000 of that victory money, when there were ways of getting
in the big game for less.

Thankfully, in 1983 there was a relatively new opportunity
to win a seat in the big game, the tournament satellite. Satellites
were the brainchild of my friend Eric Drache, who was the WSOP
Tournament Director for the Binion family at the Horseshoe casino for a number of years. Jack Binion told my biographer that
Eric might have the best personality of anybody he ever knew. A

relatively young guy in the poker world (about my age—he was 40 and I was 38), Eric enjoyed a reputation as one of the best 7-Card Stud players in the country. One of the reasons he was inducted into the Poker Hall of Fame in 2012 was because of the tournament satellites he invented to grow the sport by getting more entries per tournament. And growing the tournament beyond a few dozen players was a high priority for Jack and Benny Binion.

The idea was born when Drache saw a bunch of guys playing a cash game and he said to them, "Why don't you guys each put up a thousand bucks and the winner will get a seat in the Main Event?" That was one year before I won the satellite. Drache had the concept in place, and he decided to really push satellites in 1983. Just like the guy who later made winning satellites famous, Chris Moneymaker, I think it was a brilliant idea. The satellite route was the obvious solution for me to enter the Main Event on the cheap.

The nine-player satellite events held at the Horseshoe casino paid $10,000 to the single winner, just enough for the Main Event entry fee. Ironic, isn't it? Still, the $1,165 satellite tournament fee was a lot of money for me. And the competition was tough, I knew, because I had a list of the players signed up for the satellite I hoped to play in. One of them was a casual friend of mine, Johnny Chan. He wasn't "the famous" Johnny Chan then. He hadn't won his first of 10 WSOP bracelets and two back-to-back Main Event championships yet, but he had placed in the money in several tournaments, and I knew how good a player he was. And if I didn't have to, I'd rather not play against Johnny. So, I went up to him when he was playing in a cash game, told him I'd signed up for the next one-table satellite, and that I saw his name was also on the list. I said if you're going to play it, go ahead. But if you're going to play, I'll pick another satellite, because I really don't want to play against you. He said no, go ahead, you play, and he would wait for another satellite. I took that as quite a compliment in my poker ability, and his implied endorsement gave me a real boost in confidence.

Even with Johnny Chan not playing, this satellite was not going to be a walk in the park. A couple of guys at the table were casual friends of mine, and I knew they would be my stiffest competition. One was Jimmy Doman. He'd won a couple of WSOP bracelets in the 1980s and finished eighth in the Main Event in 1986. The other was poker pro David Sklansky, another WSOP bracelet winner who later authored *The Theory of Poker*, arguably one of the most influential books on the game.

We got down to three players left in the satellite. Of course, it was me, Sklansky, and Doman. Sklansky had the chip lead, I was second, and Doman was third. Doman went out, and I trapped Sklansky in a hand and won the satellite.

Backing up a little, before the sit-n-go $1,165 WSOP satellite, I also tried the $100 satellite tournaments held at the Bingo Palace poker room (now the Palace Station). They held four of these tournaments with 100 players, each of whom put up $110. In these tournaments, one player would win a seat in the Main Event. I didn't win any of them, but the guy I was heads-up with at the Main Event final table that year, Rodney Peate, did win one. Rod was probably even more unknown in the poker world than me at the time, but he was no stranger to me. He and I played in the same poker games around town, and we had a lot of mutual acquaintances. Like people of the same interests often do, we had talked poker a fair amount. We had a lot in common, like the fact that we both didn't have a lot of money.

Rod Peate and I had both won our World Series of Poker Main Event seats via a satellite tournament. No satellite winner had ever won the Main Event, so it was a foregone conclusion when we got heads up that the record would be broken. And that reality was not lost on the poker world. You did not have to have deep pockets or big backers. For about a thousand bucks you could win your way into the Main Event. And as the satellite concept grew more popular, it expanded. Chris Moneymaker gave the concept a tremendous shot in the arm when he famously won an $86 satellite tournament on PokerStars and went on to win the WSOP Main Event in 2003. Chris was an accountant, too, by the way. Just saying.

I felt proud to be a trendsetter in poker. And this was the first of several pioneering poker achievements in my life.

All of the World Series of Poker events except the Main Event were scheduled for two days, and only one tournament was played at a time. This resulted in a lot of downtime for the players, including me. So, I played a lot of cash games during the World Series back then. After I won my Main Event seat in the satellite, I had a few days before it was going to start. I started playing some No-Limit Hold'em cash games. I didn't think anything of it—I was playing in $25/50 ante games. That was a very big No-Limit Hold'em game back then involving some pretty good players. I told a friend I was going to go play some of these cash games to practice for the Main Event tournament, because I hadn't played that much No-Limit Hold'em. My friend thought I was a bit touched to be swimming in such deep uncharted waters and suggested I play a small game. Since I had won the Limit Hold'em event I had the money to sit down with $2,000 and not be decimated if it all went wrong. But I actually beat those games. I won a few thousand.

As I pen these words to leave a lasting record,
I wonder myself where it all began.
—Richard Peck

CHAPTER 7

The WSOP Main Event Preamble.
The First Three Years: 1970 to 1972.

I have heard this story many times, but it was verified to me (and some others) in person by Doyle Brunson. He acknowledged that this is what happened.

By vote of the players in 1970, Johnny Moss was "elected" champion of the first World Series of Poker Main Event. The following year, he won the title of World Champion, collecting all the chips from the other five players in the first "freezeout" (no rebuys, no re-entry) version of the tournament. But a "World Series" that consisted of only one table—and not even a full table—needed a growth hormone to eventually spur the tournament to the meteoric heights it has reached today. The players recognized this.

Johnny Moss was recognized as the two-time World Champion. But it was also recognized that Johnny would not be the best spokesman for poker. A quiet man, he wasn't overly literate, nor very articulate. He was a great instinctive player, but he did not have a gift of gab. There was a general consensus on the problem, but not necessarily the solution. They just knew they needed a poker ambassador who, as World Champion, could better hype the tournament.

The 1972 Main Event presented an opportunity. When it got down to the final three players, it was Amarillo Slim, Doyle Brunson, and Puggy Pearson. They got to talking, and a deal was struck. Back then, the tournament was still played with casino chips—you got $10,000 worth of Horseshoe chips for your $10,000 buy-in. It was a winner-take-all situation in theory. In practice, here's what happened.

At the time, Doyle was the chip leader, or close to it. That's when the reporters and the TV cameras arrived. Doyle didn't want the spotlight at that particular time—his family back in Texas didn't know what he did for a living, plus becoming known as a top player could be bad for business. Puggy was colorful, but he didn't have the tremendous bullshitting ability that Slim had. Slim was the best talker of the three, and he told them he really wanted to be the winner. They knew Slim had a magic gift for gab, so they made a three-way deal and agreed they would let him win.

So, the fix was in. Puggy and Doyle started playing crazy—they had to eventually lose their chips to Slim. This is when Amarillo Slim started to upset Doyle. Slim started to showboat, doing things like holding his hand up to show the crowd. He started flaunting his inside knowledge in front of Brunson and Pearson, showing off and playing up to the crowd. After a while Doyle said he couldn't stand it anymore, so when Slim made one of his showboat moves, Doyle moved all-in on him. Slim slowed down, gave him one of those looks that asks, "What just happened here?" Slim had to fold this particular hand, but he got the message.

So did Jack Binion. He saw what was happening and asked the three to meet with him privately in his office. Because Doyle didn't want the publicity, he was allowed to withdraw from the tournament with about $19,000 in chips, claiming illness like he had a stomach issue. Given Doyle's hefty stature, a stomach ailment was believable. He was probably around 6'3" and over 300 pounds at the time, I'd guess. Throughout his career he made a bunch of weight-loss bets with people, so his weight fluctuated quite a bit. Many people don't know it, but he was an outstanding athlete in his early days, and likely could have played professional basketball. But an injury was probably the best thing that could have happened to him, because he turned to poker full time, and that's where his true talent lay.

Amarillo Slim made the most of this decision for him to win. In fact, he made his whole career off that win. He wrote a book that sold well called *Play Poker to Win,* and began making appearances on TV talk shows. He appeared on the Johnny Carson Show 11 times, and it seemed like everyone was watching this show in the 1970s. He spoke to Congress, made *60 Minutes* three times, and appeared with Benny Binion for an entire episode of the *Tomorrow Show.* With this kind of exposure, Amarillo Slim had become the most famous poker player in the country, and he used his good-old-boy storytelling charms to talk up poker and the tournament. Poker was the underground national pastime, and there was a groundswell of interest as the game gained public attention. Like him or despise him, Amarillo Slim Preston gave poker and the WSOP the boost it needed. And by doing so, he changed the course of poker.

I didn't hear what Puggy got out of the deal. The WSOP was so new a title didn't bring much prestige, and making money was probably what he was most interested in. Don't forget that the very next year, 1973, Puggy did win the tournament. All three of these guys eventually got their World Series Main Event titles. Doyle won twice in 1976 and 1977, and he came in second to Stu Ungar in 1980, and third to me in 1983. Of the three 1972 final table finalists, it turns out Doyle was really the best spokesman for poker in the long run.

L to R: Amarillo Slim, dealer, Benny Binion, Doyle Brunson, unknown, Puggy Pearson. Photo: Las Vegas Review Journal.

I'd have played in this tournament for nothing . . . that's the truth . . .
just to have the opportunity to play in it. The money is important. Don't
misunderstand me, the money is very important. But I wanted to win
this tournament more than anything I've ever wanted to do in my life.
　　　　　　　　　　　　—*Tom McEvoy, as interviewed on*
　　　　　　　　　　　　ABC's Wide World of Sports

CHAPTER 8

♣ ♦ ♥ ♠

The 1983 WSOP Main Event.
How I Became Poker's World Champion.

The World Series of Poker Main Event. It's the granddaddy of all poker events. To poker players it's the Super Bowl, Kentucky Derby, Stanley Cup, Indy 500, and the Masters all rolled into one. It's the event everybody wants to win, because the winner is designated as the overall World Champion of Poker for one year.

Over 40 years ago, in 1983, there were just 108 entries into the Main Event, a number dwarfed by today's standards. To view this objectively, a little perspective is required. First, the WSOP was in its infancy, relatively unknown, and just starting to gain momentum, and the entry numbers were not pumped up by thousands of small, online, and local tournament qualifiers, well-healed celebrities, and bucket-listers. Second, imagine the size of today's field if the cost of entry had not remained the same. The 1983 entry fee of $10,000 roughly translates to $30,000 today. That's a big chunk of change, and a value that was intended to limit the field to mostly top pros, the best in the world. On a per-player basis, the overall quality of play was arguably very high. There was almost no dead money.

Yet even back then the World Series of Poker field was international. Including entries into all the events, nearly 30 foreign countries were represented. Jack Binion, the WSOP host, said, "If it's going to be a world championship, we have to have worldwide competition." He had succeeded in attracting the best poker talent from all over the globe.

The 1983 World Series of Poker was the start of a historic shift brought about by the growing popularity of satellite tournaments. For the first time there were almost as many "semi-professionals" and/or "amateurs" in the field as professionals. I was classified by most at the time as an amateur, even though I had made my living playing poker for four years. Without the satellite concept, even middle-limit professional grinders like me would not have been able to attend the big dance. And the WSOP was starting to attract high-profile celebrities, like Larry Flynt, who controversially finished 14th in 1983 (see more about this story in Chapter 30).

The four-day Main Event was a grueling test of poker skills, cunning, luck, and physical stamina. In 1983, the starting stacks were $10,000, and each player anted $10 with one $50 blind per hand (today the players get more starting chips, and from start to finish it's a two-week tournament). The antes and blinds went up every two hours, and play ran about eight hours each of the first three days. This small structure, in relation to the chips on the table, made it a slow-action tournament. My goal for the first day was to stay alive and survive.

The oddsmakers didn't give me much of a chance. Bob Stupak's Vegas World wagering form that gave odds on which players would win the Main Event didn't even have my name listed. The El Cortez wagering form had me at 60 to 1, and Rod Peate, the eventual second-place finisher, at 75 to 1. I had been playing low-limit buy-in tournament poker in Las Vegas for the past four years, so I was known in the local poker community. Still, the smart money was on the well-known, big-time players with lots of experience playing high-stakes poker.

For the Main Event, 12 nine-handed tables were squeezed into the main floor at the Horseshoe casino in downtown Las Vegas. Back then, the daily Main Event tournament format was structured on hours played versus the number of players remaining. We played a fixed number of hours the first and second days, and whoever survived played the third day. Then on the third day, we played down to the final nine. The final table started at noon on the fourth day, giving the players some time to rest up. In my case, the final table actually went into the wee hours of the fifth day.

The Main Event—Day One

Like many if not most poker players, we do things we hope will bring us luck. Some say it's superstition, but it's part of the color of the game. On one of my forays to Reno, I visited the historic old mining town of Virginia City, Nevada, with a couple of my friends. The town personifies the Old West, and I bought a black Stetson hat and a western shirt. Despite the fact that I looked like a "drugstore cowboy," I thought the western look worked for me. To personalize the shirt, I had Bobbi sew a green shamrock on the collar in deference to my Irish heritage. I wore this when I won Amarillo Slim's Super Bowl of Poker in Lake Tahoe in 1982. The Stetson and the shirt (I also had a black shirt) became my lucky outfit.

When I sat down that first day, Tuesday, May 17, 1983, attired in my lucky outfit, my table was crowded with poker legends. Three were former World Champions: Amarillo Slim, Bobby Baldwin, and Puggy Pearson. David Sklansky was also there. The room was crowded, too. Binion's Horseshoe casino, growing in stature across the globe, did not have a poker room yet. They cleared out an area from the casino main floor. It had low ceilings, no ventilation to speak of, and the "rail" where spectators could stand and watch was so close I could reach out and touch them.

Photo by Pamela Shandel.

I made up my mind before the tournament started that I was going to make a respectable showing, but I was not going to be intimidated by anybody, especially the biggest names. That first day I played very few big pots. I just hung in there and chipped up a tad to finish the day in 36th position with $12,675 in chips. The leader, Austin Squatty, had $40,325, and around a third of the field had been eliminated.

The Main Event—Day Two

On day two, Wednesday, May 18th, the blinds and antes were getting larger, forcing more play. Continuing in the tournament meant winning more chips. I broke a player with a few thousand chips, then couldn't seem to win a hand for a while. My table was consolidated, and I found myself with Doyle Brunson on my right and the eventual runner-up, Rod Peate, on my left. Plus, the legendary Amarillo Slim was at the table. Talk about tough competition! And I was down to just $5,000 in chips, half of my original stack. I was in trouble. Time to get aggressive. Luckily, I experienced a run of good cards—a rush—and won a series of pots. I was still on my rush when a hand I played made the national limelight.

One writer, Phil Hevener, managing editor of *Poker Player* newspaper and columnist for the *Las Vegas Sun*, called the hand I got into with Amarillo Slime "One of the most fascinating hands in the World Series of Poker." That's not a typo—that's just the way I feel about Slim, and not just because of this hand, as you'll see. We were the only players left in a pot of about $40,000. I had pocket Aces and raised going in. Slim called with pocket Sixes. The flop brought a 6 - 4 - 3, with two spades, setting up the possibility of a flush and a straight. I bet about the size of the pot and he just smooth called. That made my radar go off. I doubted he had a hand like 7 - 5, so I put him on two-pair or a set (three of a kind; a pair in the hand with a matching card on the board). The next card was an off-suit Ace, giving me the top set of trips. I could beat anything but a straight. That gave me the confidence to make a bet big enough to put half of Slim's chip stack in jeopardy. Again, he smooth called, reinforcing my read that he had a big hand. Slim was a gambler, but I didn't think he would take that big a chance with a flush draw. But sure enough, the last card to come off the deck was the 9 of spades. Three spades for the potential flush were on the board.

I was so confident I had the best hand that I shoved. I went all in, stood up, and in my best western drawl said to the famous Texan, "If you have a flush, Slim, you just won yourself a big pot." If he called and lost, he would be eliminated. The action was done, and Slim faced the big decision to call or fold. Everyone watching drew a collective breath. Cameras flashed. The TV cameras swiveled to Slim. All eyes were on him, and I know he loved it. So, he did what he did best. He showboated. He stoically turned over his hole cards and looked at me, showing me my read was right. A pair of sixes, giving him a set.

Slim was looking for a sign of weakness from me, the relatively unknown young poker player he knew, but knew little about. But I read it as bullying, something that makes my blood boil and brings me out of my nerdy introverted self. So, I made a move I later regretted, but the TV people and the audience loved. I countered this psychological move by turning over one my hole cards, the Ace of hearts.

Slim stared at the board, pondering his next move. Then he did what he always did when the spotlight was on him. He started jawing. We jawed back and forth for several minutes, again, his way of stalling. I remember saying, "Wake me when it's over." Finally, I had had enough, and I called the clock to be put on him. This is an infrequently used tactic when one player feels another player is taking too much time. That meant he had 60 seconds to act on his hand—call or fold. Slim kept talking as the Tournament Supervisor Frank Cutrona counted down the last seconds, but he refused to play his hand or throw it in. "So, what happens now?" asked Slim, who was well aware of the rules. "Your hand is no good," Cutrona said. Slim's hand had been declared dead, and I won the pot. Slim only shrugged. Without comment and without showing my undisclosed hole card, I stacked the chips that were pushed my way by the dealer. My other Ace, by the way, was the Ace of Spades. If Slim had made a flush, it wouldn't have been the best hand possible, "the nuts."

The hand was a dramatic moment that got a lot of publicity. It was shown on TV that night and was written up in a lot of papers. I was besieged at the next break by reporters and friends wanting to know what my unexposed hole card was. I put them off as long as I could. But many of the reporters were Las Vegas poker players, and they were my friends. I finally let on to one of them, after he promised to write it up in the *Gaming Today* newspaper, which did a great job covering the Las Vegas poker scene.

It was a mistake to show one of my Aces to Slim during the hand. My friend Al Jay Ethier, who had spent a lot of time playing poker with Amarillo Slim, was convinced seeing the Ace put too much doubt in Slim's mind to call. No Ace shown, and odds are Slim calls, I win a bigger pot, and Slim exits the tournament. Some in the poker press called this my "flair for the dramatic," but it wasn't. I showboated. I played very aggressively and in retrospect, the play probably also lacked a little common sense. But this cocky play contributed to my table image, which ultimately worked in my favor.

Regardless, the play set up the finale with Slim about 20 minutes later. I raised pre-flop with an Ace-9 of Spades. Slim moved all-in with pocket Queens, arguably the correct move with his stack size. I flopped a 9 and a flush draw. The next card, the turn card, was an Ace, and that sent Slim to watch the rest of the tournament from the sideline. And my chip stack kept growing.

Day two recessed at 8:45 p.m. I ended the day in 12th position with $38,400 in chips. For perspective, the leader had $74,300. Interestingly, the top four chip leaders after day two did not make the money. Including the legendary Johnny Moss.

The Main Event—Day Three

Day three started at noon on Thursday, May 19. I was still at the table with Doyle Brunson. Before the tournament I had only spoken with him once, when I purchased his *Super System* book four years earlier. I told him how much I admired him and considered his book the bible of the game. Doyle smiled and said thank you. His graciousness is part of the reason he has my highest respect. I believe his book helped turn me into a winning Hold'em player.

Photo by Pamela Shandel.

So now I found myself sparring with the player who would become the most famous man in poker. I moved in on Doyle a couple of times. I came over the top of him, and I didn't have a hand, but I was positive he didn't have one either. He was trying to steal, and I just knew it. This tactic was working, so I kept doing it. At one point, I had bet at him so many times and run over him so often that he looked me in the eye and said, "No man alive can do what you've been doing to me and get away with it." That made me think I had rattled him, and he was getting annoyed. Maybe. A while later, a hand came up where he showed me why he is a world-class player, when he put a stop to my constant betting and raising.

He raised the button, and I came over the top again, this time legitimately with two Jacks. He called and the flop came K - Q - x. I had about $150,000 in chips at the time, which was above average and more than enough to get me to the final table. But I just had to show Doyle how tough I was. I made a big bet and he called. Of course, I shut it down on the turn and he won the pot with a bet. I found out later he just had Ace-10, but I had allowed him to change how I was playing. I should have just check/folded the hand, but I wound up losing about a third of my stack to one of the greatest players ever just because of my ego. I wanted to be able to say that I outplayed him, but he got the best of me. He got me to lay down the best hand.

My mistake came from my own attitude. I entered the Main Event with the mentality that I wasn't going to let anybody intimidate me. But I became way too cocky, and I allowed Doyle to goad me into making a bad play. It may seem like a minor hand to some people, but that's when I learned to swallow my pride at the poker table.

The night before the final table I was, as you can imagine, a bit keyed up. TV news crews from ABC, NBC, CBS, and a Canadian network would be filming the action the next day. I was going to be on an international stage. I couldn't sleep, so for the hundredth time I read and then reread the No-Limit Hold'em section of Doyle's *Super System* book. Ironic, since Doyle had made the final table with me and would be one of my opponents on Friday.

The Main Event—Day Four

Day four, the final table, Friday, May 20. Play resumed at noon. At the beginning of the day, there were nine players left. The three chip leaders were Rodney Peate with about $360,000 in chips, Doyle Brunson with maybe $250,000, and I was running a distant third with $117,000. I thought the poker gods were smiling on me since $117,000 was the winner's share of the WSOP Limit Hold'em tournament I had won a few days ago. Freaky, but true. Paying attention to the numbers has served me well in my poker career.

Going into the last day, Doyle Brunson was the favorite to win his third world championship. At that point the line on me was 8 to 1, even though I was third in chips. Remember, I was still relatively obscure in the poker world, but not unknown to everyone. The Tournament Director, Eric Drache, took those odds and bet on me. Good for him.

In those days, the tournament was run dollar-for-dollar chips in play. One hundred and eight entrants at $10,000 each put $1,080,000 in face value of chips in play. Therefore, each chip represented its face amount in real money. At the start of the day, the remaining six players in fourth through ninth position had an average of about $60,000 in chips, roughly 5 percent of the chips in play. The blinds were going up.

Going into the last day, I was going to use the strategy I had learned and honed from my tournament poker experience. My key strategy was to avoid confrontations with the big stacks unless I flopped the nuts or a big hand. I planned to concentrate on and attack the short stacks. My plan worked, and I eliminated two of the short stacks.

The final table in 1983 followed suit from the year before, as the first six players hit the rail very quickly on the way to heads-up action. But that is where the similarities ended. In just over 20 minutes, George Huber (ninth), R. R. Penington (eighth), Austin

Squatty (seventh), Donnacha O'Dea (sixth), Robbie Geers (fifth), and Carl McKelvey (fourth), were all sent to the rail. R. R. Penington and Austin Squatty were my victims. The final three players had taken turns disposing of that unfortunate half-dozen.

So, the three chip leaders at the start of the day were now the final three players. I was the chip leader with $400,000 and change, Rod Peate was second, and Doyle Brunson third. There was no deal to be made three-handed as long as Doyle was in it. Everybody thought he would just run over us and win. The smart money was on Doyle, the seasoned veteran versus the little-known guys.

Yet by three o'clock in the afternoon, Doyle had fallen behind Rod Peate and me in the chip count. We both had about $400,000, and Doyle was behind with about $280,000. At that point he was playing an aggressive game, raising just about every flop. Doyle and I kept challenging each other, staying fairly even, while Peate watched the action. Then, at 3:21 p.m., Doyle got too aggressive by his own admission, and overplayed a hand against Rod Peate. He went all in with top pair and a flush draw after the flop, and Rod Peate's set of nines held up.

The poker world was stunned. The perspective and the buzz was that the "amateurs" had eliminated the "pros." Rod Peate and I were professionals who played poker for a living, and we had played against each other several times in the past. But neither of us had ever played at this level. Besides, the David v. Goliath angle made a better story. It was good for poker.

Comparing the two Davids, here is Johnny Chan's analysis at the time: "McEvoy is a soldier, more consistent player, more conservative. Peate is more aggressive, more of a gambler. I make Tom the favorite." He wasn't playing favorites, because as you will see in the next chapter, he had nothing to lose. Chan had 20 percent of the action of both Rod Peate and me.

We were now heads-up. I was in seat 7 and Rod was in seat 2, so we were facing each other across the broadest part of the table.

Rod had a chip lead of not quite 2 to 1. To be exact it, was 62½ percent to 37½ percent—he had $666,000 to my $414,000. We had started day four at noon, and we were now heads-up at around 3:30 in the afternoon, which was faster than expected. ABC's *Wide World of Sports* was televising the tournament, hosted by Curt Gowdy, and they wanted to be able to announce the winner on their nightly news. The previous year, the heads-up battle between Jack "Treetop" Straus and Dewey Tomko was over in less than an hour. I know—I was there. They played a million-dollar pot with A - 10 off-suit versus A - 4 suited before the flop. That was absurd as far as I was concerned. However, assuming this year would be much the same, the WSOP officials informed us that there would be a three-hour break.

Photo by Pamela Shandel.

I told them this heads-up match was not going to be slam-bam-thank-you-ma'am like last year. Neither Rod Peate nor I were No-Limit players as a rule, and our style was not to push in our entire stack on a whim. This wasn't the first time that Rod Peate and I had faced each other at a final table as the last two players. The first time was just six months earlier in October 1982, when he beat me in a tournament at the Showboat casino in Las Vegas. I knew this final table would last a long time because of our styles. I'm not Doyle Brunson or Jack Straus, and I was not going to put it all in on a draw.

I also knew I was going to have to change tactics against Rod. Up to this point I had been, in my opinion, the most aggressive player at the table. I had done a lot of leading out with marginal hands, and it had worked. But the blinds were only $1,500 and $3,000, which is very small in relation to the huge stacks we had, so we both had a lot of room to play. I now figured my best strategy would be a slow, long grind where I avoided taking any big risks. I had plenty of time to maneuver. Be patient. No need to gamble.

I didn't care if the tournament was over in five minutes, as long as I was the winner. That's all I cared about. Winning the tournament was more important to me than the money, and I knew the money was more important than the title to Rod. You can lose the money or win more, but the World Championship is in the record books forever. I knew right then and there I might never get this chance again. I knew I couldn't shrug off a second-place finish with an "I'll just do it again next year" attitude. I was absolutely convinced this was a once-in-a-lifetime chance, so I'd better win it now. No pressure. Half a million dollars on the line. To say I was a bit wound up and nervous is an understatement.

Faced with the anguish and tension of an unexpected three-hour break, I was rescued by my fairly new friend, Jimmy Langan. He was an excellent poker player and one of the top table tennis players in the world. I was a top table tennis player, too, but not as good as

Jimmy. He was from Ireland, and I, of course, am of Irish decent. I identified with Jimmy and the Irish and endorsed that pride via the shamrock sewn on the collar of the shirt I wore that day at the final table. Jimmy had played in the Main Event and busted out just short of the final table, and he was still there watching when they called the break. He knew exactly what I needed during this long hiatus to totally relax and get my mind off poker.

He took my wife and me up to his hotel room and gave me a complete body massage, head to toe. It was the best and most timely massage I ever had. It totally relaxed me. I was away from the crowd, the reporters, and the poker room, and was able to get my mind off the game. I came back to the table mentally and physically refreshed and ready to play poker. On top of that, Jimmy told me he thought if Rod Peate and I played heads-up 20 times, I'd win 19. A nice pat on the back to my poker prowess.

We resumed at around just before seven p.m. Here's a brief play-by-play of the action:

7:23 to 8:00 p.m. McEvoy doing most of the betting. Rod folding.

8:02 p.m. Tom wins $70,000 pot with A - K.

8:20 p.m. Chip count: Tom $480,000, Rod $600,000.

8:30 p.m. Rod shifts into more aggressive play.

8:45 p.m. Break. Chip count: Tom $445,000, Rod $635,000.

9:00 p.m. Play resumes.

9:04 p.m. Rod wins $150,000 pot. Chip count: Tom $300,000, Rod $700,000. Blinds $3,000-$6,000.

9:18 p.m. Tom wins $210,000 pot, which revives him. Back to more aggressive betting.

10:00 p.m. Tom forcing action and chipping away. Now up to $480,000.

10:35 p.m. Tom wins flush over flush. $200,000 pot. Tom takes lead $580,000 to $500,000.

10:36 p.m. Rod wins $200,000 pot.

10:45 p.m. Break. Chip count: Tom $440,000, Rod $640,000.

11:06 p.m. Rod rivers a 9 for trips, wins $130,000 pot.

11:08 p.m. Rod wins pot with Ace high.

11:15 p.m. Key pot of the tournament. Flop is Q – J - 5 with two Clubs.

Tom goes all-in with K - Q off suit. Rod has 6 - 7 of Clubs and calls. Pot is $748 ,000.

Tom wins.

Midnight. Two Limit Hold'em players not making a move until they are forced to. Chip count: Tom $680,000, Rod $400,000.

12:19 a.m. Both trying not to lose versus going for it.

12:40 a.m. Break. Chip count: Tom $745,000, Rod $335,000.

1:13 a.m. Play resumes.

1:24 a.m. Tom wins $160,000 pot after going all-in. Rod folds.

1:30 a.m. Blinds up to $8,000/$16,000. New record.

1:31 a.m. Final hand.

We played heads-up for 7 ½ hours until 1:31 a.m., a record that stood for over 30 years. When it was all over, a then not-so-famous Mike Sexton said we had set poker back ten years. Needless to say, we missed the nightly news. In fact, the next year ABC refused to come back and televise the Main Event because we took so long.

Some thought Rod and I were deliberately stalling to stay in the limelight, which was total BS. From the start of heads-up until about 11 p.m., he had the chip lead. Rod was aggressive, and I knew I needed to revise my strategy against him. Bobby Baldwin was one of the TV commentators, and he asked me during the break, on camera, if my strategy changed when the play got down to one-on-one. I said, "Yes it does, but I don't care to discuss it."

My strategy had been to slowly grind Rod down. But it wasn't working. He kept picking up smaller pots and increasing his chip lead. He whittled me down from $400,000 to roughly $280,000 by around 9 p.m. Things were not going well, so it was time to change tactics and get more aggressive. My opportunity to take a stand came at around 11 p.m. I flopped top pair with a K - Q on a Q - J - 5 flop. There were two Clubs on the board and Rod had the 6 - 7 of Clubs, giving him a flush draw with the possibility of a backdoor straight. I shoved all-in and Rod decided to gamble on his draw and try to take me out right there. He missed both the Club flush and the straight, and now I was ahead in the chip count for the first time since Rod had taken out Doyle Brunson, roughly $680,000 to $400,000.

Photo by Pamela Shandel.

Now my strategy changed again. I was in the lead, and I went back to trying to grind him down. This time it was working. I became more selectively aggressive. I put pressure on him. He'd call a bet and then he'd fold. I was slowing gaining chips, drinking water and eating apples while Rod was drinking cola and smoking. And

I tried to take advantage of every psychological advantage I could muster. I stacked my chips in three separate stacks and had two stacks shaped like arrows pointing at my opponent. I kept up my aggressiveness and chipped away at Rod until the break at 12:40 a.m. With the chip count favoring me at $745,000 to $335,000, I had totally reversed our chip positions.

Every time we went on break, we were besieged by the TV cameras and the reporters who were covering the event. They asked me, "Tom, are you as calm and cool and collected as you look? You nervous at all?" I told them, "The only time I'm nervous is when I'm talking to you guys." Regardless of all the commotion and hubbub, I was laser focused on the job. And I finally got it done.

At the 8:45 p.m. break, Rod was ahead in the chip count, $635,000 to $445,000. Rod and I were approached by a mutual friend, Fred David, a WSOP bracelet winner in the 1981 $1,500 No-Limit Hold'em Non-Pro tournament. He pulled us aside, and within hearing distance of anyone on the rail, he said "You guys are playing for too much money. Why don't you guys do this. How about if Tom wins, Rod, you get $350,000 instead of $216,000. If Rod wins, Tom, you get $300,00 instead of $216,000."

If Rod agreed to this deal, and came in second, he would get about the same kind of money I was going to get. Rod agreed to the deal. I was already thinking ahead, and I agreed—immediately. Fred's plan seemed to favor Rod substantially, but I saw it as advantageous to me. Here's why: Rod would have less incentive to win, because we had literally taken money out of the equation. I knew that money was more important to Rod than winning, and the opposite was true for me. Nobody remembers who came in second. The desire to win, and the heart behind it, would be on my side of the equation. It was my total focus. I had to win. And in my opinion, that edge was huge.

As the tournament progressed into the wee hours to Level 17, the blinds were now up to $8,000 and $16,000—the highest they had ever been in the Main Event (a record that held for many years, by the way). That was a cost of a little over 3 percent of my chips per orbit, so technically we still had a lot of room to play. But we had been playing for 7½ hours, it was getting late, and it was 0-tired thirty in the morning.

Then it happened. Rod was dealt a fairly strong hand, the King and Jack of Diamonds. Before the flop he raised the pot with a bet of $40,000. I looked at my cards and saw the one No-Limit Hold'em hand that scares me the most, pocket Queens. The first big pair I had all day. It's a strong hand, but also the hand that quite often gets people knocked out of tournaments. When they make a big bet pre-flop and get played with, all too often they are up against Aces, Kings, or Ace-King. Queens are a big underdog to Aces or Kings, and only a slight favorite against A - K. I had just beaten Rod the previous hand, and sensed he was tired of getting pushed around and was ready to gamble.

After Rod's $40,000 bet pre-flop, I had to give him credit for a hand. But frankly, my Queens made me nervous. I immediately decided I had only two choices—go for it or throw the hand away. My tournament life wasn't on the line, but losing would erase all of my forward momentum and put me behind the eight ball again. I made a move I had rarely made in this Main Event. I pushed all my chips into the center of the table, then leaned back in my chair with my hands behind my neck and waited.

Rod stood up, contemplating whether to call or fold, and hesitated for what seemed like all of one second before announcing he was going to call. My heart sank. I thought I had bet into the nuts. I really thought he was going to turn over two Aces or two Kings. He stood up and pushed all of his chips into the pot. We turned up our cards, and I started to breathe again when Rod surprised me with his King-Jack of Diamonds. Instead of being way behind, I was way ahead!

The flop came 6 - 6 - 3. The turn was a Jack, giving Rod a pair. The last card was a 3. My hand of Queens and sixes held up. It was over. I won this tournament because every time I played a big pot, both luck and the odds were on my side, and I did not get drawn out on. I had really won.

When this fact hit my brain, I jumped several feet straight up, so high I actually landed standing up on the seat of my chair. I swung my hands wildly, forcing a bystander to duck out of the way. I whipped off my Stetson hat, jabbed my right fist in the air in triumph, and yelled several times, "ALL RIGHT!" My coke-bottle glasses slipped from my nose. I was euphoric. I remember getting down from the chair and Bobbi grabbing my hand, but the next minutes were a blur. The noise level in the room erupted, and reporters, friends, and well-wishers rushed over to me all at once. I was choked up and had to wave them off and try to recover my composure. It was a very emotional moment for me and Bobbi, who had been sitting beside me for the entire heads-up match. It was the last time the World Series of Poker allowed significant others to sit by their partners, literally right at the table.

The reason they allowed it at this tournament was because, when we were heads-up, Rod Peate asked management if his girlfriend could sit with him at the table. He also asked me, and I told him I was okay with it as long as Bobbi could sit next to me.

Photo by Pamela Shandel.

I couldn't help but glance at the stunned look on Rod's face and feel for him. After four grueling days, and over seven hours of heads-up play, he had come so close to winning. Rod's story of parlaying a $110 buy-in at the Bingo Palace casino satellite tournament into coming within a whisker of winning the Main Event was epic. It was such a compelling story that when we were heads-up, Gabe Kaplan (star of TV's *Welcome Back, Kotter* and an accomplished poker player) told a Las Vegas reporter he wanted to buy Rod Peate's rags-to-riches story and make it into a movie. I was told that Gabe said, "It would make a heck of a movie of the week for television." I thought my rags-to-riches story was exciting, too, but Gabe didn't seem interested when I suggested it to him a few months later.

I remember working my way through the crowd to shake Rod's hand, and the feeling it gave me. Two friends, the first middle-level $10/$20 players ever to run this deep in the World Series of Poker Main Event. For the first time, two unknowns had reached the pinnacle of the game. Together, we had shown there was hope for the average poker player to reach the rarified upper level of the poker world. It was no longer the exclusive club of the "big guys." Rod and I had changed the face of the World Series of Poker.

In World Series tradition, it was time for the money. No trophy or similar fanfare. Jack Binion brought over a million dollars in bundles of cash to the table in a ratty old used cardboard box and unceremoniously dumped it onto the table. Stacks and stacks of $100 bills. I handled the money, played with, stacked it—all while the cameras clicked. The publicity people had a field day. Or night, as it was. The accountant in me fought the temptation to count it, and after a few minutes, surrounded by armed guards, the money was taken back to the cashier's cage for safe keeping.

Photo by Pamela Shandel.

Answering the reporters' questions, glad-handing, and congratulations went on for about an hour and a half. Here's what I said in my interview on ABC's *Wide World of Sports* after winning the Main Event:

I'll say one thing. Rod is one rough, tough player. And I had to do it my way, which is a slow, long grind. I have nothing but the highest respect for Rod. We were friends before the tournament and I'm sure we'll stay friends after the tournament. And I truthfully have to say that I'm glad it was me and Rod and not Doyle Brunson or any of the other Texans. I got nothing against Texans, but for years they thought they're the best in the world. Well, I'm from Michigan, and Rod's from Washington, and the Texans have got some competition. And if that sounds like bragging, well, I don't know, I'm just high as a kite right now. It's a very emotional experience. Anyone who's ever won a tournament like this before . . . I mean this is something that will last a lifetime, long after the money is spent and gone. I tell you something . . . I'd have given a lot of this prize money away for nothing . . . I'd have played in this tournament for nothing. . . that's the truth . . . just to have the opportunity to play in it.

Announcer: "It's not the money?"

The money is important. Don't misunderstand me, the money is very important. But I wanted to win this tournament probably more than anything I've ever done in my life.

It was 3:00 in the morning when the reporters asked their last questions. Then one of the most touching things happened. Still riding the euphoria of my victory, Bobbi and I walked across the street to the Golden Nugget, where I was a regular player and had a lot of friends. The card room was full, and the players had been monitoring the WSOP going on right across Fremont Street. When I walked in, the whole room stopped playing, everyone stood up—the players, the floormen, and the dealers—and gave me a standing ovation. I kind of teared up. This was proof positive to me that I had a lot of people in the poker community rooting for me, because I was one of them. It's human nature, I think, to be a bit jealous of someone else's success, but I got a really warm reception from my peers at the Golden Nugget. Berry Johnston, who is a pretty nice guy, did the very same thing three years later after he won the Main Event. I happened to be there. He basically got ignored. Berry is a really good guy who played there at the Golden Nugget on and off, so he wasn't a regular like me. I only point this out to emphasize that money isn't the only thing that motivates me. Peer recognition is important. Everybody likes to be liked, but to be respected is even more important.

The next day, I tipped the Horseshoe dealers $25,000 and the security guards $1,000 (who weren't used to getting tipped at all), the largest tips ever to date. Eric Drache, the WSOP Tournament Director, said it was the largest toke (tip) by a man who is not wealthy, a measure of the man. I deeply appreciated that.

In retrospect, my experience playing almost every tournament around Las Vegas for four years gave me more tactical tournament knowledge than most if not all players in the Main Event—but not No-Limit Hold'em experience. That—and having no common sense and no fear—is what carried me through. As soon as I thought someone was bluffing, I came over the top of them, even if I didn't have anything. Good thing they didn't call me out. No tight player has ever won the WSOP Main Event. But I never played a serious hand with Rod Peate when I didn't have the best hand—not once.

After the 1983 World Series, I was third in WSOP money earnings, behind only Doyle Brunson and Stuey Ungar.

I have been the subject of the poker press, as you might imagine, for quite some time. Here are a couple of my favorite quotes I gave them over the years, inspired by my Main Event win:

"I'd like to kiss my former boss right now. I'm never going to push a pencil again unless it's for me."

"I've never done drugs in my life, and I was on a euphoric high for the next five or six days. You'd think I had a drug-induced high, but it was better than that. It was a once-in-a-lifetime thing. I couldn't sleep, I was floating on cloud nine because I'd come from basically nowhere to win the two biggest poker tournaments back-to-back."

I may be a World Champion poker player, but I am definitely the world's worst businessman. My backers have made more money from my earnings than I have.
—Tom McEvoy

CHAPTER 9

Let's Make a Deal. When I Won, They Won More.

At the 1983 World Series of Poker, I won a bracelet for first place in two events. The Limit Hold'em $1,025 buy-in event paid $117,000. The $10,025 buy-in Main Event No-Limit Hold'em tournament paid $540,000. With a total purse of $657,000, I actually only got to keep around $200,000. After Uncle Sam and the IRS got their $40,000 check from me, I was left with about $160,000. The reason is not at all uncommon; it's just mathematically intricate.

Remember, my initial career path was in accounting, not poker. Any accountant worth his salt would never recommend a client put all their eggs in one basket. Rather, they should spread the risk. And reducing one's investment, and potential losses, is often how poker players spread the risk. Happens all the time, and I do mean *all* the time. They sell some of their "action." They take on investors that go by many names—backers, stakers, or sponsors. That's less money for the player to get into tournaments, but also less "keepin' money" when they win.

Here's the story of my deals in the 1983 World Series of Poker. Get out your calculator and play along.

Limit Hold'em Tournament Victory: $117,000

I had two large sponsors for the Limit tournament. I sold 20 percent of my action to Frank Hunter and another 20 percent to Marty Sigel (see more about this character in the next chapter, "Sigel *v.* McEvoy"). That accounted for $400 of the $1,025 buy-in. I paid the $25 buy-in fee that went to cover the WSOP overhead and profit.

I traded 5 percent to a good friend from my table tennis days in Grand Rapids, Stewart Ansteth. He had lived with me in Vegas for a while dealing blackjack, and then moved back to Michigan to get married, leaving behind some furniture he had purchased. I said I would give him a piece of my action in this tournament and keep the furniture, which was like a gift, because there was no way he was going to sell it as he had already moved. He got way more than the furniture was worth but, hey, that's what friends are for.

There's also the 1 percent I gave to my cheapskate cousin Dan Barber from California. After I survived the first day in the Limit Tournament, he asked if he could get a piece of the action. He didn't post any money before the tournament, so he wanted in after I had made it into day two. I gave him 1 percent for $20. He got $1,000 for his $20 bucks. Clearly, I should have charged him more, at least a hundred. We had already gone through most of the field. We were into day two now with just a handful of players left, and I was in the middle of the pack.

So, I entered the WSOP Limit Hold'em tournament with the ability to keep only a little over 54 percent for myself. The tournament victory paid $117,000, of which I got to keep roughly $60,000 (after generous tips of around $3,000). I wanted to keep that money for myself and my family, but I also dearly wanted to play in the Main Event. When I moved to Las Vegas, I told my friends in Grand Rapids that I would be playing in the World Championship within five years. This was year four, and I had two obstacles. I was running out of time, and I didn't have the entry money. The relatively new satellite tournament path was clearly the affordable way for me to take a shot at entering the Main Event.

Main Event Satellite Victory: $10,000

So Frank Hunter, who had 20 percent of my action in the Limit Hold'em tournament I had just won, suggested (well, practically begged) we go 50/50 partners in a Main Event satellite played at Binion's Horseshoe casino. That meant a $582.50 entry cost for each of us, which worked for me. Before the satellite started, I individually approached two players I knew who were signed up to play in the same satellite as me. They were casual friends of mine, and I knew they would be my stiffest competition. I was right. One was Jimmy Doman, who later won a couple of WSOP bracelets in the 1980s and finished eighth in the Main Event in 1986. The other was poker pro David Sklansky, another guy who would later win a WSOP bracelet. I asked both of them if they wanted to trade 5 percent if one of us wins the satellite. They both said yes. So, I swapped off 10 percent to my two friends. Now my maximum win was 40 percent, until fate stepped in.

We got down to three players left in the satellite. Of course, it was me, Sklansky, and Doman. Sklansky had the chip lead, I was second, and Doman was third. You think maybe I handicapped this satellite pretty good?

At this point, Johnny Chan came over to the table. He said "Tom, I'll give you a thousand dollars for twenty percent of your action." This was a satellite, and I didn't even have the chip lead, so at the time it didn't sound like a good business decision. Johnny had heard me say it was my dream to play in the Main Event, so he figured I had the biggest motivation to win this satellite. Obviously, my 50/50 benefactor Frank Hunter was watching (called "sweating") me at the table, and he heard Johnny's offer. I told him I thought we should take the deal because if I didn't win the satellite, it would give us the "bullet" (money) to play another satellite. Frank rather reluctantly agreed.

Doman went out third, and I beat Sklansky to win the satellite. Frank Hunter got 35 percent, Chan got 20 percent, and Sklansky and Doman (who was sponsored by Seymour Leibowitz, so he actually got the money) each got 5 percent.

Before the tournament started, I had traded 1 percent with two other friends, Don Williams and Allen Elrod. Allen had won a satellite, too, at the Bingo Palace, same as Rod Peate had won there. Don, "the world's best unknown poker player," went on in his career to win a few bracelets. At the end of the satellite, I was down to 33 percent, so I had $3,300 toward the $10,000 Main Event buy-in. If you think it's complicated now, it does get worse.

No-Limit Hold'em Tournament Victory: $540,000

So now I had the funding to enter the 1983 World Series of Poker Main Event. The $3,300 I had won in the satellite, and the $6,700 from my satellite backers, now in for the same percentages of my Main Event earnings:

20 percent—Johnny Chan
5 percent—Jimmy Doman, sponsored by Seymour Lebowitz
5 percent—David Sklansky
1 percent—Allen Elrod
1 percent—Don Williams
34 percent—Frank Hunter

34 percent—Me

Like me, Rod Peate's satellite tournament earnings covered his Main Event entry, and he, too, was willing to take on investors. One of them was Johnny Chan, who, as I said before, recognized talent when he saw it. Rod told me Johnny Chan offered him $1,000 for a 20 percent stake in his Main Event earnings. That's less than par because a 20 percent stake should be 20 percent of the buy-in, in this case $2,000. Regardless, Rod took the offer. That fact was pertinent to my Main Event financial decisions later. Unfortunately for Rod, he also sold pieces of his action to his buddies on credit, which is never a good idea. In any case, when the smoke cleared at the end of the Main Event, Rod only had about the same percentage of himself that I had of myself.

Regardless of who won, Johnny Chan had a great payday. Remember, he had 20 percent of both Rod and me, a $2,000 investment that would now pay him over $150,000. Talk about hitting a parlay! As an interesting aside, he came close to selling his interests. When we got down to a final table of nine, Mickey Appleman, a big sports bettor who has also won four WSOP bracelets, made Johnny a big proposal. He offered $70,000 to buy Johnny's 20 percent interest in both Rod and me *if* he would have no tax consequences. Johnny felt he couldn't go there, and fortunately for him, he turned it down. Johnny Chan personally made more money than either Rod Peate or I made, but he didn't get the full $150,000. Here's why.

Rod Peate and I got down to heads-up at the Main Event final table. Now technically, you're not supposed to make a deal, but it's done all the time. So, to understand what comes next, first consider the numbers that were staring us both in the face: $540,000 for first place, $216,000 for runner-up. That's a huge payday difference of $324,000. We got a break about every two hours, and during one of them I approached Rod and said, "Would you like to save $50,000?" That's all I said. I was suggesting we change the payout to $490,000 for first place, $266,000 for second. That represented a very modest savings, but it brought the payday difference down to $224,000. Keep in mind this is pretty heady money to both of us grinders at the time. Also, a strong consideration was the fact that we had both sold pieces of our action for roughly the same amount, so the offer guaranteed how much money we could put in our pockets. Well, all his buddies were convinced that he would win and coached him not to do it . . . yet. He said no deal, and I shrugged and said that's fine.

Much later, when we got to the next-to-last break in our marathon Main Event match, Rod agreed to our mutual friend Fred David's suggestion. If I won, Rod would get $350,000 (instead of the $216,000 second-place money), and if Ron won, I would get $300,000 for second place. I won and Rod got the $350,000 for himself and his backers.

Paying my backers

When you win the Main Event, they put great stacks of cash on the table, but that's just for the TV cameras and the media. The smiling winner with his/her bracelet, posing by a literal wall of hundred-dollar bills. After the cameras are turned off, they take all that cash back to the cage. You go to the cage and the first thing they ask you is how much do you want to give the staff and dealers as a tip. I tipped $25,000, which was a record for a decade or so. The $25,000 tip came off the top, so to speak, so all my backers participated in the tip. In other words, the backer percentages were applied after the tip was paid. Johnny Chan didn't like the fact that I tipped that much, since he in effect was responsible for 20 percent of that tip. The truth is I did kind of overtip, but I was sky high after winning the Main Event right on the heels of the Limit tournament.

You have the choice of check, or cash, or both. I didn't take all my winnings at once. I withdrew some of the money from the cage right away to pay off many of the people that had pieces of me. The Horseshoe casino provided me with two security guards, which I greatly appreciated. Like most tournament poker players, I knew exactly how much I owed, and to whom, right down to the penny. Everybody got paid within a week, except for one guy who falsely claimed he had a piece of my action and ended up suing me (See the next chapter "Sigel *v.* McEvoy"). I had to track some of them down, and some of them tracked me down. They all had my phone number. I asked everybody I paid to sign a letter stating that they had received X number of dollars from me. I told them nobody would see the letter unless I was brought in on some kind of audit and had to explain where the money went. Only one of my backers refused to sign, David Sklansky.

Don't forget, the tax man had a piece of me, too. Of the $540,000 for first place in the 1983 World Series of Poker Main Event tournament, I got to keep $160,000. Not bad considering that it would have taken me 19 years to earn that much at my old accounting job in Grand Rapids.

I do believe, in the case of a lawsuit,
that the truth is an acceptable defense.
—Tom McEvoy

Chapter 10

Sigel *v.* McEvoy. The Main Event Lawsuit.

Here's the story of how and why I got sued, and the case that went all the way to the Nevada Supreme Court. Proof positive that bad guys can huff and puff, but if you stand up for what's right, they can't blow your house down.

I shared in the last chapter how I needed to sell pieces of my action in 1983 in order to enter the WSOP $1,000 *Limit* Hold'em tournament. One of my backers was Marty Sigel, a guy I had played a lot of Razz games with at the Stardust casino. We never socialized, but for some reason he took a liking to me. A few weeks before the 1983 World Series, Marty overheard me talking about selling some shares of myself in the upcoming WSOP, and he offered to take 20 percent of me in two tournaments, the $1,000 Limit and the $1,000 No-Limit Hold'em (*not* the Main Event) tournaments. In other words, he would give me $200 for each tournament. I had already lost the first two WSOP tournaments I had entered that year, the Stud 8 or Better and Razz events, and I was stuck a little bit. Marty's offer was the kind of support I was looking for, so I agreed. I wouldn't have agreed had I known what kind of character I was dealing with. Marty Sigel showed his true colors soon enough, starting with the fact that I didn't see the color of his cash investment until the day I had to buy in.

Backers normally post their support money well before the eleventh hour. That's the whole idea. The player is short of money, and they need to have it up front. Instead, I had to hunt Marty down at the Horseshoe casino. That year, Marty had gotten a job working on the poker room floor at the Horseshoe for the WSOP. I'm not sure what his official job title was, but it was in a support capacity. He wasn't making decisions on the floor, and that was the only time he worked the World Series. So, he was around.

The first tournament that Marty verbally committed to investing in me was the $1,000 Limit Hold'em tournament. I didn't receive Marty's investment until I hunted him down the day of the tournament. Later, after I won, he was nowhere to be found. I don't know what happened—if he quit, got fired or just left—but in any case, he wasn't around to collect his 20 percent that evening. I looked around, but I couldn't find him.

Late that night, Marty called me up at home and was insistent that I come back downtown immediately to pay him his money. I said, "Look, I'll pay you tomorrow." I told him I was tired, and I was going to bed. I reminded him that he was also invested in the $1,000 No-Limit Hold'em tournament I was playing in the next day, so it benefited him for me to be fresh. I even offered to call the Horseshoe and authorize him getting his money from the cage, but no, he was still insistent he wanted me to come downtown right away.

Despite Marty's insistence, I didn't go downtown in the middle of the night, but I did pay him the very next day. He got his money. When I got heads up with Donnacha O'Dea to claim my Limit Hold'em bracelet, there was no deal struck that would have reduced Marty's (and all my backers') winnings, so he got full value. For his $200 investment in me in the Limit Hold'em tournament, he got in the neighborhood of $22,000. He got 20 percent of the $117,000 first-place prize, which is $23,400 minus his portion of the tip. And because a deal is a deal, I also withheld the $200 that was due me per our bargain to help pay the entry cost into the No-Limit Hold'em event that day. When I paid him, I asked him to sign for it, like I did with all my backers, which he declined to do.

This is where all the confusion starts, and this is partly my fault. When I paid Marty, he said, "Now Tom, I want twenty percent of anything you do here at the World Series." I was very clear that the No-Limit Hold'em event I was playing in that very day was to be my last event in the 1983 WSOP, and that he had 20 percent of me in that event, but none other because there was no other. At the time, it had not even occurred to me to play a satellite for the Main Event. And, I had no intention of using a big portion of my earnings from the Limit Hold'em tournament to buy into the Main Event.

So, I played the $1,000 No-Limit tournament and I lost. I didn't even think about Marty Sigel. As far as I was concerned, we had settled up our business. Then, at the urging of my friend Frank Hunter, I became the first player to win their way into the Main Event via a satellite tournament (See Chapter 6) and went on to win the 1983 WSOP Main Event.

After I won the Main Event, Marty was going around town telling people he had 20 percent of me in the Main Event. Even though, mind you, he never posted any money for the big tournament. I remember thinking, "Wait—I only had a third of myself, and now Marty is claiming he has 20 percent of me. Are you kidding me?" So, I confronted him. He claimed I said he could have 20 percent of everything I did. I told Marty, again, that when I paid him for the Limit Hold'em win, that the No-Limit Hold'em event was going to be my last event—and that was the only other tournament he had invested any cash in with me.

And then things deteriorated. He didn't do this in front of witnesses, but he threatened my life. To try and put the fear of God in me, he reminded me that he had been in combat in Vietnam and had singlehandedly killed a lot of Vietcong. I don't respond well to threats, and I lost my temper. I said, "Well Marty, you better not miss." And I walked away from him. I didn't own a gun, but I went right out and bought a Saturday Night Special. Thank goodness, I have never had to use it.

Despite all this, Marty Sigel had the audacity to sue me. Of course, I had to defend myself and get a lawyer. Cost me about $15,000 in legal fees. I told my lawyers that under no circumstances was I ever going to give Marty any money or settle with him. If we have to go to court, we have to go to court. He can go screw himself. I don't owe it and I'm not going to pay it.

My argument in the lower court was twofold. First, that Marty did not have an agreement with me for my Main Event performance. Second, regardless of that, Marty was trying to collect a gambling debt, which is illegal in Nevada unless you are a casino. The lower court agreed with the second point, ruling his claim was an unenforceable gaming debt. That part was a move by my legal team to get the case tossed out, and it worked. While I agree with the law that verbal contracts are binding, I did not have a verbal contract with Marty.

As part of this process, I had to do a deposition in front of Marty's lawyer while he was present. He kept his mouth shut and let his lawyer do the talking. I was not going to let him strong-arm me. After the case got thrown out of the lower court, his lawyer withdrew, saying he had a difference of opinion with his client as to the merits of the case. I believe Marty got a lawyer to take his case on a contingency basis, hoping I would make a settlement. That was not going to happen.

Marty didn't give up just yet. He recruited a new lawyer, a female Razz player, and filed a motion to appeal the lower court's ruling to the Nevada Supreme Court. She called me and tried to get me to make a settlement of some kind, which I adamantly declined. Then the Supreme Court, in its infinite non-wisdom, decided the case would have to go to trial:

Martin B. SIGEL, Appellant,

v.

Thomas McEVOY, Respondent.

No. 15412.

Supreme Court of Nevada.

October 23, 1985.

Reverses earlier judgment

Accordingly, we conclude that the district court erred by granting respondent's motion to dismiss appellant's complaint, and we therefore reverse the district court's decision and remand this matter for further proceedings.

In other words, the fact that there was no verbal contract in the first place was not the point. They ruled that buying a piece of a player's action in a poker tournament is a business investment that could be legally enforced in Nevada. True that, but now I was going to have to keep defending myself and go to battle to prove, somehow, that the very thing I was being sued for did not exist in the first place. And that meant more legal fees. Great.

After the Supreme Court's decision, Marty could take me back to court. But he didn't. I guess as soon as he realized he was going to have to dig into his pocket and start to actually pay a lawyer for his legal work, he dropped the case. It never went to trial. He didn't pursue it, the statute of limitations ran out, and that was the end of it.

I knew Marty's younger brother, Tommy Sigel, who was mainly a 7-Card Stud player. Despite all this commotion, we were friends. Like most of the rest of the poker community, he told me he thought his own brother really didn't have a case.

This whole episode started right after the 1983 World Series and went on for five or so years before it was finally over. As far as I know, Marty Sigel is still around, and he still hates my guts. The feeling is mutual. We occasionally crossed paths, and on one of those encounters, I told him, "Well Marty, I figure I'm going to outlive you, and I'm going to piss on your grave." Rumor was that he was going to get a poker player, a guy with a reputation for physical altercations and drug use, to harm me, but that didn't happen.

Marty Sigel.

As a poker player, I have to give Marty credit. He was mainly a 7-Card Stud player, and he played Razz, too. Marty went on and won two Stud bracelets. Rather disgusting. True to his personality, he was a very loose, aggressive player who would get ahold of chips and then bully the table. I don't abide by bullies.

I'm confident this whole chapter finally got put to bed years later when I read an article by Scott Burnham of *Card Player* magazine, where he referred to the case as part of his series on poker contracts. I contacted him and explained what happened. I also told him what Marty Sigel was really like. Here's the article he wrote, published on April 18, 2018.

Contracts and Poker: Making Contracts

In an earlier column on player deals (Card Player *Nov. 22, 2017), I reported on the Nevada Supreme Court's decision in Sigel v. McEvoy. After Tom McEvoy refused to pay Sigel a portion of his main event win, Sigel sued McEvoy. McEvoy moved to dismiss the claim on grounds that the debt was an illegal gambling debt. The court ruled that it was a business investment, thus affirming the enforceability of contracts with backers.*

McEvoy subsequently reached me, expressing concern that the court case only told part of the story. According to him, Sigel did back him in two events in the amount of $400; McEvoy won one of them and paid Sigel $22,000 (the Supreme Court acknowledged this). McEvoy claimed that was as far as their understanding went but Sigel claimed that his investment entitled him to recover a portion of all events McEvoy entered, including the main event.

After the court's decision on the motion, Sigel did not pursue the case and that issue was never resolved. I apologize to McEvoy for telling only the half of the story I knew from the public record. The full story also affirms additional advice I gave in the article—while oral contracts are generally en-forceable, they can easily lead to disputes about what in fact was agreed to.

It's alright to pass the time, but it's a shaky way to make a living.
—Bret Maverick

CHAPTER 11

♣ ♦ ♥ ♠

1983 to 1984. Life Starts to Change
After Winning the Main Event.

As so often happens, I made the mistake of equating fame with fortune, and I found out the hard way that it doesn't. I thought I would automatically get rich. Instead, the opposite occurred.

Photo by Scott Henry for the Detroit Free Press.

Mike "The Mad Genius" Caro wrote in his newspaper article after my Main Event victories that it wasn't fair that I had declared I was not going to squander the money I had won. His tongue-in-cheek contention was that every winner needed to lose the money back in order to keep the money circulating within the gaming community. Well, I didn't squander it right away. It took me seven years.

Every attempt I made to have some success away from the poker tables was met with disaster. Every single investment failed. Every person I trusted deceived me in one fashion or another. But I have no one to blame but myself. You call your own bets, you make your own loans, and you manufacture your own luck. If things don't go as they should, you have no one to blame but yourself.

That said, let me take you through the years after winning the Main Event, starting with the rest of 1983. To say the least, it was a very good year. From a poker perspective, it was the best year of my career.

—1983—

Las Vegas lives and breathes gambling, so my Main Event victory was a pretty big deal locally. Here's how my daughter Melanie remembers those next few days in the aftermath of my big win.

I was in eighth grade, living in the house now in Montara Estates. It was all very exciting, him winning this big poker tournament. I remember that early the next day, he went on the Good Morning America *TV show live. The show was in New York, and we were three hours behind them. At 5 a.m. the whole family were all in the local affiliate studio watching him give an interview.*

And he had the headlines in the paper. There was this awesome picture of him standing up on the chair with his hand in the air, and my mom is like holding her hands like she's praying . . . watching him.

We were very proud. Dad always had a very strong ego, and I remember almost every year we would drive back to Michigan in the summer and spend about three weeks driving and being in Michigan. After Dad won the Main Event, I remember making fun of him to my grandparents, saying his black cowboy hats—Stetsons—were too small for his head now. But they were really proud of him, too. My grandfather had T-shirts made for the entire family—Dad's sister, brothers, parents, and us. They said, "Grand Rapids Tom's Daughter," . . . Sister," etc.

Remember, nobody supported his decision to move across the country and start playing poker as a career choice—nobody. Everyone thought he was a lunatic . . . especially his parents. They thought he was making the biggest mistake of his life. And they weren't nice to him about it in any way. I just remember them being very very upset and completely unsupportive. He took a big risk. He had three kids and moved everyone to the unknown . . . to the great desert . . . to pursue a career. Who does that? Who did that? So, I think he took great pride in the fact that just four years later, he came back to his hometown with this amazing win. Sentiments had changed. He did it!

Even my mother had turned the corner regarding her impressions of her oldest son. When asked by a reporter she said: "I'd been a bit ashamed of what he was doing out there for the last four years. It's a strange way to make a living. But we're happy for him. I've never broadcast to anybody what Tom was doing out there. But I can't keep it from them now!"

Far From a Normal Life

It's hard to describe the month or so after winning the Main Event. For the first five days, I didn't sleep. I experienced a euphoric, nondrug-induced high. It was the closest I ever came to what I imagine drug users experience. Several players would sometimes do marathon poker sessions, and they would take drugs like cocaine to keep themselves going. I believe there is still a lot of drug and alcohol abuse in the poker world, but I've never been a part of that subculture.

I was floating on cloud nine. Physically, even without sleep, I was fine—more than fine, really. I was on top of the world. And then I started to learn the tough life lesson that fame and fortune can have a darker side.

I was getting so many money requests I couldn't set foot in a casino or card room without people asking me for a favor or money, and it was starting to drive me crazy. My whole life had been turned topsy-turvy since I won those two bracelets, and I didn't know how to handle it. I really didn't. Things were so surrealistic that I just wasn't thinking too clearly.

So in July, I opted to just get away from it all for a while, which took the form of a trip to two places I had always wanted to visit. First stop was San Francisco for three days to see the city and visit a stamp dealer to add to my collection. Then on to Hawaii for five days to get away from it all and just relax. And who suggested he take this mini-vacation with me? Just one person, the then not-yet-so-famous Johnny Chan. The same Johnny Chan I had made about $80,000 richer a few months ago.

This was two years before Johnny Chan won his first bracelet in 1985, which he followed with back-to-back WSOP Main Event championships in 1987 and 1988, and then a second-place finish to Phil Hellmuth in 1989. I knew him before he became a poker legend, and I knew how well he played—that's why I asked him not to play in the WSOP satellite I won in 1983. I respected his game, and we were on good terms, but not bosom buddies or hanging-out pals. The fact is, the only time I ever hung out with him was on this trip. Naïve, trusting Tom—I thought he just wanted to be friends.

Chan and I posed for a tourist photo.

What I didn't realize at the time was that Johnny Chan had an agenda, and that he has an agenda for everything. Back then, Johnny Chan had few personal friends. He had associates and business acquaintances. He was all about Chan and all about making money. His agenda on our trip was to try and hustle me and beat me out of as much money as he could playing heads-up poker. At his request, we started playing a bunch of freezeouts, some for $300, some for $500. But a funny thing happened. I made sure we played other games, not just Hold'em. He beat me in Limit Hold'em, which kind of surprised me. He definitely outplayed me and beat me. But he didn't do so well in the other games—Stud, Razz, No-Limit Hold'em, and so forth. I got ahead of him in the freezeouts—not for much, it was pretty close. On the flight back, he beat me and recovered some of his money, but I wound up ahead.

I also wound up with one fewer World Series of Poker bracelet. For some stupid reason, I decided not to get a safety deposit box and store my precious bracelets like I knew I should have. No, I guess I was too proud and decided to bring my two trophy bracelets with me on this trip. Bringing them on that trip just shows you how screwed up I was, because I lost one. Well actually, due to my own negligence, it was stolen.

As a way to relax and get my mind off poker, I enjoyed playing Pac-Man and had become a pretty good player. In Hawaii, I went to an arcade by myself. I was playing Pac-Man when I ran out of quarters. I had been wearing my Limit Hold'em bracelet, and my wrist got sweaty, so I took it off and set it on top of the machine. I went to get more quarters—wasn't gone more than a couple minutes, and when I got back—no bracelet. Unfortunately, I no longer have any of my four World Series of Poker bracelets, but more on those stories later.

Other than the agony of this loss, the trip was fun. We stayed in Honolulu, and I spent a great deal of time on Waikiki Beach watching the pretty scenery and enjoying the solitude of reading books. Once, I was so immersed in reading that a big wave took me by surprise and ruined my book. I had a good laugh over that. Then it was back to the mainland, and back to my new reality.

After four years of being a pro poker player in Las Vegas, I was experiencing literally overnight success. I didn't know how to handle that. It's not like I won millions. What I won was good money back then, but it wasn't enough to last forever. The declines in my wealth have not had anything to do with poker. I didn't lose all my money playing poker, yet in some ways I almost wish I had.

In my poker career, I made a lot of good decisions. In my personal life, I made a lot of very bad decisions.

One of my first financial decisions was probably a good one. When I came back down to reality, I sent a check to the IRS for about $40,000 in taxes. It was the biggest check I had ever written. My WSOP winnings represented more money than I had ever had, and I didn't want to take a chance on losing money and finding myself in a pinch to pay the tax man. In other words, I wasn't sure I could trust myself with all this money. Maybe that was an omen.

Don't forget, poker is a cash business, so please don't tell the IRS to audit me. I carefully document my gaming wins and losses and back them up with receipts, when available, to prove the validity of my claims—just like the good little accountant that I trained to be. I always file a tax return, regardless of how much, if any, money I make. Bottom line is I have paid taxes on my poker earnings, and I have filed taxes as a professional poker player every year from 1979 on.

I don't have my tax returns anymore. When I lost my house in 2017, in my second divorce, a bunch of my records got disposed of when I had to move. Good thing politicians aren't required to share their tax returns, but I'm probably too old to run for President, anyway.

Mismanaging Newfound Money

In 1979, I had left behind a life in Michigan I knew didn't want to go back to—so I tried to be a good money manager. But I failed in this partly because I didn't know any better than to be a nice guy. I loaned out money to a lot of people that I never should have. When you are winning, it's amazing how popular you become. They'd say, "Gee Tom, can you help me? I'll give it back in such-and-such time." Well, of course, that didn't happen. I was trying too much to be liked. I couldn't say no at first, and it affected me mentally. By the time I wised up, and that took a long time, the damage was already done. I was very naïve and, frankly, stupid.

I wasn't very street smart at all. I had grown up in the Midwest, and I was used to people being honest and keeping their word. I wasn't quite prepared for so-called friends knifing me in the back, which happened on multiple occasions. Over the next few years, it got to the point that I was getting two or more monetary requests a day. It was my own fault that I would find myself giving these "friends" money just so they would go away and stop bothering me. When someone owes you money they don't have, they avoid you. You magically don't see them very often. It was an expensive way to get rid of undesirable people. Very expensive. In fact, I wrote off about $46,000 in bad loan losses I suffered in 1983 and 1984. I no longer have a problem saying "NO" to any loan request. But, alas, I don't get asked too often anymore.

It's little wonder that my wife Bobbi didn't like poker players, who were most of the people in my world then, and now. She knew a lot of my poker acquaintances were putting the squeeze on me, for small piddly amounts and for big sums. One example is Hall of Famer Eric Drache, the brilliant inventor of tournament staples like satellites and the "must move" table. In 1983, he approached me wanting to borrow a sizable amount of money. I liked Eric, and so I became a reluctant loan shark. He promised to pay me $1,000 a month in interest, which he did for several months. I didn't want to charge him like that, because, to me, that's an absurd amount of interest, or "juice." He said, "No, that was what money was worth," to him. The details are fuzzy now, but eventually I needed my money. I did get the principle back, but it took a while. It's great to be in a financial position to help out a friend, but it's not good money management. With Eric, I was lucky. With many others, not so much. I did a lot of questionable, silly things like that with my money. This not only started to drain my bank accounts, but it also started to put a strain on my marriage.

And I discovered there was more than just a new financial reality after winning the WSOP Main Event. There was a new poker reality, and it began to alter my style. I became more of a known commodity. I continued to play a lot of tournaments and cash games around Vegas, and players began to gun for me. They would give me more action than I was accustomed to. Winning a pot against "The World Champion" Tom McEvoy gave people bragging rights, so they would risk more. It is harder to play against irrational players, and I had to alter my game accordingly.

I also discovered that when you have a high profile you become a target for other people's ventures and schemes. More than one guy ripped me off, and it made me a little hard and more skeptical. It seemed like everywhere I turned someone was putting the bite on me. I say again: I was far too naïve and trusting.

Bad Investments

A poker-playing acquaintance of mine, we'll call him Paul, approached me later in the year with a carrot that really intrigued me—the idea of hosting a poker tournament. Being the naïve, trusting person I was back then (versus the more skeptical human being I turned into), I fell for the bait. This guy claimed to be a "businessman" from Washington state, and said that he had some poker contacts. He maintained he had been doing well financially with seasonal Christmas-tree sales lots. He sold me on the idea of investing in a lot in Las Vegas with him. Then, in addition to making some money, he told me he would arrange a meeting with some people he knew at the casinos in Washington state to work out a deal to do a tournament. So, I went for it, and invested $5,000 of my Main Event winnings.

I found out later he had used some of my money to play blackjack while he was on his way to Washington to buy the Christmas trees. So, the whole venture started on a sour note I didn't even know about. What I did know was that once the lot was open in Las Vegas, Christmas tree sales weren't going so well. Paul then used some of the money earned thus far to run radio ads. That didn't boost sales at all. Finally, I came to the startling conclusion that this was not working too well, so I tried to get some of my $5,000 back. I went to the Christmas tree lot and confronted the guy Paul had running the place, another poker player who knew me. I told him as part owner I wanted him to give me the day's receipts, but after a long song and dance he wouldn't part with the money. After that, Paul absconded with all of the remaining money and left town, never to be heard from again.

I decided to report him to the police, but nothing happened. On top of all this, the trees were in my name, so I owed sales tax to the state, which I paid. I had to estimate the sales because the sales records were also long gone by that time. So, I got scammed by this liar because I dreamed of hosting a poker tournament. A dream that would eventually be fulfilled and bring me much joy, and much angst, in the future.

Then I tried to make another investment that didn't pan out, this time in rare stamps. I wasn't a novice collector. My experience started way back when my dad used to buy stamps for me to collect when he was a traveling paint salesman. I've been a collector ever since. Turns out I'm better at spotting crooked poker players than crooked rare-stamp dealers. The rare stamps I bought for my nest egg turned out to be a scam that sent several of the dealers involved to jail.

In 1980s' money, I invested $10,000 apiece for two stamps, using my World Series earnings. I bought these two high-value stamps that were part of what they called the U.S. Columbian Issue. They were the first of a set of commemoratives that were issued in 1893, and were issued in a variety of postage values. There were one-cent stamps all the way up: 50-cent, $1, $2, $3, $4, up to $5 stamps. Those high-dollar stamps weren't used too much, so few of them were printed. If you could get them in really good condition, the value skyrocketed. The $4 and $5 stamps I bought were both legitimate, in mint condition and unused, but they were doctored stamps. Very hard to discern unless you are an absolute expert, and even they get fooled. At the time, I knew just enough to get in trouble.

For example, stamps back then had gum on the back that people wetted to adhere the stamp to the envelope. Collectors for decades used "hinges" to display their stamps. They put a little sticker on the back to attach it to the stamp, and that left a little imprint that took away some of the gum. That chopped the value of the stamp down by 50 percent. A stamp described as "unhinged" means it has no marks on the back. In some cases, if there were light hinge marks on the stamp, the bad guys would brush them out with their lab equipment. That is what happened to me.

I already had a stamp collection of United Nations and Bahamian stamps, and some other general foreign stamps, but they weren't all that valuable or likely to gain greatly in value. So, I was excited about investing in some premium value stamps that I was convinced would appreciate in worth. I met with a dealer in California who evidently thought he could fool the stamp-collecting world. I came to learn he had a cohort inside the Philatelic Foundation, the organization that evaluates stamps, and they were able to produce false certificates, including mine. This dealer's work was expertly done, but eventually he got caught, as I learned when I got a call one day from the FBI. They caught the guy and his confederates, and they spent a year or two in jail. There was a restitution fund, and I would get some money periodically, but nowhere near what the stamps cost me. As you can imagine, learning the hard way that my investment had dropped significantly in value disillusioned me, so I stopped collecting stamps for a while . . . a couple of decades to be exact.

As the saying goes, fool me once, shame on you. Fool me twice, shame on me. In 2003, I went to a stamp show, and I started buying stamps again. Not extremely rare ones at first, but eventually I did. And the same freaking thing happened to me a second time. Within the Philatelic Foundation there was some controversy over a very rare stamp that I bought for $15,000. It was a 90-cent purple stamp from the 1880s. It was rated one of three best examples of this stamp in existence, which is still true today. It was extremely well centered, unhinged, had original gum—all the stuff that made it a huge premium. Before I bought it, I didn't even know the stamp existed in that condition. I also didn't know there was some controversary over the Philatelic Foundation certificate for this stamp. Originally, it was listed as never hinged, and then it got resubmitted by a subsequent owner as a legitimate mint-condition stamp that had what they considered to be a hinge mark on it. I examined it thoroughly and had another expert dealer examine it under a big magnifying glass, and he didn't detect any kind of brushed-over hinge mark. So, there were two certificates, one that stated my stamp had original gum and was never hinged, and another one (that I didn't know existed) that said it had original gum but had been hinged. So that chops the value down. The bottom line is this was never resolved. I ended up selling this stamp for a third of what I bought it for.

I still have a lot of stamps, but the stamp market has deteriorated because, unlike poker, there is little new blood going into collecting. Schools don't have stamp-collecting clubs anymore. Stamps don't have gum on the back anymore. The older collectors are dying off. So much for my investing expertise.

Even the "smart" things I did with my newfound money didn't pan out. I tried to put $2,000 of my winnings from the Main Event into an IRA, but the IRS wouldn't allow it. They ruled that prize money from the prestigious WSOP tournaments failed to qualify as earned income. From my perspective, poker was my full-time job, and I spent more time earning a living at the poker table each week than most people spent at their 9-to-5 jobs. My winnings were earned just as any other wages are earned, the big exception being the fact that I was risking my own money to make money. Kind of like a stock market gambler, I mean investor, right?

Three years later, in 1986, Billy Baxter, winner of seven World Series of Poker bracelets and fellow Poker Hall of Famer, was also a winner in Federal court. He battled the IRS ruling and got a U.S. District Court judge to decree the skills of a professional gambler equated to those of a professional athlete. A poker player is now considered to be engaged in a trade or business under the IRS Code. From all of us in the poker community, thanks Billy!

Fame Also Opens Doors

My poker fame began to open my eyes to a potential additional income source: Teaching. In August 1983, I was recruited by Mike Caro and his boss, publisher Stanley Sludikoff (publisher of my first book, *How to Win at Poker Tournaments*—more on this in Chapter 12), to be one of the headliner pros in a poker seminar. The subject was "Freezeout Tournament Strategy." The seminar was held at the Stardust Casino, and featured Doyle Brunson, David Sklansky, Mike Caro, and me. The attendance fee was $195. I remember Doyle was very polite to me, asking me what I thought about different poker situations, and was thoughtful when I expressed my opinion. It was a great teaching—and learning—experience. Teaching poker would become one of my most cherished pursuits, and I'm proud to say four people I gave lessons to have won WSOP bracelets, and two more came very close. I cover more of my teaching experiences in Chapter 25. My World Champion status, and the public relations opportunity it afforded, got me invited to be one of the pros at this and many other seminars. In 1983, it also got me invited to Ireland.

Irish Eccentric Club International Poker Tournament

When I won this tournament in September 1983, "King Tom Wins Duel in the Smoke" was the headline in the Dublin newspaper. That kind of journalism just doesn't fly in the United States, and maybe due to my Irish heritage, I loved it. It's my favorite headline of all the stories on me. But first a little history about the guy who originated this tournament and one of my favorite people, the eccentric, flamboyant Terry Rogers.

Terry Rogers was the best-known bookmaker in Ireland. In the late 1970s, he started holding 5-Card Draw poker tournaments for charity under the auspices of what he appropriately called the Eccentric Club. He was in Vegas in 1979 when he discovered the World Series of Poker and No-Limit Hold'em, became enthralled with both, and imported the concept to Ireland, founding the Irish Poker Open. It became the longest-running No-Limit Hold'em poker tournament in Europe and the second-longest in the world after the World Series of Poker.

Terry Rodgers, Liam Flood, and me.

Rogers befriended many of the high-stakes gamblers like Benny Binion, Doyle Brunson, and Chip Reese, by taking bets and offering mind-blowing long odds. He also brought over a few Irish players to compete in the Main Event, like Donnacha O'Dea (who I beat to win my first bracelet in the 1983 WSOP Limit Hold'em tournament) and Jimmy Langan (who won the fourth Irish Open in 1983 and gave me the massage during the Main Event break and kind of adopted me) and Liam Flood (who won the Irish Poker Open twice). Of course, being of Irish decent, I came to know these players very well, and through them, their benefactor Terry Rogers.

Terry was a brilliant promoter. It was Terry's idea to put Irish poker on the map—and in the news—by piggybacking on the growing fame of America's poker professionals and inviting several of us to what he billed as his "International Hold'em Poker Tournament" in Dublin. This wasn't the Irish Poker Open, held annually in March, but it was a clever publicity idea to draw the worldwide attention of the poker community to that country. And, of course, increase interest and participation in his annual Irish Poker Open.

Three former World Champions made the trip with me: Puggy Pearson, Amarillo Slim, and Stu Ungar. And what better way to interest the Irish press than also getting a guy with an Irish name who was the current World Champion to play. I was featured prominently in all the PR articles prior to the tournament. We all flew to Ireland together, with Puggy and Stuey playing backgammon the whole flight over.

The consummate promoter, Terry took care of us, and we were treated like royalty. I played in this tournament three times, in 1983, 84, and 87. One year Terry greeted us at the airport with a yellow Rolls-Royce. Another year Terry arrived with a white horse, which Amarillo Slim rode out of the airport. He even introduced us to the Lord High Mayor of Dublin, with photographers nearby, of course.

This first tournament event I attended was held at the Killiney Castle Hotel, a charming, stately, conservative place that was actually an old, renovated castle. My room was right out of a fairy tale. Thirty-three players were entered in the No-Limit Hold'em Main Event. Buy-in was 2,200 Irish pounds, or about $2,640. It was a two-day event set up as a "Fast Action" tournament for the first day, and then slowed down for the second day. So, it only took about six hours to play down to the final ten. On day two, however, we played from three in the afternoon until 4:00 the next morning, September 15. For the last two hours, I was heads-up with an Englishman, Michael Anderson.

Several times he had me on the verge of elimination, once drawing out on me to amass a 52,000 to 14,000 chip lead. That's when my friend George Huber, who had bet on me, said, "Don't worry, Tom. This just means you'll have to play a little bit longer." My spirits lifted, I started winning a series of pots and took the lead.

If you have read any of my tournament poker strategy books, you've seen this poker lesson several times. "When you are playing short-handed or heads up, you don't need a big hand, just the best hand." On the final hand I called Anderson's all-in shove with pocket fours, and he revealed an A - 2 off-suit. He hit a two, and my pair of fours beat his pair of twos. The odds were with me, and I was $43,125 richer.

I was wearing the same lucky shirt I wore for the WSOP Main Event that year, with lucky Irish shamrocks sewn on the shirt collars. When I won, I even repeated my WSOP winning performance by standing on my chair with my right arm outstretched. Unfortunately, I no longer have that lucky shirt. I can't jump that high anymore, either.

I didn't call home after winning the Irish tournament. Bobbi found out about it when she read it in the *Las Vegas Review Journal* newspaper. I guess I should have called her, but life on the home front was starting to unravel.

Terry Rogers was a real good guy. I loved that man. He sponsored me the next year at Amarillo Slim's Super Bowl of Poker, but I didn't cash. In fact, Terry told me he would back me in any poker contest I wished. And he did, for a while. I didn't win any money for him—well, actually I did. He sponsored me in a tournament I won. That's the good news. Here's the bad news. The guy he hired to help with the tournament and take care of the money absconded with the cash. I got my share, but Terry's share was gone with the smoke. I asked him what he was going to do about this guy. Terry said, "Well, I could have him killed." He was kidding, of course, and he basically wrote it off.

By the way, I returned in 1984 to play in Terry Rogers' international tournament, held that year on the Isle of Man. I was busted by the eventual winner, Liam Flood, an Irish Open Champion, when I misplayed my hand. I tried to trap him when an Ace and two Diamonds hit the flop, making my Ace of Diamonds with a King kicker the best hand. My mistake was slow-playing my hand by checking, and he checked back. Then the last King hit the board, matching his pocket Kings. Of course, I put all my money in then, a little late. Liam was a good guy, a casual friend, and I was happy to see him win. In 1987, my friend and roommate (whose snoring kept me up all night) Alan Elrod won the event, the only tournament of any consequence he ever won in his life.

Jack Straus World Match Play Championships

I ended 1983 at the Jack Straus World Match Play Championships in December at the Frontier casino in Las Vegas. A strange thing happened in the $3,000 No-Limit Hold'em Double-Elimination tournament. My first loss was to Benny Binion, who wasn't known as a great poker player, but he had great fun beating the reigning World Champion. But whoever put the double-elimination brackets together for the tournament made a mistake. You weren't supposed to play the same guy again unless it's in the finals or close to it. So, Benny beats me in the first round, I beat somebody in the second round, then Benny loses in his second-round match. For some reason they had us playing each other again, which shouldn't have happened. So, I played Benny a second time and beat him. I went out in the next round, losing to Stu Ungar. It was the only time I ever played Stuey heads-up. He ended up winning the tournament, by the way.

Tom playing poker at the Frontier casino, 1984.

I did pretty well in three other events (non-match play events) in the same tournament. I placed eighth in the $2,500 No-Limit

Hold'em, third in the $1,000 Razz, fourth in the 7-Card Stud Hi/Lo, and third in the $1,000 No-Limit Hold'em tournaments, netting over $22,000. It was a good end to the year.

As an aside, Jack Straus had a subsequent tournament scheduled at the Frontier when Steve Wynn, at that time the owner of the Golden Nugget, decided to launch his own tournament at roughly the same time. It was Wynn's bid to take on Benny Binnion's World Series of Poker, and he called his tournament the Grand Prix of Poker. Jack Straus had his tournament scheduled first, but the date was usurped by Steve Wynn. Everybody knew Straus wasn't going to come out well on this. They tried to get him to change his dates, but he basically said, "No, I had my dates first, let him change his dates." Fighting Steve Wynn is like trying to fight City Hall; you are not going to win even if you're right. Still, Jack didn't budge on his dates, and at the time the poker world could not support two tournaments of the same magnitude at the same time—poker was much smaller back then. Jack's tournament didn't draw very well, but Jack did a very classy thing. He came down and played Steve Wynn's $10,000 Main Event while his tournament was still in progress. Jack Straus was a class act. Steve Wynn, not so much. My Stetson is off to Jack Straus.

Meanwhile, Back in Michigan

My newfound fame had not gone unnoticed back in my home state. I was interviewed by Mark Kram, sportswriter for the *Detroit Free Press*, and was honored with a front-page photo in the sports section, and a full-page article inside the newspaper on December 18, 1983. Kram captured what differentiated me as a poker player very well:

Unlike many of his peers, McEvoy is less than extravagant in his indulgencies. Conservative by nature—though he never has been one to shy from a risk—he neither bets heavily on other forms of gambling nor uses alcohol or drugs, the weakness and ruination of many past poker champions. McEvoy is restrained, deliberate. He conducts his affairs in an orderly fashion and has applied the basic principles of business to a pursuit that years ago had been the vocation of road hustlers and grifters.

1983: Net Poker Proceeds of $253,000 (the biggest individual year of my career)
- $23,000 Limit and No-Limit Hold'em cash games
- $19,000 Various other cash games
- $207,000 Hold'em Freezeout Tournaments
- $4,000 Other Freezeout Tournaments

—1984—

Heads-up with Betty Carey

I started the year with an interesting heads-up match with Betty Carey, who in the late 1970s and early 1980s was considered the most feared female No-Limit Hold'em player on the planet by guys who should know—poker legends like Amarillo Slim and Doyle Brunson. And me. She played high-stakes poker back when women at the poker tables were most often arm candy, and never a serious threat as a player. Hall of Famer Linda Johnson called Betty Carey a "pioneer for women in poker."

The story begins with Bobby Riggs, the notorious male chauvinist who went up against Billie Jean King in the infamous "Battle of the Sexes" tennis match in 1973. Riggs was a gambler, hustler, and showman who would do or say anything for publicity—and a decade later he was still challenging women for money. He challenged Betty Carey to a $10,000 buy-in No-Limit Hold'em freezeout to be held in Aspen, Colorado. But after Riggs started hearing about Betty Carey's expertise in poker, he realized he was outmatched and that he was almost sure to lose. Rather than take another licking at the hands of a woman, he backed out of the match.

But the match was still all set up in Aspen in the height of ski season. There were no casinos in Colorado back then, so the venue was a hotel. Since I was the reigning poker World Champion, I was the alternative and got the invitation to play her. I agreed, but I told the organizers I would only put up $2,000 of my own money. If they wanted to play a match for $10,000, the rest of it would have to come from other sources. They got Bob Stupak to put up around $5,000—I'm not sure who kicked in the other $3,000. But the organizers really wanted a $10,000 match, and I found out later why they wanted it so badly.

Johnny Chan was there when I got to Aspen a day early, and he wanted to gamble with me to try and win some of his money back that I won from him on our Hawaii trip. I suggested we play Gin, and he agreed. But when we got to our playing venue, his hotel room, he wanted to change the game to No-Limit poker freezeouts. I agreed, and we used pennies for chips and played for $300 a game. I proceeded to win the first eight games, and Johnny started to go a bit ballistic. When I threatened to just stop playing, he calmed down and we kept playing. He won the next two games, and he settled down more—until he lost the next two games after that. Then he became so hot under the collar that I called it a night. Johnny hated to lose, and he was not happy.

There was a special table set up the next day, and we had a lot of spectators including Lyle Berman and Puggy Pearson watching my match with Betty. As a highlight to this story, Johnny Chan was still steaming from his losses to me in Hawaii and Aspen, so guess what he did—he decided to bet some money on Betty Carey and do a little coaching for her. He couldn't beat me consistently, so why not help her? That's the kind of fine fellow and friend Johnny Chan was.

Funny thing happened on the first hand dealt. I had a J - 10. Betty was on the button and raised and I called. With the flop, I picked up an open-ended straight draw. We both bet and the pot got bigger. The last card was a brick—I completely missed my draw. Nevertheless, I decided to move in on her. I overbet the pot and pushed all my money in on the very first hand. Betty Carey was a very pretty woman, and I remember her looking at me with her dazzling blue eyes. She said, "Well, Tom. I think I have you beat. But I'm going to let you play for a while longer." She folded because she wanted the show to go on for a while. She knew the game was rigged and that she was going to win.

I found out later from various sources that I had been cheated. Her boyfriend at the time (he had run World Match Play tournaments for Jack Straus) was a snake who ran the tournament, which made it easy for him to "prearrange" the card decks. This was otherwise known as "cold decking." I couldn't prove this or do anything about it, so I just let it slide. But about 20 years after the crime, Betty Carey got religion. She wanted to make good on bad things she had done in the past, and our rigged match was one of those bad things.

Betty sent me a letter admitting her wrongdoing, that I had been cheated, and that she would like to pay me back. I told her on the phone I had only put up $2,000 of the $10,000 purse, and that Bob Stupak and others had put up the rest. She sent me some gold to compensate for cheating me. Thank you, Betty. It takes a really big person to do something like that.

Tournaments Early That Year

1984 WSOP Program.

My legitimate tournament year started off with a second-place finish in March in the $1,000 buy-in Limit 7-Card Stud event at the Celebrity Poker Classic in Las Vegas, netting me $9,600. In May, I defended my World Champion title at the 1984 World Series of Poker at the Horseshoe casino in downtown Las Vegas. As defending champ, I was featured on the cover of the World Series of Poker program, a self-promotion medium the WSOP no longer needs. I didn't cash in the Main Event but did finish third in the $1,000 Pot-Limit Omaha event for $16,800. The final chapter records all of my tournament cashes from 1979 through 2022, and if you peruse it, you'll see the broad variety of poker games I was pretty good at.

Bad Loans Continue

The year after I won the Main Event, 1984, was pretty good financially, albeit offset by my continuing bad loan losses. Some of those losses were from my fledgling attempts to sponsor other poker pros. For example, I sponsored Robert "Chip Burner" Turner for a month or two in some $110 tournaments at the Stardust casino. I backed off after a while because he didn't do what I told him to do. In these tournaments, you could re-buy for $100, but I told him I didn't want him in for more than $300 in any event. He started getting in $500 and $600 deep and losing. Guess why he got his nickname? Anyway, that's when I said enough is enough. I lost a bunch of money with him disobeying me. Robert Turner went to California when they legalized Stud and Hold'em in 1987, where he worked to build up the popularity of these games in a lot of the card clubs in the state, acting as a card room host. In 1988, he recruited me (and my reputation as a former World Champion) to run the first poker tournament at the old Horseshoe Club (now the Hustler Casino) in Gardena, California, which turned into the royal fiasco I cover in Chapter 12.

Beating the First Poker Computer

I participated in an interesting publicity event at the World Series that year. Mike "The Mad Genius" Caro had developed the first poker-playing computer, which he programmed to play No-Limit Hold'em. He called it ORAC, which is Caro spelled backward. Since I was the defending World Champion, Caro wanted me to be the first big challenger. I beat it, and so did a lot of other players. ORAC had a losing record against top players.

1984 ORAC computer graphics

We played on the Horseshoe casino floor with a great deal of folks watching this man-versus-machine contest with great interest. A professional dealer dealt the cards, and Mike would receive ORAC's cards and type them into the computer. I remember I was ahead of the computer, and I made a play at the pot. I had the computer covered—I had more chips than the computer. We got all the money in. I had A - 9. The computer had A - Q. I caught a nine. I said this just proves that the computer is human, because it got drawn out on. As part of the publicity hype, this was billed as a $100,000 buy-in, winner-take-all freezeout. But in reality, it wasn't. I didn't put any money in, and I didn't play for any money. I just beat the computer at the first public contest.

Me holding my winning hand and Mike
Caro holding ORAC's losing cards.

Bob Stupak's America's Cup of Poker

In September 1984, I played in the America's Cup of Poker at Bob Stupak's Vegas World (which became the Stratosphere, then the Strat). At his tournament, Bob "The Polish Maverick" Stupak, a famous gambler, rustled up a man-to-man heads-up No-limit Hold'em contest. He challenged me to a heads-up match for $5,000, and I beat him. So, he immediately wanted to challenge me again for $10,000, but I wouldn't do it.

Then I was challenged by Evert Goulsby. I beat him heads-up for $5,000. He then wanted to play me again for $10,000, offering to give me back 10 percent of my money. I turned him down, too. Then I played a third challenger, Mike Cox, and beat him. I beat him twice, then gave him a rematch and he did beat me. So, I won four matches and lost one for a net gain of $15,000. Sometimes I was able to add to my poker income playing poker in hybrid ways that were not tournaments or cash games.

I also won the $500 Limit 7-Card Stud event at this tournament for $13,500, and was runner-up in the $200 Limit 7-Card Stud event for $3,320. This was the last time I wore my lucky shirt. I don't have it anymore, and my luck started really going downhill. Fortuitous? Maybe.

This is the tournament when I first got to know Ron McMillan, the man who would later sponsor me in major tournaments for the better part of a decade. He volunteered to sponsor a piece of my action in Stupak's first tournament events, which he continued to do for quite a few years. Ron is one of the finest men I have ever met. He's a good person and a good man who does what he says he is going to do. He's still a good friend, and as you will see, has become one of the key figures in my life.

Meanwhile, Back at the House

Life with Bobbi and the kids was getting rockier. Bobbi and I were both working all the time, or sleeping, or just sort of managing. We didn't really talk much, we just existed together, without communicating in any real way. We would exchange information, but that was about it. I don't recall any huge blowouts, just a steady, growing unhappiness.

1984 Net Poker Proceeds $73,000.
Non-Poker Losses of 46,000 (wrote off bad debts)

A funny thing happened on my way to fame,
fortune and serenity—I lost all my money.
—Tom McEvoy

CHAPTER 12

1985 to 1989. Book, Bracelet, and Betrayals.

—1985—

From a tournament-poker perspective, 1985 started out with a bang and then fizzled out. Dropped off a cliff, really. In January, I cashed in five events at the Stairway to the Stars tournament at the Stardust casino, each in a different poker game—Razz, 7-Card Stud, Limit and No-Limit Hold'em, and Stud/Hold'em Doubles (which I won with my partner Cheryl Davis). This was the only high-profile tournament I cashed in for the entire year.

However, I fared better this year in cash games, and not all of them in Nevada, earning about $43,000. For example, I was invited to Dallas by a colorful character by the name of Ken "What a Player" Smith. He wore a tuxedo with a stove-top hat he claimed was from Ford's Theater, where Lincoln was assassinated. He would flip his hat up when he won a pot and shout "What a player!" It was all just his schtick. At Ken's behest I flew to Dallas so Ken could sponsor me in several big cash games. He put up the money for me to play in the game, and we split the profit. I won something like $25,000, so he came out pretty good. Actually, he parlayed some of that to take some of my action in later WSOP tournaments.

Spreading the Wealth

I continued my increasingly bad habit of loaning money to dead-beats who did not repay me. I ended up writing off over $17,000 in 1985, and $23,000 the following year. I was writing off more money than my old annual salary as an accountant in Grand Rapids. As you might imagine, this was a constant irritation in my marriage. Bobbi was working hard at the post office bringing in a nice income through the front door, and I was giving it away to a bunch of losers out the back door.

But that wasn't the only way I was succeeding at spreading the wealth. If you have ever "min-cashed" in a tournament—made your entry fee plus a little more—then I could be partly to blame. I was never one to just win and sit back on my laurels. I was constantly thinking about poker, my chosen profession, and its future. I participated in the sport, in the game, and my mind often turned to ways to move it forward, to enhance its growth.

When I won the WSOP Limit Hold'em bracelet in 1983, of the 234 entrants, only nine were paid, with 50 percent going to the winner; 20 percent for second; 10 percent for third. Very top-heavy payouts. It was totally obvious to me that for tournament poker to get bigger and better, the tournaments had to pay more spots. They had to give weaker players a shot of at least cashing in these contests. The skilled players would still rise to the top, but to attract more people, they had to pay more people. They couldn't just have all the money piled up at the top so the best of the best tournament pros would get the lion's share of the money all the time. It had to be more of a flattened payout.

In 1985, I began advocating for paying more players. If there were more than 100 entrants, then they should pay the last two tables. Instead of paying 50 percent to the winner, I suggested paying him/her 40 percent, and distributing that extra 10 percent money further down the ranks. That's eventually what happened.

Some of the top players like Eric Seidel and T. J. Cloutier liked that bigger first prize because they had a chance to win it more than the average player. But they were so shortsighted. One of the reasons tournament poker got bigger is because they paid more places. Eric Drache, who was running the World Series of Poker at the time, agreed with me, because the next year the WSOP expanded the number of payouts. Eric Drache was very forward thinking, too.

I guess that means I had a hand in the growth of the WSOP. I'm proud of that. I would contribute more to its growth, I think, with my battle to end smoking in the poker room, but I'll share that story in Chapter 18.

How to Win at Poker Tournaments (1985)

I wrote the very first book on the subject of tournament poker, *How to Win at Poker Tournaments*, which was published in April 1985. I had been approached by Stanley Sludikoff and Mike Caro. It was the first time I had met Sludikoff. He was a groundbreaking publisher who printed the first gaming magazine, *Gambling Times*, one of the few publications that covered the poker scene before *Card Player*. He also started the first poker publication, *Poker Player*, which was more of a newspaper,

not a slick magazine. Sludikoff also authored and published several books on blackjack and poker.

Caro, nicknamed the "Mad Genius," was a pioneer poker theorist and author of over a dozen poker books. He was also an editor at both of Sludikoff's poker publications, and the creator of the first poker-playing computer you read about in the last chapter. They contacted me after I first won the World Series in 1983 to see if I would be interested in writing a book on poker tournaments. I told them I had never even thought of writing a book, but that I did have my own very definite opinions on the subject. So, after a little arm twisting on their part, I agreed to do it.

It turned out to be a totally losing proposition for me. I needed a coauthor/writer for the project, and I recruited Roy West. Roy was a well-known poker teacher, and later a columnist for *Card Player* magazine from 2001 to 2009. We worked together on my first book project for several months in 1984. I dictated my thoughts and ideas into a tape recorder, and Roy organized and edited the book. I paid him $5,000 out of my pocket for his services, and the deal was that after I had recouped the $5,000 from royalties, we would split anything beyond that 50/50. Well, splitting half of zero doesn't amount to much, so I lost money. The book was inexpensive, but there wasn't a great market for tournament poker books—yet. I broke the book into sections on the types of tournaments: 1) fast action, or 15-to-30-minute levels (like most satellites); 2) medium action, 40-to-60-minute levels; and 3) slow action, or two-hour levels, which at the time was really just the Main Event at the World Series. The Main Event has been two-hour levels from the beginning, and still is. This softcover book is still available in my private library, but if you look for it on Amazon, good luck.

This book was a legitimate piece of poker literature. As my first literary effort, it was okay for the time, but it was nothing great. Things are so much more sophisticated now, so it's really dated.

Basing the instruction on the pace of tournament play is no longer relevant, since virtually all major tournaments are medium-action events. But the book still has valid information in there.

On top of zero royalties, the book publisher, Sludikoff's Gambling Times Incorporated, went belly-up shortly after my book was published. Sludikoff defaulted on a handful of royalties to me. We're not talking thousands of dollars; it might have been a hundred or two. So, I ordered several copies of my own book from him. They were worth less than what he owed me in royalties. Then I told him, "Look, you owe me some royalties that I'm not getting paid for, so I'm not going to pay the invoice for the book copies." We left it at that.

That was my only real association with Sludikoff. Shortly after the book came out, he won a little freeroll (no entry fee tournament) for the media the World Series of Poker put on at the Horseshoe casino. He credited me for giving him insight into tournament poker that helped him win. He said he wouldn't have won the tournament if he hadn't read the book that he had me write so he could publish it. Ironic twist. It's one thing to report about poker, but when actually playing the game is not your main thing and you win, even something as small as this tournament was, it's a big thrill.

World Series Book Signing

Just after my first book came out, I was able to arrange permission with the Binion family to have a book signing "event" at the World Series of Poker in their Horseshoe casino. I was pretty proud of the book, and I used an empty poker table close to the tournament action to set up shop. Today you would pay dearly for the opportunity to sell your merchandise at the WSOP, but back then I was a small added attraction. And not a very good one at that—I only sold a few dozen copies. The venture was not very profitable considering the retail price was only $9.95.

Kicked Out of the Silver City Casino

I've been kicked out of two casinos in my life, but only for blackjack. Never for poker. I don't play blackjack that often, but on occasion, it is a nice break from the poker tables. But like poker, playing blackjack well takes some concentration, and that's what got me into trouble. Here's what happened at the Silver City casino in 1985.

I was playing single-deck blackjack, and a bunch of low cards came out on the first deal. That meant the rest of the deck was rich in high cards—and that favors the players. So, the dealer took the deck and shuffled up immediately. Alright, duly noted. A few deals later a whole bunch of aces and tens came out on the first deal—and that favors the house. You don't think they stopped and shuffled up then, do you? So, when the dealer was getting ready to deal the next hand, I said, "I'll wait." The dealer asked me what I meant. I pointed out the deck had been shuffled after the first hand dealt was all low cards, but when the same thing happened with high cards dealt on the first hand, the deck was not reshuffled. So, it was my intention to not play and wait until the deck was played out and shuffled again. You'd think I was trying to rob the joint! The pit boss, this young guy—it's always the young guys who are new at the job and trying to establish their authority—came over and said, "You can't play here anymore. Don't come back." I said okay, and I left. But I came back the next day. The same guy spotted me from clear across the room, grabbed security, and came running over before I could even make a bet. I'm not a huge better, by the way, usually just betting five-dollar red chips. Again, I said, "Okay, I'll leave, just don't touch me, don't lay a finger on me." They didn't. They just took my picture and I left.

My Backgammon Beginnings

I think the "luck factor" is part of the allure of both poker and backgammon, and that's why I was attracted to the game. A bad player on a good day can beat a great player. It's not that way in golf or tennis.

In 1985, I met the World Champion backgammon player, Paul "X-22" Magriel, at the poker table. Magriel arguably won more major backgammon tournaments than any other player in the world. He was widely considered the world's premier backgammon teacher, an original and clear-thinking theorist and one of the game's best players. By comparison, he was a savant in backgammon like Stuey Ungar was in poker.

We met and took a liking to each other, and we hung out together for about a year as friends. Paul wanted to become a better poker player, so he decided it would be a great idea if we could teach each other. He was going to teach me backgammon from scratch, because I knew absolutely nothing about the game. I had never played backgammon in my life, and I didn't even know the rules, let alone game strategy.

I would talk poker with him, and he developed his skills and got to be a minor success as a poker player. And I got to be a minor success as a backgammon player. But as I was starting to get better and could really use his expert coaching, he was no longer a part of my life. Unfortunately, he had started going down the drug path and I could not handle that. We backed off from each other. Sometimes relationships just fade away: they don't go out with a bang; they go out with a fizzle.

When I won the Professional Poker Players Invitational poker tournament in 2006 and beat Marsha Waggoner in the finals, Paul Magriel made the final table and was sitting next to me. Paul took his backgammon nickname, X-22, from the square occupied by the winner in a backgammon tournament he hosted from a field of 64—one player for each square on a chessboard. While playing poker, Magriel developed his nonsensical "Quack Quack!" shout when he bet. It was a reference to his X-22 nickname, since a pair of twos are known in backgammon as "double ducks" and in poker as "ducks."

Family Vacation to China

My cousin Dan was a full professor at California State University, Long Beach, and he organized and led tours once a year to some foreign land. I had gone on a very memorable tour with him in 1982 to Italy, and this year he was leading a group to China in July. Bobbi and I were excited about the trip. We felt the boys were too young to appreciate the experience, but we took Melanie, who was old enough and really wanted to go. One of my poker friends, Fred Merker, joined us on the trip. Ironically, he wound up living with us in our house on Mountain Valley Road for a year or two after he lost all of his money in the stock market. We didn't even have a room for him, so we had to partition off part of the downstairs living room for him.

We had a great time seeing the sites like the terra-cotta warriors and climbing the Great Wall. Melanie turned Sweet 16 in China. Thankfully, that was while she was still speaking to me.

A Daughter Can Be Rough on a Dad

Vacations and my poker career definitely kept me busy, but I was still the father of a sixteen-year-old daughter who was growing up in Sin City. Too fast, I feared. November marked the beginning of a whole year that my daughter Melanie didn't speak to me. When we passed each other in the hallway, she glared at me and just moved by me. She got past it, finally, and we got to be very close, as you'll see in the next chapter. But at that point in time, it was a tad icy at home between us.

I can understand why she was mad at me. I had grounded her for a typical teenage charade. She and a girlfriend collaborated so they could stay out all night doing God knows what—going to parties with boys and stuff, I suppose. She told us she was staying at a friend's house, and her friend told her parents she was staying at our house. Bobbi and I discovered this after speaking with the friend's mother. Busted. I grounded her for a week or so with the warning that if she ever did this again, I would ground her for the remainder of the school year, which was about six months.

Well, guess what? She did it again, the same thing with the same girlfriend, and we caught her again. I was under a lot of self-induced stress and pressure then, and when she misbehaved, I just went ballistic. I didn't relent on the grounding, so she was very upset with me, to say the least, and she stayed upset for a whole year.

Melanie wasn't a bad girl, just a little devious while growing up exposed to this world of unsavory lifestyles and characters and seediness that was Vegas at the time. She used to dress very precociously and go out to casinos and walk up and down the Strip with her friends just to see how many catcalls and whistles they would get. She was very good at sneaking out of the house to go to parties, where she experimented with pot and alcohol. Of course, she didn't tell her parents anything, which was really easy because we were either sleeping, working, or not paying attention—me especially. In a proud dad moment, I'll let Melanie take it from here.

In Las Vegas, you grow up very fast. Once I got out of high school I straightened up, got my act together, and started going to college. My parents told me that I didn't have a choice, that I was going to college, or I was going to have to work and pay rent. I ended up graduating high school a semester early because I wanted out. I realized all the people I knew were very toxic and not healthy, so I graduated early and started going to college when I was 17.

I started part-time because I worked. I always worked, starting with babysitting at 11. I worked at a grocery store, at a computer store; I worked my whole life. The next semester, I went full time to UNLV. My parents paid for my college—it was cheap because it was an in-state school. I lived at home because I had no desire to go live in a dorm. I flailed around a bit—couldn't decide what I wanted to do, what major—there were a lot of big decisions to make that I had no clue about. I changed my major about three or four times and then finally landed in a Women's Studies class, and then just clicked. At that point, I kind of came into my own. I was a five-and-a-half-year college student, going to school year-round and working at the same time.

When I turned 21, I got a job working at the Mirage as a "Club Mirage" girl in their Slot Club. Then I got a job a couple years later at the Tropicana. I was a "Special Events Associate," but it was really a glorified secretarial job. I was heavily into feminist stuff and Women's Studies, but for some reason they hired me anyway. My bosses were the most sexist pigs—they were terrible. But I kind of just took it all in jest. I didn't get offended, I got even. I was doing all this activism, and I was doing all these flyers that I used the Trop equipment to create and even print. They fueled my activism. They hired good-looking women, and I think I had that going for me. But I also had skills and was good with people. After graduating when I was 23, I left Vegas and never looked back. I really wanted to pursue some kind of career in some kind of progressive issues and politics. And women's issues. It was next to impossible to do that living in Vegas. I dated a college philosophy professor from the east coast whose mom worked for the League of Women Voters in Washington, D.C. He encouraged me to go there for an internship, and his mom set me up with interviews.

Today I'm married and I have my own business doing fundraising event planning. I help nonprofit organizations raise money through galas and special events. I'm a logistics master, so I coordinate all the details, do all the production, and then help them with fundraising strategy. I guess you could say I left my old life behind and moved to the opposite coast to pursue a career. Sound familiar?

—Melanie McEvoy Zuhoski

Despite her early years in Las Vegas—maybe *because* of her early years there—Melanie has been very successful, and I'm quite proud of her. She reminds me all the time of my lack of good judgment and claims she didn't get her common sense from me. We are close and can tell each other anything. Even when the truth hurts.

1985 Net Poker Proceeds of $43,000.
Non-Poker Losses of $17,000 (wrote off bad debts)

—1986—

To say that being a professional poker player in Las Vegas was hard on my family life is an understatement. Lord knows having a teenage daughter in the house is hard enough on a dad, let alone

one who wasn't speaking to me. And maybe I didn't do such a good job of listening, either. She fell prey to the teenage urge for independence combined with the seediness of Las Vegas.

But I was oblivious. Melanie told me later about what she remembers as a funny story about walking out of the house one evening. I was sitting right next to the front door, reading a book. As she was leaving, she said, "Bye, Dad, I'll see you later. I'm going out to get pregnant." Apparently, with my nose still buried in my book, I just said, "Okay. Bye."

Poker Tournament "Management"

In January, I was asked to be the "Assistant Tournament Coordinator" at the Frontier casino for their new Triple Crown Poker Classic. It was the casino's first effort to develop its own tournament format apart from the Jack Straus tournaments that had been held there. It was my first official connection with poker tournament management, but in reality, I was more of just a host. My job was to play poker and help the players enjoy themselves and have a memorable time.

I have one vivid memory of this event. As at any tournament, there were a fair amount of cash games, and I was playing in one during the tournament. For some reason I don't remember, I had to leave the game for a while. When that happened—when a player had to leave but was going to come back soon—they put a little plastic covering over their chips. The casino would let someone else sit down in the vacant seat with their own chips and play until the absent player returned.

Marty Sigel decided to play over my seat. This was during the lawsuit, so we weren't exactly best of friends, and many of the people at the table knew it. They knew there was going to be a problem when he sat down in my chair. Marty Sigel knew perfectly well that this was my seat and my chips. Unfortunately, I fell for his trap because I was really upset when I came back to the table and saw him in my seat. So, we had a small fracas. We elbowed each other a bit. No fistfight or blows struck. He left, and I sat down. Just doing my job making sure the players were entertained. End of story.

A Very Good Year for Razz

Many if not most poker players are unfamiliar with Razz, so a little primer on the game is in order here. In Razz, the lowest hand wins. It's dealt like 7-Card Stud, two cards down, four cards up, and the last card down. The best hand is the A, 2, 3, 4, 5, a hand that in poker is called the "Wheel." Straights and flushes do not count against you. So, if you can count to five, you can learn how to play Razz. You are first dealt two cards down and one up. To start the action, there is a forced bring-in bet that is posted by the highest card showing. When there are two or more of the same highest cards, the determination is based on suits, reverse-alphabetically with Spades highest, followed by Hearts, Diamonds, and Clubs. So, the highest possible card is the King of Spades. Aces play as ones, the lowest card.

In the 1980s, Razz was "spread" or offered for play on a regular daily basis by only one casino in Las Vegas—the Stardust. This casino had a well-deserved reputation for being run by the mob and cheating. In spite of that I still beat the game, even though I was definitely cheated more than once. When I arrived in Las Vegas, I was determined to learn all the poker games, and I got to be pretty good at Razz. My first WSOP cash was in 1982, when I came in sixth in Razz.

Razz is the "R" in the five-game form of poker called HORSE. Each game is played until the number of hands dealt equals the number of players, called an "orbit," and then the next game is started. HORSE consists of Texas Hold'em, Omaha High-Low Split-Eight or Better, Razz, 7-Card Stud, and 7-Card Stud High-Low Split-Eight or Better. Because of the challenge to be proficient in five diverse poker games that switch every orbit, many top poker pros consider HORSE to be the true test of a player's acumen.

Razz was very good to me in 1986. On April Fool's Day, the first day of April, I won the $200 Razz tournament at the 1986 Pot of Gold Tournament in Reno, which netted me almost $8,000. The next day, I came in second in their Limit Hold'em tournament. I still have the two trophies. No bragging intended, but I ran out of room for all my poker trophies, and I only still have about half the trophies I won over the years. This Razz trophy was the precursor to the Razz prize I would win the very next month—my third World Series of Poker bracelet.

World Series of Poker—Winning My Third Bracelet

I won the $1,000 7-Card Razz tournament at the WSOP, earning my third bracelet and a prize purse of $52,400. I elected to receive a smaller, feminine version of the bracelet, which I gave to Bobbi, inscribed with her name. I don't think she wore it more than twice in her life. This customized bracelet was less valuable than the standard bracelet—a smaller version obviously has less gold in it. Years later, she would sell it in a garage sale for $400, its value in gold at the time. Later, the buyer contacted me, but getting it back never materialized.

At the final table, I was heads-up with the wife of tournament director, Jack McClelland. Alma McClelland was quite a lady and quite a poker player. I liked and respected her. I was casual friends with the McClellands, and because of Jack's WSOP position and the fact that they both played in other tournaments, our paths crossed often. Alma won a WSOP bracelet in 1989 in the Ladies Limit

7-Card Stud event. Unfortunately, Alma was a heavy smoker and died from lung cancer in 2000. It was a great loss to the poker world. This quote from Alma shows what a classy and insightful lady she was: "The poker table is like the business world. To be successful you have to act like a lady, look like a woman, think like a man, and work like a dog." Alma came in second to me twice in tournaments. The other time was at the 7-Card Stud event at the Knights of the Round Table tournament in Las Vegas the following year, 1987.

Speaking of twice, that's how many times I got knocked out of the tournament ("went broke") to the guy who eventually won the World Series of Poker Main Event. In the 1986 Main Event, I was up against Berry Johnston. I remember the hand. He had a suited A - K versus my A - K off-suit. The flop was King high, and we got all the money in the pot. The last two cards matched the suit of the A - K in his hand, giving him a flush. Berry had caught a "runner-runner" flush. So instead of a split pot, I busted out. Berry had about 50,000 in chips and later got knocked down to about 7,000. If he hadn't won my chips earlier, he would have been out of the tournament. But he had enough chips left to come back and win the whole enchilada.

The other guy I went broke to in the Main Event was Phil Hellmuth, in 1989. By losing—having my last few chips pried from my hands—I helped create poker history for two very decent people. These were not day one losses here. I had run deep in the Main Event again and busted out before the money. I finished fortieth when they paid 36. I had the A - Q of spades, and the flop was a Queen with two small spades. I went all in, and Phil's two Kings held up. I would make the same move today. That's poker.

1986 Net Poker Proceeds of $66,000.
Non-poker losses of $23,000. Lots of bad debt write-offs.

—1987—

In January 1987, I met the man who would become my best friend for the next three years, Gene Lee, or the name he went by, Gene Rindy. He played a major role in my ultimate journey into despair—and bankruptcy. My worst enemy couldn't have caused me more damage than my so-called best friend.

Gene was the tournament director of the Super Stars of Poker tournament, which was held that winter at Caesars in Lake Tahoe. First prize in the Limit Hold'em Championship was a brand spanking new Ford Mustang, a great incentive for this poker player (who was seeing his financial reserves dwindling). Technically, I did not win the tournament. When it got down to three-handed we made a deal. The other two wanted some extra money, which was all right with me. I was the chip leader, and I wanted the car. We made a deal and chopped up the money, and I got the Mustang. They also had a first-place trophy, and we kept playing for that, which I didn't win. We had already chopped up the money and I got the car, and then I technically came in second in the tournament. That the official tournament winner didn't win the car understandably created confusion with management. Gene Rindy negotiated with the tournament officials, explained what happened, and they went along with it. Players making deals amongst themselves can complicate things.

My friendship with Gene was starting to grow. We started playing backgammon, and for a while he was beating me, and I would pay him. Then I started beating him, and, oddly, he didn't have the money to pay me back with the same money I paid him. This was a tell, an omen of things to come.

After the tournament I was going to fly back—had a plane ticket in hand—but now I had to drive back. I was going to give this new car to my daughter, who had just graduated from high school. But Bobbi said, "Oh no, she doesn't get this car, I get this car." You would think a new car would make a wife happy with her poker-playing husband. But you would be wrong.

Of the three cars that I won in poker tournaments, this was the only one I wound up keeping.

By February 1987, after getting back into the "victory circle" by winning the Mustang, I was beginning to feel the drought was over. It was hopefully the end of a long, six-month run of bad cards, and I hadn't been playing my best poker, either. I had let the cards affect my mental attitude and my money management. When you are running bad, it can seriously erode your confidence, to the point where you start to consider alternative professions. But that's when my never-say-never mental toughness kicked in, and I simply refused to be the victim of circumstances. I simply refused to quit and resolved to do better. It worked. Sort of.

In April I teamed up with the coauthor of my first poker book, Roy West, to conduct Texas Hold'em classes at the Las Vegas Hilton hotel. These classes were geared toward the low- and medium-limit players and were reasonably priced at $195 for this audience. We limited class size to the first 20 who signed up to make the ten-hour-long classes more personal and interactive versus lecture style. I also participated with six other poker pros hosting seminars at the Las Vegas Hilton for a couple of hours on Tuesdays and Thursdays. We charged $25 per session and had over 350 participants. I really enjoyed the people and the teaching, and I think I learned more than I taught. Later that year, Mike Caro sang my teaching praises in an article he wrote, saying *"You've proven yourself in poker combat again and again. You really are a special teacher to the poker world."*

Interest in tournament poker was gaining momentum. In the seminar, we calculated that a player could be expected to win one in 65 tournaments if the field was 200 and the player was twice as good as his or her opponents. At that time, I was winning one out of every 14 tournaments I entered and finishing in the money in one out of five. Yet I felt teaching more people to be better poker players was good for the game. Relatively unknown players winning might be good for poker, but it was bad for the pros like me who made a living at the game. It was good that the game was attracting more players, but that combined with the heavy luck factor was making it harder for the better-known players to repeat as champions. And I couldn't help but notice how the newer players appeared to be targeting the established pros during tournament action in order to eliminate them.

In May, I won two satellites into World Series of Poker events that were held at the Las Vegas Hilton. That paid off as I cashed in two WSOP events that year, placing seventh in the $1,500 No-Limit Hold'em event for $17,160 and fourteenth in the $1,000 7-Card Stud event for $2,590. I followed that up in June by winning the $500 7-Card Stud event at the Knights of the Round Table tournament at the Tropicana in Las Vegas, earning $24,000.

In September, I returned to Dublin, Ireland, to compete in the Irish Eccentric Club International Poker Tournament as the guest of the host, my good friend Terry Rogers. I went with my buddy Allen Elrod, the guy who I had traded one percent of my action with in my 1983 World Series Main Event victory. We shared a hotel room in Dublin, and I think it was part of his plan to throw me off my game by snoring all night. It worked. I didn't cash. But in this event, we both traded 5 percent of ourselves. This time it paid off for me, because Allen won the tournament.

Tournament poker is a physically grueling profession, and far from a nine-to-five job. I was still playing a lot of cash games back then, but I always quit play by 1 a.m. a week or so before a tournament started. I was preparing for tournaments by getting myself on the same sleeping schedule I would likely be on when the tournament began. This meant I would usually get up about 11 a.m. By then, Bobbi had already gone to work at the post office. We were seeing less and less of each other, and frankly, that was partly by design.

Another strain on our marriage was the fact that I was on the road a fair amount of time. I played in tournaments that year in Dublin, Atlantic City, Reno, Lake Tahoe, and Bell Gardens, California. Bobbi worked and took care of the kids while I was out of town, and most of the time when I wasn't. Communication between us was becoming more and more nonexistent. She was very unhappy, and I was the brunt of her unhappiness. It's hard to enjoy marriage when your spouse is mad at you four out of every five days. My marriage was becoming intolerable.

1987 Net Poker Proceeds of $78,000 (Not Counting the Car I Won). Non-Poker Proceeds of $1,500.

—1988—

In January, I was in Lake Tahoe at the Super Stars of Poker, where I placed fourth in the $500 Limit Hold'em event for $3,080. My new friend, Gene Rindy, was running the tournament. But when one of the envelopes with some of the prize money mysteriously disappeared, Gene was the chief suspect, and they were going to fire him.

I had also won a bunch of money playing side cash games and had about $14,000 in a safe deposit box, and Gene needed it to cover what he allegedly stole and what he gambled away. Gene was allegedly stealing to support his gambling habit. He liked to play Omaha, and I had begged him not to play. He ignored me and got into a big game and got a bad hand. He flopped a set of three sixes. In Omaha that isn't much—too many possibilities that can beat you. He lost a giant pot, and then he lost the prize money. And so, he was going to get fired. He had signed a marker at the cage and couldn't pay the marker.

He came up to my room, and he was desperate. He had to make this good. He knew I had $14,000, which would solve his problems. When he asked for the money, I said no. Rindy, a black belt in karate, lifted his fist up like he was going to hit me. This guy could literally kill me if he wanted. I said, look, if you hit me, it's all over between us. He thought about it and dropped his fist. But I stupidly caved in, and I bailed him out. He got fired anyway.

This was not a great poker year for me. In 1988, I only won slightly north of $13,500 in poker tournaments, and entry fees and sponsors ate up most of my tournament profits that year. It had been five years since I won the Main Event, but players remembered me, and they were gunning for me. Here's an example: In April, I played in the $200 Limit Hold'em event at the Pot of Gold Tournament held at the Hilton in Reno. Roy Ritner was a shift manager at the casino, and we ended up heads-up for the event title. In an attempt to intimidate me at the final table, when he went all in, he put all his chips on top of a copy of my book, and pushed everything into the middle of the table. It was a corny thing to do, and I'm not easily intimidated. However, he did beat me to win the tournament.

I was still playing cash games, but not fairing too well. I was running bad on the felt *and* at home.

My Marriage Is on the Rocks

The last five years I was married to Bobbi were terrible. Just terrible. She had a tell. If she walked down the steps with a raised eyebrow, it was going to be another bad day. I couldn't communicate with her. She was very unhappy, and I was the brunt of her unhappiness. My marriage had become intolerable, and I began making efforts to figure out why. I wanted to understand what was going wrong, and why it had gotten so bad.

Personal Development Assistance

Fate can sometimes be fickle. My daughter Melanie, who was in her second year of studies at UNLV, attended the first session of a large-group awareness-training seminar for personal development put on by the highly respected PSI Seminars. She came home bouncing up and down, excited and planning to make all these big changes in her life. She was 19 and not a little kid anymore, so at first, I was a bit alarmed. I feared she was being brainwashed by some kind of cult. I decided I had to check this out.

So I went to the same seminar, accompanied by Melanie. If you had paid to go to one, you could go back again to the same seminar for free as an audit. I liked the seminar, and I got a lot out of it.

And I even talked Bobbi into going to one. Between Melanie and me she was feeling left out. I don't think she found this as helpful as we did.

PSI Seminars offered more advanced seminars, and I did one of those myself. That was pretty intense—one of the most intense things I ever did. I went through two or three of these seminars with Melanie and that's when father and daughter, so estranged just a few years back, bonded for life.

Then we did another seminar called PLD—Pacesetter Leadership Dynamics. Melanie was voted—get this—the most exciting person in the whole seminar, and she got a little trophy. The young guys in the seminar were drooling over her. And I was proud of her because she was finding her direction in life. I guess you could say I was, too.

A big part of these seminars is introspection, and through them I was starting to explore why my marriage was going sour. To further this goal, I went to another seminar, this one by John Gray, the author of books I had been reading, including his bestselling *Men Are from Mars, Women Are from Venus*. The picture was starting to become clearer.

After the seminars, Bobbi and I started marriage counseling, which lasted maybe three or four months. Between counseling and the seminars, I began to figure out some of the things that were going wrong. I learned I didn't really like Bobbi very much. She had gained weight, and the physical attraction was gone. Bobbi was always a good mother, and I remember telling the counselor you can't make love to your mother. That may sound cold, but the main thing was that she was mad at me all the time.

I came to the realization I had fallen out of love with Bobbi. It's hard to love someone the way they are supposed to be loved if they are mad at you four days out of every five no matter what you do. And I made it worse by being gone and not communicating well. I took a bad situation and made it worse. But no matter how guilty you may feel, if your spouse or significant other is not happy with you, even if you deserve some of it, having them mad at you all the time . . . I don't think anyone can handle that. It took a long time for me to get to the breaking point, but I was fast approaching it.

And don't forget we had three kids, plus the fact that Bobbi wasn't crazy about moving to Vegas in the first place. On top of that she did not like poker players because I kept getting scammed by them—especially my so-called best friend—which contributed mightily to the breakup of my marriage.

We kept trying. We made it through to the end of the year. That's when we decided to separate and get divorced. Actually, I decided to get divorced, and Bobbi agreed. The divorce was final in 1990. I initiated both of my divorces; I had reached the breaking point both times.

Jerry's Nugget Prize Money Flap

I won a little No-Limit Hold'em tournament at Jerry's Nugget casino in Las Vegas in April that year and caused such a stir that I was asked to leave the premises. By some accounts I was escorted out, but you can't believe everything you read in the poker papers.

I was accused of stiffing the dealers because I refused to toke (tip) them. As Bill "Bulldog" Sykes, a poker newspaper columnist reported, *"Tom has a history of toking about 10 percent of his win."* That's true, and you've already seen how much I tipped after my big WSOP wins.

But I didn't toke this tournament because I felt the tournament management was dipping into the till, and I got in a heated argument with the card room manager, Lee Kaymar, after the tournament was over. I won the tournament, collecting all the chips in play. After the final hand, I counted all of the chips in front of me, which should have been all of the chips used in the tournament, and counted $30,500 in chip face value. That represented a prize pool of $3,050, not the $2,450 they paid out—a $600 or 20 percent difference.

When the tournament ended, there were $6,000 more tournament chips than when we started. Why? The casino accounted for the difference as the "rounding factor" that happens when lower-denomination chips are taken off the tables. This happens because as the blinds and antes increase, the smaller denomination chips become cumbersome and are no longer needed. For example, when black $100 chips are removed, and a player has two of them, they are replaced in his chip stack with one blue $500 chip (a $300 gain for the player).

- With 41 players left, they exchanged $5 chips for $25 chips. That adds $800 max.
- With 17 players left, they exchanged $25 chips for $100 chips. That adds $1,200 max.
- With six players left, they exchanged $100 chips for $500 chips. That adds $2,000 max.

The maximum the "rounding factor" could add to the tournament was $4,000, *not* the $6,000 extra we ended up with. This didn't account for the 20 percent difference in this tournament, even if every player had gained the maximum number of chips every time a lower denomination was removed from the table—and that never happens.

Bottom line—there were a lot more chips in play in this tournament than there should have been. And it was these shenanigans that I was bringing to the attention of tournament management, a situation they flatly denied. Those are the facts; you be the judge.

This all caused quite a stir in the poker community, as you might imagine, and received a fair amount of ink in the poker press. Tom McEvoy, highly regarded for his integrity, dared challenge a tournament director and suggest the presence of shenanigans. Here are two excerpts from some of the articles.

> *About 80% of the poker players I talked to about this issue believe McEvoy's version.*
>
> —*Corky Miller*

> *The sad thing about this whole affair is that two good guys, Tom and Lee, are now at odds with each other. Both have excellent reputations in the poker community, with no hint of chicanery in the past.*
>
> —*Bulldog Sykes*

Putting Tournament Players First: World Series of Poker

In the 1988 World Series of Poker at the Horseshoe casino in downtown Las Vegas, I minimum cashed in the $1,500 Limit Hold'em event for $1,500. While I basically broke even in the tournament, I was able to exert some influence that contributed to a huge positive shift in the way this—and later all tournaments—were run.

First, a little background. Earlier in the year, Jim Albrecht had taken the job of poker room manager at the Mint casino, which was located in downtown Las Vegas next to Binion's Horseshoe casino. Almost before Albrecht could learn the location of the men's room, the Binions bought the property and merged it into their casino. Jack Binion made Albrecht the Horseshoe poker room manager and director of the World Series of Poker, where he teamed up with seasoned tournament director Jack McClelland. The Albrecht/McClelland collaboration directed the next ten World Series of Poker tournaments.

Back then, the World Series of Poker tournaments, other than the Main Event, were basically one-day affairs, starting at noon and going until a winner was declared, usually around 5 or 6 in the morning. I told McClelland and Albrecht this was insane, and that the players were killing themselves, physically. The WSOP didn't stop play at, say, 1 a.m. and let the players come back the next day. Nope. They made them play straight through, because they thought it increased the big tips they received from the winners.

Here was how stupid this thinking was. They thought if they restarted a tournament the next day, the handful of people who made the final table might be excluded from playing in the next tournament. I told them if some of these guys play poker for 18 hours straight, they are going to be too tired to play again right away. How can anybody operate on three or four hours of sleep (if that) every day for a month without coming apart? In my opinion, their short-term thinking was all about greed, because they thought they wouldn't get as much money in tips. Maybe they were right, but at what cost to the players?

From my point of view, a handful of players tied up in the final table of the previous day's event would be able to play in the following day's event (maybe not from the beginning, but before the buy-in period ended), and therefore would be able to tip in both events. I told them tournament planning was also a factor. For example, when they scheduled a Stud tournament following a Hold'em tournament, a lot of the Stud players weren't going to play in the following day's Hold'em tournament anyway. I argued that giving the players a rest after 12 or so hours just made sense. At least it was obvious to me.

I wasn't just thinking about what would be to the advantage of a handful of top pros, of which I was now considered one. Maybe that's why they listened. It wasn't long before putting the players first is exactly what they did.

Gene Rindy

I was the best friend Gene Rindy ever had. But true friends don't do to friends what Rindy did to me. He lied to me, stabbed me in the back, and gut-squeezed me for money. I helped him out at the expense of my own family. And he rewarded me by making up stories to get more money out of me, cheating me, and all kinds of other things that I stupidly went along with for way too long before I woke up.

Rindy was around my height, stocky, with a little bit of a tummy on him. He really was a tough guy with his black belt in karate, and he often described with pride some of the fights he had been in. To punctuate his tough-guy aura, he would let someone hit him in the stomach as hard as they could. He would be braced for it, and he could take it. Getting the picture?

Over the course of the three or so years we were "friends," I lost over six figures—over $100,000 to him. I have already shared how he stiffed me at backgammon in 1987. And the time I bailed him out to cover his alleged stealing and gambling losses at the Super Stars of Poker in Lake Tahoe in January of 1988, even after he threatened to hit me. But naïve, trusting Tom felt sorry for him and thought he could help his friend. Rindy was married and had a son with a deformed hand. Again, I was naïve and stupid. Because Gene didn't have the money and his son needed surgery, I personally paid for two operations to help his boy. That wasn't cheap, and I actually put a big part of the cost on my credit card. Bobbi wasn't too happy with that dumb move.

That's when I still had money . . . before everything went sour. Rindy was constantly putting the bite on me for money, and I had also loaned out a lot of my money to other people. I still had some poker winnings but the money I loaned out to Rindy and other people was draining my financial resources—fast. I was starting to feel the walls coming down around me, and my whole life was starting to fall apart.

To get the money to pay me back, Rindy actually shared this harebrained idea with me. He knew of a drug dealer in Florida who had a bunch of money stashed away, and he was going to try to rob him. I considered the story to be all BS and didn't want anything to do with it. He told me later, "I just couldn't do it, Tom. I just didn't want to die." Yeah, right.

Most of the time, Gene Rindy was trying to be my friend. But his true colors would come out every so often, like the time he threatened to hit me. We finally parted ways early in 1990. I told Rindy I couldn't be around him anymore, and I just asked him to go away. He did. I think his own marriage was also falling apart by then.

Gene Rindy may have been physically tough, but he wasn't exactly smart. Here's an example I was told about. In May 1990, he took a job at the World Series of Poker working for Jack Binion as a chip runner or something . . . a lower-echelon job. Not as a dealer, although he did deal poker on and off. A guy named Johnny Joseph from Texas was playing in some high-stakes side cash games that year. He would sign a marker and Rindy would go to the cage and get money for him. Once Rindy went to the cage, forged Johnny Joseph's signature on a marker, and managed to misspell the word "Texas." So naturally they caught him right away. He had to make good on the money he allegedly stole, and in any event, they fired him. You don't hear about those kinds of things when they happen because the casino keeps it hush-hush and out of the papers. That's how guys like Gene Rindy move around the gambling community and keep getting caught with their hands in the cookie jar.

I wasn't street smart back then. There were a lot of sleazy people in poker. They would do things they considered to be part of the game, and tried to get away with whatever they could (and think nothing of it). I wasn't ever like that, and I wasn't thinking along those same lines. I was brought up in the Midwest, and this goes totally against my grain. So I would get myself in these "little" jams sometimes. I just wasn't used to people deliberately lying right to my face and trying to manipulate me and maneuver me. I had this reputation for integrity, and they didn't, but they used that against me. I made some incredibly bad decisions on who I trusted. I tend to learn my lessons the hard way—and that's an understatement.

South Bay Poker Classic Fiasco

First, some background to set the stage for this story. California legalized Hold'em and 7-Card Stud in June of 1987. The seven Los Angeles-area card rooms and the Las Vegas poker casinos were cooperating in tournament scheduling for the good of the game and prosperity for all. Despite this, bad things were happening in the poker world in 1988. Steve Wynn's Golden Nugget cancelled the prestigious Grand Prix of Poker. Then, the night before it was scheduled to start, the plug was pulled on the East Coast Players Association Tournament in Myrtle Beach. The Gulf Coast Poker Classic in Mobile, Alabama, was cancelled by the local district attorney.

This is when Robert "Chip Burner" Turner came back into my life. He had gained poker room experience going to work for Steve Wynn as a poker host at the Golden Nugget in 1977, which is where I first met him. He got credit for introducing the game of Omaha poker to Nevada in 1982. He went to California in 1987 when they legalized 7-Card Stud and Hold'em. He worked relentlessly for the Horseshoe casino in Gardena, building up these games from scratch, playing, putting people in action, starting games, keeping them going, whatever it took to grow interest and support for these "new-to-the-area" poker games.

The culmination of his 18-month struggle to turn the L.A. area with zero Hold'em and Stud games into a location where players came specifically to play them, was going to be organizing and managing the first South Bay Poker Classic at the Gardena Horseshoe (now the Hustler Casino). There he teamed up with the "Grand Dame of Poker," Marsha Waggoner, who would later be one of the inaugural inductees into the Women in Poker Hall of Fame. Together they hired me and my so-called best friend, Gene Rindy, to run the show as host and tournament director.

Rindy had been tournament director at the Superstars of Poker at Caesars Tahoe and Amarillo Slim's Super Bowl of Poker at Caesars Palace in Las Vegas. I didn't have as much experience managing a poker tournament, but they were my profession, so to speak, and my status as a World Champion was a great drawing card. Rindy and I got busy planning all the arrangements for the South Bay Poker Classic. We designed the room layout, planned the schedule, promoted the tournament in the press, called and recruited players, created and placed the advertising, and put up signs. We put a ton of work into the tournament, which was slated for November 18 to 30.

And then the Horseshoe casino parted ways with Robert Turner and Marsha Waggoner. It was reported that negotiations for their contract stalemated, and that they and the Gardena Horseshoe "came to a mutually amicable parting of the ways." In other words, they were fired. And the casino just decided to tear all the signs down and forget it. When all this happened, I was on a *Card Player* poker cruise with Bobbi, hoping a vacation might be good for our relationship. Showing his sense of fiscal responsibility, Rindy made a very expensive (guess who paid?) phone call to me to my ship at sea to let me know Turner and Waggoner had been let go, and the status of the tournament was up in the air. That news kind of spoiled the vacation. Turner left for Malta to play in the Irish Eccentric poker event, finishing third. Meanwhile, Gene Rindy and I were left holding the bag. I was in the middle of the ocean, and I was steaming. But not as much as Rindy.

After Robert and Marsha left, Rindy took it upon himself to meet with the owner of the Horseshoe, Milt Corwin. We hadn't talked about him taking that action, he just went and did it. We had made our deal with Robert Turner, not the owners, who I had never met.

Remember, Gene Rindy was a beefy guy of Asian descent, and he was a multiple-degree black belt in karate. He could beat people to a pulp, and sometimes did. The popularity of the martial-arts movies back then made him an even scarier guy. During his meeting with Corwin, the Horseshoe owner, Rindy told him we had a verbal commitment to continue plans for the tournament. And then

Rindy—the thug who wore a suit when he worked—verbally threatened Corwin with physical mayhem. That's what Rindy himself told me, not what I heard from somebody else. God knows how accurate his version is. Anything he said was suspect. Corwin decided Rindy was bluffing and cancelled the tournament again, stating "It's been cancelled due to circumstances beyond our control."

The press reported that at this meeting on November 3 the Horseshoe Club management made outrageous demands on us, like a $500 daily deposit to cover food costs and $30,000 up-front money. Plus, no cut of the profits for us from side games, as was the standard practice. They reported Rindy left the premises with the gracious help of the security guards. Makes a great story, but I wasn't privy to any of this.

I had a poker-playing lawyer friend who tried to help us by putting a little legal pressure on the Horseshoe Club. He talked with Milt Corwin, and the communication went something like this. "Why don't you let these guys have the tournament? If you don't, the only one who is going to make any money is me, because we are going to sue you." Corwin stuck by his guns, and that's how it came out publicly that Rindy had threatened him. My lawyer friend later said, "These two guys. One guy thinks he's the brains of the outfit, and he can't spell the word *cat* if you spotted him the *C*." That was his take on Rindy.

During all this, I had never met with the owner. The only time I met him was when I took him to Small Claims Court. Corwin showed up when I sought a judgment against him. You are not supposed to take your lawyer with you, but he pulled in his lawyer as a "witness." The judge assigned some cases to others, but he thought this case would be interesting and he wanted to do the case himself, so he called us into his private chambers. Representing myself, I showed him all the stuff that had been used with my name to promote the tournament. And I won the judgment against the

Horseshoe casino for reneging on their contract. In Small Claims Court back then, the maximum you could get was $1,500, and that's what I was awarded. And they paid it, eventually. Quite a while had passed and I hadn't received a check, so I had to contact them and reminded them the law said I could go after them for even more if they didn't pay. The money was nothing to them, but they dragged their feet paying me.

Why did the management decide to cancel? I don't know. They had never had a tournament there before, and Robert Turner had talked them into it. And then after they fired Robert Turner, they just decided to cancel the tournament. We had signs up and ads placed and all that stuff. What they did was extremely stupid and shortsighted. They should have just let us go on with the tournament. They would have made money. I talked to a guy that worked there, and he actually said all the staff wanted us there to do the tournament. They knew they were going to make more money, more tips, and they weren't happy that this tournament got cancelled.

Meanwhile, I was going into a depressed funk. I had to let people know they had cancelled us. In the meantime, Gene Rindy was up to his usual tricks, scamming me to pay him back for the "tips" he supposedly paid a couple of people that worked in the casino to support our tournament bid. When we thought were going to run the tournament, Rindy needed new outfits, so I bought him some new clothes. With him, it was just endless BS. It's obvious to me now that I wasn't thinking clearly; I was too trusting. He lied to me and fabricated stories to get money out of me. And I fell for it.

Rindy came into my life at the absolute worst time, when everything was falling apart. And he just piled on. He was actually the final push that ended everything for me. All the money I gave Rindy really upset Bobbi, and she had every reason to be upset. It was the last straw for my marriage.

Card Player **Magazine**

Phil and June Field founded *Card Player* magazine in 1988, and June invited me to write an article for the first two issues, which I was pleased and honored to do. Of course, the publication went on to be a great success, and is still in circulation today. A few years later, I knocked June out of a Limit-Hold'em tournament, and as she was leaving, she popped a balloon behind my head. I nearly had a heart attack, thinking I had been shot. Don't ever do that to anybody, please!

1988 Net Poker Losses ($3,134), my first losing year.
Non-poker losses of ($40,500), mostly due to Gene Rindy.

By my calculations, I had lost north of $125,000 over the last five years or so from bad loans and losses that offset my entire poker earnings. These losses do not include interest on credit cards. The losses were for money that I loaned out for the most part. It's even worse than that, because I included some of my income from miscellaneous sources like giving poker lessons or appearance fees to offset some of my write-off losses. By now I didn't have much money left, and I couldn't loan out what I didn't have.

—**1989**—

The Reprieve

Just when things were at their bleakest, I received a call from the Bell Gardens casino in Gardena offering to let us have the tournament there. We quickly agreed, and I announced that the recently cancelled South Bay Poker Classic had been revived, renamed, and moved to the Bell Gardens in California. The California Bell Tournament would be held February 16 through 26, 1989.

Given such short notice, we nevertheless drew a really good turnout with a strong field for our tournament. Some well-known names included Mike Sexton, 1990 WSOP Main Event runner-up "Tuna" Lund, the 1991 WSOP Main Event champion Brad Daugherty, and my 1983 World Series Main Event opponent, Rod Peate.

I was just kind of winging it and trying to deal with this resurrected tournament and everything else happening in my life all at the same time. Pat Martin got us in the door at the California Bell Tournament mainly because he wanted to have a hand at running it. He had a lot of ideas, most of which were not very good, but as the liaison with the casino, he established his authority, although it was never clearly defined. In retrospect, I let Martin have too much influence over what was going on. Right out of the gate, in the very first event, he delayed the start by over 30 minutes for some fabricated reason. The players were getting antsy, and so was I. I finally overrode his stalling tactic, and we got the tournament started. But this beginning had not gone over well with the players. The attendance on the first day of the tournament was really good, but after this inauspicious start, the attendance was not so great. For that you can thank Pat Martin and Gene Rindy.

What was the first thing Rindy did as the tournament was starting? Without consulting me because he knew I wouldn't go along with it, he apparently skimmed off around $600 worth of buy-ins. We were still playing dollar-for-dollar on the chips at the time, so it was easy to add up.

Tuna Lund made the final table, and he's friends with Brad Daugherty, who I coauthored two books with later, and they brought the situation to my attention. The chips were counted, and the chip count didn't balance with the buy-in money—it was short a few hundred dollars. "Bad news Tom, you're short," they told me. I said if that was the case, we would have to make it good. By this time, I already suspected what Rindy had done. I'm no saint, but I'm not a thief. My reputation was on the line here, too.

This was like a $200 tournament, which was modest even back then. So, we charged maybe $225 to play with a $25 entry fee. As part of our renumeration, we split the entry fee money with the house. So, Rindy just kept about three of the buy-ins. But the players were smart enough to count down the chips in play at the final table, and that's exactly what happened. So now I was in this dilemma.

Halfway through the tournament, Rindy actually told me he had swiped the money! He was helping collect the money and just pocketed some of it. So now what? The only thing I could think of was to short-change my own chip stack to cover it. He had really put me between a rock and a hard place, and I was glad the chips were counted so I could make it good. It was just another one of several things that Gene Rindy did that made me finally ask, "What the heck am I doing with this guy?" I was so naïve and stupid and trusting it was mind-boggling. How could I ever get involved with a guy like Rindy?

At the same time our tournament was running, the cross-town poker competition, the Bicycle Casino (the "Bike") was still hosting nightly tournaments. We did outdraw the Bike and their tournaments, and we took a handful of their players away. George Hardy, who ran the Bike, and his general manager came to our club that first night to see what was going on. George dressed like the character Diamond Jim Brady, and that's the name he later gave the big tournaments that he ran in August at the Bike.

Out with the Old, In with the New

Meanwhile, in the midst of all this Gene Rindy mess, I was dealing with a personal mess (or two) that had me verging on a nervous breakdown. Just before the California Bell Tournament began, In January of 1989, my wife Bobbi and I separated and were on the road to divorce. I moved out of my house and rented a cheap apartment.

When I got back to Vegas after the tournament, I needed a real place to stay. A poker-playing friend of mine, Bob "Coach" Ciaffone, offered to let me live with him in his house. Bob authored *Robert's Rules of Poker,* which set the standards for poker tournament play and served as the basic guidelines for the Tournament Directors Association years later. Ciaffone also became famous in the poker world for his long-time role as a card columnist for *Card Player* magazine. Bob was no slouch as a poker player, either. In 1987, he placed third in the WSOP Main Event. I lived with Bob Ciaffone for six or seven months in 1989, along with another poker-playing roomie, Bob Walker. I didn't see that much of Walker—he was a poker pro who traveled a lot and eventually amassed over $350,000 in tournament poker winnings. When it came to poker players, I kept good company. When it came to women, not so much.

I had met another woman who factored very big in my life. Her name was Vicki Rose, and she had been dating a friend of mine, another poker player, who turned out to be not such a nice guy. Vicki was fun to be with, and after they broke up, I started seeing her while I was living at Ciaffone's place. More on the saga of Vicki Rose in the next chapter.

For perspective, I never dated much before I got married. Bobbi was only the second woman I had ever dated. Outside of poker, I never had much of a social life. At this point, I was 44 years old, and looking back on it, I guess I must have been going through a mid-life crisis, fueled by extenuating circumstances that were happening all at once. My whole life was falling apart. I was on the verge of bankruptcy and divorce at the same time, and I was near to a nervous breakdown. My best friend stabbed me in the back and could not have caused more damage to my life than my worst enemy. I also wasn't doing well at poker. Surprise, surprise. All this grief was happening at the same time, so I was looking for a little happiness by starting a relationship with Vicki Rose.

Does this justify my behavior? Probably not, but I'm only human.

Hall of Fame Poker Classic

In December, I won the $2,500 Pot-Limit Omaha event at the Hall of Fame Poker Classic for $70,000, which was kind of a big deal. At the time, the Hall of Fame Poker Classic was arguably second in status and size only to the World Series of Poker. A win at this tournament event was the equivalent of winning another bracelet. Before and after this year, the prize was a watch instead of a bracelet. But this was the only year they awarded Horseshoe trophies for the event winners. A big giant trophy with a big giant horseshoe on it made of 32 ounces of silver. So, there are only about 14 of these trophies in existence, and I have one. Actually, I gave it to my son, Patrick, to keep and enjoy.

The Binions put on the tournament at their Horseshoe casino on Fremont Street in downtown Las Vegas. It was called the Hall of Fame Poker Classic because it was run in conjunction with the induction of a new player or players into the Poker Hall of Fame. They didn't do it at the World Series like they are doing now. In 1989, Fred "Sarge" Ferris was inducted. Doyle Brunson and Jack Straus had been inducted the year before.

I had played with Sarge several times. In fact, I learned a life lesson from him when he beat me in a big pot after I overplayed my hand in a Limit Razz cash game at the Frontier. It was the biggest negative in my Limit Razz career because it was the only time in my life I played $400/$800 Limit Razz. Some of the legends of poker were playing in that game: Sarge and Doyle Brunson and Chip Reese. There was one "live one" in the game, too. That's what we called a player with lower skill and lots of money. It was the biggest cash game I ever played in. I was winning—beating the game—when the live one left his chips on the table and left the game for a while. So, I quit for a little to wait for him to come back. My mistake was deciding to get back in the game before the live one came back. I went from plus $15,000 to minus $4,000, a $19,000 swing. That's when I realized that a high-stakes $400/$800 game was not something I should be playing with these guys.

Sarge knew who I was and that I had won the World Series. You know what Sarge told me one time? He said, "McEvoy . . . " in that slow delivery he had, "you're just a babe in the woods." I didn't think much of it at the time, and then I realized later that he was right. From then on, I pretty much stuck to my lower-limit lane.

A Little Perspective

Just to give you a perception of the size and scope of poker in Las Vegas in 1989, there were 13 tables at the Aladdin, 12 tables at the Dunes, and only ten tables at the Frontier. That year the Horseshoe added four tables, bringing their total to 19. Poker, as we know it today, was still in its infancy.

On a Sad Note

Benny Binion, a giant in the poker world and the originator of the World Series of Poker, passed away on Christmas Day 1989 at the age of 85. The very next year, he was inducted posthumously into the Poker Hall of Fame for his contributions to the game. It broke my heart when I got the news. I remain a great admirer of Benny Binion, and he will always have my undying gratitude.

1989 Net Poker Proceeds of $42,442.
Non-Poker Proceeds of zero.

As they say about pocket Aces, they really look pretty and you certainly can play them, but don't fall in love with them.

—Unknown

CHAPTER 13

♣ ♦ ♥ ♠

1990 to 1994. A Divorce, a Rose, a Bracelet, and Bankruptcy.

—1990—

"We Back Jack"

1990 started out on a sour note. Benny Binion had just died in December, and the Culinary Workers Union went on strike in January. They were the most powerful union in the state of Nevada and were always a major force the casinos had to deal with. Picket lines had formed at Binion's Horseshoe Club as more than 1,000 union members walked off their jobs.

Benny was still revered, as he still is to a certain extent to this very day. And all the poker players liked Jack Binion, Benny's son, who was running the show now, as well as the World Series of Poker. You would never know Jack was a billionaire. He was very down to earth. You could talk to him. He didn't put on airs. He would talk to the little guy just like he talked to a big executive. We poker players were loyal to the Binions, and we were going where the action was. So, we crossed the picket lines wearing buttons that read "We Back

Jack." It's no surprise that the strike didn't hurt attendance at the games.

Target Practice in the Desert

The cancelled tournament at the Horseshoe casino last year in Gardenia had left a terrible taste in my mouth and saddled me with the special plaques I had ordered and paid for out of my own pocket. There were multicolored plaques for first, second, and third in all the events, each inscribed with the tournament name and date, and each included a horse emblem significant of the host location. Now they were worthless, and I couldn't recycle them.

Back in Grand Rapids, I had won over 200 table tennis trophies, and I actually recycled some of them by applying new plates. I loved winning trophies, but after you accumulate a houseful of them, they start to diminish in importance, and get tarnished and banged up. So, I came up with the perfect way to dispose of all my unwanted trophies and the new useless plaques: Target practice.

I still had two pistols, a 22-caliber I had inherited from my father (a family heirloom I passed on to son Patrick) and the 38-special I had purchased for protection against Marty Sigel. I took them to a shooting range out in the desert on the way to Red Rock Canyon. Kids like to shoot guns, so I took my two teenaged boys with me. I figured I could use the target practice, because frankly, I wasn't a very good shot, which I demonstrated that day.

It was the perfect way to let off a little steam during an ugly time in my life. Some of the strangers at the range were curious about my shiny targets, and a couple of them asked if they could have a few to shoot at themselves. I didn't bring anything home—everything I took was blown to bits.

Divorce

Bobbi and I tried reconciling. We got back together, and I moved back into the house for another five or six months. We went to marriage counseling for a while. That didn't work. Too much water under the bridge. I admitted to having the affair with Vicki to Bobbi and the three children, who were old enough—21, 18, and 16 at the time to understand. Melanie, the oldest, was living at home and attending UNLV. Mike, our middle child, had graduated high school and was living at home. Patrick, the youngest, was a junior in high school.

The last five years of our marriage, my own children will tell you, were pretty bad. It was a very stressful home for them. Patrick told me that, in his opinion, I should have gotten divorced from Bobbi five years sooner than I did. Was it Bobbi's fault? No. She had married an accountant from Grand Rapids, Michigan, not the professional poker player I had become. If I had stayed as an accountant in Michigan, she would have been okay with that. But I wouldn't have been happy. Do I realize that some of my thinking and actions are a little bit controversial? Yes. Quirky, perhaps. But like the Sinatra song, I did it my way.

Our divorce was final in June 1990. I was feeling good old-fashioned Catholic guilt. Even though I was no longer a practicing Catholic, I still tried to be a good Christian and actually live a good Christian life, which is what most Christians try to do (except on Sundays, in my opinion). By then I was totally broke. There was nothing to fight about. I left with a used car and my clothes and virtually no money.

I turned over every marital asset to Bobbi. She got the house and the Mustang convertible I won at the tournament in Tahoe. I got the debts. I moved the mutual credit cards out of her name and into mine. So, I took all the heat for my utter failure to manage my money properly. I was on this massive guilt trip (that lasted for years), and I was trying to do the right thing. Bobbi kept the house for a while, until she remarried in less than a year and her new husband moved into her house. Later they got their own house and sold the house that was ours to our son, Mike.

I did have one thing going for me, though. I was now established as a poker player, so I still got sponsored at different times. I still had my abilities as a player, although self-doubt was beginning to creep into my head. I had a pretty good year at the poker table—you couldn't say I wasn't running well—yet I was trying to figure out what I should do next. With everything falling apart around my head, I began to reevaluate whether or not to leave poker. I was actually considering getting a job and doing something else with my life. I even talked this over with some close friends. I was good with numbers and could do other things besides accounting work. And then I realized that this kind of radical change was not what I wanted. I recognized that I did not want to go back to working for somebody else. So, I just basically knuckled down and rededicated myself to poker, which gave me something positive to put my energy into, while my personal life was, well, difficult to deal with.

Vicki Rose

Vicki had flaming red hair, and a disposition to match. As I said, she was dating another poker player friend of mine who was divorced. Vicki told me he had been violent sometimes to her, and when they broke up, we got to know each other better. She was a very attractive woman, very fetching, and we had a very strong chemistry. From the first time I met her, I was attracted to her, and, well, one thing led to another. I was 45, she was 37. I started having an affair with Vicki while I was still married . . . something I will always feel guilty over and regret, but I did do it. I never claimed sainthood. I try to be a good person, and an honest person. Honesty sometimes has warts, and I'm sharing mine.

Since things with Bobbi were now at a finale, I moved out of the house and moved in with Vicki. Her parents owned the house she was living in, but they weren't living in Las Vegas at the time. I ended up living with her for three turbulent years. I'm not sure why I stayed as long as I did, but she was exciting to be with, in many ways.

Vicki was a firebrand drama queen. She had one minor problem that I couldn't overcome . . . she was, in my opinion, clinically insane. But history—my history—repeats itself, and it took me a long time before I realized she was too unstable, and that I couldn't handle the constant drama of this relationship. I'll give you a few examples, starting with one story my friend Dan Alspach relates.

I met Vicki in 1992. I did not play much poker. I was president of a technology company that did anti-submarine warfare. For one reason or another my wife wanted to take a vacation, and there was this Card Player *cruise to the Mexican Riviera, so I said let's do that. Something to do to entertain me while she was doing stuff with the kids.*

The first night I sat down at a poker table, and I didn't know anybody. Tom was sitting on my right and this very beautiful, very sexy girl was sitting on his right. Very striking. Red hair. And I thought how lucky he is to be with her. After about five hands, she lost all her chips with a bottom pair and no kicker against three of a kind, a set. Tom tried to tell her to try and be a little tighter because she needed to make her bankroll last for the whole trip. And then she started to loudly rip and berate him and let him know what she thought of his advice, and that it was none of his business. He knew she had a limited bankroll, which she managed to lose that first night. By then I thought if she was with me, I'd either jump overboard or I'd throw her overboard.

Here's another example. About a year or so after I was divorced, I took Vicki to Michigan with me to meet my family. My father liked her and really thought I should get married to her. I was actually engaged to her for a while, and I gave her an expensive diamond pinkie ring that I had converted into an engagement ring. (I never got that back). After she met my parents, other than my father, the rest of the family was so-so, not convinced either way that she was the right person for me after my divorce. Vicki was dramatically different than Bobbi, emphasis on the dramatic. Evidence what happened on our way home.

We were flying back to Vegas from Grand Rapids, and we had to change planes in Minneapolis. While we were in the air terminal, I got a hot dog because I was hungry. I don't remember what was said between us, but they called for the boarding of our plane, and she started hissing at me like a cat. I asked her to stop, but she kept it up while we were walking onto the plane. I warned her that they were going to throw us off, but she was used to talking her way out of trouble. Vicki was one of those people who, you know . . . she was attractive, smart, and glib. She was hissing like a cat at me all the way to our seats on the airplane, which were near the front. I was a bit frantic, and I didn't know what to do. I sat down, and by now I was begging her to stop. To make matters worse, the neighbor that I used to beat out of his paper route money playing poker as kids, was on the same plane with his wife. Vicki was now hissing louder and clawing the air. I was going crazy. I was horrified. I didn't know what she was going to do next, because she was unstable and crazy and she was going off. Then Vicki stood up and started shrieking at the top of her lungs.

I don't care how charming you might be, you can't do that. The pilot came out from the cockpit and told us he was going to get security and that we would be asked to leave the plane. I said fine. The airline folks don't care what your reason is, you can't do that. Period. We hadn't taken off yet, and she was trying to talk her way out of it. The pilot didn't blink, did not smile. There was no appeal. We were gone at this point. Of course, our luggage had been transferred to the Vegas-bound plane from our Grand Rapids flight.

Sure enough, we got kicked off the flight. Now what? We found out there was another flight to Vegas eight hours later that day. I asked if there was any way to get on this flight. The airline told us we could get on this flight if we agreed to sit on totally opposite ends of the plane and not next to each other. I said, "That's fine with me!" Vicki was crying now and saying, "I just want to go home." That was definitely the craziest of all the things she did while we were together.

Besides Vicki, there was another issue I was also dealing with. I knew there was something wrong with me, but I didn't know what. After my divorce, sometimes I would hardly leave the house for what seemed like months at a crack, except to go to the occasional movie or to go get food. I was suffering from bipolar disorder (although not severely like my mother), which wasn't diagnosed, let alone treated, for another eight years. When things went wrong in my life, I would often find myself in a depressed funk. I was a bit of a mess and wasn't using the best judgment. No excuse, but it was part of the reason I did some of the stupid things I did. I would go on swings of high and low, but I was never suicidal. Some of the best poker I ever played was when I was in what they call an elevated state. I've been treated for bipolar disorder now for 25 years and it's pretty much under control now.

In the meantime, after Bobbi remarried, her new husband joined her and the kids in her house. My youngest son Patrick didn't like her new husband much: He was a nice guy, he just wasn't Dad. He was about 20 years older than me, and his personality was far less strong than mine. Patrick started acting up and misbehaving. Since they weren't getting along, Patrick moved in with me and Vicki for his senior year of high school. He got along famously with Vicki, and she liked him, which was one of the bright spots in our relationship.

Right after high school, Patrick enlisted in the Marine Corps, where he spent five-and-a-half years. Bobbi and I had to sign the papers to allow him to go into the military. I told him not to feel pressured to go into the service, that I would come up with the money and we would pay for him to go to college if he wanted. He said,

"No Dad, this will make a man out of me. I want to do this." Thank goodness he didn't have to shoot his weapon in combat—this was between wars. But he patrolled the jungle in Panama for drug dealers on the border, so that had to be a little scary.

Within a year of leaving the service, he joined the police force in California as a San Diego County deputy sheriff. He spent his first four years in the county jail system—that's what they did with their recruits back then. Then he was in a patrol car, then he was on the SWAT team, and now he is a captain. He's still in San Diego with his wife and my two grandkids. After being married and raising a family, he spent six or seven years working to earn his bachelor's degree, and then he finished his master's degree. I'm very proud of him.

My relationship with Vicki Rose just got worse and worse, and we were on and off for the three years we were together. She was a heavy smoker, which I couldn't stand. And she was very possessive. She wanted to put her little brand on me, so she talked me into getting a little rose tattoo. It's on my butt cheek. Easy to see without undressing. My son Michael made it a family tradition at Christmas for years to have me slightly lower my pants and show my tattoo to various friends and family members who happened to be around at the moment.

The drama and the belligerence kept growing. When I needed Vicki to be stable the most, she was out to lunch . . . consumed by her own issues and problems. I warned her that I couldn't take very much more. As things deteriorated, a couple of times I threatened to leave if she didn't stop throwing temper tantrums and start acting more reasonably. Instead, she started taking my stuff and breaking it. Throwing things, smashing things, destroying things. My stuff, not hers. One time, she grabbed the 38 Saturday Night Special five-shot revolver I had purchased years before after Marty Sigel threatened to do me in and started waving it in my face. I didn't know if it was loaded or not (turned out it wasn't). That was no idle threat, and it created the only time I ever laid a hand on her. In self-defense I backhanded her—not hard—and grabbed the pistol from her hand. Thinking about that still gives me shivers.

Despite being so unstable, Vicky became a student teacher at a grade school. The day she found out her contract for the following year had not been renewed, she came home to an empty house. I had moved out. I had warned her the day that I left that, if I left, I wouldn't come back, and that's what happened. She called me in tears about her school situation, not realizing she had already pushed me over the edge. I had rented a small condo across town, where I lived for about a year. I did not give her my address. I didn't even tell any of my friends or family where I'd moved.

I drifted away from everyone. I had retreated into my shell, traveling a lot to poker tournaments, and trying to grind out some small wins in cash games.

Vicki eventually tracked me down and tried to get me back, but to no avail. She was too unstable and I couldn't handle this relationship . . . this constant drama . . . anymore.

Her father passed away just after we broke up in mid-1993, and her mother moved into the house in Vegas. I've lost track of Vicki, and that's got to be a good thing.

The moral: As they say about pocket Aces, they really look pretty and you certainly can play them, but don't fall in love with them.

Poker Is the Bright Spot in My Life

Despite all the turmoil in my life, 1990 was a good year for me playing tournament poker. In January, I won the $300 Pot-Limit Hold'em event at the Fourth Annual Super Stars of Poker in Lake Tahoe for over $23,625, and finished second in the $300 Limit Hold'em event and sixth in the $2,500 No-Limit Hold'em tournament. I cashed in events in several tournaments: the Winnin' o' The Green and the Diamond Jim Brady in L.A., the World Series of Poker (eighth place in the Limit Omaha event), a satellite at the Gold Coast and the Maxim U.S. Open in Vegas, and the consolation tournament at the Final Four of Poker at Harvey's Resort in Lake Tahoe. I was making money, but it wasn't enough to pull me out of debt. It allowed me to make interest payments, but the credit card debt alone was eating me alive.

These poker accomplishments didn't go unnoticed within the poker community. Jack McClelland, who had his finger on the pulse of the Vegas poker world since he began directing tournaments at the defunct Golden Eagle in 1979, noted my poker successes this year, saying, "The comeback player of the year is Tom McEvoy. After his 1983 World Series of Poker win, he went flat, but he's playing as sharp as ever now."

Right then, though, I was broke. But I knew I was not going to stay broke. One of the reason's I've been successful is I'm not willing to just lay there on the carpet and die . . . I won't do it. I have the drive to get up and try again. And I'm not a miserable person just because I don't have what I used to have. I'm not rich, but I've had a blessed life.

1990 Net Poker Proceeds of $28,000.
Non-poker proceeds of $4,400. And no more Rindy.

—1991—

Poker in general, and tournaments specifically, were growing in popularity. So casinos were beginning to get creative and try new tournament concepts. In January, I participated in a unique two-person team concept at the King of the Hill tournament at Harvey's casino in Lake Tahoe. The idea was that one team member would play Hold'em, and the other would play Lowball. I partnered with Herb Chessler—he played the Lowball leg and I played Hold'em. We placed third for $660. Not a lot of money, but it was a fun partnership format.

Bankruptcy

"Fun" was not the operative word for this point in my life . . . I was dead broke. At one point I literally played with my case money (i.e., my last dime), because I had to make 200 bucks to pay for my daughter's tuition. I put my last 200 bullets on the table, and I had to win playing $5/$10 7-Card Stud to pay her tuition and still have enough to continue to play on. That's the kind of pressure few feel. I won, but that illustrates how I was scraping the bottom of the barrel.

I was hoping I could have a breakthrough at the 1991 WSOP and avoid bankruptcy and pay off my credit card debt, but I had a bad tournament. That was my one big shot each year to make some serious, life-changing money, and I failed. I won $5,600 in a couple of events at the U.S. Open tournament in Las Vegas, but it only scratched the surface of my debt, which at this time was approaching $90,000. Now I was at the end of my rope. I was borrowing on credit cards to make minimum payments on other credit cards. That only works for so long. Without a major influx of cash, I was done. It didn't happen, and I had no choice but to file for bankruptcy.

Part of my debt was to my dad—he had bailed me out a couple of times with some loans that I now could not repay. As part of the bankruptcy, I had to send a letter to everyone that I owed money—including my dad, which took him by surprise. He wasn't upset. My family was always worried about me. I went belly-up, and that got me out of hock.

I had finally had the ego beaten out of me. A divorce—after 23 years of marriage—four-flushing friends, a cold streak, and a bankruptcy will do that to you. Still, if things don't go as they should, you have no one to blame but yourself. The decisions that brought me to this point were mine. I had manufactured my own luck.

Yet I was determined to demonstrate that misfortune is an opportunity for personal growth. Like almost every other poker player in the universe at one point, I was broke (this was just the first time). The idea is you have to keep getting up off the floor and fighting. Usually that means making some adjustments.

Rethinking My Poker Tournament Strategy

Casinos had started to favor medium-action one-day events. These tournaments ended faster, which created more side-table action. They did this by shortening the level times to less than an hour and raising the blind amounts faster (only the WSOP Main Event retains the slow-action format of level increases every two hours). This increases the luck factor at the expense of the skill factor. In other words, weaker players were helped by a faster format. I thought this was a key reason my performance had been declining.

In most medium-action tournaments, about 20 percent go out in the first two rounds. This makes it important to do better than simply survive. Extremely tight play won't allow you to survive with enough chips to be in position to contend. Loose play early either gets you an early exit or lots of chips.

Despite my lobbying attempts, faster medium-action tournaments were here to stay, so I had to revamp my play and learn to adjust. After a lot of analysis, I changed my tournament style and started getting better results.

Ending the Year on a High Note

The changes started to work. Starting to steer my financial boat back in the right direction, in December, I won the Pot-Limit Hold'em event at the National Finals at the Maxim casino in Vegas for a very nice payday of $24,480. I had gotten back up off the floor, and I was itching for more.

My Sponsor, Ron McMillan

All of this was good news to Ron McMillan, who had volunteered to become my full-time major tournament sponsor. He had been taking pieces of me here and there since the Bob Stupak tournament in 1984. Now, he agreed to pay my entry fees and expenses, which was a godsend to me. He was in on my winning my fourth and final bracelet the next year. In fact, that got us in the black . . . for a while at least.

1991 Net Poker Proceeds $19,500
Non-Poker Proceeds $4,100

—1992—

Starting the road to recovery, this year started out pretty good, poker-wise, with two fourth-place finishes, one in the Pot-Limit Hold'em event at the Queens Poker Classic II in Vegas in January, and the other in the No-Limit Hold'em event at the Peppermill Spring Tournament in early April in Reno. The $10,000 I won in these tournaments set the stage and heightened my confidence level for the 1992 World Series of Poker.

1992 World Series of Poker: My Fourth Bracelet

It paid off. First, I won my last WSOP bracelet in the *Limit Omaha High* event, a game that is not even played any more at the World Series. I was on a hot streak and busted seven of the final nine players to get heads-up with Berry Johnston. Berry was the 1986 Main Event Champion and a future Poker Hall of Fame inductee (2004). For 29 years, Berry cashed in at least one WSOP event, which I believe is still a record. It was one of the few times that two former Main Event Champions got heads-up in another World Series event.

I asked Berry, before I asked permission from the Binions, how he would feel if I allowed my dog to sit on my lap He said, "Well, the place is going to the dogs anyways. Might as well. Fine." The Binions recognized a good PR opportunity when they saw it and agreed. Poker Hall of Famer Linda Johnson, who would become the owner of *Card Player* in 1994, took a photo of me and my dog, Suki, and it was used on the cover of the magazine.

Berry and I went heads-up for over two hours. I remember thinking, "Here you've got to be lucky, you've got to be at the top of your game, and you've got to play mistake-free. One mistake and you're out the door, or severely crippled." He had me nine to one at one time, but I beat him. I bluffed him in one key pot and turned it around. To me, it was the ultimate test because I was playing one of the best poker players in the world, and one of the best Omaha players out there, so I was really proud. I was also very proud of the $79,200 payday, and, of course, the bracelet.

But it wasn't my only WSOP payday this year. I also placed second in the 7-Card Stud event, finishing second to Men "The Master" Nguyen for $60,000. I had an interesting run-in with Nguyen later, which you can read about in the "Famous Poker Player Stories" chapter. After this cash, I went from tenth to seventh on the all-time WSOP money winner list.

Poker Results Were Improving

The evolution of my poker strategy continued to pay off. I cashed for over $31,000 in five different poker games at the L.A. Poker Classic, the Diamond Jim Brady Tournament at Bell Gardens (which was won by my good friend T. J. Cloutier), the Peppermill Fall Tournament in Reno, and the Hall of Fame Classic at the Horseshoe in Vegas. Even though I didn't have much money anymore, I was able to sell pieces of my action because people still liked my play, and I had a really good track record from my heyday as a poker player. At age 48, I had won four WSOP bracelets, one Hall of Fame Classic, and one Superbowl of Poker championship. I kept making scores, so I was able to "stay in action," as they say. And I was gradually getting back on my feet again.

My two ambitions as a poker player were first, win the WSOP Main Event again, and second, to become the first player specializing in tournaments to be named to the Poker Hall of Fame. Like a good businessman, I had set goals for myself. Lofty goals, but goals, nonetheless. To reach those aspirations, and despite my poker success, I knew I could still improve my game. For example, I took 7-Card Stud lessons from one of the best players in that game, Rick Greider. In my mind, even the best can always get better, and I still believe that.

1992 Net Poker Proceeds $47,000
Non-Poker Proceeds $13,000

—1993—

Four Queens Poker Classic III

In early January, I placed fourth in the Omaha High/Low Split event at the Four Queens in downtown Vegas after a brutal 13-hour session. It was exhausting. I was so tired I started to head home without my fourth-place prize of $5,493. I was stumbling toward the door when the tournament director caught up with me and reminded me to go to the cage. Can you imagine?

Dad Passed Away

Dad and I had planned for him to visit me in Las Vegas in January. Just before his scheduled flight, he called to tell me he just didn't feel very well, and he didn't think he could make the trip. He wanted to send my brother Steve out in his place—back then you could give your plane ticket to another person to use. Shortly after Steve arrived, we got a call from home telling us Dad had been diagnosed with liver cancer. Steve and I took a red-eye flight to get back to Michigan immediately. Of course, the airline gouged us on the ticket prices, even for a trip like this.

All his children were there, and we physically carried our father out of the hospital to his favorite chair at home, where he held court for the last four days of his life. He knew was going to die, and he wanted to die at home. I vividly remember an incoming phone call that one of my brothers answered. He told Dad so-and-so was calling, and Dad said, "Tell him I can't come to the phone. I'm dead."

We all heard that, and we were stunned at first. Then we started laughing. My dad was a fussbudget all his life, but in the end, he tried to make it easy on everybody. To the last hour of his life, he was dictating instructions to my brother Steve, who was going to take over the knife business (which I had no interest in whatsoever). He said goodbye to Mom, who couldn't really comprehend what was happening.

My father passed away on January 29, 1993, eight days after being diagnosed with liver cancer. He hadn't known he had it, and it metastasized quickly through his system. At least he didn't suffer much.

My dad worried about Tom. Dad set up his estate so that Tom would not get one lump sum, a different trust arrangement than the other siblings. He got his money doled out annually because Dad didn't trust him with the money. Dad and Mom were proud of Tom, but they were worried about him. His life and his world were completely foreign to them. They saw it as gambling, not as professional poker.

—Alan McEvoy

Mom Joins Me in California

My mom finally got to watch me play poker, although I'm not sure she was totally cognizant of what was happening. After Dad died, I took Mom with me on a train trip (she had a phobia about flying) to California in March to watch me play in two tournaments, the first Masters of Poker event at the Normandie casino

in Gardena (fifth of 469 entries in Limit-Hold'em, sixth of 369 entries in Lowball), and at the Bicycle Club's March Madness in Bell Gardens. The latter is where she got to see me win first place (239 entries) in the Hold'em event to the tune of $19,800. This picture was taken at the Bicycle Club. Phyllis Caro, Mike "The Mad Genius" Caro's wife, was the tournament director and did an excellent job.

Commemorative Chips and the 25th World Series of Poker

This was the Silver Anniversary of the tournament, and the leading casino chip manufacturer, Paul-Son Gaming Corporation, was commissioned to produce a commemorative set of chips with the faces of all the World Champions, plus Benny Binion. There were 1,000 sets of 20 $2.50 denomination chips, and they sold out in 45 minutes. I still have the set I bought.

I am a chip collector. I used to collect low-denomination "race off" tournament chips, the chips that are taken off the tables once the antes get so high they become irrelevant nuisances. I took them off my own stack, but I got caught doing that early on at the Bicycle Club and got in a little hot water, and that ended that.

Then I started collecting interesting chips, specializing in commemoratives with a poker theme. To me, collecting chips is like collecting history. Through my interest in poker memorabilia, I became acquainted with my biographer, Brad Smith, who is the publicity director for the Casino

Collectables Association. At his request, I attended their annual "World's Largest Casino Collectibles Show" several times as a featured VIP. The show is held every June in Las Vegas, and it's a must for anyone interested in poker and casino history.

On My Own Again

After I escaped from Vicki Rose, she had no idea where I had gone. Vicki wanted to reconcile, and in August, she tracked me down in California, because she knew I played in the Bicycle Club tournament every year. We had a pleasant visit, but it wasn't enough. I realized she hadn't changed.

After the divorce and my relationship with Vicki ended, I had a whole bunch of different relationships I used to get teased about. A friend said, "McEvoy, you change girlfriends every other week." I did date a lot of ladies at different times with different degrees of intensity. I discovered in my middle age—from 45 on—that women were actually attracted to me, something that seemed to have escaped me for most of my life.

Business Agreement with Phil Hellmuth

I have known Phil Hellmuth for a long time, and I consider him a close personal friend. We had talked before about the possibility of him sponsoring or staking me, and he had indicated he would consider it as soon as his bankroll would allow it. At the time, Ron McMillan was already staking me, and when he had to put a halt to our arrangement in 1993 due to a temporary situation, I let Phil know. He contacted me during the Gold Coast Open in July and asked me to join a group of poker pros he was staking. I agreed, and our business relationship started the next day and lasted for about two years. Phil knew me, liked me, and knew I was always going to watch his back. I actually helped him keep track of some of the other people he was sponsoring.

Hellmuth suggested our financial arrangement. He would advance entry fees and travel expenses to me, and we would share winnings equally after expenses were reimbursed. When I lost, the fees and expenses were put "on make-up," or banked and carried forward to the next tournament. I liked this arrangement because it worked well for both of us. It kept my risks at a manageable level and gave Phil the possibility of a good return on investment. His R.O.I. odds were good because I had a track record as a winning player, and my results had been fairly consistent over the years. At the time, I had placed in the money in 19 percent of the tournaments I had entered and won 7 percent of them.

Phil was backing me in the bigger, major tournaments, not the smaller tournaments around Las Vegas that I still played on my own dime. Usually, we would gather together at these bigger tournament venues, when the whole group of players he was sponsoring would all be playing, and hammer out any details.

In every tournament, no matter who you are or how good you are, you're a substantial underdog to win. Phil and I were stuck almost $60,000 after I lost events in two World Series. But Phil never lost faith in me. He told me if I got to $150,000 stuck, he might have to reconsider, but not to worry about the $60,000 and to just keep playing because he had faith I would win for him eventually. We once went through a dry spell of over a year without either of us making money, but Phil never lost confidence in me, which gave me confidence in myself. "Tom," he said, "I've stuck with you through thin and thinner!" His faith was justified. He said, "Honor is everything in the poker world. That's why I eventually got into business with Tom McEvoy—he has both honor and potential."

The next year, Phil branched out and formed a partnership with Herb Bronstein, who was also backing players, by splitting the costs of other players with him. Phil shared me with Herb, and Herb shared two of his players with Phil, and they added another player to their roster. They each kept one other player for themselves, sort of hedging their risks. As Phil put it, "I supply the money, advice, and emotional support that my players need, while they supply the time and the talent. It's a mutual trade."

Our arrangement was forged on the basis of trust: a handshake agreement; no written contract. I'm very proud of that. I'm also very proud that Phil made money on me and didn't lose a nickel.

After about two years, Phil came to the conclusion that staking all of these players was disrupting his game too much, and he decided to stop sponsoring all of us.

Phyllis and Milt Meyers

To subsidize my income, I started giving lucrative one-on-one poker lessons. That's how I met Phyllis Meyers and her husband Milt. Phyllis contacted me because she wanted to learn how to play

No-Limit Hold'em. She was a good 7-Card Stud player, but this Hold'em game was new, interesting, and growing in popularity. I started giving her lessons, and she progressed to become a pretty good Hold'em player, winning a few smaller tournaments and cashing in several others.

Milt was an eye doctor in Detroit and had the contract for the optometry needs for General Motors employees. He was extremely intelligent, a renaissance man, and a super nice guy. He had his own plane, and once flew me to Grand Rapids from Vegas on his way to the East coast. Milt Meyers was never comfortable playing anything higher than $20/$40 Limit Hold'em. It wasn't the money; he just wanted to win. I gave him some lessons, too, but mostly I was teaching Phyllis. I got to be very good friends with both of them. I was giving lessons out of my inexpensive rented condo when Phyllis came up with the idea of buying a nicer condo, for the express purpose of renting it to me. I thought it was a wonderful idea. They bought a condo on Indian Princess Drive, and I moved in early the next year, 1994. I lived there for the next six years until I bought a house. It's great to have great friends.

Michele Johnson (not the famous actress)

In October, I went on a *Card Player* Poker Caribbean Cruise on the Carnival Cruise Lines *Celebration* bound for Puerto Rico and the Virgin Islands (I went on a lot of *Card Player* poker cruises) with my brother, Alan. I was the cruise "triple threat," winning at poker (heads-up against Robert "Chip Burner" Turner), Gin Rummy, and Backgammon. It's also the cruise where I was lucky enough to meet Michele Johnson. She had been married and divorced from the same man as Linda Johnson, which is how they shared the same last name. Michele worked in the magazine's distribution department. That's when we began a relationship that lasted about a year, and she moved in with me for a short time in my new condo on Indian Princess Drive.

Michele liked me because she thought I was a nice guy. When we met, she had no idea I was a famous poker player—she lived in the "real world." I took Michele with me to Grand Rapids in the summer of 1994. Mom was living at home, which was risky in itself, and was now so far gone she had to have constant care. Mom put a huge guilt trip on my sister and made her promise she would never put her in a nursing home. Mother eventually became a danger to herself. She would wander in the neighborhood, forgetting where she lived. When things progressed to the point that she didn't recognize her children, her children unanimously agreed that Mom belonged in a home.

On this trip, I wanted to give my brothers and sister a break from her caregiving, so we stayed at the house. Mom was a strict Catholic, and Michele and I stayed in separate rooms, but that didn't stop her from pegging Michele as a "hussy." My siblings were unhappy I had brought her there because of Mom's reaction. Sometimes you can't win for losing.

Michele wasn't really a bad person, but we had two incidents that created trust issues between us. The first one caused me to question her reliability. I was going on a trip to California, and I had sent a check to cover my play in a backgammon tournament. For one reason or another—my fault—I discovered I didn't have enough money in my checking account to cover this check, and I had run out of time to get to the bank. So, I gave Michele a check from another account to cover the first check and asked her to please deposit it in the bank. Instead of doing so, she pawned the chore off on a third party who didn't deposit it in time, so my check bounced. That put me in an embarrassing situation in California, which infuriated me. I thought I could rely on her, but I should have just done it myself.

Earlier, Michele had gotten into a little bit of a financial jam, and she hit a jackpot that bailed her out for around $4,000. Then she got into another jam, and, without asking, she "borrowed" $800 from me. She thought she could hit another jackpot. She intended to replace the money. She was going to successfully gamble at the slots. Really? That's a plan?

When I began writing my second tournament poker book, I had originally done a dedication page for the book and said some nice things about Michele. They got edited out before the printing stage. We broke up in 1994. She later followed me on a cruise to Alaska, where we had a brief reconciliation, but it was over between us.

Tournament Host in California

In November, I was hired to serve as the tournament host at the debut of the 1st Annual L.A. Poker Open at the Normandie Casino in Gardena, California. It had been scheduled in the vacant time slot created by the cancellation of Binion's Hall of Fame tournament that year. As part of the effort to attract players to this "replacement" venue, I was featured with my photo in literature and ads in the newspapers and *Card Player* magazine (where I was now a staff writer). The casino wanted a host who knew—lived and breathed—poker, a well-known name and face and a friendly winning personality. I had experience hosting tournaments at the Frontier and the Bell Club, so I fit the bill. Basically, I served as a sounding board and technical advisor. And, I was a playing host, so I also competed in the tournament, which was one of the attractions for the other players. The tournament was a huge success.

1993 Net Poker Proceeds $26,000
Non-Poker Proceeds (-$3,000)

—1994—

In March, I joined John Bonetti (winner of three WSOP bracelets) and Herb Bronstein (eight major tournament wins) as hosts of the third annual Masters of Poker Championship at the Normandie

Casino in Gardena, California, where we kicked off the tournament with a big celebration party event. The casino management promoted the event by saying: "By having pro players as liaisons, we are better able to keep our operations directly tuned to the needs of the tournament players." I won the $500 Limit-Hold'em and $300 Omaha events and cashed in four other events to capture the "Best All-Around Player" honor. Since I would be turning 50 that year, in July I qualified for and participated in the First Annual Seniors Championship of Poker in Oceanside, California, finishing sixth in the No-Limit Hold'em event.

Winning My Second Car

In August 1994, I won my second car at a unique competition at the Diamond Jim Brady Tournament, held at the Bicycle Club in Bell Gardens, California. The prize was a 1994 Lincoln Mark VIII. They called the contest the "Brilliant All-Around Poker Points Championship," and the car was awarded for the cumulative honor of best all-around player. Points were given for a player's finish in the different tournament events, and the nine players with the most points got to play for the car in a special tournament. Each player got chips based on their performance in the previous tournaments. I wasn't the chip leader going into this playoff, but I played well and won the car.

Phil Hellmuth was sponsoring me, and at that time I was on "make up" with him. So, before I could pocket any renumeration, I had to pay him back for previous losses. That day, Phil was with me at the Bicycle Club, playing in a cash game. After I won the car, I reported it to Phil. He asked, "What are we going to do with it?" Ted Forrest (31 WSOP cashes), who was in the cash game with Phil, overheard this and said he would like to take a look at the car, and possibly buy it. And he did. Because the car was technically in my name, he went with me to the car dealership to look it over. He decided he liked the car, and he bought it. I believe he spent in the neighborhood of $31,000 for the car, in cash. That got me off "make up." Phil Hellmuth got all the money. I won the car, but I didn't get to drive it or keep it.

I also won the $1,000 buy-in Limit Hold'em event, netting over $41,000. *Card Player* magazine reported I told them I had "promptly dedicated the win to [my] new girlfriend, Michele Johnson, whom he met on a recent *Card Player* poker cruise."

The Houseguest from Hell

The poker community is my world, and I have met and become fast friends with many of the great people who associate with the game. Playing the poker circuit tournaments involves a fair amount of travel, which has an associated expense. To keep these costs down, many players would "bunk" with friends from time to time, and I'm no exception. Sometimes, funny things happened.

In July 1994, during the Gold Coast Open, one of my closest friends, Neil Campbell, stayed with me in Vegas, as I often stayed with him when I traveled to Los Angeles. Neil was a big guy, over 300 pounds, and he woke me up at 6 a.m. one morning, hollering, "Get in here quick, the toilet is overflowing!" Sure enough, the fragrant blue chemical in the tank was running all over and staining my new beige carpet. In our frantic effort to stave off disaster, Neil broke the toilet paper dispenser, and then attempting to make repairs, I broke part of the toilet. I went to the tournament while Neil stayed home to manage the plumber I called. Repairs were made, but the carpet was a goner.

The next morning, Neil required nourishment in the form of three cinnamon rolls, heated in the microwave on my best crystal plate. Two minutes is overkill, but my guest discovered too late the plate was too hot to handle and dropped it and its sticky contents on my tiled kitchen floor. We were both barefoot and only in our boxer shorts, and being more agile than my corpulent companion, I was able to jump out of the way. Pieces of glass bounced off the floor and attached themselves to various parts of Neil's ample anatomy with amazing accuracy, leaving him bleeding in several strategic areas. Using tweezers and a washcloth, I removed the glass from his feet, legs, and other areas. Undeterred, we dashed to the Gold Coast to get there on time for the tournament.

It was really funny—later—when we reflected on it when I stayed at his place the next month to play in the Diamond Jim Brady tournament. Unfortunately, and to my deep regret, Neil Campbell passed away later that year on December 10, 1994. I still miss him, his large spirit, and his loud, booming voice.

Incidentally, we tournament poker circuit pros mostly stayed in hotels rather than bunking with friends. The hotels offered special rates to players coming in to play in their poker tournaments, and we always got a poker rate—usually between $18 to $40 a night, depending on where you were. These rates were advertised, encouraging players to get their reservations in as soon as possible for the tourney and the room.

First Annual Queen of Clubs Tournament

This was a tournament for ladies only held at the Bicycle Club in Bell Gardens, California, in early September. I was invited to be part of a special seminar for the players entitled "Tournament Tips from the Pros." Speakers included myself, Mike Caro, and the well-known female pros Susie Isaacs and Marsha Waggoner.

Sal's Town Desert Classic

I got offers to host poker tournaments from large, well-known casinos, and from small, relatively unknown ones. One of these was Sal's Town Card Club Casino in Rosamond, California, in the middle of nowhere about 50 miles north of Los Angeles. I was their featured pro host for their October tournament for a couple of years, until I apparently upset the owner, Sal Martinez. Then he sold the place.

Participating in Fundraisers

I received many requests to participate in fundraising events for worthy causes, and I tried to help out whenever I could. In October, I was happy to be part of a poker seminar with Mike Caro, Mike Sexton, and video producer Ben Tracey. A member of the *Card Player* staff, production manager Maryann Gruberman, had recently been hospitalized at a very young age for a heart attack. I was a columnist for the publication, and I knew Maryann and thought highly of her. To raise money for Maryann's medical expenses, the magazine organized and promoted the seminar, held at the Gold Coast casino in Vegas on October 20. The $20 ticket proceeds were given to Maryann, along with 20 percent of the proceeds of a poker tournament that followed the seminar.

Hosting the Second Annual L.A. Poker Open

The first L.A. Open at the Normandie casino was so successful they asked me to come back and host it again in November. This is where I first spoke with and started to get to know Kathy Liebert, who would become a big part of my life in the late 1990s. That's covered in Chapter 16.

Oktober Pokerfest

Also in October, I won the $200 Limit-Hold'em event at the Bicycle Club's Oktober Pokerfest tournament in Bell Garden, California. Along with the prize money of $11,520, I won one of my favorite trophies, a German stein chalice. It's one of the relatively few trophies I still have today.

World Poker Finals

In early December, I won the $100 Omaha and the $500 No-Limit Hold'em events at the World Poker Finals at the Foxwoods Resort Casino in Mashantucket, Connecticut. I ended the year running pretty good, which made my sponsor very happy.

Hall of Fame Classic

I finished 1994 with a good showing at the annual Hall of Fame Classic tournament at Binion's Horseshoe in downtown Vegas in late December. I came in fifth in the $1,500 No-Limit Hold'em event and ninth in the $5,000 No-Limit Hold'em event, where I made the final table along with poker notables Annie Duke, Dewey Tomko, Mansour Matloubi, Huck Seed, and Seymour Leibowitz. Pretty stiff competition.

In early 1994, I had moved into the condo on Indian Princess Drive owned by the Meyers, right around the same time I started working on my next book with Dana Smith, the subject of the next chapter.

1994 Net Poker Proceeds $3,000
Non-Poker Proceeds (-$100)

*Books are like people, in the sense that they'll turn
up in your life when you most need them.*
—Emma Thompson

CHAPTER 14

Dana Smith, My Coauthor.

When it comes to impacting my life, no one has played a greater role than my writer, friend, and confidant Dana Smith. So, she gets a whole chapter. Our relationship is an interesting one, and can be described with many words—close, volatile, siblinglike, quarrelsome, to name a few. If it wasn't for her, I wouldn't have written 14 poker books.

Dana was born April 28, 1937. For a number of years, she taught school as an English teacher in California. Her first marriage didn't last long. She met her second husband, a very prominent doctor from Bakersfield, California, at a ski lodge. He had some children that lived  with them, including an 18-year-old son who committed suicide. Their marriage collapsed after that. Dana has no natural-born children of her own, but while they were married, they adopted a son, John, who now lives in Ithaca, New York, with his wife. John and Jennifer have one now-adult child, who recently married.

Dana played poker in Bakersfield and used her poker playing, book editing, and writing skills to write a couple of poker books. She wrote under the pseudonym Shane Smith because she believed being a woman would hurt sales, a fair assumption given the times. One book was about Low-Limit Omaha 8 or better, which she played a lot in Bakersfield. Another book she did was called *Tournament Tips from the Pros*, in which she quoted me extensively along with quite a few other famous poker pros—without any formal permission, she just did it. I was flattered that she had included quotes from me that she had pulled from articles and my first book, *How to Win at Poker Tournaments*. Other than these two books, there were no other books specifically on poker tournament strategy. Frankly, I had always thought I could do a better job than I had done with my first book, but that would be a labor- and time-intensive endeavor I wasn't going to attempt unless I could make some money . . . something I was severely lacking at the time.

Dana Smith moved from Bakersfield to Las Vegas after her second marriage to the doctor fell apart in 1994. Recently divorced, she was ready for a change in her life, I think. When she was with the doctor, she was pretty well off. Now she was on her own and had to earn a living again. She was no longer teaching, so that meant writing. She told me she came to Vegas to see if, among other things, she could find me and convince me to do another book on tournament poker.

I met her for the first time when we ran into each other at the Mirage casino—not prearranged, just in the poker room. She told me how she was hoping to meet me when she moved here, and that she would like to work with me on another tournament book, with her as ghostwriter. I didn't know her from Adam, and I wasn't sure another book would make any money this time. So, basically, I gave her the brush off. Fortunately for both of us, she didn't give up.

Dana got busy making a living doing book edits and other things—including putting together a new Tom McEvoy tournament poker book business plan. Six months later I ran into her again, again not prearranged. At this point in my life, I was dead broke and going through a very rough patch. I had declared bankruptcy in 1991 and I was still struggling to get back on my feet. My romantic relationship with Vicki Rose had fizzled, my dad had died the year before, and my mom had Alzheimer's and was going downhill fast. And then Dana reappears.

She pitched me again. But this time she was prepared with a typed-up business plan. She showed me her projected net income was at least $25,000 each. Now she had my attention. This looked like a nice chunk of money, and I could do something I had wanted to do—put together a better tournament poker book.

This time I listened and agreed to give it a try. But I gave her a lot of grief at the beginning of the process, insisting we do this my way and on my time schedule, which was wrong on all accounts. I started to dictate the book into a tape recorder without any plan. I gave the first tapes to Dana, and she promptly complained, and rightfully so. She said it was an unorganized mishmash with no flow. Basically, she said, "This is not working, you idiot."

At this point I followed her advice, and we did it the right way. We took a step backward and developed an outline I could follow to organize my thinking as I dictated. Once we hammered that out, I started to work in a logical, organized fashion. Then the book started to fall into place.

The broad concept I came up with was to use my World Series of Poker experience to cover tournament play in several different poker games. I had a first- or second-place finish in six different World Series events, in six different games. Nobody else had so many multigame poker successes. I had won four World Series bracelets, and even Phil Hellmuth with his current 17 bracelets, didn't have them in six different games. So, that's how we did it.

But for the seven months it took me from start to finish on this book in 1994, I was starving to death. I spent the lion's share of my time working on the book, which cut into my poker time tremendously. To be fair, I hadn't been doing very well lately in poker, anyway.

Word had started to get out that I was doing this new, expanded book on tournament poker. Some of the big-name players didn't like the idea that I was going to wise-up a bunch of people. Eric Sidel said to me, "Tom, I heard about your book. How much money do you think you're going to make on the book?" I told him what Dana had calculated we would make. He said, "Tom, I'll give you $25,000 if you don't publish it." We hadn't printed it yet, but we were getting close. I thought about all the work we had done, said thank you, and turned him down. It was a nice gesture and a nice offer, but we had come too far to abandon the project. By the end of 1994, the manuscript was finished.

Tournament Poker was published in early 1995, and it was an instant success, an immediate poker bestseller. There was nothing out there like it. Dana was slightly off in her projections of how much we would make on the book. I stopped counting after we had made over $100,000, and we ended up making a lot more than that. We were selling the paperback version for $40, and sold 200 hardcover issues for $60 each. I still have the first hardcover issue, sealed in a clear plastic box. The book was even translated into French.

On the heels of the publishing of *Tournament Poker,* I started writing columns for *Card Player* magazine. One of the driving reasons for doing the columns was to get publicity for the book. But it went so well I ended up continuing as a *Card Player* columnist for about ten years. I dropped writing these to pursue other interests.

The book money was coming in when I really needed it. I will never be able to thank Dana enough for being a huge part of my getting back on my feet. Success breeds success, and after we made so much money on this book, it was only natural to do another one. This time we invited my good friend T. J. Cloutier to get involved, and together we wrote *Championship No-Limit and Pot-Limit Hold'em.* Pot-limit was being played at the time, but not very much No-Limit . . . except at World Series time. A lot of people consider this my best book with T. J., which may account for why this, my third book, was even more financially successful than the last one. We split the proceeds by thirds between Dana, T. J., and me. I wound up doing four books with T. J. and Dana. We did a Limit Hold'em book, which got a little bit of criticism. We did an Omaha book, and a tournament hands book, *Championship Tournament Practice Hands.* To keep the money rolling in, we lowered our price per copy from $40 to $30, and we were getting it! We self-published these books, so there was no middleman.

I moved into the two-bedroom condo that the Meyers bought and rented to me in 1994. After our book was published in 1995, Dana's lease ran out on her apartment, and she ostensibly needed a place to stay. At her suggestion, she moved into the second bedroom in my place. She was well aware that my romantic interests lay elsewhere and that I was dating other women. Nevertheless, in so many words she pointed out to me that since we got along so well, and worked together so well, it might be a good idea if we made our relationship permanent. The problem was, I was not attracted to Dana. I liked her as a business partner—she was great—and we had a very good business relationship, but I didn't want it to go beyond that. Once, she even contacted the Meyers and told them I was ruining my life because I was dating a stripper (more on her in the next chapter), but that plan backfired. Dana lived with me in the condo for one summer, and when she figured out I wasn't going to do what she wanted me to do, she moved on.

But we continued to successfully write books together, and we have maintained a strong yet sometimes strained friendship. Dana didn't want to be single the rest of her life, and she met and married her third husband, Don Vines, in about 2000. I was casual friends with him, and we got to be better friends after they married. They used to go out six days out of seven and play video poker machines, where they perfected the basic strategy to be "break-even" players. If you study video poker, know the right machines, and know what you're doing, the goal is to break even because the profit margin is the comps you earn. Don Vines thought it was ridiculous to ever pay for a meal in Las Vegas. When they were married, I went out with them a lot, and frankly took advantage of their meal comps. Don and I co-wrote a book, *How to Win No-Limit Hold'em Tournaments,* in 2005. He was a smoker, and he unfortunately got throat cancer and passed away in 2011. His buddies included a lot of policemen, and they held an annual poker tournament and named it the Don Vines Memorial Tournament. I donated to his tournament for a lot of years, and played in it, too.

Dana co-wrote a couple of books with some other famous poker players besides me and T. J. Cloutier. She wrote a book with Byron "Cowboy" Wolford in 2002 titled *Cowboys, Gamblers & Hustlers: The True Adventures of a Rodeo Champion & Poker Legend.* She also coauthored *The Life and Times of a Gentleman Gambler* with "Oklahoma" Johnny Hale in 1999. Johnny was not exactly an upright fellow, and he and Dana had a falling out about some of the royalties she felt she was due but never received, since she had done the lion's share of the work. The book was self-published, and Dana dumped off her remaining copies at his place and that was it.

Truth be known, Dana Smith and I have a sort of love/hate relationship, maybe more along the lines of a brother/sister relationship. I'd do anything for her, and she for me. Over the years, I have been invited and briefly lived with Dana three times, and she has asked me to leave her home that many times as well. She helped me with arrangements to get my current home and has helped me innumerable other times as well. And as a former English teacher, she still corrects my grammar ad nauseam. Dana has continued to play a big role in my life, and I'll cover that chronologically later in the book. She recently moved to New York to be with her son, and I miss her.

Life is what happens when you're busy making other plans.
—*Allen Saunders*

CHAPTER 15

1995 to 1998. Books, Major Tournament Manager, Prop Player, Bipolar Diagnosis, and the Stripper.

—1995—

Tournament Poker

My second poker book, published by Cardsmith Publishing, became available on March 1, 1995. As I mentioned before, it was an immediate bestseller and a lifesaver for me financially.

I had asked Phil Hellmuth to do an introduction for the book. By then, Phil was a rock star in the poker world. He agreed, but he didn't want it edited, and I said fine. The introduction was a little egotistical, but that's my good friend Phil.

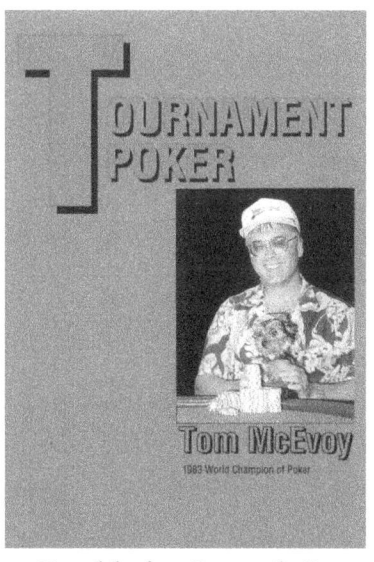

I sold autographed copies at the Gambler's General Store in Vegas and Reno, the Bicycle Club "Winnin' O' The Green"

tournament in Southern California, and at Binion's Horseshoe at the World Series of Poker.

But one of the biggest promotional efforts was through *Card Player* magazine, which was purchased by Linda Johnson, Scott Rogers, and Denny Axel in November of the previous year. Mike Sexton did a two-page review of the book in the magazine, and we ran ads with an order form for readers to send in to buy the book.

In December, I was welcomed as a *Card Player* columnist by Linda Johnson. My new column was titled "Tournament Talk," and I continued as a bimonthly column contributor for the next ten years. The columns were mostly about tournament strategy, but occasionally they gave me the opportunity to rebuff my occasional critics. One example is Mason Malmuth, and you can read about that article in Chapter 30. They also gave me the opportunity, in the little bio at the end of my columns, to promote my books. My pay for each column wasn't that much, but the PR exposure was priceless.

The Stripper

During the spring I met Kathy Mitchell, an intriguing young lady and poker player from Columbus, Ohio. She initiated a conversation with me at a poker tournament at the Gold Coast Casino in Las Vegas. I was on the escalator going down to the poker room, and she was on the escalator going upstairs. When we passed in the middle, she started to talk to me. She was really hot, so when I got to the bottom of the moving stairs, I immediately took the escalator back up. We started talking, and we hit it off. She was headed back to Ohio, so we kept in touch on the phone. That's when I learned she was a divorced mother of four, and a professional exotic dancer. Or stripper, as Dana Smith referred to her. In Ohio back then, a stripper couldn't even go topless, so this was a very mild sort of stripping.

She came out to California in May when I was hosting a tournament at the Normandie Club, where we started dating. Ours was a long-distance relationship, and when she went back to Columbus, I decided to go pay her a visit. I got to see her dance one time, and to me it was pretty mild stuff, not at all like the strip clubs here in Vegas today (or so I'm told). I also played poker there in some home games and a charity tournament. Kathy was a rock-and-roller, enamored with the rock group AC/DC. She was a groupie and followed them on tour.

Like most long-distance relationships, ours didn't last much past the summer. Even after we broke up, she would occasionally show up in Las Vegas and we would go out again for a little bit. Once she came out for the smoke-free tournament I hosted at Sam's Town Casino in 1999 and stayed with me in the condo. She stayed with me again for a brief time in 2000 after I had just purchased a new house, and I helped her get a job at the World Series of Poker as a brush (money runner). Twice I tried dating Kathy Mitchell, and each time she did things I didn't like, so I called our on-again, off-again relationship permanently off.

At the tender age of 50, I was beginning to realize I was more attractive to women than I had previously thought. Even imagined. My poker notoriety no doubt contributed greatly to my attraction, but I was only too happy to find myself appealing to the ladies.

26th World Series of Poker

The $70 Million "Fremont Street Experience" canopy was under construction during Binion's World Series of Poker and completed later in the year. Despite the noise and the hubbub, I finished third in the $1,500 Omaha Pot-Limit event and netted a little over $35,000.

Ten Main Event champions. Photo taken by Larry Grossman in 1995. L. to R., Me, Johnny Chan, Stuey Ungar, Russ Hamilton, Johnny Moss, Puggy Pearson (dressed like an Indian), Berry Johnston, Jim Bechtel, Phil Hellmuth, and Jack Keller.

Masters of Poker Championship III Tournament

Taking advantage of my increasing exposure as a best-selling author, I was invited to host the Normandie Club's Masters of Poker Championship III in May in Gardena, California. My photo was featured in the advertising for the tournament, which proved to be a pretty good draw. Kathy Mitchell got to watch as I managed to eke out a first-place finish in the $50 buy-in No-Limit event for $4,325.

Seniors World Championship Hall of Fame

"Oklahoma" Johnny Hale founded "The Seniors" World Championship of Poker Players Hall of Fame in 1994, inducting one member, Johnny Moss. I turned 50 in November of 1994, which was the youngest age of eligibility. In 1995, Hale put himself in the

Senior Poker Players Hall of Fame along with eight others, includ-ing me. We were honored because of "our poker playing ability and our contributions to the game of poker."

On a related note, Hale also started the Seniors World Championship of Poker Tournament at the Hollywood Park Casino in Inglewood, California, first held in July 1994. Later, some of the tournaments were held on cruise ships. I liked Johnny Hale, but he was a poker player I didn't totally  trust. Hale always put a positive spin on things, even though he was known to stretch the truth a bit. The Seniors World Championship of Poker was the grandiose title he bestowed on his tournament. He tied his "seniors" concept into what he called "The Senior Charities," except I'm not sure who the charity recipients were. A little shady? Perhaps.

Birth of the Legends of Poker Tournament

Since 1985, one of the most prestigious tournaments on the circuit was the Diamond Jim Brady, held at the Bicycle Club in Bell Gardens, California. For a number of years, I would participate and spend the whole month of August there. The tournament was the brainchild of George Hardie, the casino's founder and general manager. For the tournament, George dressed like the reincarna-tion of Diamond Jim Brady, the legendary character in poker from the past, complete with topcoat, stove-pipe hat, and diamond stick pin. George was a pretty well-known guy in the poker community and was even nominated for the Poker Hall of Fame once or twice. For some reason, Hardie's contract with the Bicycle Casino was not renewed, and my old friend Robert "Chip Burner" Turner was asked to create a tournament that could match the prestige of the Diamond Jim Brady.

His concept was the Legends of Poker tournament. He came up with the idea to have top poker pros each host one of the tournament events. He recruited a bunch of us players who were big names in poker to launch the tournament including Phil Hellmuth, Johnny Chan, Susie Isaacs, Vince Burgio, Max Shapiro, Mike Sexton, Ted Forrest, Cindy Violette, Barbara Enright, Herb Bronstein, and me. The Bike would comp the entry fee for the event each hosted. Pretty brilliant. They knew these top pros would stick around and play in the other events, which was a big draw for the tournament.

I actually won the 7-Card Stud event I hosted at the inaugural Legends of Poker, where I was up against Sam Grizzle, Scotty Nguyen, and Chris Furgeson. In poker, the proof of a good idea is longevity. The Legends of Poker has been part of the World Poker Tour schedule since 2002 and remains one of the most highly anticipated poker tournaments every year. The concept originator, Robert Turner, who was also the tournament director and a player, would soon factor into my life yet again.

15-Year Career Summary

At this point in my little over 15 years as a professional poker player, I had played in 3,200 tournaments/satellites. I had placed first 230 times and placed in the money an additional 372 times. I won the tournament once out of every 14 entries for an average win rate of 7.2 percent. I had an 11.7 percent win rate in my other "in-the-money" finishes. When you add the two together, my win plus money finishes rate was 19 percent, which is an important number when you consider the following.

Ron McMillan Becomes My Sponsor—Again

After Phil Hellmuth, Ron McMillan stepped back into the picture as my sponsor. I don't remember when it was exactly. Ron is a rare breed—businessman, entrepreneur, and an all-around fine man who is fun to be around. He is affectionately known as "Mr. Mama," because he owns an award-winning restaurant by that name, specializing in breakfast—they also do lunch, but close at 3 p.m. I still eat there often, and highly recommend the place.

Ron backed me from 1996 through 2002—about six years. And he spent much more than he made staking me in poker tournaments. For example, Ron sponsored me in the $10,000 WSOP Main Event every one of those years, and I didn't cash even once. Six or seven years of $10,000 losses and you're talking *real* money. So, it was kind of like starving to death . . . I was on make-up, and when I had a tournament score, I had to give it to him to make up for the losers. Still, I don't know how I will ever be able to repay Ron for his sponsorship or his friendship.

As an aside, I have Ron to thank for hooking me up with my second wife, Yolanda, in a strange, roundabout way. Yolanda's ex-husband's brother was married to a relative of Ron's, and through him she contacted Ron to see if he knew of anybody in Las Vegas with a room to rent. Ron did: me. That's covered a little down the road in Chapter 23.

Sponsors and Some Financial Perspective

If you compare my tournament poker winnings as reported by the Hendon Mob (the world's premier poker ratings site) in the last chapter of this book, and the net poker proceeds I report at the end of each chapter, you'll often see a huge disparity. For example, in 1995, Hendon Mob documented my tournament earnings of $143,500, while my records show net poker proceeds of just $39,000.

I want to explain why. I calculated that in 1994, playing most major events on the tournament circuit and most of the minor ones cost about $175,000 for buy-ins alone. One year, Mike Sexton calculated he spent almost the same for his entry fees alone. Beyond the upfront costs just to enter, tournament earnings don't equate to net profits for three more reasons. First, sponsors get their share of the profits after they get the cost of the entry fee back. Second, there are deals. Many if not most tournaments are "chopped," like I did in my Main Event victory. That is, an agreement is arrived at by the remaining few players as to how the prize money will be chopped up or divided. This lowers the remaining players' risks, as the first out are guaranteed more money while the eventual winner agrees to take a smaller cut. I would say 75 to 80 percent of the time, some kind of a hedge or deal was made.

The other factor that eats into net poker proceeds are the costs involved with travel, lodging, and food. Sometimes a sponsor will cover these costs, which are repaid out of prize money. While my win plus money finishes rate of 19 percent was very good, it still means that 81 percent of the tournaments I played netted me zero return. Sponsor expenses not repaid by tournament prize money were not absorbed by the sponsor—they went on "make up" to be repaid by the prize proceeds of future tournaments. My winnings totals at the end of each year in this book reflect all of these factors.

Busy End of the Year

In November, I captured two first-place victories at the World Championship of HORSE tournament in Inglewood, California. The first was in the $300 Razz event, and the second was in the $300 Omaha High/Low event. Combined winnings were about $15,500. I was also named the "Best All-Around Player" at the Hollywood Park Sport of Kings Poker Classic. In December, I hosted the First Annual Mountain Classic at the Top of the Vine cardroom in Bakersfield, California. For this, I was paid with a very nice poker table that I kept for years.

1995 Net Poker Proceeds $39,000
Non-Poker Proceeds $4,500

—1996—

Poker Book Number Three: *No-Limit and Pot-Limit Hold'em*

For about a year after the publication of *Tournament Poker,* my writing was limited to my *Card Player* column. Sometimes Dana Smith would pinch hit and write a column for me, usually when I was goofing off or traveling to a tournament, for example, when I spent the whole month of August at the Bicycle Club in California.

But as the old adage goes, strike while the iron is hot, and Dana and I began contemplating another book. I suggested enlisting the help of my friend T. J. Cloutier, who was considered not only one of the best tournament players but also one of the best No-Limit Hold'em players out there. He was the best all-around player that had never won the World Series of Poker Main Event but had come ever so close. He had two seconds, a third, and a fifth. He was the logical choice, and when we reached out to him, he agreed immediately.

At the beginning of the book project T. J. and I were what I would call "casual friends," but once we started working together our friendship became much deeper. We became the best of friends. We dictated the book together, with Dana there the whole time listening, directing, moderating, and making suggestions. T. J. and I were just talking poker, but the partnership worked because of Dana. She was the driving force behind getting the material organized and flowing and properly smoothed out. It worked.

We didn't start the third book until the second half of 1996. T. J. would travel from his home in Texas and spend time in Vegas. I put him up more than once. I'd say we did the book in about four or five months. *Championship No-Limit and Pot-Limit Hold'em* was released January 1, 1997. And it became the best-selling book I would coauthor.

World Poker Industry Conference

Poker as an industry was gaining awareness and momentum. *Card Player* magazine witnessed this firsthand as they gained circulation and advertising dollars. On March 27 and 28, the magazine hosted its inaugural annual World Poker Industry Conference at Treasure Island casino on the Strip in Las Vegas. I attended the conference as an opportunity to promote myself. With the help of Dana Smith and her Cardsmith publishing, we produced a flyer promoting my skills and availability as a tournament host, coordinator/director, consultant, and seminar speaker. Of course, my success as an author was part of my bio, which supported the credibility of the next book that was under way with coauthor T. J. Cloutier. I was able to rub elbows with a sizable gathering of current and future poker influencers. Self-promotion is out of my comfort zone, but I took one for the team.

Son Mike Marries

In August, my son Mike married Shannon Lenhart in a ceremony at the Tropicana in Las Vegas. They were both 24. The marriage lasted only about four years.

Shannon is from Las Vegas, and her parents had a reception party for the newlyweds at their home. In my zest to toast the couple, I jumped up on a chair to get everyone's attention, which was a move the Lenharts did not approve of. One of the many times in my life I didn't exactly think before acting, but I was very proud of Mike and so happy for him.

Mike had started working at the age of 14 or 15 in one of the lowest jobs in the kitchen at Tillerman's, which was a fine dining restaurant where I used to eat often. By the time he was 25 or 26, he was general manager of the place and able to buy the former McEvoy house from his mother. That's where he fell down the stairs and broke his ankle. He was prescribed pain medication, and unfortunately got hooked. That's what started him down the path of drug abuse.

Mike is very intelligent, attractive, hard-working, and a bit of a bad boy. Shannon was going to law school and Mike was working in a restaurant. There were some differences there, obviously, in the direction their lives were going. I liked Shannon, and I even had lunch with her occasionally. She told me her biological clock was ticking when she divorced Mike, and she remarried and had a whole bunch of kids.

I hadn't seen Mike for seven years. Right before this book was published, I finally met with him again. My daughter Melanie arranged our meeting in Vegas on the High Roller Wheel, the largest Ferris wheel in the United States. It takes an uninterrupted half hour to go around, which gave Mike and me a lot of time to talk. It was very emotional for both of us. I told him I wanted my son back, and I wanted to put the past behind us. He said he wanted his dad back. We are planning to spend time together and get to know each other all over again. Thanks, darling daughter Melanie!

The 1996 Tournament Trail

Dana Smith figured that I was traveling three to five months out of any particular year "traversing the tournament trail." In addition to Las Vegas, I was able to cash in tournaments this year in California (Los Angeles, Gardena, Bell Gardens, Oceanside, and Lake Elsinore) and Atlantic City. I won the $500 No-Limit Hold'em event at the August Sizzle tournament in Lake Elsinore, and the $220 Hold'em/Stud Tag Team event at the LA Poker Open IV in Gardena.

1996 Net Poker Proceeds $30,300
Non-Poker Proceeds $0 (Book Proceeds NOT included)

—1997—

17th World Series of Poker Millionaire

After taking a *Card Player* Panama Canal poker cruise, I finished so well in three events in the April/May 28th World Series of Poker that I became the 17th WSOP millionaire with total earnings of $1,045,397. I earned a second-place finish in the $3,000 Hold'em Pot-Limit for $102,000, losing to Phil Hellmuth as he earned his sixth bracelet. I finished third in the $2,000 Hold'em Pot-Limit event for $46,930 (won by Britain's David "Devilfish" Ulliott, his only WSOP bracelet), third in the $1,500 7-Card Stud event for $36,622, and ninth in the $1,500 Razz event for $3,600. The 1997 World Series of Poker Main Event final table was televised on ESPN under the new Fremont Street canopy. Stu Ungar won.

My First Tournament Manager Gig

The Queens Classic tournament, held at the Four Queens casino in downtown Las Vegas, was arguably the second-largest poker tournament in the world at the time. It was conceived and directed by Gene Trimble, who left for greener pastures at the Fiesta Hotel Casino and was replaced as the poker tournament director by Steve Morrow. He created quite a brouhaha at the January 1997 Queens Classic VII by changing the payout structure so that three tables were paid—roughly 8.5 percent or 27 of the 315 entrants. First place was reduced from 40 percent to 27.5 percent of the purse, and second place was reduced from 20 percent to 17.5 percent. It was one and done for Steve Morrow at the Four Queens.

That opened the door for me. Finally, I got the opportunity I was hoping for: the chance to actually run a major poker tournament. I was hired to be the Tournament Manager/Director and Host of the Queens Poker Classic Summer Edition IV that ran in August and into September at the Four Queens.

I was hired because of my backgammon associate, Howard Markowitz. He had run some backgammon tournaments at the Four Queens, where he became friends with the executive who made the decisions as to what events they were going to have and who they were going to hire to run them. They hired Howard to be in charge of the poker tournament. But he was a backgammon tournament expert, which is a lot different than a poker tournament. He played a little poker, enough to know he didn't have the experience needed to run a poker tournament. He knew of two people in the poker world who were capable, me and Bob Ciaffone. While Ciaffone was a very good backgammon player, and a good poker player, he picked me because I had poker tournament experience. And I lived in Las Vegas.

This gave me the opportunity to implement some major tournament changes that I felt would benefit both the players and the casino. My goal was to create a different atmosphere—to make the player-experience lighthearted and fun instead of blood and guts like so many tournaments were. I wanted to please as many players as possible, including myself. To show everyone involved I was serious, I dressed in suit and tie instead of my usual more casual attire (I was often teased as being "a spokesperson for Goodwill's fashion department"). Here are some of the changes I made:

1. Starting the tournament on time, which actually drew applause from the players.
2. Increasing the number of starting chips.
3. Beginning with 45-minute levels, then increasing them to an hour at the crucial halfway mark, giving players the opportunity for a little more "play." This increased the skill factor and reduced the luck factor.
4. Adding a few more levels into the tournament.

Working with Howard Markowitz, we put in 16- to 20-hour days planning and running the tournament. We were exhausted, but it was so successful that I was hired to manage next year's Queens Poker Classic VIII tournament the following March. The two years I ran these tournaments, they were not nonsmoking tournaments, but I knew the change was coming. I remember the last time I ran the Four Queens tournament, I walked around and told the players that I hoped they were enjoying their cigarettes because this was the last time I was ever going to work at a tournament that allowed smoking.

My Next Poker Book

Poker books were becoming nice income makers for me, until *Championship Stud: 7-Card Stud, Stud 8 or Better, Razz.* In concert with Dana Smith's Cardsmith Publishing, we enlisted the help of two poker pros who were experts in their games. Linda Johnson covered Razz, Max Stern covered Stud 8 or Better, and I covered 7-Card Stud. It was the worst book I ever produced. These were individual efforts, and the book lacked the teamwork camaraderie that I had enjoyed with T.

Dr. Max Stern • Linda Johnson
Tom McEvoy

J. Cloutier. Max had to type out his part on a computer. Linda, if I remember right, just mostly dictated her part. We gathered together a few times, but mostly we worked independently.

The timing for the book was unfortunate for me. I was busy as tournament director at the Four Queens at the same time Dana was pressuring all of us to finish this book. Basically, I was only able to work on the book on and off. So, it was not one of my best efforts, and regrettably we didn't make much money on it. It was published and released in January of 1998.

The book, specifically my part, was the recipient of a fair amount of criticism, specifically by our poker book competitors, David Sklansky and Mason Malmuth. The competition was healthy, even expected, as these guys frankly just didn't like me. And the feeling was mutual. Sklansky took exception to my math in the book. I felt that two-thirds of the time when the door card (the first card up) is paired in 7-Card Stud the player would make three of a kind. The math was closer to 60 percent than 67 percent. Sklansky was correct. I was off a bit. It was on me, and I should have researched it better. The disagreement was voiced to the poker community in such avenues as letters to the editor in *Card Player*, where I was still a columnist, which gave me a chance to rebut. When I think back on it, the vocal disagreements probably benefited book sales for all parties. To see more about why David disliked me, see Chapter 30.

1997 Net Poker Proceeds $39,000 Non-Poker Proceeds $300

—1998—

My New Poker Profession: Prop Player

My old friend Robert Turner had moved from his marketing director position at the Bicycle Club to the Crystal Park Casino & Hotel in June 1997, to develop the top-notch poker area the casino was opening that month. This is the same poker-savvy guy who created the Legends of Poker tournament at the Bike. After the successful Queens Poker Classic ended in October, Turner reached out to me and asked me if I would like to move to California and become a "prop player" for him at Crystal Park just outside of Los Angeles. That's short for "proposition player," a player paid an hourly wage by casinos to help boost traffic at the poker tables. Being a prop player was a different way to make a living playing poker, so I thought I'd give it a try. I started in January.

Prop players don't play with the casino's money; they play with their own bankroll. Most importantly to my bottom line, I would be responsible for my own wins and losses, and I was confident that I would be a winning prop player. You know who the ideal prop player is? The guy that plays in the games and loses his money. That's the perfect prop player. But how long can you afford to be a prop player if you're losing more than your salary? I was a winning prop player.

I got a salary of $25 an hour. The most common game I was playing was $10/$20 Limit Hold'em, but I was free to play other poker games as well. We prop players didn't have an exact set schedule, we just kept track of our hours.

Turner actually did a decent job of handpicking a crew of pretty good prop players to play for him that year. But being a prop player is a total grind. There's a lot of downsides to it. It's like punching a timeclock in a factory, only you are playing poker. It's tough because a lot of times you have to play short-handed games, you have to start games, and you're playing with some of the other props who are all pretty good players. As the game gets good or if there's a waiting list of new players who want to play, it's understood you are supposed to give up your seat and then help start other games. Getting paid to play poker as a prop player is not so glorious.

When I came out to California, I rented an apartment. Later that year, Kathy Liebert moved in with me (not to be a prop player) and we split the rent. That didn't work all that well, as you'll learn more about in the next chapter. I kept my condo in Las Vegas that I was renting from my friend Phyllis Meyers and her husband Milt. My roommate there, Bob Walker, was paying half the rent. So, I was paying rent on two places at once, which was a drain.

While a prop player, I was still competing in major tournaments like the World Series of Poker and the Carnivale of Poker in Vegas, as well as other tournaments in California. Leo Chu, the guy that owned Crystal Park, was very flexible . . . he was a good guy to work for, actually.

I was a prop player there for ten months. Then I was given the opportunity to be a prop player at the Hollywood Park Casino and Racetrack in nearby Inglewood, California. Rod Peate was working there, and so was Phyllis Caro (the former wife of Mike Caro), who later became director of poker operations there. This casino was a step up because it was much bigger and better than Crystal Park, with more tables and more customers.

But being a prop player there was déjà vu all over again, and I decided I just didn't want to be a prop player anymore. Ten months at Crystal Park, one month at Hollywood Park, and then I quit. I had enough of it. And it's not because I lost money. It was just a total grind. I didn't like living (or driving) in L.A., and I missed Las Vegas. So, by the end of the year, I was back in the town I loved. And I was finally in a financial position to buy a house.

Being Diagnosed as Bipolar

In August, during the Legends of Poker tournament at the Bicycle Club in L.A., I played tennis doubles against Kenny "Skyhawk" Flayton (a top pro poker player who never beat me in a single set of tennis, ever). He was teamed with a guy I didn't know well, Dr. Paul Fischman. I can't remember who my doubles partner was, but we thoroughly trounced Ken and Paul. Paul was a poker player, too, of course, and had mentioned he was a psychiatrist. When we talked after the match, I told him I thought something was wrong with me. I explained how I was okay now, but that I would go into these mood swings when I didn't function too well. I didn't feel suicidal, but I did get depressed. I talked about my mother a little bit because, to me, it was a virtual certainty she was bipolar, but her symptoms were far more severe than mine. Paul gave me a long medical explanation for why he thought I had a milder condition than bipolar. There was a long medical name for it, but it amounted to almost the same thing, but to a lesser degree. He told me this would likely change, but even if I wasn't doing anything to trigger it, my biological rhythms would be such that I wouldn't be stable indefinitely.

Right after this, I went to Foxwoods in Connecticut, rooming with Kathy Liebert. Temporarily, as it turns out, as she got mad at me and got her own room. So much for sharing expenses. This was about the time that Kathy Liebert and I were going from poker friends to romantic friends. Kathy has been—and still is—a very important person in my life. So important in fact that I've devoted the entire next chapter to her.

Dr. Fischman was also there, playing in the poker tournament, and when Kathy kind of threw me under the bus, I was already cycling into a very negative situation. Paul recommended I see somebody, adding, "Tom, I can be your doctor or your friend. I can't be both, and I'd rather be your friend." So he sent me to somebody who gave me an initial diagnosis of bipolar disorder and prescribed the wrong medication for me: Lithium. The cure was worse than the disease. For some people, lithium works. In my case, it just weirded me out far worse. I only saw that psychiatrist once. Paul then directed me to another psychiatrist at home in Las Vegas. I went through three of them, one who died and one I fired. I finally got the right doctor and the right medication.

More on Dr. Paul Fischman

I deeply admire Paul Fischman. He was on a medical team in Africa that helped eradicate the very last case of smallpox. Once he was in the middle of a poker tournament and literally dropped everything to make phone calls for a friend of mine that had suddenly gotten sick. He found the right physician and drove the ill man to his office, sacrificing his afternoon for a total stranger. There's the Hippocratic Oath, for sure, but only one in a million poker players would do that.

He is calm and cool at the poker table, too. I gave Dr. Fischman extensive poker lessons. He finished third in the Seniors WSOP tournament one year. His favorite game is Big O, which is Omaha 8 or Better with five cards dealt to each player. He's a winning player now. He didn't used to be. He was in games with the likes of Hall of Famer Dewey Tomko and other bracelet winners back in his home state of Florida, which is why he sought lessons. He lost a fair amount of money to those guys, but after the lessons, he won most of it back. Paul is right all the time, which I hate. He went with me to Michigan once, and my family all liked Paul. He joked he could continue his practice with multiple clients, or he could devote his time and energy just to me, because he couldn't do both. Note he was retired at the time.

The First Major Las Vegas Nonsmoking Poker Tournament—Almost

My gig at the Four Queens opened the door for me to run the tournament of my dreams. I was approached by Nick Gullo, the casino manager at the Showboat Casino in Las Vegas. He asked me and Debbie Burkhead (renowned in the poker community as a player, *Poker Player* newspaper columnist, and later co-founder of Poker Player Cruises) to host a tournament there. We agreed, and we also agreed to bill the Showboat Poker Spectacular as the first nonsmoking major poker tournament in Las Vegas. The tournament was to kick off with an all-day poker seminar put on by Mike Caro, Mike Sexton, Roy Cooke, Lee Jones, and myself.

Poker writer Max Shapiro wrote in May, "*The first major non-smoking poker tournament in Las Vegas will be held in November at the Showboat, thanks to the innovation of poker legend Tom McEvoy.*"

But the poker gods were against us from the start. The Showboat's poker room closed at the end of July, but management decided to go ahead with the tournament as planned November 1 to 15. Then the Showboat was sold to Harrah's Entertainment, and Nick Gullo was let go and took off to run the poker room at the Casinos Europa in San Jose, Costa Rica. I had a contract to host the Showboat Poker Spectacular, so I met with Harrah's people. They were squeamish about the nonsmoking aspect of the tournament—its big selling point—and feared attendance would be poor and they would lose money. Exasperated, I put out a plea to the poker community to fax Harrah's or call them to support the tournament.

Harrah's attempted to void my contract by claiming that I did not have a gaming license to run the tournament, which was hogwash, and they knew it. This issue had never been raised at any other of the properties where I ran or hosted poker tournaments. Tommy Lopez, in his "Poker Beat" column in the September 15-21 issue of *Gaming Today* wrote, "*It's doubtful whether any poker tournament directors, or poker room directors who run daily operations, have gaming licenses.*" Nevertheless, on October 2, one month before it was to start, Harrah's cancelled the tournament.

Tom McEvoy Poker Spectacular

When one door closes, another opens. Within a few hours of the cancellation, Robert Turner asked me to host a tournament back where I was a prop player at the Crystal Park Casino—during the same timeframe as the cancelled tournament, starting November 5 and running through November 13. And the kicker—the tournament was to be called the "Tom McEvoy Poker Spectacular." He offered me $5,000 to use my name as tournament host. How could I refuse? My calendar was free.

Robert Turner knew an opportunity when he saw one. I was a tournament draw, I could recruit a lot of players to attend, and he knew many players who had allocated the time to play at the Showboat were now free to travel to Los Angeles to play at Crystal Park, which he billed as L.A.'s only hotel and casino. I actually cashed in the tournament, taking sixth place in the Razz/Omaha/Stud event. The Tom McEvoy Poker Spectacular tournament was considered a raging success and would be held under the identical name at the same location in 1999, and for two years after that at Crystal Park's sister casino, the Hollywood Park Casino in Inglewood, California.

The day after the tournament, I was a speaker at a seminar put on by Mike Caro's University of Poker at Hollywood Park. I was joined by Mike Sexton and Lee Jones, the author of *Winning Low-Limit Hold'em*.

I ended November as co-host of the Seniors V World Championship of Poker at the Pechanga Resort Casino in Temecula, California, alongside "Oklahoma" Johnny Hale.

Ladies' Challenge Tournament

I concluded the year with a first-place finish in the Half Omaha High/Low Half Hold'em Tag Team Event at the Ladies' Challenge tournament at Crystal Palace in December with my good friend and partner Bonnie Domiano. The tournament was on her birthday, so I arranged for a cake to be brought into the tournament, and then we played it and won. Bonnie is quite remarkable—more on her later.

1998 Net Poker Proceeds $24,700
Non-Poker Proceeds $24,400

I'd rather regret the risks that didn't work out
than the chances I didn't take at all.
—Simone Biles

CHAPTER 16

"Chatty" Kathy Liebert, the First Woman to Win Over a Million Dollars at Poker.

Spoiler alert. Kathy Liebert and I have a history. We dated on and off for six years, breaking up it seems like about 50 times. I was between wives and other girlfriends when we started dating in the late 1990s, and we broke up for good in January 2003. We are still good friends today, but we're better off not being together.

Kathy Liebert photo by Interpoker.

Kathy is very smart, one of the smartest women I have ever met, and I've always been attracted to smart women. Look, a lot of men are intimidated or don't like women that are actually smarter than them. I'm just the opposite. I always have been. I don't suffer fools lightly, and right or wrong, I tend to quickly grow impatient with dumb people.

Kathy is a top-notch poker player. For years she was the all-time leading money winner among female players, and she is still number three behind Vanessa Selbst and Kristen Foxen. As the first woman to win over a million dollars at poker, she got to be very famous among the lady players and feared at the tables by everybody. In my opinion, there is no woman more deserving to join me in the Poker Hall of Fame than Kathy. Unfortunately, sometimes Kathy rubs people the wrong way, and I think that has kept this multitalented lady out of the Hall of Fame. And that's a shame.

I first noticed "Chatty Kathy "in 1994 at the poker room at the Gold Coast, which doesn't spread poker anymore, but did back then. This woman I had never heard of was talking up a blue streak. She got heads-up in not one but two tournaments. In one, an Omaha 8 or Better event, she was up against a friend of mine, Don Vines. It's truly a small world, since I coauthored the last book I wrote with Don, and he later married my other coauthor, Dana Smith. Don beat Kathy, and then she also finished second in the other contest, a Hold'em tournament. I remember wondering who's this girl . . . she's just yackety, yackety, yack . . . talking incessantly all the time at the poker table. Something she still does.

A few months later, also in 1994, I was hired for the second time to host the L.A. Open tournament at the Normandie Club in Gardena, California. By then Hold'em was legal there. And this noisy, smart girl that I was curious about and attracted to showed up for the tournament. Pretty soon she was going to all the same tournaments I did. It was at a tournament at Foxwoods that we really started talking and getting to know each other. Since we were traveling quite a bit, we used to spend hours and hours on the phone talking about poker strategy. We started having a few dates. The attraction grew, and over the next six years we dated—on and off.

We tried living together in 1998. We rented an apartment for a year while I was a prop player at Crystal Park in Los Angeles. That didn't work too well. I tried that twice again with Kathy, living with her for a few months, and each time it ended badly. Every time we broke up, I wouldn't talk with her or call her. She would call me on some little pretext and open the door a crack hoping I would push through. And I did, I kept doing that, the same thing. Things would be alright for a while, and then we would go back to not getting along.

The final breakup happened on New Year's Eve 2003. I was the defending champion of a little home tournament of a friend of mine in Long Beach, California. Kathy had a condo near the Bicycle Club in Bell Gardens, which was within driving distance. Kathy was supposed to join me at this game, but decided at the last minute not to go, despite my pleading. She's stubborn that way, even though people were hoping she would be there. She and her dad had been there the previous year when I had won, but unfortunately, she had lost her father just a month before this.

So now I had to borrow her car to get there. I went and didn't do well, surprise, surprise. We had a big fight when I got back to the condo. I asked her if she would take me to the airport the next day so I could get a flight back to Vegas. She said no, you're on your own. I had to call a friend in the middle of the night, explain that I was stranded at Kathy's, and ask for a ride home. She picked me up at around three in the morning at a nearby little donut shop. She dropped me off at my Vegas house at the crack of dawn, then turned around and drove back to California.

That was the final straw for me with Kathy. I was not going to go back to dating her again. My friends didn't believe me because they had seen this before, but this time I meant it. And we never did start dating again, but we have maintained a friendship.

There were a lot of smarts in Kathy's family. Her father was a college professor and wrote all kinds of books that were used as texts on heavy subjects like Developmental Psychology. He moved to Las Vegas and actually lived with me for a few months until Kathy got him settled into one of the rental properties she owned. We got to be pretty close, and he was hoping Kathy and I would get married; he liked me that much. Her grandfather was well off, and she inherited money from him. Kathy is an expert in the stock market and invested wisely. She made big profits on her stock market and real estate investments and playing poker. I said she was pretty smart. She is a very good money manager, too.

A few months before we had broken up for the last time, I had arranged for her to get a freeroll seat from a friend of mine, Texan Larry Wright. He sponsored her with the $10,000 buy-in for the first PartyPoker Million Limit Hold'em, a million-dollar tournament hosted by *Card Player* Cruises and held on a Carnival cruise ship bound for the Mexican Riviera. Kathy won the tournament, becoming the first woman to win a million-dollar first prize. Second place got only around $90,000, because the tournament wanted the publicity of a guaranteed million-dollar payout to the winner. That big purse created the opportunity for a lot of deals and "saves" along the way, and Kathy only pocketed a small percentage. I had a small piece of her action, and I got $20,000. Larry Wright got a much bigger piece. Nevertheless, she made the final table alongside notable players like Chris Ferguson, Mel Judah, Ken Flaton, Mike Yuwiler, Scott Buller, Bruce Yamron, and Phil Hellmuth.

I've been friends with Kathy, on and off, for almost 30 years. I always said she was a good friend, but not the best girlfriend for me. I still feel the same way. Like the good friend she is, when I lost my house in 2017 and was having marital problems, Kathy offered to let me stay at her house for about four months. And when she goes out of town for poker tournaments, I go over to her house every other day and look after her six cats. I'm a cat whisperer . . . not just a cat guy. She knows I talk cat.

*Not in doing what you like, but in liking what
you do is the secret of happiness.*
—J.M. Barrie

CHAPTER 17

1999 to 2000. New Look, New Books, New House, and a Vegas First.

—1999—

Lasik Surgery

In early February, I finally did something that had been on my wish list for quite a while. At age 54, I got rid of my big, thick coke-bottle glasses that I had worn to correct my extreme near-sightedness since fourth grade. Some thought they had made me look "studious," but I thought the correct word was "nerdy."

I had been following reports on a procedure to correct vision problems like mine called radial keratotomy which involved cutting into the eyeball, the cornea. Mike Sexton had that done, and it was successful for him. But the idea of anybody cutting into my eyeball was appalling to me. When Lasik surgery came along, it was a big improvement, shooting a laser beam into your eyeball, not cutting it.

As the reports on Lasik kept getting better and better, I decided to do it. I didn't have a lot of excess funds at the time, but I splurged and spent $2,000 per eye to correct my vision. I went to the Wellish

Vision Institute in Las Vegas, and they did a wonderful job. They did both eyes at the same time. Completely painless and a complete success. The surgery center used my story and my photo in their advertising, including an ad in *Card Player* magazine. I didn't get paid, but I gave them permission because I believed in the procedure.

Recovery took about a month or so to really stabilize. Shortly after the Lasik surgery, I went to California for my son Patrick's graduation, where I learned really fast that I had no business driving on a freeway at night. It was scary with headlights all around me and cars zooming past.

Son Patrick Graduates

On February 12, my son Patrick graduated from the Regional San Diego Law Enforcement Academy. He has had a terrific career in law enforcement and I'm very proud of him. The San Diego

County Sheriff's Department has over 4,000 employees, and he is one of only 15 captains. He's in charge of a district, one of eleven in San Diego County. They recently sent him to the FBI Academy for three months for technical advanced training. I figure they don't do that unless they have their eye on you for bigger and better things. Patrick is adamantly nonpolitical and plans to get his 30 years in before retiring, when he hopes to do some police-training teaching.

My Second Book with T. J. Cloutier

Our second book together, *Championship Omaha: Omaha High-Low, Omaha High and Pot-Limit Omaha,* was published on February 28, 1999. This poker game was quickly gaining popularity, and we were able to parlay T. J.'s WSOP bracelets in all three forms of Omaha, and my Omaha bracelet, into the definitive guide to winning Omaha cash games and tournaments. With our continuing editorial guidance from Dana (a.k.a. Shane) Smith, this book was another money maker for us.

Mom Dies

Marie McEvoy passed away on April 19 at age 88, just a month or so shy of her 89th birthday. I went back to Michigan for the funeral, of course. It's always very sad and tough to lose a parent, made even worse by the fact that she didn't recognize any of her own children in the last couple of years of her life. Alzheimer's ultimately killed her. She just kind of drifted off without any physical pain and suffering, thank goodness.

Australia and Darrel "Dazzler" Lanyon

I was contacted by Linda Johnson and Jan Fisher about a great and sudden poker/travel group opportunity. Somebody had won a poker trip, then decided at the last minute they didn't want to go and had put it up for sale. So, for a very discounted price, I bought a ten-day trip to Australia and New Zealand that included entries into a big poker tournament in each country. Being single and available, I could do things on short notice, which in this case was about eight days. The flight was about 25 hours, which was a bit of an ordeal, but it was worth it. It was the only time I was ever in that part of the world, and the trip was a whole lot of fun.

The first six days were spent in Melbourne, Australia. I stayed at the Crown Casino and Hotel, the first and only time I ever stayed at a five-star hotel. I liked my hotel room so much I didn't want to leave it, even to go down and play the cash games. I enjoyed just hanging out and taking in the great view. Typical me. The group did some fun things like visiting the Melbourne Zoo (where the monkeys hurled "natural" fastballs at us) and attending a totally different sporting event, a football game that wasn't our football and wasn't soccer.

The poker experience was memorable, too. They fussed over me as the first former World Series Champion to attend their Crown Australian Poker Championships tournament, which was still in its infancy. Now it's a major stop for a lot of people. I was the bubble boy in the Main Event. The tournament's major promoter was Darrel "Dazzler" Lanyon, the editor/publisher/owner of *CARDS* magazine. He was Australia's most colorful player and the driving force behind the growth of poker Down Under. Dazzler was one of those "poker wannabes" who dressed like a cowboy, complete with a fake pistol. He got me involved in a challenge match, where he said, "You're not gonna let me win, are you?" I said, "Nope." He called my raise with the 10 - 5 of Clubs and then got all his money in with a flush draw. He hit it and beat me, which I'm sure was the highlight of his poker career. After that I never saw him mentioned again.

The tour group also visited New Zealand for four days and played in the first New Zealand Cup of Poker at the Christchurch Casino. Jan Fisher likes telling the story of the riverboat trip we took there. The boat jockey was zooming at high speed right next to some huge rocks. I must have flinched a few times, and from the look on my face they thought I was terrified. When we were done, I shook the boat driver's hand and told him that was the best trip I ever had! That cracked up Linda and Jan, who thought my experience was just the opposite.

The First Major Las Vegas Non-Smoking Poker Tournament—For Real This Time

After the initial attempt at the first Las Vegas non-smoking poker tournament at the Showboat was cancelled, I was approached by Dick Gatewood, the poker room manager at Sam's Town casino on Boulder Highway in Vegas. I occasionally played poker in his room, and I had gotten to know him. Dick liked the smoke-free idea, and he had gotten permission from casino management to do a smoke-free tournament, and he asked me to host and run it. I was immediately all in, and the Sam Boyd Poker Classic was scheduled for November 5 to 15, 1999 (named after the casino owner). Sam's Town hosted little daily tournaments sometimes, but this was the first major tourney. And also, the last one—not sure why, but they just did it once.

The non-smoking aspect of the tournament was the promotional hook to hype the tournament, and we got lots of publicity. The Sam Boyd Poker Classic was the cover story of the September 28 issue of *Card Player* magazine. Erik Seidel wrote an article for the magazine supporting the non-smoking tournament. We even got coverage from the fledgling internet poker websites. We got a lot of favorable publicity, and the event took on a life of its own.

The main draw was that smoking would not be allowed in the tournament area, which was segregated from the live-action area and the hallways where smoking was still permitted. Several smokers threatened to boycott the tournament, but most of them played anyway. What happened was what I thought would happen. Players who had stopped playing tournaments because they couldn't stand the smoke anymore came back.

We had an excellent turnout of 3,603 entrants for 20 events and paid out $725,000 in prize money. Many of the players expressed extreme delight with the non-smoking environment, and we didn't hear a peep from the smokers. Most of them realized it wasn't that terrible to go out in the hallway to smoke. Confidentially, the smokers actually liked the idea themselves, most of them, because they were having a hard time with secondhand smoke, too.

For Las Vegas, Sam's Town was the first battle, the first victory, the first step that started to get casino managements' attention. The next step was to convince casino management that the majority of poker players themselves were in favor of non-smoking tournaments. The petition drive to do just that is covered in depth in the next chapter.

I Continued in Demand as a Poker Host

I was developing quite a reputation as a successful poker tournament host. In September I ran the well-named Tom McEvoy

Poker Spectacular for Robert Turner at the Crystal Casino & Hotel in California (I was a groomsman in his wedding the following year), and the Seniors VI World Championship in early December. With all this hosting and traveling about, it wasn't a big year for poker winnings. I only cashed in three tournaments the whole year, placing no higher than fourth.

Net Poker Proceeds (-$4,100) Non-Poker Proceeds $19,000. Salary from my tournament host and prop player salaries.

—2000—

Harrah's Entertainment Cancels Me—Again

In January, I came in second in the $500 Pot-Limit Omaha event at Harrah's Carnivale of Poker III tournament in Vegas, winning $17,400. Later, in May, Harrah's asked me to be the tournament manager for the following year's tournament, the 2001 Carnivale of Poker IV. Hoping I could make it smoke-free, I agreed. But for months, the 2000 tournament was being roundly criticized for the effect of smoking in their low-ceilinged, poorly ventilated tournament room. So in May, they announced they would move the tournament venue internally to their grand ballroom, which would be entirely non-smoking. Alas, there was still some management trepidation about the concept. They just weren't totally convinced non-smoking was the way to go, so before the end of the year, Harrah's just threw in the towel and cancelled this and all future tournaments. Drats, foiled again.

A House of My Own

In 2000 I was able to put together enough money to make a decent down payment on a house. I had book royalties coming in, some inheritance money, and payments for hosting tournaments. In February, I moved into my newly built four-bedroom house on Gisborn Drive. It's the house on the left in the photo. I was the original owner of this 2,100-square-foot home, and so I got to choose some of the décor like flooring and wall colors, and so the interior was bright and sunny. When I purchased the house, it was with the intention that I would live there the rest of my life. It had a downstairs bedroom, so the plan was when I got older, I wouldn't have to deal with steps. I lived there for 17 years, the longest I lived in any one place in my life.

Later, in 2008, I would buy the house pictured on the right as a rental property. They were identical models, except the rental had a bigger garage and no downstairs bedroom. It played a pretty big role in my life, as you'll see.

Shortly after I bought the house, Dana Smith hosted a house-warming party for me. She noted in her invitation that "Tom needs stuff . . . the usual things that guys never have enough of. Towels, sheets, dishes, etc." As usual, she was correct.

Mi Casa es Su Casa

I wasn't exactly rich, so my friends helped supplement my income (and make my mortgage payments) by renting a room and living with me. I had become friends with George Fisher, who was a customer when I was a prop player at Crystal Park. He decided to move from L.A. to Las Vegas with his girlfriend, Sandra Green, and they were looking for a place to stay. George contacted me and I rented them the downstairs bedroom for a couple of years. They were still living there when George died. He played a big negative role in my life, as you'll see.

Not only did I rent rooms out, on quite a few occasions I had house guests. I constantly had a stream of visitors. At one World Series, I had the master bedroom for me, Bill Mullins and his wife were in one of the other bedrooms, and another couple was in the third upstairs bedroom. Downstairs on the couch I had Casey Kastle (of the non-smoking petition fame you will read about in the next chapter) and Robin Biroc sleeping on opposite ends of the couch. Vince Burgio was there, too. When I had a house full of poker people, it was a lot of fun.

My Third Book with T. J. Cloutier

The book-dictating collaboration with T. J. Cloutier and Dana Smith continued with our third book, *Championship Hold'em*, which was published April 1, 2000. It, too, was met with criticism from some quarters. Seemed T. J. was not fond of two-card Hold'em hands with "connectors" (sequential cards, like 6 - 7 or 9 - 10) whether they were "suited" (of the same suit) or not. The statistical gurus (like Sklansky and Malmuth) were quick to point out that suited cards have a slight advantage, and they were correct. But there is no "right" way to play Hold'em—that's what makes the game so fascinating. Statistical odds are just one factor that players have to weigh along with stack sizes, player tendencies, position, stage of the tournament, etc. T. J. Cloutier had proven results in hundreds of tournaments, while the critics, well, not so much. Poker players bought books to learn about the playing thoughts and strate-

gies of winning players. That's why this book was so successful.

We also still had the benefit of my columns in *Card Player*, which was growing in circulation along with the growing popularity of poker. Each column ended with an editor's note about my latest book, and how to order one.

Costa Rica

After Harrah's Entertainment bought the Showboat Casino and the non-smoking tournament was cancelled, the manager who had recruited me to run it, Nick Guillo, went south to work at the Casinos Europa in San Jose, Costa Rica. It was the country's premier casino, and they were able to attract a lot of big-name poker players to come down by offering to pay for room and airfare in exchange for X amount of hours playing cash games. They also got poker notables like Susie Isaacs, Linda Johnson, and even T. J. Cloutier to headline "Celebrity Poker Challenge" tournaments, and in August 2000, they invited me and Kathy Liebert to come down as special guests. I went down there several times as a player. I was a big deal to the players down there—they had never played with a guy who had won the Main Event. They had some pretty good home-grown players in Costa Rica, like Humberto Brenes, who was nominated for the Poker Hall of Fame several times.

New Meaning for WSOP

Truth be known, I don't like to shave. In December the poker media spotted me at the Pot of Gold Tournament in Reno sporting a new white beard, where I was being teased for growing it to get a backup job as Santa. And a really clever journalist dubbed me as the WSOP—the World Santa of Poker. Today I still proudly (or maybe lazily) occasionally wear the white beard.

Poker's Base Was Shifting

Following a protracted eight-year legal battle for control of the Horseshoe among Benny Binion's heirs, his son Jack Binion sold his interest in Binion's Horseshoe to his sister, Becky Behnen, in 1998. He retained 1 percent interest in order to lawfully retain his Nevada Gaming License. Included in the deal, of course, was ownership of the World Series of Poker. That meant that Becky Behnen and her husband Nick were in charge of the largest poker tournament in the world. I didn't really know the Behnens at this time, but I would get to know them very well the following year.

I was not a fan of Nick Behnen. Nick hated poker players—he made that quite clear to me. I said, "Well, you know, poker is what made Binion's famous," and he replied, "I don't care." He didn't think poker players gambled enough and they didn't dress very nicely. Ironic, isn't it, that the thing that put Binion's on the map was the thing he hated? The Behnens never could have gotten the

WSOP to the size it became on their own . . . they didn't have the expertise.

In 2000, the World Series of Poker was four times bigger than the next-biggest tournament on the poker circuit, domestic as well as international. But after the 2001 tournament, the couple in charge were facing anger from the poker community. They had advertised that 3 percent of the event prize pool would be withheld for tournament personnel. Instead, the Behnens distributed cash withheld from the World Series prize pools to a wider range of Horseshoe employees including those on the fringes like security guards and switchboard operators. They fired card room manager Cathi Wood, who argued the money should have been divided among tournament dealers and bosses, the key players in a smoothly run poker tournament. The Nevada Gaming Control Board investigated the distribution, which was not good publicity for the tournament.

As this was happening, Las Vegas, as a poker destination, was starting to slide. At one point there were eight major tournaments in Vegas, but by this time we were down to three—the World Series of Poker, the Orleans Open, and the Tournament of Champions. Southern California was becoming the poker capital of the United States, hosting large and small poker tournaments almost nonstop all year long. And, California had adopted some non-smoking laws (while WSOP players were still playing in the fog of smoke). Plus, new competition, in the form of card rooms, were opening all across the country.

In 2001, I got involved in the fray.

Net Poker Proceeds $15,000 Non-poker Proceeds $10,600

Much smoking kills live men and cures dead swine.
—George D. Prentice

CHAPTER 18

Poker's Anti-Smoking Petition Drive.

Back in the Day

When I arrived in Las Vegas, smoking was more or less synonymous with playing poker. But as the turn of the 21st century approached, the proof that inhaling secondhand smoke was a cause of cancer and heart disease was becoming more and more known. Media coverage of the dangers of secondhand smoke was growing exponentially. Public awareness of the downside of smoking was becoming common knowledge. And on top of the health hazards, smoking stunk.

Poker's Anti-Smoking Initiative

I'm proud to say I was on the forefront of the effort to ban smoking from the poker room. Players were getting sick, and not just a few, including the players that smoked themselves, from the effects of secondhand smoke. I personally have known three or four poker players who didn't smoke yet died from different forms of cancer caused by the secondhand smoke they endured at the poker tables.

At the World Series of Poker, in particular, it was a huge problem. People were getting sick right and left. At the Horseshoe casino where the WSOP was held until 2004, the players called this affliction the "Horseshoe Crud." Players were getting all kinds of bronchial problems, bronchitis, and other things—coughing, hacking, spitting up. There was just no escape from it. People were sitting at the tables smoking—in many cases chain smoking—and it was just horrendous.

I never got a penalty in my life for my tournament play. But I got a warning once that was related to the smoking issue. A penalty means you have to sit out a certain length of time, either a round of play or a time limit like 20 minutes. I've seen people get penalties that cost them the tournament. Once a player got a penalty when he was heads-up at the final table, and he lost a bunch of chips that got blinded off because he wasn't there. So, a penalty in poker is no trivial thing.

You can guess what caused the warning. It was in 2001, the last year smoking was permitted at the tables in the World Series of Poker, and I was playing in a WSOP tournament event. Sitting close to me was a professional player, a bit of a jerk, Chris Tsiprailidis. I was counting his cigarettes—he was on his 29th cigarette—and oblivious to him, his smoke was coming straight into my face. I had put up with this long enough. So, I asked him very politely, if I gave him a chair to put behind him, would he please put his ashtray on the chair so his smoke wouldn't come into my face because it was making me sick. He started cursing at me. Another guy at the table, who was a cigar smoker, said, "Wait a minute. Tom asked you very politely to do this, and I think you should do this." My antagonist said he'd been smoking since he was 14 years old, and that nobody was going to tell him what to do, blah, blah, blah. After he started cursing me, we got into it and I started arguing back. The floor man came over and said, "You guys need to stop this now. Put an end to it." So, we stopped for about five seconds. The floor man walked away, and we started after each other again. It was mostly him. I was reacting. I was polite to begin with, but when he started to attack me, I was no longer polite. I wasn't so nice anymore, I was pissed. The testosterone levels had gone up. The floor man came over a second time, and this time he laid down the law. "Alright boys," he said, "if this doesn't end right now you both get a penalty." We both shut up and no penalty was given. That's the closest I ever came to getting a penalty, all due to secondhand smoke.

This is an example of what was going on, the constant warfare between the smokers and non-smokers. In my early days in Vegas, most poker players were smokers, so I had been enduring it to the detriment of my health for years. By 2000, I'd say about 75 percent of the players didn't smoke anymore. In California at the time, they had outlawed smoking in public buildings. The time was ripe for a change. I was never so sure of anything in my life.

I helped pave the way for this change. After what was to be the first non-smoking poker tournament in Las Vegas at the Showboat Casino was cancelled in 1998, I persevered and ran the actual first non-smoking tournament in Vegas in 1999 at Sam's Town. Following this trend, Mike Sexton, a non-smoker, made his 2000 and 2001 Tournament of Champions non-smoking. Both smoke-less tournaments were a big success, and they got the conversation ball rolling. I started talking at length with my friends Casey Kastle and Paul Ladanyi about the smoking problem, both while playing and privately away from the poker tables. I had multiple conversations with them and several other players. There was a consensus that we needed to do something about the smoking problem at poker tournaments.

At the World Series a player's options were very limited. You either had to put up with smoking at the tables or not play. Every self-respecting poker player loves the World Series of Poker. This is what we shoot for, what we dream about. Most players wanted to play yet felt smoking at the table was not acceptable. Now we had to prove it.

Non-Smoking Petition Drive

There was really only one way to demonstrate to poker tournament management that the recent trend in non-smoking tournaments was in the cards for the future. The writing was on the wall, and we players needed to put the consensus of the players in writing, too. So, a petition was written, and it was 2001 to 2002 when the poker players' non-smoking petition drive took place. I don't remember who had the idea for a petition, but it was a good one. Paul Ladanyi, Casey Kastle, and I were the three biggest instigators that actively went out and got people to sign. But we had plenty of help.

I believe Paul drafted the petition. He brought it to us—we reviewed it and together decided what we wanted to say. Paul lived in Hungary but was well known in the tournament poker world at the time. Casey was also well known on the poker tournament circuit. He's a longtime friend of mine, and back then I played with him on a regular basis. He has dual citizenship with a European country. It's interesting that two guys from Europe were instrumental in getting smoking banned in U.S. poker rooms, because it took about eight or nine years for European casinos to follow suit. I never claimed to have originated all of this, but I was behind it all the way and eventually helped get the concept over the finish line.

The Kastle /Ladanyi Players Petition

We the undersigned poker tournament players feel the time has come for casinos to provide a pleasant, healthy, and smoke-free environment for tournaments. We are no longer willing to endure the annoyance, irritation and health risks brought about by being forced to inhale secondhand smoke. California has led the way and we have learned how much more pleasant it is to play and be able to breathe clean air, and we applaud the Tournament of Champions and Sam's Town for going smoke free. So strongly do we feel about this issue that we declare our intention to patronize only non-smoking tournaments and to boycott those that continue to condone this unhealthy habit.

I retained the actual petition documents.

The first petition document was totally handwritten and signed first by Paul Ladanyi. It was signed, in order, by Max Shapiro, Barbara Enright, (two illegible names, imagine that?), John Juanda (who wrote "smoker" in parenthesis after his name), and Alan Cunningham. We were off to a good start.

Then the petition text was printed. This made for a more formal petition and made it easier to distribute and solicit subsequent signatures. The first signature on page one of the first printed version was Casey Kastle. His was followed by poker greats Daniel Harrington, Eric Seidel, Kathy Liebert, Doyle Brunson, Gabe Kaplan, Chip Reese, Ted Forrest, Vince Burgio, and Ray Zee. The petitions asked each petitioner to print their name on the left and sign their name to the right of their printed name.

There were two copies of the printed petition version, apparently so more than one person could take it around for signatures. The signature "drive" went on for several months. The petitions were circulated not only at the World Series and other big tournaments, but at some of the smaller tournaments in Vegas, too. We had no deadline in mind—just the goal of getting as many signatures as possible.

It was really easy to get signatures. A lot of smokers signed this petition—some of them even put their name and wrote in parentheses "smoker" beside it. Even they had had enough. I had a lot of help getting the signatures. Paul Ladanyi and Casey Kastle, in particular, were instrumental in getting the signatures, as well as myself. We carried the petition around asking our peers to sign it. We asked wherever we were playing, at cash games around town as well as at the World Series. We waited until the person was not in a hand to ask, hey, could you sign this. If one person with a big name, like Doyle Brunson for example, signed the petition, other people at the game would say, hey, let me sign it, too. Others assisted here and there, talking with players and asking them to please sign this petition. We ended up with approximately 550 signatures on the petitions. A few were duplicates—I guess they were really passionate about the cause! Remember, there was no formal organization conducting this—just a bunch of poker players who were winging it.

When you look at the signatures, many of them are extremely well-known poker players. Hugely successful pros and bracelet winners. Can I remember the names of the people I personally signed up? No. A lot of these names aren't familiar to the general poker-playing public today, but many if not most were among the top-notch players of the time. There are world famous players with recognizable names on every page. There are also signatures of many amateur "man on the street" poker players who played cash and tournaments.

An Infamous player signed, too. Russ Hamilton, the 1994 World Champion whose picture was taken off the wall of fame at the World Series of Poker. He was involved with the online fiasco at Ultimate Bet. He was cheating, basically—he could see his opponent's hole cards. He and some of his confederates were ripping the players off. I don't care how talented you are as a player, if your opponent knows what your hole cards are, you're in trouble. I cover more about my involvement in bringing Russ's cheating to light in Chapter 22.

The biggest fear of tournament management and casinos was losing the business of a significant percentage of their players—smokers. Some of the smokers were telling us that if smoking were banned, they wouldn't play. But our thinking was that if given the choice of not smoking at the tables—going outside the poker room to smoke—or not playing poker, even players who smoked would not stop playing the game they loved.

We were right.

The intention was to present our petitions to the people who ran the tournaments and had the final say—poker room managers, tournament directors, and the management of casinos that were hosting tournaments. So, we presented the petitions to them in person, talked with them, and shared the petitions. We didn't give them the petitions; we kept the originals.

We also told them we had history and precedence on our side. Smoking had been banned several years before in the confined space of Bridge card game tournaments after attendance started falling off. After the ban, Bridge tournament participation shot up.

Our anti-smoking group was thinking bigger picture than just poker tournaments. Banning smoking in all poker rooms would have been nice, but we knew we could only do something about the tournaments to start with. Most of the signatories were tournament players. That gave us leverage to threaten to boycott tournaments if they didn't do something about smoking. But our effort needed a final boost. I was fortunate enough to be in the right place at the right time to provide it.

No tournament was bigger and more influential than the World Series of Poker. If they agreed to ban smoking, we thought, the other tournaments would eventually fall in line. At that time the WSOP was no longer run by the Binions, Jack Binion in particular. Jack Binion is practically worshipped to this day by poker players and people who know him. He is a genuinely good guy, and I have nothing but the highest respect for him. His sister and her husband Becky and Nick Behnen, not so much. After a somewhat hostile takeover, they had wrestled control from Jack, and were now in charge of the Horseshoe, and the World Series of Poker.

In 2001, the Behnens hired me to be the poker room manager at their Horseshoe casino in downtown Las Vegas, of which I have less than fond memories, covered in detail in the next chapter. Nevertheless, it did give me some say in the WSOP tournament. I planned and put together the schedule for the 2002 World Series. But the coup de grâce was a discussion I had with Benny Binion's grandson, Benny Behnen (Benny Junior, they called him). He was a poker player in his mid-twenties, and a smoker, too. I made a deal with him. The deal was that I would give him free poker lessons if he would go along with—convince his parents—to make the World Series non-smoking.

It worked.

Now they didn't make the cash games non-smoking, and people watching could even smoke on the rail. While it defeated part of the purpose, it was still a huge improvement. So, in 2002, I was instrumental in getting the World Series of Poker to go non-smoking for the first time. They have been non-smoking every year after that.

Some of the smokers weren't happy. But they realized they didn't have to stop smoking, just had to go smoke outside the tournament area. So, there was no big ruckus at the WSOP when this new policy was announced. I played in the 2002 WSOP. Were people talking about the new rule? That's all they were talking about. It was overwhelmingly successful, so much so that once we did it the first time, that was it. After the 2002 WSOP implemented the change, other casinos fell into place. It spread all over. The East coast had a lot of tournaments, and they went non-smoking. There was a domino effect. Europe was a holdout for about eight or nine years, but eventually they came around, too.

Here is a partial list of "famous" signatures on the document:

Poker Hall of Famers
- Doyle Brunson (1988) (WSOP World Champion 1976 and 1977) (d)
- Chip Reese (1991) (d)
- Jack Keller (1993) (WSOP World Champion 1984) (d)
- Russ Hamilton (WSOP World Champion 1994)
- Johnny Chan (2002) (WSOP World Champion 1987 and 1988)
- Berry Johnston (2004) (WSOP World Champion 1986)
- Barbara Enright (2007)
- Dewey Tomko (2008)
- Henry Orenstein (2008) (d) (Creator of the Poker Hole-Card Cam)
- Dan Harrington (2010) (WSOP World Champion 1995)
- Erik Seidel (2010)
- Tom McEvoy (2013) (WSOP World Champion 1983)
- Scotty Nguyen (2013) (WSOP World Champion 1998)
- Daniel Negreanu (2014)
- John Juanda (2015)
- Dave Ulliott (2017) (d)
- Phil Ivey (2017)
- Huck Seed (2020) (WSOP World Champion 1996)
- Layne Flack (2022) (d)

Women in Poker Hall of Famers
- Marsha Waggoner (2008)
- Cyndy Violette (2009)
- Kathy Liebert (2010)

Other Poker Notables, World Champions,
  and WSOP bracelet winners
- Andrew Bloch
- John Bonetti (d)
- Chad Brown (d)
- Vince Burgio
- John Cernuto
- David Chiu
- Bob Ciaffone (d)
- Allen Cunnigham
- Brad Daugherty (WSOP World Champion 1991)
- Ivo Donev
- Chris Ferguson (WSOP World Champion 2000)
- Ted Forrest
- Prahlad Friedman
- Phillip Gordon
- Oklahoma Johnny Hale (d)
- Thor Hansen (d)
- Dan Heimiller
- Paul Magriel (World Champion Backgammon Player) (d)
- Mason Malmuth
- Mike Matusow
- Men "The Master" Nguyen
- Dan Robison (d)
- Gavin Smith (d)
- Mike Svobodny (World Champion Backgammon Player)
- Robert Turner

- Amir Vahedi (d)
- David Williams
- Cory Ziedman

Celebrities
- Gabe Kaplan
- Frank Mariani
- George Marlowe

Poker exemplifies the worst aspects of capitalism
that have made our country so great.
—*Walter Matthau*

CHAPTER 19

2001 to 2003. Hired, Kicked Upstairs, Fired, and Hired.

—2001—

www.tournamenttalk.com

In April, I got outside of my comfort zone (waaay outside) and started a website called Tournament Talk. The concept was to provide an opportunity for people to "Talk Tournaments with Tom" at my website devoted entirely to tournament poker. I paid a lady to set this up and help me with it, and she kept it going for a few years, but neither one of us was internet savvy enough to make it work. Or maybe she just had a bad client. The site lacked for content, and my attention. I'm just not good at some things, and new technologies I don't totally understand like this website is one of them.

I didn't really understand the amount of time and energy building and promoting a successful website entailed, and I had precious little of either to put into it. Plus, in my opinion, I'm just not good at marketing myself. With the stuff I've done in poker I should have become a bigger force than I was, but I'm not kidding when I say I'm too much of an introvert. Some of the biggest names in the game got that way by seeking opportunities for the spotlight. But that's just not me.

Hired to run the Horseshoe Card Room and the WSOP

By this time, I was highly focused on my efforts with the petition drive to get poker tournaments smoke-free when the opportunity to close the deal with the WSOP presented itself. Free poker lessons for Benny Binion's grandson, Benny Binion Behnen, Jr., the son of WSOP owners Nick and Becky Binion Behnen. All he had to do was help convince his parents, recent owners of the World Series of Poker, to make the prestigious tournament smoke-free. I knew in my heart if the WSOP eliminated smoking at the tables, all the tournaments would follow suit.

Becky Binnion Behnen and
Benny Behnen, Jr.

The timing was perfect. After the 2000 WSOP controversy, the Behnens fired their card room and tournament manager, Cathi

Wood, and the position was open. Benny Jr. recommended me to be the new card room manager, and after a meeting with him and Nick Behnen on June 16, I was hired. I was to embark on a major career change as the Poker Room Manager and World Series of Poker Tournament Director at Binion's Horseshoe in Las Vegas, after I returned from a *Card Player* poker cruise on the Queen Elizabeth II (probably the nicest ship I was ever on, and certainly the biggest) on July 10. At age 56, I would be the first World Series Main Event winner to oversee the poker room or the WSOP tournament. I hadn't had a regular job in 23 years, and I had never run a card room. Gulp.

Linda Johnson warned me not to go to work for these people, but I couldn't resist. Too big a carrot, so I did it anyway. It's not like I had any great trust in these people—I was on my guard. But they turned out to be even worse people than I thought.

I had always wanted to take a crack at running a major poker room, almost as much as I had always wanted the opportunity to run the World Series. I felt fully qualified for both. With all my experience, I was an expert on tournament structure and what events to put together to match the venue. Along with the preplanning, I knew I could make good game-day floor decisions.

Card Room Changes

Downtown Vegas had become a tough draw for poker. The Horseshoe poker room was struggling to attract high-stakes players, hurt by competition from the Mirage casino (recently sold after a decade of ownership by casino guru Steve Wynn) and the Bellagio, which had just opened two years earlier. Plus, there was competition for lower-stakes players from local casinos closer to the homes of Las Vegas residents. So, I had my work cut out for me.

The Horseshoe had one big poker room with at least a dozen or more tables. To build tournament traffic, I planned to create a market niche between the low-cost tournaments, like those offered by the Orleans casino, and the $100-plus events held by the Mirage. Unfortunately, I wasn't able to make tournaments happen, but it wasn't for lack of trying. To recapture some of the mid- and high-stakes cash-game traffic, I introduced the cheapest maximum rake (the amount the card room takes from each pot) in the world at $2 per hand. For high-stakes players ($100/$200 or more), the games were rake free. I also increased the variety of poker games and limits offered, including No-Limit Hold'em, Pot-Limit Hold'em, and Razz.

WSOP Changes

The changes I had planned and promoted were threefold. First, to double the guarantee and pay next year's champion $2 million. Second, to make the entire tournament room (normally the casino's bingo room) smoke free. Third, to add four new events, extending the World Series by one week. I felt these changes would help overcome the bad feelings among the players from last year's controversy, so the tournament would be bigger and better than ever.

One other relatively small change that year ended up changing the course of poker history. While I had planned the 2002 WSOP tournament, I didn't have anything to do with this decision. ESPN decided to install pocket cameras for the first time to allow them to show (on tape delay) the players' hole cards, although only for the Main Event.

I would have been 100 percent in favor of this decision. The hole-card camera wasn't new and had been first used three years previous in England. That's about how long I had been saying that poker would never be a spectator sport unless people could see the hands and what was going on, so they could start to understand the strategy and the thinking. Otherwise, watching poker was like watching paint dry.

Not everyone agreed. Jack Binion was skeptical that players would let you look at their hole cards, and he felt he misjudged how much the poker players would eventually enjoy the publicity. Players who had concerns soon discovered that TV coverage was in their best interest because it generated a steady stream of new players. Eighteen years after I won the Main Event, television would finally emerge as a major contributor to the growth of the game.

The First 53 Days on the Job

I rank these as among the worst 53 days in my life. I was trying to oversee the daily operations, initiate new ideas, work on WSOP plans, and deal with personnel problems, all while dealing with Nick Behnen. I was told later by another employee that the expectation was that I would work 10- to 12-hour days, from morning till like 7 p.m., which wasn't going to happen. I didn't perform up to these expectations, and I didn't do things quite the way I should have most likely, at least in their opinion.

STEVE ANDRASCIK/REVIEW-JOURNAL

Binion's Horseshoe poker room manager Tom McEvoy fans out cards in front of photos of past World Series of Poker World Champions. McEvoy won the world championship in 1983.

I was given a starting salary of $60,000 a year. I found out later that my predecessor was only getting $40,000 and that's what they really wanted to pay me, but I was offered $60,000. I had an office at the Horseshoe, up on the second floor where the buffet area and bingo room were, in the area above the old Mint casino. I had a computer at home, and also in my office, and at this time internet poker was in its infancy. It was poker, it was new, and I was attracted to it like a moth to flame. The first site was Planet Poker, which I played a little bit, but it wasn't very good. Paradise Poker had recently started and was making big inroads. I had an account, so a couple of times I played there in my office. That didn't sit well with people. I got ratted out, probably by George Fisher.

What I didn't learn until later was that my "friend" George Fisher, who played at the Horseshoe a lot and knew everybody there, was continuously undermining me because he wanted my job. George and his girlfriend were still living with me, renting a room in my house, so he knew everything that was going on, all my weaknesses, and he had gotten to be good friends with Nick Behnen. Over a year later, I finally learned I had a mole living in my house who had done everything in his power to get me fired. At the time I trusted him. Stupid me.

Kicked Upstairs

In early September, I was informed by the Horseshoe casino manager Blaine Benedict that I was no longer the card room manager. They didn't want me running the World Series of Poker myself from the floor. Benny Junior told me, "I think this would drive you crazy, and we don't want you to run the tournament." So, on Thursday, September 6 I had a man-to-man talk with Nick Behnen, and I told him that day I was very interested in continuing on as a consultant and WSOP Tournament Director. After the meeting I proposed several things to him that evening in an email, after which he agreed:

1) I would assume the title of Director of Poker Operations and WSOP Tournament Director.
2) I would direct the 2002 WSOP and do the scheduling (already done) plus the structures to be used. I would also act as a consultant for the WSOP and daily poker room duties.
3) Bob Dunning, who had been working for me, would be appointed Poker Room Manager. One of many mistakes I made.
4) That Billy Gwynn would be let go. I didn't trust him, and I was right. He later stole some money, confessed, and left town in the dead of night.
5) That George Fisher and I would have the use of two tables to run games the Horseshoe had not previously spread, with

the proceeds to be split equally between George, myself, and the Horseshoe.

6) That George and I would get paid by check every two weeks, the same as all other employees.

So, after 53 days, I was kicked upstairs to be Director of Poker Operations, a new title, and WSOP Tournament Director. So now I was to oversee the poker room and the WSOP, but not run either one. They kicked me upstairs since firing me would make them look very bad and fly in the face of the positive publicity about me being their poker room manager.

The Four Queens Poker Classic was currently in process in downtown Vegas, and I was one of the several celebrity hosts along with eventual Poker Hall of Famers Phil Hellmuth, Linda Johnson, and Layne Flack. I felt we could capture some of this business right away for the WSOP if a new agreement could be consummated with the Behnens right away. And it was—an agreement with a handshake.

We made it official in the home of Nick and Becky Behnen on 9/11, the day the crap hit the fan. It exploded on the TV and like the rest of the country, we didn't know what was going on. What a topsy-turvey day. With one eye on the scary day that was unfolding, we talked things over, finalized things, and I was hired, or well, rehired. I was still dating Kathy Liebert at the time, so my love life was a bit topsy-turvey, too. Talk about a coincidence. I used to say I don't believe in coincidences, but . . .

As WSOP Tournament Director, my first responsibility was to hire someone to run the tournament, two people actually. One was Steve Morrow, who is no longer active in poker and hasn't been for 20 years. He worked as Jack McClelland's assistant for the 17 or 18 years Jack Binion ran the Series as Tournament Director. I wanted to give him a shot at running the tournament, so I made him co-director with Matt Savage. Matt was clearly (to me) the Alpha person in charge.

Matt Savage would have worked for free at the WSOP just to have it on his resume, and he cheerfully gives me credit for launching his big-time tournament directorship career. He was getting solidly established as a front-line tournament director. I knew his capabilities, having attended tournaments he had directed, so I knew he was entirely qualified. Later this year he founded the Tournament Directors Association (TDA) along with Linda Johnson, Jan Fisher, and David Lamb. He was on the microphone to call the 2003 WSOP final hand when Chris Moneymaker defeated Sammy Farha. Currently he is the Executive Tour Director of the World Poker Tour.

I did the entire structure and schedule for the 2002 World Series of Poker. What tournaments were going to be played and when they were going to be played. I spent untold hours in executive sessions and management meetings to hash it all out. All the events were played in the same room, and never more than one tournament at a time. Most of the tournaments lasted more than one day, so they would have a tournament every day with the finals of the tournament going on the same day the next tournament started.

The fact that Tom McEvoy—whose name is synonymous with honesty, integrity, and the World Series of Poker itself— was slated to direct the 2002 WSOP, held the promise of restoring much of the sheen to this event. After all, players, dealers, and management alike respect Tom, and he's been part of the WSOP for years. Moreover, his creativity, together with his management skills, seemed to breathe new energy into the planning for next year's event.

—Lou Krieger, Editor of *Poker Player* newspaper and author of *Poker for Dummies* in *Poker Player* magazine, 9/11/01

Probably my biggest legacy in the 2002 WSOP was the change in the tournament policy to ban smoking at the tables. It would be a while before people watching from the rail and people playing elsewhere in the casino in cash games were prohibited from smoking, but it was a start. I am very proud to have been instrumental in getting the World Series of Poker to go non-smoking for the first time. They were non-smoking every year after that.

> *The decision to go non-smoking for the 2002 WSOP tournament was, "the biggest step we have ever taken, and I support it completely."*
> —Benny Binion Behnen, Jr. *Poker Digest*, 1/24/2002

2001 Net Poker Proceeds $3,600
Non-poker Proceeds $1,000

—2002—

Active on the Tournament Trail

Planning the 2002 World Series of Poker still gave me time to play tournaments, and I was able to cash in the January World Poker Challenge in Reno, the February L.A. Poker Classic, the March Casinos Europa Invitational in Costa Rica, and the inaugural Bellagio High Buy-in Tournament in Vegas in April. I was keeping my ear to the sentiment of the poker world, and most of my many poker acquaintances were excited about the upcoming smoke-free WSOP, and my management of the tournament.

Fired as the WSOP Tournament Director at the Eleventh Hour

I got fired the day before the 2002 World Series of Poker started, on April 18, 2002. The day before the show started! The day before—who does that? It cost me untold thousands of dollars from tips and other renumeration that I was then deprived of. I got no thanks, no nothing. They used my entire tournament plan and schedule even though I was no longer involved.

Why was I fired so unceremoniously one day before the world's biggest poker tournament, the one I had meticulously planned for months? I don't know. The owners didn't give me an explanation why I was fired, and I didn't ask for one. And at that moment, frankly, I was shell-shocked.

The day I got the shocking news George Fisher told me I had better get off the property pretty quick or they were going to escort me off. Which I think was probably not true—a bluff to get me off the premises. I'm not a troublemaker who throws a hissy fit. I said, "Well, can I still play in the event, George?" He said, "Yah, sure, just get out of here now." He wanted me to go quietly, and I did. I did play in the WSOP that year, finishing 32nd in the Seniors event. I also finished third and in the money in an event that was my invention—that I planned and added into the World Series—the $2,500 No-Limit Hold'em Gold Bracelet Match Play event. There were 29 players, and you had to be a WSOP bracelet winner to play. That meant that three got first-round byes. I was not one of them. I beat Captain Tom Franklin in round one, Jennifer Harmon in round two, and Phil Ivy in round three. That put me in the semi-finals against Phil Hellmuth. My suited A - Q lost to Phil's pair of Jacks. I would have had about 90 percent of the chips if I had won this "coin flip." Sometimes it seems I have nothing but bad luck when it comes to winning a race when it really counts. Hellmuth lost to Johnny

Chan in the finals. This event was one and done, never to be held again. And, once again, I tried but did not cash in the Main Event.

George "Judas" Fisher

Most poker players have nicknames, and that's my nickname for the guy who betrayed me. I don't know exactly what George Fisher did, but I now know he was working behind my back almost constantly to get me out because he wanted my position. He had the ear of Nick Behnen, and every chance he got he said a lot of negative things about me to the Behnens, always suggesting I was the problem, and he was the solution. He saw me as a threat, figuring they didn't need him if they had me. And all the while he was doing this, he was living in my house!

George Fisher wormed his way into my position as the Director of Poker Operations and WSOP Tournament Director. He was aided by his girlfriend, Sandra Green, who was also living with him in my house. She worked for nothing at the WSOP, like an unpaid assistant and gopher. She wasn't super smart like he was.

Fisher was there for the beginning of the 2002 WSOP and through the 2003 WSOP when Chris Moneymaker won. And all that time George and Sandra were still renting a room from me. That's how long it took me to figure out what George had done to me. I can't believe I was as dumb and naïve as I was for as long as I was.

But in the end, perhaps he got what he deserved. George was a 60-something-year-old marijuana smoker. He actually grew a marijuana plant in my backyard he called his "exotic fern." But he neglected to tell his heart doctor about this little piece of information when he had to have heart surgery. He died on the operating table, leaving me stuck with his jobless girlfriend at my house.

Took me awhile to figure out what had happened, and I finally did. I verified George's evil plot with Matt Savage, who was surprised I didn't know what was going on. "Well," Matt said, "you turned out better than what happened to him."

In an interview for this book, Matt said George thought he didn't need any help, but Matt soon learned he definitely did. He felt George didn't really have a firm grasp on the industry at the time, like I did. So, hiring Matt to run the tournament that year gave him the opportunity to cover up some of the shortcomings of George Fisher.

An Act of Disgust

I was so disgusted after I was fired from the 2002 World Series of Poker that the remaining WSOP bracelet I still had in my possession, my Main Event bracelet, felt somehow tainted. Note this was before the modern era of bracelets. They were not fancy and elaborate, just very simple and elegant, a style I like better than the new ones, actually. The bracelet style had not changed in the nine years since I won my first one in 1983. Back then they didn't even inscribe your name on it. In my appalled state I decided to replace the memory with something new—like that was even possible.

I visited a local jeweler who was a poker friend of mine (sound familiar?). He showed me this beautiful ruby ring that I fell in love with. It looked almost too pretty, and it was too pretty. I thought the ring was worth more than it was, and the bracelet was worth less than it was. So, I traded the bracelet along with a bunch of casino and World Series chips for the ring, which I still have. Years later I paid for it to be checked out by an expert. Turns out it was manufactured in a lab. I got screwed over by the jeweler (again, sound familiar?).

In just a matter of months I settled down, and I realized I'd like to get the bracelet back. I had help getting it back, and once I did, I wanted to change it—to make it better. I had it all buffed up, had my name inscribed on it, and added six diamonds on each side. Years later, to help make ends meet, I sold the bracelet on eBay in a package deal that included three of my books and some other personal memorabilia, a decision I will always regret.

Parting Ways with My Sponsor Ron McMillan

This story starts with Larry Wright, a well-heeled Texan I had met playing a cash poker game downtown at Binion's. We struck up a conversation, and he told me he and a friend were going to get a cab and go down to the Strip. I offered to take them, and we became friends. You'll remember from the Kathy Liebert chapter that I arranged for Larry to sponsor her in the first Party Poker million-dollar Limit- Hold'em tournament held on Linda Johnson's cruise ship. I had already won a seat online for this tournament, and Kathy wasn't going to play unless someone sponsored her. Larry and I became even closer friends when Kathy won the million-dollar first prize in April 2002, shortly before the WSOP.

I had already won my seat in the 2002 World Series Main Event, and I was playing for my sponsor, Ron McMillan. Then I became a victim of circumstances, and in the process did something that upset Ron. Larry asked me if I would play a satellite for him to try and win a Main Event seat for him. Of course, I said yes. But I knew I had better let Ron know, and when I called Ron before I played, I got his voice mail. I left a message, telling Ron I was only doing this at Larry's request, and this was not something I would have played on my own. I won the satellite, Larry got his seat, and Ron dropped me shortly thereafter feeling that I cost him $10,000. He had the right to drop me—I can't argue with that. But to feel I cost him ten grand—no, that's not right. I made it clear on my phone message. I was very specific about that because I didn't want any misunderstandings. This was just one more instance where I had the best of intentions and managed to get my butt in a sling.

Regardless, Ron McMillan and I are still friends. Even after we went our separate ways, post 2002, a couple of times Ron volunteered to take a piece of me in a tournament or two, but we didn't cash when he did it. I never asked him for anything, ever. He did it for other people, too, I wasn't the only one he'd take pieces of. Unfortunately, his funding of tournaments for me has been nothing but a losing deal for him overall.

The Door Closes for One and Opens for Another – Bonnie Damiano

The only bright spot about my dismissal from the 2002 WSOP is that it helped create an opportunity for others, notably Bonnie Damiano. She became an assistant tournament director for the Series and the Hall of Fame. Later in September, she ran the Four Queens Poker Classic, which ended October 6, and then became the first to take a poker tournament to an island with her Caribbean Classic that started two days later in Aruba. Quite a few poker pros joined me by hopping a midnight flight to play in the second leg of the back-to-back tourneys, including Phil Hellmuth, Russ Hamilton, Annie Duke, Howard Lederer, Linda Johnson, Scotty Nguyen, and Men "The Master" Nguyen.

Bonnie was an idea person, a hustler, and she had a lot of concepts and big plans that fizzled out. I once invested in one of her ideas, a lingerie line for larger ladies and, to the chagrin of myself and others, lost my venture capital. Bonnie would play a big role in my life in several ways, as you will see.

Beat Texas Hold'em

My seventh poker book, *How to Beat Low-Limit Poker*, came out on September 14. It was written by Dana Smith, with a little help from me. Literally. I didn't really do much on this book. Dana, who was still using the pseudonym Shane, thought there was a market for a pretty basic book for beginners and relative newbies. She was wrong because it didn't sell much. This experience level wasn't my forte. I enjoyed the more technical writing that employed strategies and deeper thinking for more advanced players, or players trying to get advanced.

World Poker Tour

2002 was the inaugural year for the World Poker Tour, which debuted at the Five Diamond World Poker Classic at the Las Vegas Bellagio casino in December. At the request of my good friend, Mike Sexton, I played in this tournament, finishing 13th in the $1,000 Pot-Limit Hold'em event.

Mike Sexton was one heck of a guy—a gymnast from Ohio, a U.S. Army paratrooper, co-founder of PartyPoker.com, and a Poker Hall of Fame inductee in 2009 (not to mention a good friend and pallbearer for Stu Ungar). He was there when I won the World Series, and a couple years later moved to Vegas to pursue a career in poker. Mike began as the television commentator for the WPT in this tournament and continued for a total of 15 seasons. His lifetime of advocating for the game of poker earned him the apt title of "Ambassador of Poker."

2002 Net Poker Proceeds $2,200
Non-poker Proceeds $3,700

—2003—

Emergency Surgery at Jack Binion's Tournament in Mississippi

In January, I played in the World Poker Tour's second televised tournament at the Fourth Annual Jack Binion World Poker Open at Jack's Horseshoe casino in Tunica, Mississippi. Before I left Vegas, I was experiencing gallbladder discomfort, so I went to two doctors for an opinion. One warned me I likely had gallstones, and the second said I didn't have anything too serious. He was wrong. Shortly after I arrived, I had a massive attack that sent me to the hospital.

It took three agonizing days before they decided that my stones weren't going to pass naturally, and I had to have them surgically removed. Two gallstones about the size of a robin's egg. I saved them for a while. They were brown and hard as a rock and resembled little turds. I spent three more days in the hospital and then a couple of days in my hotel room recuperating. Then I had a decision to make.

I had won a satellite for the $10,000 No-Limit Hold'em Main Event. Jack McClelland, who had run the World Series for Jack Binion, followed him to Tunica as his tournament director. He very graciously offered to roll over my satellite entry so I could use it the next year. I wasn't 100 percent, but I didn't need or use the heavy-duty pain pills they gave me, and I wanted to battle through this thing and play. I finished in the money in 19th place, making $9,162. It was slightly less than the buy-in, but I was glad I played.

The gallstones were caused by too much fat intake in my diet. After the surgery I developed irritable bowel syndrome (IBS), which I have had ever since. I love to eat, and I really have to watch my food intake, and these two factors are often unpleasant crossroads in my life. I love prime rib, but it doesn't love me. Sometimes one just has to pay the price of enjoyment.

While I'm talking about Mississippi, how Jack Binion got to Tunica is an interesting story. The 1988 Indian Gaming Act had cracked open the door for casinos to be established in more states than just Nevada and New Jersey. As Jack told my biographer, he investigated riverboat gambling in Iowa and wasn't convinced it was going to work. Then he went down to Mississippi looking for a gaming opportunity and found it. Nobody but Jack in the Binion family was interested in going out of state. This was after Benny Binion had passed away, and the other two Binion's stockholders were his mother and brother. They approved Jack using the name "Horseshoe" but not "Binion's Horseshoe." So, he opened the Horseshoe casino in Tunica, Mississippi, and started a whole new company. He cut a lot of his family members—children, grandchildren, nieces, and nephews—in on the franchise. Jack's Horseshoe ended up being worth much more than Binion's Horseshoe downtown.

Internet Poker Is Taking Off

PokerStars, UltimateBet, and Paradise Poker all started in 2001, with Full Tilt Poker launching in 2004. Dan Goldman, the Vice President of PokerStars, summed it up when he was quoted in 2003, saying, "Poker is experiencing a worldwide boom of epic proportions." And this was before the Chris Moneymaker "boom." The internet poker sites were beginning to compete with brick-and-mortar poker rooms, and the whole professional poker community was watching with great interest.

Representing PokerStars

On March 28, 2003, I announced my new role as the only official host for PokerStars.com, calling it "an outstanding online poker site." At the beginning of our association, the weekly online tournament points leader got to play me a $1,000 freeroll in the game of his or her choice. These heads-up matches were held every Sunday. When I won, the money rolled over, and the following week's match was for $2,000, and so on.

I will go into detail on my brand representative role with PokerStars and other companies, in the next chapter. These endorsements made a significant impact on my life.

The Championship Table: At the World Series of Poker (1970 to 2002)

My next poker book, *The Championship Table: At the World Series of Poker*, covered the final tables of the World Series of Poker from its inception in 1970 through the 2002 championship. It was a collaboration of Dana Smith, Ralph Wheeler, and me, released on April 1, 2003. Ralph had approached Dana to do the book, and he did the lion's share of the research, which was spot-on accurate.

Unfortunately, maybe this book came out a few months too soon. It may have been much more popular if it had come out after the 2003 Main Event, for the reasons described below. So, under the brand of the Championship Series, we did an update the next year to cover the 2003 Main Event final table, and a third update in 2009 to add coverage of the Main Event tables through 2008.

2003 World Series of Poker—the Moneymaker Effect

When Chris Moneymaker won the 2003 World Series of Poker Main Event it was like an electric shock—like lightning stuck an entire industry. The amateur accountant with the magic name captured the imagination of everyday poker players all across the world. If he can do it, why not me? If the runner-up, poker professional Sammy Farha, had won there never would have been this kind of explosion—what some called the "Moneymaker Effect."

Moneymaker was an accountant, just like me. He played a lot of poker, but it wasn't his profession. He was a working guy with a regular job and a regular family. After he won, he thought he was going to go back to his accounting job—he actually said that. But I knew Chris had no idea what was in store for him. I could say from experience his life was never going to be the same.

He actually did go back to his job, for a few weeks anyway, but he was being bombarded by offers. PokerStars was actively recruiting him, and he soon became their second—and primary—host. Overnight he was famous, and he was swamped with offers. It was magic for him, and for poker as a whole.

As an example of how poker exploded, there were 839 entrants in the 2003 Main Event. The next year the number of players tripled, to 2,576. The year after that, the number of entrants doubled again to 5,619. Tournament entries grew exponentially all across the country. It was the "Moneymaker Effect."

For me, I cashed in the $1,500 No-Limit Hold'em and the $1,500 Limit Omaha events. I was around, but not in the room at the Horseshoe when the planet shifted for poker. But I was on one of the limited-edition collector chips that featured all 31 WSOP millionaires that the Series made available that year.

Son Patrick Marries

On August 30, 2003, my son Patrick married Vanessa Coffeen in a wonderful ceremony in San Diego. She was a part-owner in an insurance agency, and he was a San Deigo County deputy sheriff. The two of them are really something. They both had full-time careers and found time, somehow, to further their education with, for

Patrick, a bachelor's degree, and then for both of them, a master's degree—all while also starting a family. Today I have two of the greatest grandchildren, Marissa and Chayse.

As soon as the wedding was over, since I was already in California, I made the hundred-mile trip north up the coast to the Bicycle Casino in Bell Gardens as a seminar speaker along with T. J. Cloutier and poker up-and-comers Jennifer Harmon and Daniel Negreanu. Life was good!

Championship Satellite Strategy

My ninth poker book, *Championship Satellite Strategy,* came out on October 1, 2003. This was my first book partnering with Brad Daugherty, who I consider to be the epitome of the forgotten World Champion. I had written four books with T. J. Cloutier, and Dana Smith and I discussed doing a new book with someone else. I was friends with Brad and considered him a really good player, so we contacted him and we agreed to work together on two books. This first effort with Brad was one of my best books, in  my opinion, and I'm very proud of it. I remember when we finished this book, we weren't sure how to put the sequence together. So, I spread out the typed pages for the entire book on the floor at Dana's place and I put that thing together like a puzzle to get the right order—and it flowed.

2003 Net Poker Proceeds $(-$10,000)
Non-poker Proceeds $21,500

Your brand name is only as good as your reputation.
—Richard Branson

CHAPTER 20

♣ ♦ ♥ ♠

Poker Brand Representative. Wearing the Logo.

A brand representative is a professional who promotes a company or product with the goal of building the brand's positive image and increasing its awareness. Spokesman, ambassador, team pro, whatever you chose to call it, being a poker pro brand representative was a very important part of my life for many years. It was the best job I ever had.

PokerStars: 2003 to 2011

For me, it all started with PokerStars early in 2003. I was their first official pro host, the first pro they universally recognized. I say this because the first poker pro they actually contacted and recruited was Amarillo Slim, who wasn't even computer literate. He only lasted a couple of months before they had to get rid of him. He was supposed to be playing cash games online under his name on their website, but it didn't take long before they realized he wasn't even playing. He had someone else—a friend or relative—playing for him online.

At that time, PokerStars' bankroll was a whole lot bigger than their name awareness. So, after the Amarillo Slim fiasco they needed to get a professional poker player with a recognizable name who would do what he was supposed to do. So, they contacted me.

I didn't know anybody at PokerStars until their marketing guru (and poker player) Dan Goldman contacted me and offered me the position. I wasn't a very good negotiator. I just thought this looked like something I would like to do, and I took the first offer they made. No written contract, just a verbal agreement. I liked Dan, and we became good friends. We are still friends today.

It was a great partnership, and we were all very happy together. I was PokerStars' dedicated Team Pro for eight years, and I could not have been more delighted. It was a deal made in heaven. It started with a monthly salary of like $2,000, and I was able to work my way up to $4,000 a month. I got a bonus for any tournaments, live or online, where I made the final table, and got to pocket any money I won. On top of that, they paid my entry and all associated travel expenses into three major tournaments a year—the $10,000 WSOP Main Event, one major European tournament, and the PokerStars Main Event in the Bahamas. I got to see more of the world, like the Caribbean, Denmark, and Germany—all on PokerStars' dime.

Primarily, all I had to do was play poker and wear PokerStars branded clothing. That included playing live cash games on the PokerStars website under my own name for at least 15 hours a month, with my own money. I did anything they asked, from making TV commercials to special promotions, often timed around major tournaments like the World Series. For example, PokerStars would host online contests, and the winners would get to play me. They made a big deal out of the heads-up matches by bringing two computers into the same room, where we would play online while physically facing each other. I did all kinds of little things they asked me to do—that was all part of the job. And I loved it.

Here's another example. As a publicity gambit, the PokerStars Team Pro would face off against the poker pro who had the best tournament successes in the past week in a freezeout game of their choice, for a prize of a thousand bucks. If I beat the player, the prize purse would go up to two thousand for the next week, and so on. At one time I faced Michael "The Grinder" Mizrachi, the only time I ever played against him. We played for $5,000 because I had won this innovative PokerStars event four weeks in a row, and he was my fifth opponent. When I beat him, he wasn't happy. On PokerStars, you could play heads-up matches online if you wanted for whatever stakes the players agree on. Mizrachi said he was so displeased with the $5,000 loss to me that he went on PokerStars and put up his own $5,000 to challenge someone else to a heads-up poker game. He won, so he got the $5,000 he didn't get from beating me by beating someone else. Pretty much portrays the poker world.

This short story illustrates how much the dynamics of the poker world is misunderstood, sometimes even within the industry. One time I didn't get my monthly online playing time in because I was busy playing World Series of Poker events. Sure enough, I got a call from an accounting clerk who informed me that I hadn't fulfilled my contract because I hadn't logged enough hours this period. I politely informed her that my job was to represent PokerStars, and that I was representing PokerStars by playing in the World Series of Poker. And that was a hell of a lot more important than me playing online for a few extra hours. That was the last I heard of that nonsense. Can you imagine? In the middle of the WSOP?

I was the first official PokerStars host in 2003. The second host was Chris Moneymaker. He won the World Series of Poker Main Event that year after winning his seat on PokerStars, and they immediately made a deal with him. He became the head host, and I got more or less shoved into the background, which I completely understood. After that PokerStars added all kinds of ambassadors. They started recruiting Main Event winners like Greg "Fossilman" Raymer in 2004 and Joe Hachem in 2005. They kept expanding with noted pros like Daniel Negreanu, who was one of their main pros for years. PokerStars even paid some pros for prominently displaying their logo. They sponsored Kathy Liebert in the Main Event a couple of times, even though they didn't sign her up as a team pro. PokerStars understood the value of promotion, and it served them well.

By the end of my tenure as a PokerStars team pro, my gig was worth about $100,000 a year considering the salary, tournament buy-ins and winnings, and reimbursed travel expenses. It all ended thanks to Black Friday, April 15, 2011, the day everything changed for online poker in the United States. That's the day the Federal Government shut down the domestic online poker industry, including my employer, PokerStars. Because PokerStars was well funded and honestly run, they were the first major poker website to make U.S. player accounts whole, probably why they are the most popular place to play poker in the world today. I was glad to help them in the early days, and no one was sadder to see them gone from the U.S. market. Financially, things really went south for me after losing this income.

After Black Friday, PokerStars kept Negreanu, Moneymaker, and some of their other poker pro ambassadors on the payroll for a while. I was able to stay with PokerStars for the remainder of 2011. They didn't actually fire me, but I knew I was going to get a reduced deal.

Face Up Gaming: 2011 to 2012

That's when I was approached by my friend Bonnie Domiano, who had left her position at UltimateBet's sister online Blackjack site and was now working for a relatively new online site called Face Up Gaming. They offered me the head pro position for a salary plus what was really important to me—the $10,000 WSOP Main Event buy-in. They started the novel idea of winning prizes and tournament seats via a poker club that charged a $24.95 monthly fee. I helped them hype this on YouTube, and even started a league called "McEvoy's Poker Aces" that rewarded winners with seminars in Aruba. But that site fizzled out after about a year, and they went out of business owing me a bunch of money.

DeepStacks University: 2011

DeepStacks University was created as an online poker training site founded by Chris Torina, a former SWAT team member and instructor, and his partner, an ex-military training expert. They put together "Team Deepstacks"—a whole group of top-notch big-name live and online poker players serving as university professors. World-class players like T. J. Cloutier, Mike Matusow, Michael "The Grinder" Mizrachi, Justin "Boosted J" Smith, Adam "Roothlus" Levy, Matt Graham, and me. It was a pretty impressive group. All told, the instructors had seven WSOP Main Event final table appearances, 16 WSOP bracelets, multiple WPT final tables, and over $30 million in tournament winnings. Who couldn't learn from this group? I know I did.

In addition to the online videos we did, DeepStacks University also hosted live classrooms or seminars around the country. These seminars were promoted by the University, which signed up the students, collected the tuition money, found and equipped the locations, and often put on a post-seminar student tournament.

I remember one seminar in Buffalo, New York. It took place about five years after I had broken up with Jennifer Snyder, who lived there, an ex-girlfriend who would have become Mrs. McEvoy if I had had my way (my romance with Jennifer is covered in the next chapter). She was married then, but stopped by to say hello and actually gave me a lift to the airport after the seminar was over. We are still friends to this day.

I also remember DeepStacks University classes being held in Bakersfield, California, and at the Commerce Club in Los Angeles. There were several other stops, but I can't remember all of them. I was a professor of "pokerology" for a couple of years. Unfortunately, the concept didn't really take off and just kind of fizzled out. I think they paid my expenses and like $500 to a $1,000 a seminar. It wasn't big money, but it was a lot of fun.

WPT Boot Camp: 2005 to 2007

The World Poker Tour Boot Camp was the brainchild of a couple of self-professed poker junkies in 2005, who patterned their concept after baseball, football, or hockey camps. They were two-day camps with live lectures, archived WPT video footage, game play, and personal tips from poker superstars. That's where I came in.

And this gig was fun, too. Unfortunately for my participation, it was something that only lasted for a couple of years. At that time, I was one of maybe 20 instructors. The two or three "camps" I was involved in were all conducted at the Atlantis casino in the Bahamas. They did a really good job of recruiting a lot of students. The camp included a tournament for all the students, who competed for a "season pass," which was about a $100,000 worth of buy-ins for big WPT and WSOP events. We instructors were paid a fee and had our expenses paid. Not a huge money maker for me, but they were well-run instructional camps that are still offered today. I would highly recommend them to the serious player looking to ratchet up to the next level.

Poker Samadhi: 2021 to Present

In 2021, I was asked by my good friend Danielle Striker, a Las Vegas businesswoman and semi-pro poker grinder, to be a poker guru for her new concept, Poker Samadhi. The word "Samadhi" [suh-mah-dee] is an Indian Sanskrit word relating to the process of joining all aspects of who we are—physically, spiritually, mentally, and emotionally—to attain a state of heightened concentration and awareness. In poker parlance, some call this" getting into the zone."

Poker Samadhi is a concept designed to help poker players find success through positive thinking. My role is to share my knowledge in various ways via poker mantras that are intended to help tune the brain's vibrations into a state of poker clairvoyance—and to sell hats, T-shirts, books, poker chips, magnets, mugs, wristbands, and other merchandise branded with the mantras of Poker Samadhi's gurus, available at the business website.

The whole idea is to help players live their best life, not just play their best poker game. There are so many things that can make you successful in poker that can make you successful in life, and vice versa. For the record, I'm still an unpaid Poker Samadhi contributor, not an investor, so unlike the other brands I represented, I have no financial interest in the business.

If every conceivable precaution is taken at first, one
is often too discouraged to proceed at all.
—Archer John Porter Martin

CHAPTER 21

♣ ♦ ♥ ♠

2004 to September 2008. Fizzled Opportunities, Incarceration, Smitten at Home and Abroad, and a Big Investment.

—2004—

Poker Testimonials that Amounted to a Hill of Beans

Because of the combination of my fame within the poker world and the exploding popularity of the game (i.e., the "Moneymaker Effect"), I was the fortunate recipient of endorsement offers. Some supplemented my income nicely, and some were a complete bust. But many were interesting.

For example, in early 2004, I was asked by an entrepreneur, Stuart Krasney, to be the star in his television commercial to promote his "Poker Smarts" product, the "Texas Hold'em Super Pro Chart." It was a packaged set of the odds involved in Hold'em, retailing for $14.95, designed to help players make statistically correct choices. I was paid, as I remember, $5,000 up front, with the contractual promise of royalties of 3.5 percent. I even went to New York with him once to attend a book convention, to help him promote the merchandise. I shipped some of my books there and nobody bought a single book, although one guy talked me into giving him one. I didn't get any royalties because the idea never caught on.

Some endorsement deals included a dose of humor. Another business entrepreneur, a New York businessman, wanted to sell his product, a replica of a World Series bracelet. He had made some kind of endorsement deal with Johnny Chan, but he claimed Chan reneged, so he contacted me. I agreed to meet with him, expecting a businessman in a suit. He was anything but—a slightly pudgy guy wearing a tank top, the opposite of what I expected. He had contacted me in part because I had a reputation for being easy to deal with and cooperative. I did a bunch of promotional stuff for him, and he paid me $5,000. It wasn't a big money maker for him, but he hadn't forgotten the slight from Johnny Chan. He had some toilet paper made up with Johnny Chan's face on it, with the legend "Wipe your can with Johnny Chan." He passed these out at the World Series. He spotted Johnny at a cash game playing with Doyle Brunson and some other big names, and he passed out his specialty butt wipes as Johnny was sitting there. The entire table thought this was laugh-out-loud hilarious, except Johnny Chan. I'm sure Johnny just wanted to punch him out. But he did bring it on himself.

Bonnie Domiano came up with the idea for a poker-education website called "Poker Professor," starring me as the poker professor personified. One of my poker students, Susie Isaacs, for years had called me "Professor McEvoy." But Howard Lederer had already usurped the nickname "Professor." So, like a lot of Bonnie's ideas, this one went nowhere. Accolades to Bonnie, though—she just kept trying.

Harrah's Buys Binion's, Moves the WSOP

Since its inception in 1970, the World Series of Poker had been held each year at Binion's Horseshoe casino on Fremont Street in downtown Las Vegas. After the 2003 World Series, Harrah's Entertainment, which later became Caesars Entertainment, purchased the Horseshoe and WSOP brands. They understood the world's biggest poker tournament had outgrown its place at Binion's, and the leadership of the Behnens.

As plans were already in place, the 2004 World Series of Poker was played at the Horseshoe, but starting in 2005, Harrah's moved the WSOP to the Rio casino, a venue with more space, where it stayed until 2022, when Caesars Entertainment moved it to the newly renamed Horseshoe on the Strip.

Every event of the 2005 WSOP was played at the Rio, with one exception. At the request of Las Vegas Mayor Oscar Goodman, to celebrate the 100th anniversary of Las Vegas, the final table of the Main Event was played downtown at Binion's Horseshoe. Won by

Australian Joe Hachem, it was the last time a WSOP bracelet event was played at the iconic casino. I was on the rail at the final table, and a part of me grieved that this was it for the WSOP and the Horseshoe, the location that had had such a large impact on my life. But I knew it was time to move on.

The United States Poker Association

Enthusiasm for poker was exploding, and new players were attracted like moths to a flame to the thousands of hometown tournaments sprouting up all across the country. A guy by the name of Tommy Eubanks formed an organization called the United States Poker Association. It was to be a nonprofit organization to support and promote poker as a recreational sport. I was asked to join a board of folks representing players, the casino industry, the media, and tournament directors. Like so many ideas that were cropping up at the time, this one sounded good but didn't amount to anything.

Hobnobbing with the Stars

In July, I participated in the Celebrity Pro-Am Poker charity tournament that was held at the Hard Rock Casino. I really enjoyed the opportunity to mingle with movie stars like Lou Diamond Phillips and Gary Busey, as well as up-and-coming poker stars like Antonio Esfandiari. I remember Gary Busey not understanding the rules of poker tournaments and creating a scene. He had left the table, and his stack was getting blinded off, and he objected when he returned to find his chip stack wasn't as big as when he'd left it. He was known to have a bit of a substance-abuse habit, so he might have been on something more than just tilt. Regardless, just like everyone else, I enjoyed pressing the flesh with movie stars—and poker stars.

Final Table Challenge: A Made-for-TV Tournament

This was another attempt to take advantage of the "Moneymaker Effect" that amounted to nothing. A friend of mine, Kerry Davis, came up with this idea for a new poker tournament concept specifically designed for TV. It got some media attention from *Canadian Poker Player* magazine. They ran an article promoting the event, with Kerry and me featured on the cover of that issue. I was hired to be the tournament television broadcast analyst. It was an intriguing idea. They would hold and televise ten single-table tournaments, basically what we call "sit-and-go" tournaments, each held at participating Las Vegas casinos. Each table would have nine invited pro players and one amateur "wild card" player chosen from people who signed up by visiting finaltablechallenge.com and submitting a video audition. The wild card entrant was chosen by a studio audience the week before and flown to the appropriate casino. The winner each week would pocket $50,000 and advance to the Final Table Challenge Grand Championship and play for a $250,000 first-place prize. Sounded good, right?

The first episode was played at Sam's Town on September 14, with the play-by-play commentary supposedly to be provided by Susie Isaacs and me. I had just returned from the World Poker Tour UltimateBet Poker Classic in Aruba, and I was feeling the effect of jet lag. On top of that, they wanted us at the casino early in the morning (I still don't do early mornings well). Then they made us sit around doing nothing for 12 hours before they finally got around to doing a little ten-minute thing with me and Susie. The whole thing fizzled. One episode and done.

2004 Net Poker Proceeds $31,200
Non-poker Proceeds $36,200

—2005—

My Big and Profitable TV Break—That Got Postponed

It was the early days of televised poker tournaments, and once again I was the victim of circumstances. In 2004, The World Poker Tour created a made-for-television spinoff called the Professional Poker Tour (PPT). They promoted it as the first professional poker league and was limited to invited players who had gained fame with high finishes in major poker-circuit tournaments on the World Poker Tour or the World Series of Poker. Five shows were taped every three months starting in June 2004. The final five-player table was to be the sixth and final event. Each event was held at a different high-profile casino including the Bellagio, Mirage, and the Bay 101.

I was among the poker pros invited to the third PPT event, a freeroll for the profession headliners. It was held in March at the Bay 101 along with their famous "Shooting Star" tournament, which had become a World Poker Tour event in 2003. I was no stranger to this tournament, having participated in the very first Bay 101 Shooting Star tournament back in 1997. It became the major "bounty" tournament, where players earned extra prize money by knocking one of the celebrity poker stars out of the tournament.

There were a lot of big names in poker involved in my event—160 players, with the final table including Alfredo "Toto" Leonidas, Casey Kastle, Hoyt Corkins, and backgammon whiz Paul Magriel. I got heads-up with Marsha Waggoner and beat her to win the $200,000 first prize, a $25,000 seat for the championship event at the WPT Five Star World Poker Classic tournament at the Bellagio in April (in which I cashed for $30,000), and the opportunity to play against a short but tough field on TV. The winners of the other four PPT events, where most of the high-profile players of the time had competed, were John Juanda, Erick Lindgren, Lee Markholt, and

Ted Forrest. A final table event with those guys and me would have been epic.

The plan was to broadcast all the events on the Travel Channel later in the year. The bad news was that the WPT sued the Travel Channel for breach of contract, and even tried to shop the show to ESPN. The show went black. Even worse, the final table with all the PPT winners never happened. The good news was twofold. First, the show was revived after the lawsuit was settled and integrated into the WPT broadcast schedule in 2007-08. So, I eventually did get some TV time, although by then the results were ancient history (sort of like watching a football game after you already knew who won). Second, I made enough money from the freeroll tournament to pay off the mortgage on my house on Gisborn Drive (and a few years later, to make a real estate investment in the house next door).

How to Win No-Limit Hold'em Tournaments

My final strategy poker book, *How to Win No-Limit Hold'em Tournaments,* was written with Don Vines and released on August 2. Don, as you might remember, was Dana Smith's husband. As a longtime professional poker player specializing in Hold'em and Omaha, he was also a personal friend of mine. He was a fierce competitor who was also a great tennis player and was once a member of the Canadian Davis Cup team. Don saw his wife and me collaborating with Brad Daughtery and T. J. Cloutier on

HOW TO WIN NO-LIMIT HOLD'EM TOURNAMENTS

MAKE MILLIONS OF DOLLARS AT THE WORLD'S MOST EXCITING POKER GAME

Don Vines & Tom McEvoy

so many book projects that he decided he wanted to do a book, too. We collaborated on a pretty good book.

Another Flop—the Poker Quest of Champions

Try this tournament concept on for size . . . a whopping size. For starters, the buy-in was going to be $250,000, with a maximum field of 100 players. Then the originators, Poker Quest, Inc., would do a TV taping of 12 episodes at the Palms Casino Resort in Las Vegas. The big money would create interest in watching the show. To start the ball rolling, they had a freeroll satellite for the tournament and invited the cream of the crop to compete in it—big names like Barry Greenstein, Ted Forest, Layne Flack, Kathy Liebert, Freddy Deeb, Men the Master, and Thor Hanson.

But not Tom McEvoy.

At the last minute somebody cancelled, and they called me to be a replacement. Sounded good, I was free, so I was in, and I went scurrying across town to play. And I won.

What I won was a satellite for a $250,000 seat in a tournament that never happened. Seems the buy-in was a bit prohibitive. I also won 100,000 shares in Poker Quest, Inc. That was very nice of them, but 100,000 shares of nothing is still nothing. I tipped $400 when I won and got this obelisk trophy, one of the nicest trophies I ever won, that reads "Poker Quest Pro Shootout Champion Labor Day Weekend 2005. Palms Casino Resort, Las Vegas." Just a few years ago, I found an identical trophy in the gift shop at the Bellagio with a price tag of $1,000. Seems I have number 58 out of the 450 trophies created by a guy named Jay Strongwater.

Incarcerated in Japan

Here's another opportunity that came my way that escalated into to one of my "truth is stranger than fiction" stories. In March, I was invited by a Japanese TV show to come to Tokyo, all expenses paid (plus a little spending money) and appear on their show. I love to travel to new places, and I had never been to Japan, so I packed my bags and my passport and took off out of L.A. for the Land of the Rising Sun. My five-day adventure had begun.

Going over to Japan, I must have had to present my passport at least five or six times, including when I was at the top of the gangway and about to step on the plane. Getting situated, I stuck my passport in my bag, which I put in the overhead bin. An hour or so before the plane was to land, I noticed a guy was going through the bin up there. I assumed it was for his own stuff, and I didn't even think twice about it. But about 30 minutes out, I brought my bag down to prepare for customs inspection. And my passport was gone. I don't know if the guy swiped it or if I somehow dropped it. I was all alone in a foreign country with no passport. Panic started to set in.

I immediately told the crew my passport was missing. After landing, they did a search of the plane and they even called back to L.A. to see if it was dropped back there, but I told them I had to show it to get on the plane so it couldn't be in L.A. I could prove who I was. I had my driver's license and I had brought a few copies of my books that all had my picture. The first instinct of the authorities was to put me back on a plane to the United States. But the TV people were there to greet me, and they soon learned of my situation. They didn't want their show ruined, so somehow a deal was worked out.

I was incarcerated for one night in a hotel room. Some other guy was incarcerated, too—I don't know what he did—in a nearby hotel room. A guard was posted outside our rooms; that's how serious the situation was. I remember I kept a roll of toilet paper as a souvenir. It was so rough I thought I'd get a sore butt if I had to use that stuff every day.

The next day they released me to the TV station folks, and we went directly to the U.S. Embassy to get a temporary passport, good for a year. They were very helpful and empathetic, and they expedited the process. For a few days all I had was my driver's license for an ID, but I got the temporary passport just in time to go home.

The TV show was interesting. The premise was that they had a panel of well-known contestants; comedians and actresses if I remember correctly. One of them would "win" an all-expenses paid trip to Las Vegas and an entry into the WSOP Main Event—they really hyped the chance to win the $5 million first-place prize. It was my job to choose the winner. Each of them presented his or her case as to why I should choose them, which often brought howls of laughter from the studio audience. Of course, there was a language barrier, but the TV show folks made it very clear to me who they wanted me to pick.

I picked this pretty lady—I guess she was an actress of some kind. When she arrived in Las Vegas, the Japanese TV crew was there, and we staged the arrival with the Strip in the background. They also filmed me taking her to her seat in the Rio casino. I made sure I was playing the same day she was going to play so that I could be there to keep an eye on her. I didn't really give her any lessons, but she must have studied. She got through day one and went out on day two. A very respectable showing, as getting through day one is not all that easy.

Before I left Tokyo, I did use a little of my money to sightsee. I was going to do a tour group of the city, but it started at 9 a.m. I'm a night person, and I thought I'd be half-asleep all day, so I skipped it. I did go to the atomic museum, where I stood out as an American and I got a few looks directed my way, but nobody said anything to me. That was the only thing I did that was any fun. I enjoy history and I liked doing that, but I regret not taking the city tour.

Print Media Darling

The media was hungry for poker content, and I didn't turn down their offers. This year I was featured in player profile articles in the *Poker Player* newspaper and in the new *All In* magazine that was founded in 2004. I was also interviewed in *Bluff* magazine. I was asked to do a poker strategy article for Avery Cardoza's *Player Magazine,* which he had launched at the end of 2003. The following year, I had a three-page article in the premier issue of *American Poker Player* magazine on "How to Win at Texas Hold'em."

Some of the other publications that interviewed me for articles over the years include *Fast Company, Red Streak, Fifth Street,* and *Poker Europa.*

Book Rebranding

Dana Smith sold the rights to publish our poker books to Avery Cardoza of Cardoza Publishing. He wanted to reissue some of the books with changes that addressed some criticisms of the originals. So, four of my books were updated, rebranded "*The Championship Series,*" and reissued this year. *Winning Satellite Strategies*, my first book with Brad Daugherty, was retitled *Win Your Way into Big Money Hold'em Tournaments* and published February 1. The name, as you might guess, was to attract readers eager to become the next Chris Moneymaker.

My first three books written with T. J. Cloutier became the next books in "*The Championship Series*" released as *Championship No Limit & Pot Limit Hold'em* on April 1, *Championship Omaha* on May 3, and *Championship Hold'em* on October 26. *Championship*

Tournament Practice Hands was rebranded *Championship 107 Hold'em Tournament Hands* in 2011.

After they were rebranded, we made a little in royalties, but not much. Basically, I have no more income from prior books. Please tell your friends to buy a copy of this book. Shameless, aren't I?

2005 Net Poker Proceeds $178,000
Non-poker Proceeds $40,000
My second-best income year. It only took me 22 years
to finally earn over $200,000 for the year.

—2006—

Bitten By the Love Bug, Again

In January, after returning from the *PokerStars* Caribbean Adventure World Poker Tour tournament in the Bahamas, I was off to the Seneca World Poker Classic in Niagara Falls, New York, where I met a very special woman who was not a poker player—and fell in love.

I did a little seminar at the tournament with Phil Laak, the "Unabomber." Afterward, I went to this nice gourmet Italian restaurant in the casino. I was there by myself having a nice meal—I'm okay eating alone and reading a magazine. The restaurant wasn't busy, and the waitress kept coming over to my table—way more than normal—which got my attention. I was between girlfriends at the time, and I remember thinking she was really cute. I had never hit on a waitress until I struck up a conversation with Jennifer Snyder.

We talked about why I was there for the seminar and the tournament and that I'd be there for another four or five days. I asked her if she had a boyfriend or a husband, and she said she had neither. So, I asked her out to dinner. She said yes, and we went out two days later. We had a couple of dates, nothing physical, and then I had to leave, but I kept in touch with her. We talked on the phone a lot, and I was falling for this waitress who lived in Buffalo, New York. I was able to—finally—convince her to come out to Vegas for a visit, staying with me in a separate bedroom. We went to a show six nights in a row . . . never did that before and never will again. We went everywhere and she had a great time.

It was a long-distance relationship, but we were getting along grand. I was trying hard to convince her to give me a chance. She came out for a few more visits, and I took her on a poker cruise, along with my brother and sister-in-law. I think they had the same concerns as Jennifer's family when she introduced me when I visited her in Buffalo. They were shocked that she was dating a guy 25 years older than her.

I asked her to marry me and live with me in Las Vegas. I for sure was not going to move to Buffalo. But Jennifer was a Buffalo girl, born and bred. You can take the girl out of Buffalo, but you can't take Buffalo out of the girl. After we had dated on and off for about a year, she ditched me for good. I was in love with Jennifer, but she was not in love with me. She told me she was afraid of me. I think I was too intense.

We are still friends to this day, and she calls me once in a while when she needs a sympathetic ear. She married a guy who called me once out of jealousy, until I explained I was no threat to their relationship. I saw her once again in 2013, when she and her mother came out to Arizona for a family funeral, and they drove over to Vegas. We had dinner and a nice chat.

On a side note, Jennifer and I helped Des Wilson, the author of *Ghosts at the Table: Riverboat Gamblers, Texas Rounders, Internet Gamers, and the Living Legends Who Made Poker What It Is Today,* with some of the research for his book. Wilson, who is British, acknowledged both of us in his book for helping him with his research.

Poker Training

I was recruited to be an instructor for ProPlay, which at the time was a new and innovative way for players to learn winning poker strategy. It incorporated advanced poker training through online videos from pro players that included Anne Duke, Greg Raymer, Erik Seidel, and me giving our personal insights on a variety of poker games. Last I looked, the website was still up but not active. Needless to say, the concept was not a stunning success.

More Poker Broadcasting Flops

It was nice having my time in such demand. In addition to poker-training invitations, I was sought after by the burgeoning poker broadcast media. *CardPlayer.com* started a new radio show called "*The Circuit,*" hosted by Mike "The Mouth" Matusow as he toured the world poker tournaments, and I was interviewed as a seasoned poker pro that frequented many tournaments on "the circuit." The show didn't last long.

I was a guest on the first season of *Pokerbeat*, a half-hour television show released in November. It was primarily filmed at the Wynn, Sunset Station, and Plaza casinos in Las Vegas. The format was to showcase up-to-the-minute poker news alongside strategies and insights provided by the game's top players and industry insiders. The producers of the show promoted it as the way to get the inside scoop on poker. It ended up being another one and done.

2006 Net Poker Proceeds $34,000
Non-poker Proceeds $28,000

—2007—

Parting Ways with *Card Player* Magazine

Tom McEvoy's
Tournament Talk

I had been a regular columnist at *Card Player* magazine for over a decade. I really enjoyed receiving emails from players that posed interesting questions that formed the basis of many articles, as well as relating my own experiences on and off the felt. Typically, I would type the column as an email (you might remember I was a top typist in high school!) and send it in to the editors. They have their deadlines, so sometimes I would have Dana Smith ghostwrite a column for me; more than once when I was doing a tournament or something, and I just didn't have the time she would bail me out, but I wrote most of them. This was all after my good friend Linda Johnson had sold the magazine to the Shulmans in 1999.

I was paid about $100 an article, but the real benefit wasn't the money. It helped my recognition as a relevant poker pro some 20 years after winning the Main Event, it gave me a writing outlet and the ability to teach the game I love, and it provided the opportunity to get some free promotion for my poker books. Upon reflection, maybe I should have paid them.

Then they did something that made me furious. The coauthor of my first book, Roy West, was also a columnist and still a pretty good friend. He had also been a writer for the publication for a decade or so and they decided they were going to eliminate his column. So, he asked them would it be okay, not for pay, if he could write one last column thanking all his faithful readers. Steve Radulovich, who was the editor-in-chief at the time, said no. I'm not sure if he had the final say or not, but he delivered the message.

It was right about the time that competition in the form of new poker magazines was coming on the scene. For example, *American Poker Player* magazine had launched in October of this year. I was a popular poker author, and I had been asked to write a few articles for other poker magazines. Radulovich didn't like that. He felt that was disloyal. That's when I explained to him about loyalty. I said Roy West had asked for one last little column to thank his readers and you said no, and you expect loyalty when you did that to a guy who was your faithful, loyal worker for all that time. I basically politely told him to go pound sand. Writing for another magazine, that was my decision. I only wrote a few articles anyway. Regardless, the magazine had the audacity to accuse me of disloyalty. But *Card Player* didn't like my answer (or, apparently, my attitude), and we terminated our relationship right there on the spot.

WPT Poker by the Book: Chapter 2

Poker book authors, Top L to R: Johnny Chan, Dan Harrington,
Daniel Negreanu, Me. Bottom L to R: Barry Greenstein
and Antonio Esfandiari. Photo: World Poker Tour

On April 29, I mixed it up with five other poker-book authors in the World Poker Tour's second "Poker by the Book" specialty No-Limit Hold'em tournament, "Chapter 2." Frankly, I was a bit miffed at not being invited to the Chapter 1 tournament, since I had authored or coauthored more poker books than anyone in either "chapter."

The competition was remarkable (and entertaining, with a lot of ribbing going on), featuring three former WPT winners (Daniel Negreanu, Barry Greenstein, and Antonio Esfandiari) and three former WSOP champions (Johnny Chan, Dan Harrington, and me). The first-place prize in this "made-for-TV" single-table shootout was a $25,500 entry into next season's WPT World Championship. Barry Greenstein won entry, and the rest of us earned a hearty pat on the back.

To win, Barry had to beat the runner-up, me. I made two big moves against him, and he picked them both off, to which Greenstein noted, "Most people don't know that Tom has that move in him." Bluffing is a big part of the game for all of us. So are side bets, and I'm sure there were side bets made that were higher than the prize purse, but I wasn't in that game.

From Russia, With Love

Early in the year, I took on a student who came to my house for a few lessons. He was on the verge of breaking up with his girlfriend and he kept raving about this "tour" he was going on to Russia to meet eligible ladies. This was after Jennifer Snyder from Buffalo dumped me, so I was between girlfriends once again and maybe a little distraught about my female-companionship situation. The more I thought about it, the idea appealed to my love of travel and the ladies. It sounded interesting and fun. So, I enlisted the help of my student and made arrangements to go to Russia with him on the same tour. He directed me how to sign up for the tour, get a visa, and all the stuff you had to do. Then, at the last minute, he reconciled with his girlfriend and cancelled. I never saw him again. Undeterred, that summer I went to Russia by myself.

During the trip I carried my passport on a lanyard around my neck. I had lost/misplaced/had it stolen before on my trip to Japan, and I wanted to make sure that never happened again. On a bus leg of the trip, I put the lanyard on a hook in the bathroom stall at a rest stop. And, you guessed it, walked out without it.

I realized when we got to the hotel 30 miles or so later what I had done. You can't get out of the country without your passport, so now I was starting to freak out. I talked to the tour guide, who was able to get me a cab driver (who didn't speak any English, of course), and tell him where to take me. I didn't have any choice, I had to do this. Before we got there, he had a flat tire, a blow-out on the highway; just what my nerves needed. When we got to the rest area, my passport wasn't in the stall any longer. There was a little stand there where you could buy snacks, and I went to inquire, and sure enough, they had my passport. Along with the passport on my lanyard I had some money, and it was all there. I tipped the lady—she didn't want to take any money—but I gave her what probably amounted to a month's salary. I cannot describe how happy I was to get it back. Seems I have a propensity to misplace my passport.

I think we stopped in one small city, but mainly the tour was to go to St. Petersburg. I never got to Moscow. I went to the Hermitage Museum and to the Peterhof Palace, both spectacular places. Some of the sites I visited with the tour and some on my own. Before I went to meet any Russian ladies, the tour people introduced us to our female interpreters. One of them was perky, smart, worldly, spoke excellent English and a few other languages, was well-traveled, obviously educated, and very smart. She immediately caught my eye. The tour put us up in a hotel and threw a couple of parties where you could move around and meet different ladies. But the only one I really liked was one of the interpreters, Irina Shilova. I asked her if she was interested, and when she said yes, I asked her out. With her leading the way, we went to a few restaurants and visited Peterhof Palace. I was only there for a week, but I really liked Irina. She was about 34 and had never been married. She wasn't a beauty queen, but she was cute. I was 63 years old at this time. Are you sensing a trend here?

A couple of times in a public place when I was going to say goodnight to her, I tried to give her a little kiss on the cheek. She turned her head, which in my country has a meaning. I wasn't attempting to make any sexual advances, so I shrugged it off. We had talked a lot, and it seemed to me that we had hit it off. After I left Russia, we kept up the communication on the phone. I was older than her, and if she wasn't interested, okay, I could understand. But I really liked her, and it sure seemed like she liked me.

After my trip to Russia, I only saw her one more time. I was working for PokerStars, and I had a trip they had paid for, as well as my entry fee into a tournament in Copenhagen. Irina had some kind of passport that allowed her to travel—I guess travel wasn't quite as strict as it used to be under the Communist regime. So, she came for a few days, and we stayed at the same hotel. Again, nothing physical. She had her own room. And we went out nightclubbing and for a few nice dinners. She was only there a few days. Me, too, for the tournament. I didn't fare well at that tournament in Denmark—I guess my thoughts were elsewhere.

So that contact kind of kept things going. I made it quite clear neither one of us had any obligations. We talked about it, and both decided the next step would be for her to come to the United States So, I spent the better part of a year getting her a fiancée visa. She had been to the United States once before as a tourist, so she was somewhat familiar with America, and I think she liked the idea of leaving Russia and living here. She had also worked in the past as a travel agent, or something connected to that, in Bermuda. I told her if she came to Las Vegas, she would have her own separate room at my house, and we would see how things developed. She agreed to the trip, so I worked with an agency that specialized in helping with this process. There was a lot of red tape and expense—several thousand dollars.

During that year, we were talking on the phone quite a bit. There was a 30-year gap between Irina and me in age. She did tell me she wanted a child. I could produce this for her, but I thought about it and wondered if it was right for us. I realized that this was part of the deal, and I didn't slam the door on it. Still, everyone in my life at the time thought me bringing a Russian girl here was a terrible idea.

We finally got Irina's fiancée visa in September 2008. With this visa, you can come for 90 days. And you either have to be married by the end of those 90 days, or you have to go back home. Then do it all over again if you want. I made it clear that neither one of us was committed. When I asked her how soon she would like to come, I was hoping she was ready to hop aboard the next plane. But she said she wanted to finish her work contract that ended in another four months before she came over. I wasn't crazy about that, but I told her if that's what she wanted to do, I was okay with that.

That delay was a mistake. In that time, another woman had come into my life, Yolanda, who would become my second wife (Chapter 23). Not once had Irina said anything affectionate like "I love you" or anything like that. There was never any of that kind of talk. Still, I felt I had to tell Irina about the new woman in my life, so I gave her a call. Irina said, "I know exactly what she did to get you." Now she started telling me that she told people at her work that she had found somebody she loved. I said, "You never said one word. I never had any idea how strong your feelings were." Regardless, Irina wasn't going to trust me again, I felt guilty, and I knew this romance was over.

In the meantime, she had told the people she worked for that she planned to go to the United States, and they got her replacement all lined up. If she hadn't told them her plans, she would have been able to keep her job. Her contract would have been renewed, but evidently now it wouldn't, and she lost her job at the end of her contract. That made me feel really guilty and lousy, so I sent her $1,500 twice just to help her. That was a lot of money over there. I had the money wired to her bank, and even then, she had problems before they would release the funds to her, but they did. If Irina had come right away, my life might have gone down a different path.

2007 Net Poker Proceeds $11,000
Non-poker Proceeds $52,000

—2008—

This was a pivotal year in my life. In May, I submitted my report on the scandalous online poker cheating going on at UltimateBet.com, which I cover in-depth in the next chapter. In June, I cashed in two events at the 39th World Series of Poker at the Rio casino, the $1,000 No-Limit Hold'em Seniors event (28th for $7,669), and the $1,500 Pot-Limit Hold'em event (24th for $5,547). I met my next wife, Yolanda DeHoyos, which I will cover in-depth in Chapter 23. I continued to represent PokerStars online and at live events (Chapter 20), and I spent a lot of time making money teaching poker, which I'll talk about in Chapter 25.

Good Investment, Bad Timing

I had purchased my house on Gisborn Drive in 2000, and my $200,000 freeroll cash at the WPT's Professional Poker Tour event in 2005 gave me the funds to pay off the mortgage, with quite a cushion of cash to spare. I made $62,000 in both 2006 and 2007. In other words, for the first time in many years, I had substantial funds in the bank.

Then, in the late summer, good old Tom McEvoy karma descended on me again. My next-door neighbor and his wife were getting a divorce, which was no big surprise to me. This guy and I had had very unpleasant confrontations on more than one occasion. He was part of the reason I spent a couple thousand dollars and had the brick wall surrounding my backyard raised a couple of feet all over for added privacy. I had a hot tub back there, and when I had parties, it annoyed the heck out of him. If we were a little loud after dark, he would yell and scream at us.

I still had the pistol I had bought after Marty Sigel had threatened my life. My neighbor was a big tough guy who could mangle me in a fight. One time he came over and was banging relentlessly on my front door. Scared me. I retrieved my pistol, and if he busted through that door, I was going to shoot him in the leg. Only time in my life I thought I might have to use it. So, you see, there was no love lost between us.

When his house went on the market my first thought was "good riddance." Then, I thought, why not buy it as an investment property? The house was the same model as mine, except I have a downstairs bedroom and my nasty neighbor was a handyman-type guy who had a really big extended garage instead of the bedroom. He also had a small waterfall pond in the back and a nice tree. And, after all, this is Las Vegas, and the value of real estate always goes up here. Right? Sure.

So, I bought the property next door for $353,000 in July. On September 29, the stock market crashed, and the bottom fell out of the real estate market. I paid too much for the second house, inadvertently doing my blankety-blank neighbor the biggest favor of his life by purchasing his house when the market was high. If only I had held off for just a month or two and bought it after the market crashed. My timing was just incredibly bad on so many things.

*Cheats prosper until there are enough who bear grudges
against them to make sure they do not prosper.*

—Peter Singer

CHAPTER 22

The Saga of Russ Hamilton, WSOP Champion and Online Cheater.

The beginnings of online poker got off to a tragic start after three of the big five poker sites, UltimateBet, Absolute Poker, and Full Tilt, were involved in cyber-cheating fiascos. Party Poker and PokerStars remained above the fray. Russ Hamilton, the 1994 WSOP Main Event World Champion, was one of the own-ers of UltimateBet. He and his  confederates were ripping online players off because, unknown to their opponents, they were able to see their challengers' hole cards. Some estimates put the insider fleecing of players at over $20 million. I know for a fact the cheating happened, because he paid me handsomely to do an audit that he hoped would document no dishonesty was occurring. Much to his chagrin, my analysis documented outright fraud was taking place. Here's what happened.

Buzz was gaining momentum within the online poker community for several years prior to the end of 2007 that the hot new poker venue, online poker, was becoming more and more, well, suspicious. That's when top pro high-stakes players exposed the cheating scandal, via poker forums like Sklansky and Malmuth's *Two Plus Two*, after their fishy experiences on UltimateBet. Speculation was that nobody could beat top pros at the rate they were getting spanked. It was impossible. Something was going on. The online poker community was beginning to smell a rat.

By now it was all over the internet that many were questioning the integrity of the UltimateBet site. People that were losing online had records of some of the hands played that didn't make sense to them. They suspected cheating, and they were right! The anonymous players behind the screen names—Russ and some of his confederates—were making impossible plays that couldn't logically happen unless they knew exactly what type of hand they were up against. At first, the company refused to acknowledge the accusations. That's when Russ contacted me, I believe, in an effort to prove the company innocent.

I had heard some of the rumors going around. There was something afoot and there was a growing feeling that something was not right. But I knew Russ, and he was one of the likeable guys I had gotten to know in the poker community. The best con men are likable people. That's what makes them good con men. At this time, I had no clue that Russ himself was the chief suspect in all this.

Before the crap could totally hit the fan, Russ devised a plan to put this controversy in check. He went to his employee, Bonnie Damiano, who was running a sister UltimateBet site for blackjack. Bonnie was a good friend of mine who had hosted a HORSE league I played in for several years (and went on to gain fame hosting several major poker tournaments). Bonnie told me Russ came to her with the idea of doing a hand-analysis audit and asked her for the name of the most honest person she could think of to carry out this unique mission. Someone honorable, well-respected in the poker community, with the experience and capability to do this type of analysis. She told him the first name that came to mind was Tom McEvoy. Russ got honesty, alright. More than he bargained for.

Speaking of bargains, Russ then came to me and asked if I would be interested in doing the UltimateBet audit and wanted to know how much I would charge. At the time I was getting $200 an hour giving poker lessons, so I said I would do it for that. And he said, fine, okay, you're hired. Later, when all the hours were tallied, my fee amounted to $50,000. And I did get paid.

Why did he hire me to do an audit on his crooked accounts? It took me awhile to figure all this out, but here's what I think. Russ Hamilton was very street-smart. He knew that I was a square shooter, with a reputation to match. Russ must have thought, what better way to give UltimateBet a clean bill of health than an audit from a poker expert who was known for his integrity, like me. I think he wanted to be able to say, "Well, we hired McEvoy to do an audit, and he says everything's okay."

Russ Hamilton thought naïve Tom McEvoy could be manipulated. He told me he didn't think there was any cheating going on, but he wanted me to take a look at it. He kept implying that everything was on the up-and-up. He told me if he liked my report, he had another $200,000 to $250,000 worth of work for me. Understand the subtlety of that? It's not like he offered me money to write a favorable report—it wasn't like that. It was more subtle, just little hints here and there . . . future work and future benefits. I wasn't financially broke at the time, but an additional quarter-million dollars would have been a big chunk of income for me. He wasn't talking chump change. I think the reason he hired me was that he thought he could con me into giving a very favorable report saying that there was no cheating going on. But I was never even tempted to do a false report. My reputation was worth way more than any money he or anybody else could pay me.

By the way, paying me a couple hundred thousand on top of what he did would have been a drop in the bucket compared to what he stole.

Russ gave me over 10,000 hands, all typed up on sheets of paper. The whole play of the hands from start to finish. I analyzed them over several months, starting in early 2008. I kept track of my time. I went a little over 250 hours, but I charged him exactly $50,000.

Of those 10,000 hands I examined, most played out normal. However, I discovered approximately 1,000 hands that were questionable. About 10 percent. And of those questionable hands, I narrowed it down to about 100 that were absolute, outright fraud. About 1 percent. I'm sure now that a lot more hands were influenced by a crooked player's knowledge of the opponents' hole cards, but I outlined and wrote up the hands I knew made no sense at all individually. So, I had about 10 percent of the hands as questionable, and at least 1 percent that were clearly cheating. And I wrote up the report that way. (I still have the entire report.)

I was not given specific players' names. Most played under fictious names anyway—both those being conned and those doing the conning. Turns out that Russ and his coconspirators were using several screen names.

After compiling the audit over three to four months, I gave the finished report to Russ Hamilton, my employer. After he read it, he paid me. I guess he figured it would look bad if it got out that he hired me and then stiffed me. He complimented me and told me the report was very well done, and that he was going to forward it the Gaming Commission in Canada. Of course, he just stuck it in his safe and it never saw daylight. I found out later why. Russ was the chief culprit and chief suspect.

At this point, nobody knew exactly who did what. That is, until one of Russ's confederates who was trying to protect his own fanny secretly taped a conversation that took place in their lawyer's office. Then he decided to share it with the poker world. On the tape, Russ Hamilton admits to his lawyer that, yes, he did cheat, just like the poker world was saying he did. Then Russ says, in effect, let me make one thing perfectly clear. I'm not going to make good on this. I understand my name came up during the taped conversation. The collaborators were fearful of my report, and that I might start connecting the dots, which I did eventually. Took a while. Like I say, I was a little bit naïve, to say the least.

It turned out Russ Hamilton never had to go to court. Even though he was guilty as hell, this brave new online poker world was all uncharted territory, and the legal system didn't know what to do with him. The Gaming Commission that Russ told me my report was going to go to was in Canada, so maybe there was a jurisdiction problem. There were a lot of legalities involved that I don't fully understand, but the bottom line is that Russ never got prosecuted. Technically, he got away with it. And he destroyed some people financially, and emotionally, too, at the same time. Yukon Brad Booth, a Canadian, was an example of a guy who was considered a top player that Russ kept challenging to play heads-up and kept beating. Mike Matusow was another one that kept playing him. These guys apparently just couldn't imagine how they could keep losing, you know? Unfortunately for them, they paid a price for their stubbornness and, some could say, their stupidity.

When the taped confession came out, my report became redundant, and I didn't feel the need to prove or publicize it. The fact that I did a report did eventually come out. Somebody I don't know was doing an exposé, and he surmised that since the report never saw daylight, I had basically acquiesced to the chicanery. He was under the wrong impression that because of my previous friendship with Russ Hamilton, my report had favored him, and when I got in touch with him, he started to question my integrity. Obviously, he had not seen or read the report. I offered to give him a copy of it. Or, since I had given a separate copy to my friend Wendeen Eolis, a high-powered New York executive, he could get a copy from her. I told him I stated in the report that there was cheating going on—no ifs, ands, buts, or maybes. I made it as clear as possible that in my opinion there was hanky-panky happening. He must have believed me because he said he didn't see the need to see the report. I think he was a bit disappointed there was no new addition to the scandal story.

Could be this reporter knew that Wendeen Eolis was above reproach. She created the legal search industry when she started the first search company exclusively for attorneys and founded the National Association of Legal Search Consultants. This high-powered lady was connected in both the political and poker worlds. She was a special advisor to New York Mayor Rudy Giuliani, and once kept Vice President Al Gore's phone call on hold because she was in the middle of a poker hand. She is a friend of mine and my daughter, Melanie, and she spoke to my integrity and the Russ Hamilton story at my Poker Hall of Fame induction ceremony. Wendeen is the kind of friend who flew from a humanitarian mission in Ecuador to attend my second wedding, played in my poker tournament the following day, then flew back to South America. She is also the first woman to cash in the World Series of Poker Main Event more than once.

As an aside, I want to address the involvement of Phil Hellmuth in the UltimateBet scandal. Or rather, his lack of involvement. When the poker site first started, Phil, the all-time leading WSOP brace-let winner, was a chief spokesman with a piece of the action. But about six months prior to my little audit, and before the poop hit the propellers, he had resigned and stepped away from UltimateBet. He escaped any kind of real negative fallout. People knew he was connected to the site, obviously, but they also felt he wasn't involved in any of this scandal, and they were right! Phil Hellmuth has done a lot of things, but cheat? He would never cheat anybody. Never. He thinks he is the best player in the world, so he doesn't have to cheat. And wouldn't, even if he could. Phil is a totally honorable guy. I don't know and have never asked him if he had an inkling something was not quite right, or what. As usual, his instincts were right.

My father gave me the best advice of my life. He said,
"Whatever you do, don't wake up at 65 years old and think
about what you should have done with your life."
—George Clooney

CHAPTER 23

♣ ♦ ♥ ♠

October 2008 to 2010. I'm All In.
A New Lady and a Wedding.

In November 2009, I turned 65. It was quite a year. But first we are going to go back to late 2008.

The Last Three Months of 2008

Not long after I bought the house next door to mine on Gisborn Drive in Vegas as an investment property, it was available for rent. One of my first tenants would become my second wife. Yolanda Stock was 37 years old. I was 64.

Yolanda's story

Yolanda was a single mother of Mexican decent, and she and her son Ronnie lived in Texas. Yolanda has always been resourceful and full of ideas to make ends meet. She got permission to sell tacos outside a nightclub in San Antonio owned by Ron Stock, a single divorced father with a couple of daughters. He was an attractive, athletic guy who owned more than one nightclub. Ron noticed Yolanda, this hot Mexican babe, bought some of her tacos, and soon they were dating. Ron really liked both Yolanda and her son Ronnie. He proposed to Yolanda when Ronnie was either three or four because he felt the boy needed a dad, and Ron wanted to be that dad. They got married, and Ron adopted Ronnie.

Then, disaster struck. One of the other nightclubs Ron owned was in Little Rock, Arkansas. There was a murder on his property, a shooting in the parking lot. Not his fault the rednecks decided to shoot it out. After a lawsuit, he was forced to declare bankruptcy. On top of being out of the nightclub business, he developed throat cancer. And he never smoked.

Meanwhile, he and Yolanda were starting to have problems. They used to go to Tunica, Mississippi, and Las Vegas all the time. Yolanda liked playing slots, and Ron loved to gamble—everything—craps, horse races, poker. Like most gamblers, he was not successful. They were living in Texas, and he was struggling with lawsuits and bankruptcy. That's when, as Ron told me, Yolanda, for a lot of reasons, decided to break up with him. Then Ron was diagnosed with stage-four throat cancer that the doctors said was going to kill him. Even though they had split up, Yolanda, admirably, decided to prove the medical profession wrong and nurse Ron back to health. So, they got back together, with her basically as his nurse. In my mind she gets a lot of credit for that—not many people would have done what she did. Ironically, Ron's younger brother also got cancer at the same time, and he passed away. But not Ron; he got through it. Cancer did not kill Ron.

It was now 2008 and Ron had recovered. He was going to live now, but he wasn't in great shape. Not too many people survive stage-four cancer. He did. Ron and Yolanda were still married, but according to Ron, she told him she wanted her life back. She wanted to leave it all behind and start afresh by moving to Las Vegas.

In September 2008, Yolanda had separated from Ron and headed west to Vegas, and she needed a place to live. Her ex-brother-in-law was married to a relative of my good friend and previous tournament sponsor Ron McMillan, so she asked him if he knew of any places for rent. He called me to see if a room in my second house was available and let me know he had a friend looking for a place. I asked him to send her on over.

Yolanda came to the house and brought her aunt with her. I was a PokerStars pro at the time, and when she knocked on the door, I was playing in an online poker tournament. I let them in, briefly explained why I was busy, and let her know the room for rent was upstairs in my house next door. I gave her the key and asked her to go check it out to see if she liked it. Her aunt thought I was crazy. Who hands their house key out to a total stranger? Are you sure you want to do this, her aunt asked? Yolanda said she thought I looked harmless. I finished the online tournament and went next door to the house to see what she thought. She had decided to take the place, but she negotiated with me first. She claimed she didn't have enough money to pay the full rent but was good at cleaning and pointed out that my bachelor-pad house and my rental house both looked like they could use some house cleaning. I agreed to knock $75 a week off the rent price if she would clean my houses. She agreed on the spot.

I had another renter using the other bedroom in my rental, a former student of mine and her boyfriend. They didn't exactly hit it off with Yolanda. Not long after she moved in, she was fulfilling her obligation, cleaning my house. I started talking with her, and being free that night, asked her to dinner. Yolanda was a poker player, too, but for small stakes, and my poker notoriety was a big attraction to her. Plus, I wasn't unattractive and was reasonably well off, compared to her current modest standards. It became obvious to both of us that night that things were going to get personal. Even after I told her about the Russian woman, the fiancée visa, and her imminent visit, Yolanda decided I was available. It didn't take long before she determined that she would prefer living in the main house . . . with me.

I pushed back a little, to see if she was concerned about the big age gap of 26-plus years. That didn't deter Yolanda. She set to work implementing Ron McMillan's advice. She asked him how to get to me, and he told her I like head rubs and good cooking. So that's what she did. Yolanda was still technically a tenant, but she had other plans. (If you think men are in charge you are sadly mistaken.) Women decide what they want and have a way of achieving their goals when they set their mind to something. Men are not in charge, just allowed to think they are. The month after the stock market crashed, in October 2008, Yolanda was living in my house. And not in the spare bedroom.

Shortly after that, Yolanda landed a great job as a hostess in the high-stakes slots area at Caesars Palace. The job was all about taking care of the customers, making their stay comfortable and enjoyable. Get them show tickets, make dinner recommendations and arrangements, things like that. Her job was to be their best friend in Vegas. A couple of times I had dinner with her and one of her customers who wanted to show their appreciation. Sometimes the high-roller slot customers would give a little gift to the hostess, or even slip her some money. It was an excellent job at a great casino with nice fringe benefits.

2008 Net Poker Proceeds $3,600
Non-poker Proceeds $16,400

—2009—

Yolanda was busy in Las Vegas with her new full-time job at Caesars at the beginning of the year, and I was busy with my poker career. She didn't come with me when I went to the Dominican Republic for a World Poker Tour Boot Camp at the end of 2008, or when I went on the road early in 2009. In January, I cashed in the *PokerStars* Caribbean Adventure tournament, entry paid by *PokerStars* (of course), held on Paradise Island in the Bahamas. In April, I also cashed at the European Poker Tour tournament in San Remo, Italy. Entry also paid by *PokerStars*. Yolanda was not in Vegas when I won the World Series of Poker "Champion of Champions" tournament in May that pitted previous Main Event winners against each other—the subject of the next chapter—she was visiting friends in New York. It was possibly just as well she wasn't there. I probably did a better job without her as a distraction.

At this point, Yolanda's son Ronnie was still living in Texas with his adopted dad, Ron Stock. Like any mother, she wanted her nine-year-old son to live with her. So, Ron and Ronnie moved to Las Vegas and got a place that was within easy walking distance of my house. Ronnie floated back and forth for years between my house and his adopted dad's. After we were married, he spent most of his time with us.

This was when I first got to know Ron Stock. Evidently our paths had crossed years back when he had come to Vegas and played Limit Hold'em. I had no recollection of him, but he remembered playing with the world champion. Very typical. People remember playing with Tom McEvoy the World Champion, but Tom McEvoy has no clue who they are.

It didn't take long for me to literally become Ron's best friend, who at the time was technically still Yolanda's husband. People don't understand that, but if you know me and my character, you know I have deep empathy for people in need. Ron went from being a big shot, then lost his nightclubs and his health. He was down and out and he just couldn't crawl out of it, just couldn't handle it when his life went south. He basically threw in the towel for the last decade of his life. I could relate to being down and out, financially at least, and the more I got to know Ron, I discovered I really liked him. And due to the situation with Yolanda and Ronnie, we talked quite a bit and we got to be very close.

In June, Ron and Yolanda were formerly divorced. They were making a quiet dispersal of their marriage, and I was the witness to the divorce in a lawyer's office in Las Vegas. Before the papers were signed, Yolanda was talking with the lawyer in a different room, and I was all alone with Ron. I said, "Ron, this is your last chance. If you want to stay married to Yolanda, say so. Now's the time." He looked at me. He was quiet. Then he raised his voice with an "OHHH NO!" He didn't want to stay married to her.

Perhaps my friends and family had a feel for why. Almost all of them tried to talk me out of marrying Yolanda. They didn't see us as a match made in heaven, given her fiery personality and the age difference of almost three decades. And they expressed serious doubts about her intentions. But I had made a commitment to Yolanda to spend our future together, and I wasn't going to go back on my word.

In August, ESPN aired their coverage of the WSOP Champion of Champions tournament, and we had a big party at my house to celebrate. I used this very public special occasion to formally propose to Yolanda. We had shopped wedding rings, so I was pretty sure what the answer would be. As to the ring, it was down to two choices, but I got the hint. I bought the expensive one for $14,000. In retrospect, it was a stupid move on my part, to spend that kind of money. She has long since sold it. But I was in love. Or maybe in love with being in love.

Yolanda is a great cook, better than most restaurants at preparing south-of-the-border cuisine, and she loved to plan and host parties. This party had about 40 guests, including her now ex-husband Ron. He and I went out to get some ice, and I said to him, "Ron, I'm thinking about formally proposing to Yolanda at the party in front of everybody, including you. But, if that's something you are not comfortable with, I will do it privately." He said, "Nah, go ahead, and get her a little flower, too," and so we stopped on the way back and I got a single rose for her. I went down on bended knee and almost got trampled by the women at the party. It was a mob scene when they rushed forward, gushing over the ring.

I believe that Yolanda really did love me. She also liked my poker legacy and the comfortable lifestyle I lived, owning two houses and hosting a fair number of parties. My best guess is that my net worth at that time was in the range of $600,000 to $800,000, which was the high point of my life, financially. To protect my real estate assets, at the recommendation of my family, I transferred the deeds for both properties into a living trust.

PICClub.com

The Unlawful Internet Gambling Enforcement Act of 2006 (UIGEA) prohibited gambling businesses from "knowingly accepting payments in connection with the participation of another person in a bet or wager that involves the use of the Internet and that is unlawful under any federal or state law." This vague law, hastily tacked onto the end of unrelated legislation, was passed before anyone on the Senate–House Conference Committee had even seen the final language of the bill. It didn't make internet poker illegal, but it made U.S. banks stiff-arm the use of credit cards to fund their customers' internet poker.

That's when the Players Investment Company (PIC) Club was formed as a legal way to facilitate players getting their money into—and out of—over 100 internet poker websites. In 2009, I joined the PICClub.com Pro Team, uniting with my good friend T. J. Cloutier and nine other pros. To promote the concept, they held online bounty tournaments, hosted by the pros, as part of the *Bluff Magazine* Poker Tour. Unfortunately, the writing was on the wall for internet poker in the United States.

Busy Poker Year

It was a busy year on the poker circuit. I cashed in the $2,000 No-Limit Hold'em event at the 40th World Series of Poker in June. In July, I hosted a WPT satellite tournament held onboard the Palm Beach *Princess Casino* cruise ship that set sail out of

Florida. In August, I played in the first Binion's Poker Champions Tournament in Mississippi, followed by the first "Latin Series of Poker" event in San Jose, Costa Rica. At the October Poker Fest held at the Poker Room at St. John's Greyhound Park in Florida, Susie Isaacs and I conducted a Boot Camp with a $200 admission fee. And I participated in the Borgata Open in November in Atlantic City, New Jersey.

Net Poker Proceeds $43,000   Non-Poker Proceeds $19,500

—2010—

I started the year cashing in a couple of events at my now annual trek to the *PokerStars* Caribbean Adventure tournament in the Bahamas and scored another cash in the NAPT Deep Stack Extravaganza in February in Las Vegas. Also in February, I was on hand at the grand opening of the Choctaw Casino Resort in Durant, Oklahoma, hosting celebrity events along with T. J. Cloutier and Kathy Liebert. Early in March, I was "Cruising with Bonnie" for a week, sailing from San Diego to Acapulco with the Nevada Poker League and Bonnie Dominano-Leinhos. On May 14, Mike "The Mouth" Matusow and I put on a one-day Power Poker Course at the Daytona Beach Kennel Club & Poker Room, presented by DeepStacks Live. I was sitting pretty again financially. And then I decided to make a sizable expenditure.

Yolanda started the year with a venture into real estate. She purchased a property on Ronald Street (ironic, since her son and ex-husband are both Rons) in Vegas from our poker friend J. J. Liu, which she and her sister fixed up and flipped at a profit. She took one of the worst houses in a marginal neighborhood and turned it into the best house on the block. Quite an accomplishment for a novice who also had a full-time casino job.

McEvoy's Ultimate Gamble

On May 24, just a few days before the World Series of Poker began, Yolanda and I tied the knot, ending my 20-year run as a bachelor. Ron Stock, of all people, gave away the bride. After we were pronounced man and wife at the church, Ron jumped up, yelled, "Wait!" then proceeded to put a ball and chain on my arm. The pastor, who was in on the joke, quipped, "That's Tom's new World Series bracelet."

It was a "destination" wedding. The reception was in Paris, and the honeymoon was in Rio.

The reception was at the Paris casino in Vegas, a property owned by Caesars, Yolanda's employer. We had over 200 guests, so many that Yolanda and my good friends Buddy Ashmore and Candace Smith stayed up all night with Yolanda working on the seating charts. Too much for me—I gave up and went to bed. The planning worked without a hitch (pun intended). The party was epic, with food and entertainment, including my cousin Mark Hinds, who was a professional Kenny Rogers "know when to hold 'em, know when to fold 'em" impersonator. Brother Steve was my best man. With well-wishers all around all night, I never had a better time at a wedding or a party. I just wished I wasn't the one all-in for $60,000 or so for the grand event. Thank goodness Yolanda got an employee discount.

"All In," by the way, was spelled out on our wedding cake. And what other way is there to cap off a poker-themed McEvoy wedding than with a poker tournament. Yolanda wanted to host the tournament we called "McEvoy's Ultimate Gamble" as part of the celebration, and we held it the next day at Caesars Palace. The buy in was $230, with $200 bounties on T. J. Cloutier, Barry Shulman, Chad Brown, Dennis Phillips, Kathy Liebert, Susie Isaacs, Barbara Enright, Mike Matusow, Wendeen Eolis, and me. Wendeen had come all the way from Ecuador to be part of the festivities.

I had a great time throughout, and I was repeatedly asked where I was taking Yolanda on our honeymoon. I kept saying, "Rio." Not Rio de Janeiro in Brazil—the Rio Hotel & Casino, home then to the WSOP. Do you think I would leave town for a honeymoon during the World Series of Poker? I had my priorities straight.

Married life was good at first. If I was home too much, Yolanda would order me out of the house to go play poker and bring home the bacon. Yolanda's job at Caesars was going well and she was getting noticed by management. Her son Ronnie was spending more and more time with us, and we were having what I suspect are normal stepson issues. For example, he would play what I called the "Food Game." When we were ready to go out to eat and he didn't want to go, I said okay, but made it clear we were not bringing any food back with us, so he could go with us or fend for himself. This happened more than once until he finally changed his tune. I made it quite clear to Ronnie—his adopted dad was his dad, not me. I was not trying to replace him, and his dad was welcome over to the house any time. We got through it, and today the adult Ronnie and I get along famously.

By the way, prior to the wedding, Yolanda and I agreed to a five-year prenuptial agreement. In the event of a divorce, both of us were to retain ownership of the assets each had prior to the marriage, except Yolanda would get the house next door. With death, the surviving party would have all control of property, less personal family items. The prenup eventually expired with no action.

One month after we were married, Yolanda requested a leave of absence from Caesars to buy and flip houses in San Antonio, Texas, where she bought and fixed up two houses. Yolanda was working these real estate ventures basically on her own, with very little input from me.

Net Poker Proceeds $11,000   Non-Poker Proceeds $28,000

If you're a true warrior, competition doesn't scare you.
It makes you better.

—Andrew Whitworth

CHAPTER 24

♣ ♦ ♥ ♠

WSOP Champion of Champions Invitational Tournament.

The New York Times, June 2, 2009

Tom McEvoy Is World Series of Poker's Champion of Champions.

Tom McEvoy has been crowned the champion of champions at the World Series of Poker after beating previous main-event winners in a special tournament. McEvoy won the title early Tuesday after a two-day tournament that started with 20 former winners of poker's richest event. The field included Doyle Brunson, Johnny Chan and 11-time bracelet winner Phil Hellmuth. McEvoy did not win a gold bracelet for the event which was created for the series' 40th anniversary. He took home a restored 1970 Chevrolet Corvette worth $50,000 [I got $27,000 for it] *and the Binion Cup.*

For a few years in the mid-2000s, the World Series of Poker was run by Jeffery Pollack, who had the title of commissioner. He had a sports-marketing background and was always striving to get media attention for the WSOP. Pollack may be most remembered for his decision in 2007 to increase TV ratings by creating the "November Nine," postponing the broadcast of the final table from July to November. It worked.

The Champion of Champions Invitational Tournament was his brainchild. The idea was to celebrate the 40th anniversary of the World Series of Poker by inviting all of the living WSOP Main Event champions to a winner-take-all event. Pollack told me his plan was not to hold this every year, but to do it maybe every five years. Unfortunately, it was never held again. So, I was the first and last winner. A few weeks after I won the tournament, I had a big party at my house, and Pollack was invited. That's where he presented me with a really fancy WSOP Hall of Fame winter-weight jacket. I still use it when I visit my daughter in New York in December.

At that time, there were 25 living Main Event champions who were invited to compete in the two-day Champion of Champions Invitational Tournament. Twenty showed up to participate. This was a special event and not a bracelet tournament. Instead, the winner received the first-ever Binion Cup, a big silver loving cup trophy, named for the Binion family, who founded the World Series of Poker. Jack Binion, son of founder Benny Binion, presented the cup to me. I remember remarking, "This is the first time he handed me a trophy instead of money." In addition, the winner got a beautiful vintage 1971 cherry-red Corvette, which had been part of the Imperial Palace casino's auto collection. The car had been restored to showroom condition and had zero miles.

Can you imagine the poker talent at the tables? A historic photograph was taken of the past champions, and you could literally feel the electricity in the air. Everyone wanted to win the title, the cup, the car, and, not least of all, the bragging rights. I cannot remember facing a tougher lineup in my entire poker career.

The tournament started with three tables. After two players were eliminated, we went down to two nine-handed tables. Jamie Gold, the 2006 champion, had the unfortunate distinction of going broke very early in the first level of play. After that, one by one, the remaining players went broke until we got down to one final table of 10 players. That final table would come back to play the next day in front of the TV cameras, with ESPN airing the show a few months later. I have been at three televised final tables, finishing with two firsts and a second. I'm kind of proud of that.

The blinds started at $25/$50 with one-hour rounds. We battled for almost six hours the first day before we finally got down to the final eleven. One more to go to make the final table. Phil Hellmuth was determined to make the TV table, and after 2005 champion Joe Hachem went broke with slightly more in chips than Phil, the "Poker Brat" got his wish. Before play resumed the next morning, Doyle Brunson quipped that Phil had confirmed what he knew all along—that Phil would do anything to make the TV table. Doyle was in a humorous mood that day; he also said, "Where are all the internet players? Oh, there he is." He was referring to Peter Eastgate, the youngest player at the table, and the reigning champion.

Hellmuth, by far the shortest stack, drew the big blind on the very first hand. Carlos Mortensen, who busted Phil when he won the 2001 championship, would do it again by raising and putting Phil all in. He hemmed and hawed for a minute, then said that he would have to call with practically any two cards, and then did so with a suited 10 - 5. He was happy to see he was up against Carlos's pocket deuces. However, he didn't improve and was out on the first hand dealt. Phil was very gracious as he left the table, shaking everyone's hand and wishing us all good luck.

Peter Eastgate went out a few hands later. He raised preflop with 8 - 7 suited and got reraised by 1995 champion Dan Harrington. Peter thought about it for a while, then pushed all in. Dan rather humorously said, "Well, everybody has to take a stand sometime," and then called—with pocket aces. Peter flopped a pair with an open-end straight draw when the flop came 8 - 6 - 5. With two cards to come, Dan sweated it out, and Peter got no help. He went out in ninth place.

Along the way, I eliminated Doyle in eighth place. Later on, 1986 champion Berry Johnston, short-stacked to begin with, finally went broke to Carlos, and was soon followed to the rail by 1996 champion Huck Seed. I won a few pots against Carlos to become co-chip leader with Harrington. Then Carlos made top two pair against 1993 champion Jim Bechtel, but Jim had flopped a set, and Carlos went out in fifth place.

A Tom McEvoy mantra is, "Put yourself in a position to get lucky." In this tournament, I did. I put myself in the position to make the wrong play at the right time and get lucky.

With four players left, Robert Varkonyi, the 2002 champion, was on the short stack with a suited ace and made a raise. I was on the button with A - K off suit and reraised. Jim Bechtel, in the big blind with pocket kings, shoved, and Varkonyi quickly folded. I called and promptly discovered I was in worse shape than I thought. However, the poker gods smiled on me that day, and the flop revealed one of the two remaining aces in the deck. My hand held up, Bechtel was out, and I now had over half of the chips in play. I held the lead the rest of the way, but Harrington and Varkonyi were only one double-up from taking the lead.

We played three-handed for almost three hours before I busted Harrington with the K - Q of diamonds against his pocket nines. I called his all-in bet on a flop containing an ace and a queen. Dan is not known to be a big bluffer, so I knew he had a hand. But I decided, well, even if he had an ace, I had at least five outs with two cards to come. Still, I was fairly confident he didn't have an ace, and if he didn't, I had him. I was right, and my pair of queens held up.

If the players had bet on who would be the last two standing, Robert Varkonyi and Tom McEvoy would have been the long shots. But our colleagues didn't know our mindsets. I told the ESPN crew in my pre-tournament interview that nobody was more determined to win this event than I was. Why? Because I wanted to reestablish myself as a top-notch player who could still compete against the toughest competition. I also felt that Varkonyi, who played excellent poker the entire tournament, had something to prove. In my opinion he was a very underrated champion who wanted—and deserved—a higher level of respect from his peers. I knew that he would be tough to beat.

The tournament lasted a long time, finally ending at around 1 a.m. in the 12th level of play. When we got heads-up, I had almost a three-to-one chip lead, but I knew I was far from having this tournament locked up. I was right. Robert won a series of pots right off the bat with his aggressive play, and almost got even with me. I started to battle back, and then we played a huge pot that put him all in. He was basically on a semi-bluff with a straight-flush draw, but I had the top end of it blocked and had already made the nut straight, so he had only one out when he went all in. My hand held up, and I had the title of Champion of Champions. That is something I will cherish for the rest of my life.

It is interesting to note that the older players clearly dominated the final table. I hope there is a second Binion Cup, maybe to celebrate the 55th World Series of Poker in 2024. Wouldn't it be something to see if the old school of poker still rocks?

I remember thinking, when I initially saw the first-place prize, that beautiful red car, that I had always wanted a Corvette when I was younger. Now, if I had kept that car, one of two things would have happened. I would have earned way too many speeding tickets, because that's exactly the "go fast" brand of car that the police seem to zero in on, and I have a bit of a lead foot. Or I would crash and burn and likely kill myself. I was 64 years old when I won, on the verge of collecting Social Security, so I was no longer so interested in having a super-fast sports car.

If you are wondering what happened to the vintage Corvette, I sold it to Amarillo Slim for $27,000 cash. I got an offer the very next day for $1,000 more, but I keep my promises. If it had been Slim selling the car, there's no doubt in my mind, even after a verbal agreement, he would have sold it to the highest bidder. With Slim (or anybody else) I couldn't do that. But because I didn't trust Slim at all, I did do something that I'm sure irked him. He paid me in bundles of $2,000—not $5,000—each with a bank wrapper around it. When he gave me the money, I counted every bill in front of him. The total was correct; he didn't shortchange me. I knew he had shorted other people whenever he could, so this was my little insult to him. I understand he bought the car because he wanted it for his son.

Binion Cup Inscription

Binion Cup
The Champion of Champions
The 40th Annual World
Series of Poker
"Champion's
Invitational Winner"
In Honor of Poker's
First Family
June 1, 2009

Being able to help someone learn something is a talent.
—Margaret Riel

CHAPTER 25

Teaching and Coaching the Game I Love.

This seasoned poker coach is still available if anyone wants to hire me.

You may have noticed my end-of-the year "Non-Poker Proceeds" summaries have looked pretty good for the last four or so years. They do not include any royalties from my books, but for these years most of that extra money came my way from teaching poker. This took on many forms—seminars, private group sessions, and individual one- and two-person lessons.

I had an active teaching career for about 40 years. I've taught everyone from total novices who hardly knew what beat what, to pros who simply wanted to get better. Most of the people I taught were reasonably experienced poker players who knew their game was lacking and sought to improve. They didn't necessarily want to be professional players; they just wanted to be winning players. That was my only guarantee, that when the teaching was over, my students would be better poker players.

Seminars

I was asked a lot of times by people who were organizing poker seminars to be one of their speakers. For a while that was a major source of extra income for me. These seminars took many forms. Sometimes I would host seminars myself, but most of the time I worked in conjunction with other people, casinos, or organizations. Often the seminar was put together in combination with a tournament to help promote it and increase entries. The Wildhorse Resort in Pendleton, Oregon, marketed my seminar and their tournament by putting me on a $5 chip!

Most of the time, the seminars were intended to be money makers. Organizers would hire several speakers, usually pros, and I would be one of the pros. They would do all the advertising and marketing, facility arrangements, recruit the students, collect the money, and then pay me for my appearance. Depending on the type of seminar, I would prepare and teach on certain requested poker topics, like cash games or tournaments, or particular games such as No-Limit Hold'em or Razz. So, there was a fair degree of preparation required, but sometimes all I had to do was show up and answer questions from the audience.

A lot of times in my seminars I would use the *PokerStars* website to demonstrate my lessons. I remember I played Vanessa Rousso heads-up one time in a seminar on the *PokerStars* site. We were both part of the same seminar, but they put us in different rooms to play online. The match was hyped and there was speculation as to who was the favorite and all that. I beat her in one hand that I shouldn't have. I semi-bluffed a hand—actually, I had meant to check it but hit the wrong button, moving all in instead. She folded. I had King high and a busted flush. In this case, the lesson was on me, which illustrates my next point. By teaching poker, I often felt like I learned more than I taught. As the adage goes, Hold'em takes a minute to learn and a lifetime to master. I'm still working on it.

Group Lessons

Sometimes I was able to offer my own group training in connection with poker tournaments. For example, as part of Hollywood Park Casino's "Sport of Kings" poker tournament series, I was able to offer poker group training, charging $449 for a full day.

T. J. Cloutier and I did a lot of joint private lessons together, many times in my home. For an afternoon, with a small group of a dozen or so players, we would earn up to $2,000 each. On top of the teaching, a lot of the time was spent answering lifestyle questions, telling stories, and socializing.

Here's another example. I was invited to Ohio for many years in a row to spend several days teaching a group of guys. They paid all my expenses plus my fee. I would teach a while, then play little freezeout tournaments. Then I would go one-on-one with each player privately and evaluate their game. Sometimes the evaluation would be in a group session discussing where they needed to improve and so forth.

Sometimes I taught group lessons by playing online events, like a one-table sit-and-go. The students could see my cards and I would discuss what my thinking and strategy was. They loved it when I would win, which happened a fair amount. I remember one session when I folded A - J, and my students were perplexed, asking why on earth I would throw away A - J? There were three of us in the pot, one went broke with A - Q and the other won with A - K. I would have been third. I explained why, and I could see light bulbs going off in some of the students' heads. I can't tell you how gratifying it is when all of a sudden, a student is starting to get it . . . to really understand. It's not just your hand you are playing, it's the broader perspective of other factors such as your opponents' hands, their tendencies, table position, and table situation. Poker is so much more than the cards in your hand.

Private Lessons

I've given private lessons to at least 100 different people one-on-one or two-on-one. After I bought my house in 2000, I had a steady stream of people coming over for lessons. These students found me mostly by word of mouth, from previous happy customers telling their friends. I was charging $200 an hour, and there were no complaints. Well, a few complaints. I returned a student's fee once after his lesson was interrupted by an urgent phone call and then an intruding houseguest who thought he knew more about poker than me.

I started my training sessions with new students by first talking a bit to get a feel for how advanced they were. Then I patterned my lesson to be in stride with their level. In the beginning, I used to have to deal out hands and then talk about situations: What would you do when you were first to act, etc. Sometimes I would prearrange the cards, and other times they would be random.

When internet poker got rolling, it was a lot easier to teach private students. Playing real poker for real money in real time on the internet was a great teaching tool. I would sit down at the computer, and my students would sit down beside me and watch and listen. This method of instruction improved my teaching technique. And I could get a lot more training hands in a session than I could just randomly dealing physical cards. I evolved as a teacher as poker on the internet progressed.

One of my best students, Danielle Striker, found me by searching "online poker coaches." She was amazed to learn I lived only a few blocks from her. I had a website for a while that I didn't do much with, but some students found me that way. Another student, Sam Waldner, also found me online. I made a lot of friends teaching poker, and today Sam and Danielle are among my very best friends.

Free Lessons

It wasn't all about getting paid. I was approached by a friend to be the grand prize for a Long Beach, California, elementary school's fundraising effort. The winner got a trip to Las Vegas, paid for by the school, along with a little Vegas hospitality and a poker lesson from me. Getting involved in charity events has always given me great satisfaction.

Becoming a Winning Player

By my guestimate, only around 10 to 15 percent of casino poker players are profitable players, after the rake (the money out of each pot the casino collects as their profit) and dealer tips. Fact is, because of the rake and tips, you have to be a winning player just to break even. In other words, most people who play poker for money lose. Many play more for entertainment and camaraderie than to make money. Most poker players like to win, but most don't do what it takes to consistently win. Because it takes too much effort.

I have always maintained that to be very successful at poker, you have to be dedicated almost to the point of fanaticism, to have a real thirst to examine your game, seek to understand your weaknesses ("leaks"), and continue to get better. Once I decided to be a professional poker player, I dedicated my whole life to it. I know what it takes to get to the top, but most people aren't willing to make that kind of sacrifice.

I've had some students who *were* willing. I never had a student who worked harder than Danielle Striker. She is highly intelligent, much smarter than I am. She needed guidance on how to get better. Once she started playing poker, she became enamored with it, studied hard, took lessons from multiple pros, and now she crushes cash games. Frankly, she has progressed way beyond me.

And I've had several students who became successful tournament players. Four have won World Series of Poker bracelets—Kathy Liebert, Larry Wright, Louis Asmo, and David Perry. Two people I coached extensively have finished third in separate years in the WSOP Seniors event, Barry Bounds and Paul Fischman.

I always considered poker more of a mental sport than a physical sport. Tournaments are very much both, from an endurance standpoint. But from the mental aspect, there are some players today who think way beyond my capabilities. They think in different layers. The sophistication level of poker players has risen so dramatically in the years since I first got involved. The game has evolved and grown, and I am proud to have done my part to further the game I love.

Winning Advice

1. Be dedicated to the point of devotion.
2. Slow down. Think it through.
3. No bad gambling habits and other leaks (like, in my case, women).
4. Make poker a lifelong learning experience. Read, study, get coaching. I even had some coaching after I won the World Series.
5. Never gamble on credit.
6. You must want to win—to kill them.
7. Learn how to lose.

If you're going through hell, keep going.
—*Winston Churchill*

CHAPTER 26

2011 to 2013. Black Friday and Other Bad Tidings.

—2011—

As marital responsibilities go, Yolanda and I had anticipated a more or less traditional marriage. Poker was my career, and it was my job to bring home the bacon. From Yolanda's perspective, I was a "manly man," and as such, wanted to be the breadwinner. She knew I didn't cook or clean, so that would be her responsibility. I paid the household bills and Yolanda worked full-time to pay her own way and to afford her luxuries. In addition to that, Yolanda has great taste, and she made our house a home by redecorating. Shortly after we got married, she did a lot of things I really liked, like redoing the stairs in a fashion that was a homage to poker and adding new showcase shelves to show off my trophies. Our 2,100-square-foot home became sort of a shrine to my poker career and accomplishments, something we were both proud of.

Early on, I looked to help my new wife as best I could. I bought Yolanda an inexpensive foreign car. She was having problems with her credit, and I helped by paying off several thousand dollars of her debt. In turn, she hosted, catered and, frankly, cleaned up after the many parties we had for my poker friends.

The first year after we were married, we both put on some extra weight. Yolanda's cooking was fabulous, and now I was eating regularly and well. Some people say that's what happens when you're happy.

Was it all cake and roses? No. Yolanda is a fiery, hot-blooded Latina, and sometimes she would communicate her point of view very loudly. I was becoming better acquainted with a personality trait that would eventually be part of our downfall. Yolanda had the highest respect for her own opinion. She would be doggedly determined that her viewpoint was the right one, no matter what kind of arguments I or others had to the contrary. On top of that she had a temper—one time while we were still engaged, she took off the engagement ring and tossed it at me. But I didn't want a wimpy-type wife, and I got what I wanted. Yet these were the core differences between us that, unfortunately, would grow.

After we got married, we started going out for meals more and more. Looking back, I probably spent way too much money on dinners and stuff. I like to eat well; I always have. My favorite thing to do in this world is to go out for a quality dinner with good friends and enjoy good conversation. Bottom line was that we were establishing a lifestyle that we stubbornly refused to abandon when times suddenly got tough.

Black Friday

Online poker was booming across the globe. Huge sites like PokerStars, Full Tilt Poker, UltimateBet, and Absolute Poker were raking in the money, and even smaller sites like Doyle's Room were flourishing. I was a benefactor, earning close to $100,000 a year in salary, tournament entry fees. and related expenses from PokerStars.

Then, on April 15th, 2011, Black Friday, the poker world went into shock. When I logged in that day, I learned what online poker players all across the United States learned. The Department of Justice had seized the site, and we could no longer access our accounts—or our money.

A few months after this infamous date, PokerStars gave their players access to their money. Players on the other major sites had to wait, some for years. After Full Tilt paid their principles nearly $100 million in bonuses, and zero to their U.S. customers, they became the pariah of the poker world. PokerStars bought them the next year and paid back the American players.

But as of Black Friday, PokerStars was out of the U.S. market. And by the middle of the year, I was out of the best job of my life. I was very vocal about how I felt about this. I thought it was stupid beyond belief that the U.S. Government was criminalizing online poker. Our federal and state governments were always looking for new sources of revenue, and the online sites were a huge, missed opportunity. Black Friday sent all that money elsewhere. It was like Prohibition, where they tried to legislate morality; it doesn't work. I feel the same today—people have the right to do what they want with their own money inside their own homes.

I have a tremendous respect for PokerStars and everything they did and have done for online poker. And for me. But when the bottom dropped out, I knew they were not going to need me and a lot of the other professional players on their roster. Sure enough, they cut me loose mid-year. Actually, they offered me and others a dramatically reduced employment package. This represented a big loss to my income, and I was wholly unprepared for the devasting financial impact.

I honestly feel my life would have been dramatically different—better—if PokerStars had not been shut down in the United States by the government. It started the downward financial spiral I endured.

Face Up Gaming

At the urging of my poker pal Bonnie Domiano, I accepted an invitation that was better than the new PokerStars offering to become the head pro advisor and instructor for Face Up Gaming in June. In response to Black Friday, their concept was to provide a 100 percent legal nonwagering subscription-based poker site where players competed for monthly cash and prizes, tournament event seats, cash freerolls, and even poker cruises—a concept that was ahead of its time. Heavily advertised in *Card Player* and *Bluff* magazines were the free monthly lessons I gave to "platinum members." The big benefit for me: They paid me a tidy sign-up bonus as well as my entry into the WSOP Main Event. Of course, they promoted my association heavily and said really nice things about me.

For example, Felix Elinson, the CEO of Face Up Gaming, said, "Tom McEvoy is one of the most recognizable names in the poker world and a true gentleman of the game. Tom has an undeniable reputation for integrity and is a world-class poker player."

The new job kept me busy, but the reduction in renumeration was dramatic, and I didn't replace it. I lost my ability to be the breadwinner. And that put a strain on my marriage. On top of that, Yolanda thought I was a little lazy during this time period, playing a lot online and still giving lessons, but I didn't want to go out and ply my poker trade, or "hustle," in person much anymore. She told me many times to get out of the house and go play poker, which is the exact opposite of what most guys have to deal with. I still had money in the bank, and I was sort of coasting.

High on the Hog

Frankly, Yolanda and I were living beyond our means, and even though we understood what had happened, we did not cut back as we should have. I resumed investing in stamps, figuring incorrectly—again—that I was making a reasonable investment. And we were racking up credit card debt. I was still active on the poker tournament circuit, and neither PokerStars nor Face Up Gaming had paid my buy-ins or expenses to the less prominent of them, and I was playing without a sponsor most of the time. Playing and cashing in tournaments in Oregon, Oklahoma, and Aruba this year didn't cover expenses.

Net Poker Proceeds $(-8,800)
Non-Poker Proceeds $27,000

—2012—

Home Poker League

I had been one of ten players in a home poker league for a few years, hosted monthly at one player's home per year. This year the league moved to my house. I collected five dollars from every player for food, which didn't cover costs because Yolanda was such a phenomenal cook. She made all the food and catered everything herself—even decorated the place to make things special.

Each player put $250 in the pot per session for ten tournament sessions, with points awarded based on how each finished. My friend and poker student Danielle Striker won the league and a seat in the 2013 Main Event. I was lucky enough to come in second, which partially funded my WSOP tournament entries that year. Each winner got 50 percent of their own action, with the remaining league participants vested proportionately in the remaining 50 percent.

As host, I was treasurer of the league, and to evidence my dwindling financial situation, I sometimes took temporary "loans" from the league to pay my monthly bills. I was completely transparent about this, and all the players were fully aware. These loans were repaid in full by the end of the league, as promised.

The Biggest Tournament in Slovenia

Casey Kastle and our ride to Slovenia.

One of the benefits of being a professional poker player was the opportunity to travel and see the world. In late April, I played in the European Poker Tour event in San Remo, Italy. I was there along with my friend Casey Kastle, the antismoking petition coauthor. Casey cashed in the event; I didn't. Casey was a dual citizen of the United States and Slovenia, and he and I were invited to the biggest tournament in the country of his birth at the Perla Casino in Nova Gorica, Slovenia. Perla is touted to be the biggest gaming and entertainment center in Europe, and it was really something. Casey and I drove over nine hours from Italy to Slovenia, and Casey let me know how obsessed he was with winning that tournament. And he did. I didn't fare too well, but the Slovenians were very nice, and they fussed over me. I was the first Main Event winner they had seen in person, and I was treated like royalty.

Poker Situation

I was not running good, and without a sponsor, I was playing in a lot of small buy-in ($100 to $350) tournaments. I finished first in the $200 HORSE event at the Grand Challenge Tournament Series in Vegas for $2,892, and first in the $200 Pot-Limit Omaha event at the Chop Pot Poker Classic in Reno for $1,534. So, I wasn't winning a lot of money playing poker tournaments, and Yolanda and I continued to spend more than we earned.

Poker Cruise Clash

Here's a funny story that illustrates the fixes I seem to inadvertently get myself into. This year, Susie Isaacs asked me as a favor to go on a Panama Canal cruise she planned to host. I had been on over 30 cruises, and the worst one I ever did was a Panama Canal cruise. But she was a friend, they were going to pay my way, and I said okay. Shortly after that, another friend, Debbie Burkhead, asked me to do her a favor and come along on a New England Fall Color cruise she was planning to host. Now, that was a cruise I had always wanted to take, and I said yes.

Guess what? After making two promises before the sailing dates were finalized, I learned the two cruises were scheduled at the same time. When I talked it over with Yolanda, she clearly wanted to do the New England one, as did I. At the time, Debbie Burkhead had a vote in the Poker Hall of Fame as a media member, and that was a goal I had been campaigning to achieve for four years (as you'll see in the next chapter), so I didn't want to upset her. I apologized to Susie, telling her I agreed to both cruises not knowing they would be arranged for the same date, and that both my wife and I preferred the New England cruise. Unfortunately, Susie thought this was a terrible betrayal on my part and didn't speak to me for years. The bad news was neither cruise ever happened. The good news is that Susie and I are friends again.

Marriage Situation

After I lost my job at PokerStars, Yolanda and I kept spending money at the same pace, in effect spending money we now didn't have coming in. I did some additional negligent spending on my own, too. Here's the whole truth. I was still very avid with my stamp collecting. I would bid on auctions, and I wound up with more successful bids than I should have. At that point in time, with my income in an unstable place, spending money to add to my stamp collection was not the brightest thing I've ever done. Stupid, really. I had the cash to cover these purchases, but plastic had become the universal way to pay, and I wound up using my cash for other purposes before the credit card bill came in the mail. I had fallen into the credit card trap—buy now and put off paying until later. Then I bought a very expensive nineteenth-century stamp on credit. It was like a little piece of art. I bought it for $15,000 and agreed to make installment payments. Eventually, I sold it for a third of what I paid for it when the certificate became questionable. This irresponsible spending, that was all on me.

Face Up Gaming Goes Face Down

To add to our downward escalating financial situation, Face Up Gaming abruptly folded in the middle of the year, and I no longer had an online poker "job." They paid my $1,500 monthly salary by crediting that much to my online account with them. When they ceased operations, a significant amount of my earnings became inaccessible.

I wasn't making money at poker this year, either. Most of my assets were tied up in my two houses, and my liquid assets—my cash reserves—were fading fast. I had continued giving poker lessons, which helped to buoy our finances, perhaps giving us a false sense of security. Yet, we didn't cut back enough on our lifestyle. This was an impending crisis that, unfortunately, Yolanda and I did not face as a team.

Net Poker Proceeds $(-2,200) Non-Poker Proceeds $28,700

—2013—

Yolanda Rejects New Job at Caesars

In 2013, Yolanda was offered the kind of job most people in Vegas could only dream of. Caesars Palace offered to make her head of a new department they were creating because she could speak Spanish and English flawlessly. The job was to take care of high rollers, entertain them, and comp them things. Often, the wealthy patrons would give their hostess presents—expensive presents.

I saw this as a tremendous opportunity. But she felt that since the job didn't come with a raise, it was a lateral promotion. So she turned it down. Given our financial situation, I urged her to take the new job, but as was happening with more and more frequency, disagreeing with her about anything just led to a loud confrontation. Trying to get her to see another point of view was taken as criticism, which just really annoyed her.

But I think the big reason she declined this job offer was that her priorities in life were shifting, and she had an alternative income option. Her son Ronnie was living with us most of the time now, and he was going to start his freshman year in high school. Yolanda is a caretaker by nature, and that made a big difference to her. She was concerned about being a working mother when her son would need her, and she wanted to be home for him. And she had an alternate way to make money and still be at home, or so she thought.

Goodwill Hunting

Yolanda has two sisters who were building a business doing online selling, and she had been watching them and learning how to do it. She made the decision to open her own online auction business out of our house. She began amassing inventory from all kinds of places—garage and estate sales, Goodwill, other thrift stores, and the like. She invested in some kind of machine that helped her evaluate stuff so she could buy low and sell high.

There were several problems with this new business venture. First, we had no place to store her growing inventory of stuff, so she literally turned our house into a warehouse. Eventually her merchandise just took over the house. It got to the point where you could barely open the front door. There were boxes and stuff *everywhere*. And any time I would complain about this or question anything that had to do with her business, she would get highly defensive, which led to an argument. I'm nonconfrontational by nature, so I mostly avoided this growing problem. I should have taken a stronger position, but I couldn't handle fighting all the time.

Another issue was that Yolanda was building her inventory much faster than she could sell it. She would buy a whole bunch of stuff and then not sell it quickly because of the time and effort it took to list it—that's a lot of work, taking multiple pictures of items, writing descriptions, evaluating items, and creating "good deals," etc.

Yolanda is a hard worker—but not necessarily a smart worker. She's more street-smart than business-smart. I told her she was operating in a dust storm, working extremely hard, but the growing lack of space in the house was evidence that she wasn't working really wisely. These issues were becoming a multi-year, slow-motion train wreck for our marriage.

Inducted Into the Poker Hall of Fame

On Saturday, October 19, the World Series of Poker officials announced that Scotty Nguyen and I would be the 41st and 42nd inductees into the Poker Hall of Fame. It was a glorious time for me, and I was surrounded by family and friends at the induction ceremony on November the third. Next to my World Series Main Event victory and the birth of my children, election into the Poker Hall of Fame was a major event in my life. My Hall of Fame journey is covered in the following chapter.

Poker Results

I ended the year on a high note, finishing second in the $580 No-Limit Hold'em event at the WSOP circuit event in San Diego in December for $10,903. This was the only sizable tournament I cashed in this year, other than the $739 I earned in June at the Rio Daily Deepstacks. But I was not cashing in a lot of freezeout tournaments, and did not cash in any WSOP events, including the Main

Event (which I had played in continuously since 1983). To say the least, in poker I wasn't running good.

Net Poker Proceeds $ (-12,600)
Non-Poker Proceeds $7,750

To reach the pinnacle of success, you have to cross the
treacherous valleys of failures and discontent.
                                   —Debasish Mridha

CHAPTER 27

Poker Hall of Fame.

**The 2023 Qualifications for the Most Prestigious
Honor in Poker**

To be nominated, a person must:

- *Have played poker against
  acknowledged top competition,*
- *Be a minimum of 40 years old
  at the time of nomination,*
- *Have played for high stakes,*
- *Have played consistently well,
  gained the respect of peers,*
- *Have stood the test of time.*
- *Or, for non-players, have
  contributed to the overall growth and success of the game
  of poker, with indelible positive and lasting results.*

The Nomination Process Has Evolved: A Brief History

The WSOP Poker Hall of Fame was created in 1979 by Benny Binion to preserve the names and legacies of the world's greatest poker players. After the WSOP and the Poker Hall of Fame were sold to Caesars (then Harrah's) Entertainment, a group of selected, but unnamed, members of the media voted for inductees into the Poker Hall of Fame. Then a committee of Harrah's executives made the final determination. In 2009, to increase the interest of the poker community, the Poker Hall of Fame began accepting nominations from the public. This prompted online poker sites to promote their professional representatives, and PokerStars heavily pushed me. Following the public nomination process, the names of the top ten players with the most votes were given to the living Hall of Fame members, as well as a select group of media. Each member of the voting panel received ten points to cast for up to three individuals. The two who received the majority of the votes would then be inducted.

That year, the ten public fan favorites included 23-year-old online poker professional Tom Dwan. As a result, a new age requirement known as the "Chip Reese Rule" was added in 2011. It established a minimum age of 40 to be inducted into the Hall of Fame. This new requirement delayed the nomination of some players who were public favorites and regular nominees over the previous years, such as Phil Ivey and Daniel Negreanu. Both were eventually inducted when they came of age. Today, the only people who are allowed to make the final selection are people who are already in the Hall of Fame. The media and the WSOP management no longer have a vote. Each current Hall of Famer has ten votes, and they can split their votes among as many as three nominees.

Currently, only one person is added to the Hall of Fame each year, which, in my opinion, is a mistake. Hall of Famers become influential spokespersons for the sport. As of 2023, 61 people have been inducted into the Poker Hall of Fame, 31 of whom are still living. So, it just makes sense to have more people in the Hall of Fame versus keeping it a small group. We are probably going to lose on average one person a year, so you have a net gain of zero. A lot of us are getting old and we're not going to last forever. WSOP, I hope you are listening.

My Hall of Fame Journey

When the WSOP began accepting nominations from the public in 2009, I was among the first people up for consideration. That happened for the next three straight years. For four years, I failed to garner enough votes to be inducted, which was incredibly frustrating. Getting into the Poker Hall of Fame would be the frosting on the cake of my poker career, and it was extremely important to me.

For four long years I got outside of my comfort zone and put a lot of energy and effort into campaigning for myself to be chosen for the Poker Hall of Fame. Openly asking people to support me and vote for me was a new experience and, frankly, it was uncomfortable. But I really wanted that honor and told people I'd rather be in the Hall of Fame than win another bracelet. And it was the truth.

I certainly felt like I deserved it. On top of my four World Series of Poker bracelets in No-Limit Hold'em, Limit Hold'em, Razz, and Limit Omaha, I've had a lifetime of accomplishments beyond being a player. In fact, some of my proudest accomplishments had nothing to do with being a player. To help others improve, I authored more than a dozen poker-strategy books and countless poker columns, when improving the competition went against conventional wisdom. But perhaps my most lasting impact on the game may be felt in the lungs of poker players. In 1999, I hosted the first nonsmoking tournament in Nevada history and was a leader of the movement to get the World Series of Poker to go nonsmoking in 2002.

I remember a guy coming up to me during a WSOP tournament and shaking my hand—this is when they were still balloting nominations for the Hall of Fame—and he said, "I want to thank you for your proudest poker accomplishment. Do you know what it is?" And I said, "I sure do. It was getting the World Series itself to go nonsmoking."

I didn't get inducted until my fifth try. That year, 2013, I have to be honest and admit that I had given up. I didn't tell anyone I was even nominated again. Of course, that's how it goes sometimes. It's like when you are looking for a relationship, it's difficult to find one. Then when you aren't looking, you suddenly meet someone. Needless to say, I was thrilled when my turn finally came.

The Announcement

On Saturday, October 19, the World Series of Poker officials announced that Scotty Nguyen and I would be the 41st and 42nd inductees into the Poker Hall of Fame. We were the consensus of the vote from a 37-person panel that included the living members of the Poker Hall of Fame and various media personnel. We were to be inducted as part of an invitation-only awards ceremony at the Wine Cellar in the Rio All-Suite Hotel and Casino in Las Vegas on November 3. When the Binions owned the World Series of Poker, the enshrinement ceremony was held during their Hall of Fame Poker Classic tournament at the Horseshoe Casino in November. Now it is held in concert with the final table of the Main Event of the WSOP, which from 2008 to 2016 was held separately from the rest of the summer WSOP events in November and called "the November Nine."

I was 68 years old, and I had finally made it.

The Enshrinement Ceremony

Me, Scotty Nguyen, Phil Hellmuth, and Mike Sexton.

I was introduced by T. J. Cloutier, who told the audience he credited me with helping save his life by eliminating smoking in poker rooms. My good friend Wendeen Eolis, the first woman to ever cash in a WSOP Main Event, spoke on my behalf. My daughter Melanie had the audience in stitches talking about our early years in town. Phil Hellmuth introduced Scotty, but not before exiting the stage to come over and congratulate me with the kind words, "Tom, you so deserve to be in the Hall of Fame. You and I did business for a lot of years together. Your record, your integrity—is perfect. You know, perfect integrity is a beautiful thing in our business . . . for all these years, with everybody watching. Congratulations."

My son Patrick was there, with his wife and my two grandchildren. My wife Yolanda was by my side. All to see me receive what I considered to be my own personal lifetime-achievement award.

In addition to friends and family, the event was attended by some of the most prestigious names in poker, including Hall of Fame members Barbara Enright, Mike Sexton, and Eric Drache, as well as the 2012 World Series of Poker Main Event Champion Greg Merson, poker dignitaries Nolan Dalla and J. J. Liu, past WSOP Tournament Director Matt Savage, and a select group of poker media.

> *When the two were inducted in the Poker Hall of Fame Sunday, they had one major characteristic in common—emotion. Both players choked up as they spoke of how important joining the greats of the game was to them. McEvoy had trouble getting words out. Nguyen teared up. And the audience lapped up stories about their past.*
>
> *The 68-year-old McEvoy, who won the World Series of Poker Main Event in 1983, didn't try to hide the emotions coursing through him. "I was emotional when I heard the news and I'm emotional now," McEvoy added. "This is something I'll treasure the rest of my life."*
>
> *—Vin Narayanan, Gaming Guru*

My Speech

I gave a heartfelt speech at my induction into the Poker Hall of Fame.

> *"I would like to thank everyone for making my election to the Poker Hall of Fame possible. It was a very emotional day for me when I got the news. I consider this the highest honor*

a poker player can receive next to winning the Main Event of the World Series of Poker. I feel both deeply honored and humbled to be included with all the other poker greats. This is truly the frosting on the cake of my poker career."

Now I Get a Vote

Since now only the current members of the Poker Hall of Fame can vote on the next inductee, I get a vote. Well, ten votes actually. T. J. Cloutier and I always discuss it and vote the same way. In 2022, all of our votes went to Kathy Liebert, who I felt totally deserved to be in the Hall of Fame. She went for a long time as the all-time leading female money winner and is still number three. We don't have enough women in there.

During the WSOP Hall of Fame Bounty event, the newest member of the Poker Hall of Fame is announced. Two years ago, I voted for Layne Flack and Michael Mizrachi. Layne was elected posthumously the following year. Last year, 2023, I voted for Kathy again, as did T. J.

When you reach the end of your rope, tie a knot in it and hang on.
—1946 West Coast Folklore Book

CHAPTER 28

♣ ♦ ♥ ♠

2014 to 2017. Loss of Health, Assets, Keepsakes, and My Marriage.

—2014—

Marriage Counseling

Things were getting tense. Finally, we said we better get a marriage counselor and talk some of our problems out. We found one, a nice guy of Mexican descent. I was quite happy with him. He had a strong personality, and he knew his stuff. But we only had one session with him, because Yolanda didn't like him. Well, the problem was, he didn't 100 percent buy her point of view and said some things she didn't like hearing that I felt were true. She said nope, we gotta find somebody else. Then we found a Casper Milquetoast marriage counselor that she liked, for obvious reasons. We went to several sessions with this counselor, and finally ended them. We remained married, but there were still a lot of unresolved problems.

At this point, I was trying to salvage things. I'm not a quitter. And I don't just run out on my obligations. I did my best to keep us going. But I felt I was bailing the boat slower than it was filling with water.

Gambling Propensity

Like millions of Americans, Yolanda loves to play slot machines. She comes by it honestly, because many others in her family love to play them, too. How much money did she lose playing slots over the course of our marriage? I don't have any idea. How much of her business earnings, if any, went into the machines? I don't know that either. But I do know she got all kinds of comps from the casinos, which you don't get unless you are gambling quite a lot. I never put any money into slot machines, but I did benefit from and enjoy some of Yolanda's comps, so this was not a habit she hid from me.

Poker Tournaments

In January, I was one of the featured poker pros, along with Marsha Waggoner and Susie Isaacs, at the Senior Poker Tour event held at the Horseshoe Casino in Tunica, Mississippi. In April, I teamed up with T. J. Cloutier and WSOP commentator Lon McEachern to put on a free seminar at the Masters Poker Series, which was held at Dover Downs Hotel & Casino in Delaware. In June, it was downtown to Binion's to participate in the Legends Classic Series tournament.

I was on my own this year to fund my entry fees and travel expenses. I was getting more and more desperate to win, which may help explain my dismal results. Plus, frankly, the fields were getting larger, and competition was getting much stronger. Players had learned from a multitude of available poker literature, and they were gaining tons of experience online and at the growing number of casinos and poker clubs throughout the country. I made less money this year than last, and my expenses were greater than my earnings, which continued my downward financial spiral.

Further and Further in Debt

I was still buying stamps, which was a money-losing investment. Yolanda was buying and selling a lot of inexpensive items, spending a great deal of time processing orders with small markups. At one time, she tried to get me involved by helping her, but that was the last thing I wanted to do. She bought massive amounts of stuff, and her listings weren't keeping up with her purchases.

In spite of all this, we continued to live beyond our means, and I continued to watch as she made some very bad decisions. I took the easy way out and just let her do her thing instead of enduring more endless arguments. That's on me.

Net Poker Proceeds $ (-$6,600)   Non-Poker Proceeds $9,000

—2015—

Selling My Rental House

Our debts were continuing to mount, and I was more or less forced to liquidate a big part of my personal wealth—my income-producing rental property next door to my home on Gisborn Drive in Vegas. I bought it for $353,000, and I sold it for about $175,000 to my friend, poker pro J. J. Liu, in June 2015. I had decided to put it up for sale, and since J. J. had a real estate company, I asked her to list it. Instead, she offered to buy it and gave me my asking price without any realtor fees. It was the best deal I was going to get. At the time, Las Vegas was in a real estate slump, ranked last in a report on housing-market health. If I could have hung onto the house for a few more years, it would have gone way up in value, but I desperately needed the cash. One more time, I destroyed a bunch of money and didn't do it losing at poker.

The sale did not get us out of debt, but it gave us some breathing space for a couple of years. Yolanda's business was not exactly flourishing—she was making *some* money, but not enough. Of course, I did not have any big poker scores, and even with my poker teaching, I wasn't contributing much either. After the loss of the house, tension grew as we continued falling more and more into debt.

Net Poker Proceeds $7,600   Non-Poker Proceeds $5,400

—2016—

Poker

I had some good poker results this year, placing second in the 2016 Binion's Poker Classic 7-Card Stud. I also cashed two World Series of Poker events, the $1,500 Pot-Limit Omaha and, most importantly, in the $10,000 Main Event. I was staked in these tournaments, of course, because I could not afford the entry fees myself.

Starting to Get Sick

My mental anguish at my financial and marital situation was starting to affect me physically. I was getting more and more stressed out and had developed many of the symptoms of Parkinson's disease, like trembling hands. So, I went to my doctor for help. I was misdiagnosed with Parkinson's and prescribed the inappropriate medicine—really strong stuff that just made things worse. On top of that, I was still seeing the psychiatrist who prescribed my bipolar medications. When we talked about my marital situation, he even said the situation I was in was not good. I was edging closer and closer to a nervous breakdown. I had trouble concentrating, sleeping, working—I was just existing.

Our marital relationship had changed dramatically. I was no longer capable of being the breadwinner. I believe that frustrated my bride and probably angered her, too. Our unhappiness manifested in a growing number of arguments. I just let Yolanda wear me down. Let me be clear that I don't think she was doing this maliciously. She was always there, always made sure I was fed, gave me foot rubs and head rubs. She was dedicated to me, but our two personalities had become like oil and water.

Net Poker Proceeds $9,700   Non-Poker Proceeds $300

—2017—

By this time, we were desperate for money, and with Yolanda's guidance, we listed and sold my World Series Main Event bracelet on eBay in a package deal that included three of my books and some other personal memorabilia. I got $9,000 for it, and today, I wish I had it back. A few years earlier, I was offered $15,000 for the bracelet by an acquaintance, if I made it into the Poker Hall of Fame. When I tried to track this potential buyer down, I found out he had died. Just my rotten luck.

I used the money to pay off a loan from Yolanda's sister. At this point, I was also selling some of my stamp collection, likewise at rock-bottom prices. I used to have an extensive dragon figurine collection. Now it's a fraction of what it was—Yolanda sold a lot of it, along with other stuff that I would have liked to keep but we really didn't need. Like my copy of Doyle Brunson's *Super System* I, the only issue that had been signed by the publisher, Avery Cardoza, in addition to every contributor to that famous book. By then, Chip Reese had died, so it could never be duplicated.

Selling important keepsakes—that's scraping the bottom of the barrel. All these sales helped us stay afloat a little longer, but it was just postponing the inevitable. We were close to $100,000 in credit card debt, and as you can imagine, the stress on our marriage was unbearable.

The Big Dilemma

We kept afloat until we could no longer stay afloat. That's when I tried to refinance the house. I did everything I could to save it. I went to Bank of America, where my credit was good, but my ratio of income-to-debt was not acceptable. I went to some private lending companies. I had my credit checked so many times it started to count against my credit score. Same story everywhere. My credit was great. I hadn't missed a payment on anything, but my debt kept getting bigger and bigger.

Now my choices were to either sell the house and pay off my creditors or declare bankruptcy again. By this time, I was really upset with Yolanda, and I couldn't see her potentially getting half of the house in a divorce I had begun to think was inevitable, so I decided to save my credit and pay off the credit card companies rather than go through bankruptcy again and ruin my credit forever.

I sold my house, closing in May. All of my family members offered to take me in. But I hate winter, so I didn't want to leave Las Vegas and move to New York or Michigan. And the last thing I wanted to do was *be* a burden. But just before the house was sold, Yolanda and I agreed to *take on* a new burden.

Yolanda's Ex, Ron Stock, Moves in with Us

Around February, Yolanda's ex-husband, Ron Stock, moved into our home. His health had deteriorated to the point he had to take food directly into his stomach through a feeding tube, and he didn't have any money, either. At this point, Yolanda was already taking care of her son Ronnie, a senior in high school, and I wasn't exactly 100 percent healthy. We were both concerned about Ron, and I suggested we have him come live with us. She could have declined to take care of Ron, too, but she didn't, which to her credit was very selfless.

Ron had become a good friend of mine, odd as that may sound. I saw how hard it had become for him to handle things after his life had gone south. He basically threw in the towel for the last decade of his life. He remembered what he was and could not adapt to what he had become. The downstairs bedroom where I thought I would be spending my elder years was unoccupied, and we put Ron there—downstairs, where Yolanda's stuff was everywhere, and it was difficult for an able person to navigate.

Then, catastrophe struck. For some reason, there was a load of merchandise on a wheeled desk chair, and when Ron stood and put his weight against the chair, it rolled, and he fell—right in front of me and a visiting friend of mine, Vince Burgio. Watching Ron fall was like watching a train wreck in slow motion. I still don't why he put his weight on the chair—there was no apparent reason for doing this. He didn't fall far, but he was laying there in pain. He said, "I broke my hip." I said, "Really, you didn't fall very far, are you sure?" He was sure, and he was correct. That sent him to the hospital for several months, and unfortunately, he never left.

After the fall, Ron knew he wasn't going to last long, and he told us he wanted to live long enough to see his son graduate. Ronnie was 18 now, and the day he graduated that June, he went to Ron's hospital room with his cap and gown and diploma. Ron didn't get to go to the ceremony, but he got to see his son on his graduation day.

Selling My House

Soon after Ron went into the hospital, I officially sold my house, in the middle of the World Series of Poker. The guy I sold it to bought it to use as rental property, and we became his first tenants. I needed to concentrate on the WSOP, not moving, so I had to rent my own house for $1,500 a month for two months.

The World Series at the time started at the tail end of May, Memorial Day weekend. It used to run mid-April to mid-May, but after Caesars bought the tournament, they changed the date and added events, which added several weeks to the duration time.

I did not make a penny in the WSOP that year, and in June, I got busted out of the Main Event. Afterward, I went to dinner at my favorite Italian restaurant with Yolanda and my good friend

Peter Victor. That's where we got the phone call to inform us of Ron Stock's demise. Turns out he died within 15 minutes of the time I was eliminated on the third level of day three of the Main Event. I had a really tough time with that.

Moving in with a Friend

The World Series ended in late July, and that's when we packed our personal things. I was experiencing back pain at the time, so Yolanda did most of the packing. I was in no condition to supervise this, and when some of my personal records and stuff got misplaced, I had no one to blame but myself. Both my friends Peter Victor and Dana Smith had offered us a temporary place to live, but I chose to make a deal with my friend Dan Alspach to move into his house with him and his daughter. I moved there on August 1, residing in a small bedroom on the second floor. Yolanda went to Texas for a few weeks where she had things to attend to. When Yolanda got back from Texas, I quickly felt trapped. I was in a little room in a house I didn't want to be in, and our fighting resumed. It was a nightmare.

Here's an example of the stupid stuff that caused arguments and drove me crazy. When we sold the house, without discussion, Yolanda took down all the vines growing in our backyard. I tried to convince her she couldn't salvage them, but she had made up her mind. She insisted on bringing some of them over to Dan's house when we moved there, which created problems with his Homeowners Association.

She just wouldn't listen to me. I kept asking her to just quit haranguing me. She was yelling at me all the time now, and I told her she had to stop. In her defense, she was miserable, but so was I. On top of the incorrect yet strong meds I was taking, all this friction was taking its toll.

What else could go wrong? Well, during that same stretch, about the middle of August, I wrecked my car. I had a big lunch, fell asleep at the wheel, and rear-ended a guy. He wasn't hurt, yet he got $25,000 from my insurance company for "personal injury," because even though insurance companies know claimants are trying to scam them, they would rather pay than fight. I bruised my sternum, and just suffered in silence for about five weeks. The insurance company decided the car was a write-off, and I used the money I got for it to almost pay off Yolonda's truck, which she used to buy, sell, and haul around all her merchandise. She had branched out and was selling furniture now, too, not just dishes and small things.

Around late August, Yolanda's son Ronnie, who I still love dearly, had his life upended, too. He had signed up for ROTC to get his college paid for, and after graduation he went to Georgia for basic training in the National Guard. He was about eight weeks through a 12-week basic training when Ron Stock died. Yolanda wanted him to come back to Las Vegas, so instead of finishing, he came back here for the funeral. That meant he would have to start all over again with basic training. Well, that never happened. Instead, his girlfriend had moved to Midland, Texas, to live with her mom, who had just gotten a new job there. Ronnie moved to Midland to be with her, but recently the relationship ended.

The End of My Second Marriage

Dan had offered to let us stay in his home for as long as we wanted. I had prepaid rent for August and September, but by mid-September 2017, I could not take it anymore, and I moved out on my own. I just don't think Yolanda saw that I was at the end of my rope. It was time to leave or end up having a nervous breakdown. So, I left.

When that happened, Dan thought I was going to die. He swears he had written me off. He thought I had Parkinson's and wasn't good for another month. Many of my other friends thought the same thing. That's how bad I looked. Dana Smith told me she thought I was not going to live much longer, and offered to take me in, which Yolanda has never forgiven her for. I didn't file for divorce from Yolanda until I moved in with Dana, and I lived there for the next year.

I have had to start over from zero before, but this time, I was *below* zero. I took the equity money from the sale of my house and liquidated as much of the credit card debt as I could. I wasn't able to cover all of it, but I have since paid off everything I owed.

We Were Both at Fault

Whenever a couple breaks up, it's never the fault of just one person. We were no different. I made a lot of mistakes. I stood by and watched her make some very bad decisions. I took the easy way out and just let her do her thing instead of starting the inevitable arguments. I never felt Yolanda was entirely to blame, and I still don't, but she contributed heavily to our demise of our marraige.

Was the fault 50/50? I don't know. Where was all the credit card debt from? Both of us, but a lot of it was for her. My family places most of the blame on her, but I don't. Yolanda alienated all my family. She knows my family doesn't like her, and she blames me for not standing up for her. Well, I don't think I should ever have to stand up for her. She destroyed her relationship with my family by her own actions, which they personally witnessed.

My friends and family think I should be a lot angrier with her. I understand that. They don't want me to be hurt anymore. I'm not so stupid that I haven't seen for myself how she is and how she can get. Yet, we both have our regrets, and today we are friends, but without the strife. And that's a good place to be. In my heart, part of me still has strong feelings for her.

> *Women haven't changed. When you're single, you'll be appealing to a lot of them—all that money, easy come, easy go. But when you marry, you'll be lucky if you have found the one woman out of 1,000 who can tolerate "the Life." The actual odds of finding this woman is one out 32 women, computer calculations courtesy of Tom McEvoy.*
>
> —Vince Burgio

Poker

Naturally, when it all ended, I wasn't playing poker. But the breakup afforded me some time to start healing. I got off of the incorrect meds, and I started playing again. I won the $400 Pot-Limit Omaha Bounty event at the Deepstack Extravaganza in November and placed eighth in the $400 No-Limit Hold'em Double Stack event at the December Extravaganza. Both tournaments were in Las Vegas, so thankfully I didn't have to travel far.

Net Poker Proceeds $1,600   Non-Poker Proceeds $8,300.

In the end, it's not the years in your life that
count. It's the life in your years.
—Abraham Lincoln.

CHAPTER 29

2018 to 2023. Bumpy Ride, Soft Landing, TV Pilot, and More.

—2018—

Yolanda broke down multiple times when I decided I had to leave her for good and get a divorce. She cried and said she was so sorry she didn't listen to me, but it was too late. We were divorced in February 2018, after seven-and-a-half years. I was so broke that my son Patrick and my daughter Melanie paid my divorce lawyer. After the divorce, I began the road to recovery.

I stayed with Dana Smith for most of the year. Dana is very neat, organized, and orderly. I'm not, to say the least. With her, I had to walk on eggshells a lot of the time. If a chair was slightly out of place in the kitchen, she would bring it to my attention. I can't handle that. But Dana was great and when I lived there, I was well fed and generally taken care of. I was the problem there, not Dana, and toward the middle of the year, Dana asked me to find somewhere else to live. Kathy Liebert took me in for about four months, but that didn't work for me, and I moved back to Dana's again in December.

I didn't set the world on fire playing poker, but I did make a deep run in the WSOP Main Event in July, finishing 430th for $29,625, marking the fourth time I have cashed in the Main Event. My old friend Phyliss Meyers staked me, and after I cashed, she would only take her $10,000 buy-in as renumeration. For me, that extra money went a long way toward paying off the remainder of my credit card debt.

Net Poker Proceeds $9,700   Non-Poker Proceeds $7,500

—2019—

My second stint living with Dana lasted over a year, until Covid hit in early 2020. For the 36th time, I played in the World Series of Poker Main Event, the one tournament I never wanted to miss. The only year I hadn't played was 2015, when I didn't have any money or a sponsor. I didn't make the money in the Main Event this year, but did manage to play in 11 WSOP events, minimum-cashing in three No-Limit Hold'em events.

After the WSOP, while I was staying at Dana's place, I injured my back helping her move some furniture. What started out as twinges kept getting worse and worse, and I was in agony for the better part of six months. I could hardly walk across the room without pain. That curtailed a lot of my poker that year. To this day, I am very careful about lifting anything heavy.

Net Poker Proceeds $(-$3,100)
Non-Poker Proceeds $(-3,600)

—2020—

Covid Hits

When Covid hit in early 2020, like so many other older folks in the country, Dana became a hermit. She did not want me leaving the house and potentially infecting her, but my back pain was lessening and the temptation to sneak a gourmet meal with friends (who, unfortunately, like to post on Facebook) or even a hamburger and fries now and then was irresistible. Spooked by Covid, Dana told me in no uncertain terms if I couldn't live by her Covid rules—no going to public places—I would have to find a new place to reside. So I got kicked out—again.

Buddy's Place

Buddy Ashmore is a poker and backgammon friend from Edmonton, Canada. Several years before, when Buddy was shopping for a condo in Las Vegas, he asked if he could rent a room at my house. I said no, no rent, come and stay as long as you want. And he did for a month or so. He found and bought a condo, and he and his lady Candace Smith would come down from Canada and live there during the winter, many times enjoying the Christmas holiday here. I first met Buddy in 1987 in Reno at a backgammon tournament. I had lost my first match, and then won 10 straight matches after that to become the Intermediate Division Consolation winner. Buddy was one of my victims.

Buddy is better at backgammon, and I am better at poker, and we became good friends and helped each other improve in our respective games. We still play backgammon in person and online. He's higher rated than me, so it drives him crazy that I have won more than I have lost over the past few years. But according to Buddy, I'm still a little behind after 30-plus years.

When Dana booted me out around June, I moved to Buddy Ashmore's unoccupied condo, where I spent most of the year. I was still suffering with nagging back pain from bulging discs, and I went to see a back specialist. He told me they could do this little procedure where they give you a couple of shots that provides relief for most people, but not everyone. So, I gave it a try, knowing that if it wasn't helpful the next course of action was surgery. Luckily, it did the job.

Covid Poker

I had been playing poker online for the better part of two decades, but never exclusively. In 2020, the casinos, and the WSOP, were closed to in-person poker, so I had little choice. This was the first and (thankfully) only time the World Series of Poker had been played virtually. I did not play in the Main Event but managed to cash in three online No-Limit Hold'em events for a little over $3,000.

Covid wasn't going to last forever, and when it was over, I knew Buddy would be coming back to his condo in Vegas. Dana took pity on me and let me move back with her for a third time. Health issues followed me. This time it was my prostrate, complete with a weak urine stream and embarrassing dribble issues. I had a horrible surgical procedure that worked, but if I had to do it again, I'd think twice about it.

Net Poker Proceeds $2,200   Non-Poker Proceeds $400

—2021—

Practically penniless after going through a second divorce, I had moved seven times over the last three and a half years until I finally got what I hope will be my last home. In February, I moved into a 1,348 sq. ft. double-wide mobile home in a gated senior citizen park in Las Vegas. It's no Taj Mahal, but it fits me perfectly.

I got this place because I have nine family members who all agreed within a 36-hour period to give me the money to buy it. Family—my sister Marcia and her husband, Terry; my brother Steve and his wife, Carol; my brother Alan; my daughter Melanie and her husband, Greg; and my son Patrick and his wife, Vanessa. They told me it was not a loan, but I have a different viewpoint. If I ever score again, I'm going to pay everybody back. I know who paid what. I have the best family and the best friends. I lucked out.

I'm close to all of them. One of my friends, my next-door neighbor Paula, was a huge help and very instrumental in my getting this place. My new home also came with a new friend. I inherited a cat, Shotsky, from whom I am inseparable.

TV Pilot *Un$uited*

I have a budding career as a poker consultant with a part-time role in a TV show called *Un$uited*. Once again, it seems my future is dependent on finding a sponsor. So, once again, I'm a long shot.

Strategically, the concept is a TV series about the poker world that both the gaming industry and general audiences will embrace. The show's producers view it as a good way to bridge the broader public to the poker community and bring them together. It's a new and novel concept.

The show is about a terrible poker player who envisions himself to be great at the game, like his hero, Tom McEvoy. The son of a successful business owner, he gives up a bright future to go to Las Vegas to seek fame and fortune (ahem, of course, only a knucklehead would do something like that). In my view, the show had to be funny, quirky, and "poker realistic." Two episodes have been filmed, and I appear at the poker table in the main character's dream sequences.

The poker scenes were filmed at a friend's house in Las Vegas. I've made genuine contributions trying to make sure the poker is accurate. For example, the script had me calling the main character's bet with trips, three of a kind. I had them change it to make sure they paired the board, so I had the top full house, which was reasonable against his royal flush. That's a little out there, but those things happen in Hold'em. I wanted the scene to make poker sense. I told the producers right up front, look, you're using me and my name for whatever good that does you, so the poker has got to be real.

> *Working with Tom has been great. He's been a lot of fun and he has educated us on a lot of different aspects of the game and he has been a huge supporter. I think he wants to get this done as much as I do. He has pointed us in the right direction and introduced us to some of the right people, and those people have been trying to help us as well.*
> —*Producer Thomas Baldinger, 624 Productions LLC*

I introduced 624 Productions to Ty Stewart, Executive Director of the WSOP; Poker Hall of Famer Mori Eskandani, President of PokerGo; and folks in the poker media like Chad Holloway, Executive Editor U.S. for *PokerNews*. I also helped them get access to people in the industry I don't even know personally. They have all been very helpful, but none of them wanted to put up the big bucks necessary to fund a modern-day TV series.

Five seasons (ten 20- to 30-minute episodes per season) have been written, and 624 Productions is in the process of trying to sell the series. They would like to find an individual or a company to financially back Season One and/or put it on their website, such as a poker website looking for content for the poker community to watch. And/or form a coproduction deal with another company that is looking for content, preferably a company that has a distributor such as Hulu, Netflix, or Amazon.

There are some pretty well-known actors involved. Mark Riccadonna is a standup comedian who tours all over the country; Tony Denison, who played John Gotti in *Getting Gotti;* and Dan Lauria, who played the father in *The Wonder Years* TV series. I even got parts as players in the poker scenes for some of my good friends.

TV series projects can sit on a shelf for years, so there is still hope they will find the right people who want to partner up with them and get on board with this type of show. As far as I know they are still trying, even today. Here's an example—in 2023, during the World Series of Poker, there was a special showing of the pilot by invitation in a little room at the Horseshoe casino next to Jack Binion's Steak restaurant that I didn't even know was there. The two episodes were condensed into one 45-minute segment. Afterward, my good friend J. J. Liu hosted a charity tournament at her home for select invited guests and cast members. $150 buy-in. About ten of us were comped for the first buy-in. I went broke and rebought, ultimately chopping the tournament four ways.

I hope the series gets sold. If it does, and they keep me on the cast, we would be shooting In Vegas and New Jersey, going back and forth as far as the story is concerned.

I had to sign a Non-Disclosure Agreement when I got involved with the show, but they have graciously allowed me to tell you about it.

Net Poker Proceeds $(-900)   Non-Poker Proceeds $100

—2022—

My Poker Recovery

You could say that after a divorce, multiple moves, and finally having a place of my own again, I was a bit, well, shell-shocked and lethargic. What I needed was to get out of the house—and play poker. My friend Dan Alspath convinced me to start playing poker at the South Point casino, at which I didn't play often because it's off the beaten path from my house.

South Point has one of the nicest poker rooms in town, and I am treated kindly and, for an older poker pro, with a fair degree of respect. On the first of September, they started a promotion in which you could earn entry into a freeroll tournament based on the number of hours spent playing in the poker room, which motivated me to play more. They offer a wide variety of poker games, too. My friends kept talking about it and I decided to give it a try. Playing poker at South Point invigorated me—it has made a huge difference in this later stage of my life.

WSOP Hall of Fame Tournament

This was the first year the World Series of Poker moved from the Rio casino to what is now the Horseshoe casino on the Las Vegas Strip. I played in five events and did not cash in any. One of the events was a freeroll for me, the Hall of Fame bounty tournament, where all Poker Hall of Famers are invited to play with a bounty on their heads. I had no money or sponsor this year for the Main Event, which turned out to be fortuitous because just beforehand I caught my first case of Covid.

2022 Hall of Fame Tournament bounty victims.

The Casino Collectibles Association

The public relations director for this international collectors' club reached out to me and asked if I would attend their annual show in June for a few hours and do a meet-and-greet. Being a poker-memorabilia collector myself, I jumped at the opportunity. I said I would do better than that—I volunteered to be there for the whole three-day show, along with my friend Danielle Striker, to chat with people and peddle some of my books and her Poker Samadhi merchandise.

That's where I got to know Brad Smith, PR Director, and his friend Gregg Fisher. We poker players hit it off, and I invited them to my house to see my collections. Brad shared several articles on Las Vegas history he had authored, stories about casinos I had never even heard of. I liked his writing style so much I asked him to write this book. I now count him among my best friends.

Net Poker Proceeds $1,900   Non-Poker Proceeds $200

—2023—

U.S. Open Intermediate Backgammon Championship

March 29 through April 2, I competed in the U.S. Open Intermediate Backgammon Championship that was held at the Westgate casino in Las Vegas. For perspective, this tournament is one notch below the Championship event, where all the biggest names in backgammon play. So, it is the equivalent of Triple-A Baseball—one notch below the Major Leagues.

I won my first several matches, and then I lost in what amounted to the quarter finals. So now I had to go into the consolation side. I could still win the tournament, because you have to lose twice before you are eliminated. I got through the other players on Saturday. I won my last match on Saturday, which was against the guy who had previously defeated me. He finished third in the tournament, which was a money finish, and I got to the final match, which was scheduled to start on Sunday at noon.

I'm (still) a night owl, so that night I did something I rarely do—I set my alarm. Sometimes, when I don't wake up on my own volition, I'm a little dizzy at first. I usually just sit on the bed until it passes, but that morning I got up and headed to the shower, figuring that that would wake me up. I turned on the water and the next thing I knew I was lying on the floor of my very narrow shower with a badly bruised buttock and a swollen toe that was turning a nice pretty purple hue. I had fainted and broken my toe. At the time I didn't know for sure my toe was broken, but I was having a hard time walking. Yet I was determined not to miss out on my backgammon final match.

The guy who got through his matches undefeated was, of course, in the finals, and he got a cash bonus for doing that. The rules are that the Sunday finals are single elimination. So, I didn't have to beat him twice, I only had to beat him once.

My finals match was fairly close. I was suffering with toe and butt pain, but I managed to basically block it out. I think I might have taken a couple of ibuprofens. I focused on the tournament, blocked the pain, and managed to win the match. I won the U.S. Open Intermediate Backgammon Championship, and the first-place money. You won't be surprised to learn I hedged a little bit, making deals with my last two opponents.

After the match was over on Sunday, the pain came back in spades. A few days later, I showed my foot to my good friend Sam Waldner when we were at South Point playing poker, and he immediately took me straight to the hospital. I spent about 40 hours there, two days and two nights, and they pumped me full of antibiotics, as I had developed cellulitis. Without the treatment, Sam was pretty sure I would have lost my foot.

Even with that victory, backgammon is my second-favorite game, and I am still striving to get better. In May, I started working with Steve Sax, trading poker lessons for backgammon lessons. He's a world-class backgammon player, a really good teacher, a good guy, and very smart. He's better at numbers than I am by a large margin, and I was always pretty good at numbers. He's a whiz.

World Series of Poker

I played in my 38th WSOP Main Event in July, a record surpassed by only Doyle Brunson and maybe Dewey Tomko and Berry Johnston. I lasted to day three but didn't make the money. Shortly after I was eliminated, I caught the dreaded Covid bug—for the second time. It was miserable, but I think being double-vaccinated made it less traumatic.

First Wife Bobbi Passes

On August 24, two days after she had turned 81, my first wife and the mother of my children sadly passed away after a prolonged illness. I had the chance to visit with her in Michigan, which was tough, and attending her funeral was no easier. Bobbi had preplanned her own funeral very well, and she wanted it kind of lighthearted. Patrick and Melanie both told humorous stories about their mom that I had never heard. Her sister Judy did the same, and everyone was laughing. The reception was held in the basement of the church, and people were saying this was the best funeral they had ever been to—not in a morbid way—because Bobbi had wanted it that way. She got her last wishes, got her last birthday in, and was surrounded in the end by her loving family. I was so sorry to see her go.

Poker Leagues

I played in two poker leagues this year. I partnered with Vince Burgio in one and Sarah Casey in the other. One league has 16 players and will pay six prizes, the top two being $10,000 seats into the WSOP Main Event. The other pays five prizes and one Main Event seat. Both are roughly $300 per monthly session and will run for ten months. There are very talented and pro-level players in these leagues, so wish me luck.

I've been playing in poker leagues since 2012, other than when Covid shut us down for almost three years. Over the years, I have had several first-place finishes and have also won other WSOP event seats. I really enjoy the competition and the camaraderie of these leagues.

And of Course, This Book

I've spent over a year working on this book with Brad, and we have both enjoyed it immensely. This book is my last major project. After that I'm going to do what I like to do best—goof off, play poker, and watch Netflix. Because of my IBS, I don't like traveling a lot. I used to love going to tournaments, but not anymore. Plus, my stamina is such that, well, the only tournament I really care about is the World Series. To my dying day, I will still want to play WSOP events.

Net Poker Proceeds $(-4,000)   Non-Poker Proceeds $5,500

In Conclusion

A lot of people would go nuts and be miserable after going from very comfortable down to where I am now. But I'm not an unhappy person. I never let failure keep me down because failure to me is like success—it's temporary. I don't know if I'll ever have any money again, and if I don't, well, money was never my god to begin with and never will be. But it's nice to have it. I'm all in favor of money, I'm just not willing to do what some people do to get it. Like cheating people or screwing people over . . . or doing questionable things just to improve their financial situation. I'd rather be me. I don't have any real issues with my conscience because I know I am trying to do the right thing. I know I haven't always succeeded, obviously, but, like the famous song says, I did it my way.

If you are ever in Vegas, look me up. And if you need poker lessons, I'm still available.

I think the best stories always end up being about the people rather than the event, which is to say character driven.
—Stephen King

CHAPTER 30

Stories of Famous Poker Pros.

Alphabetical List of Poker Pros:

- Benny Binion
- Doyle Brunson
- T. J. Cloutier
- Eric Drache
- Larry Flynt
- Phil Hellmuth
- Phil Ivey
- John "Austin Squatty" Jenkins
- Gabe Kaplan
- Mason Malmuth
- Men "The Master" Nguyen
- Mike Matusow
- Rod Peate
- Walter "Puggy" Pearson
- Amarillo Slim Preston
- Erik Seidel
- Mike Sexton

- David Sklansky
- Jack "Treetop" Straus
- Jack Straus and Crandell Addington
- Stu Ungar
- Byron "Cowboy" Wolford

Benny Binion

Benny had enough foresight to, first, see the potential for a poker tournament as a draw for his Horseshoe casino, second to name it the World Series of Poker, and third to recognize that it could develop into something big. And as so often happens, it developed into something far bigger than the originator ever anticipated.

I really liked and respected Benny Binion. On top of that, I *loved* the guy. Benny was a fantastic individual with an endless repertoire of stories. He'd hold court on a frequent basis in the downstairs restaurant at the Horseshoe. I remember one day I was just walking by the restaurant, and Benny looked up and saw me. We both knew each other, of course, and he didn't speak, he just pointed to a seat as if to say "sit." And I sat down. He told story after fascinating story, and he was fabulous. Without him and his charisma, the World Series of Poker never would have happened. I wonder to this day what Benny would think about his daughter, Becky, and her husband, Nick, selling off the World Series rights so cheap. They threw mega-millions out the door.

My good friend Dr. Paul Fischman was invited by Dewey Tomko to witness the World Series of Poker early on. Here's his recollection of Benny Binion:

> Benny Binion used to treat us all like kings. He had a farm in Montana. Beef and all kinds of stuff. He put out a spread for all the poker players and it was free. If you were in

the tournament or he knew you, you were eating on Benny. I got to meet all the poker legends that were around back then and got to be friends with those guys before I met Tom.

This is how I met Benny Binion. I went down to the Horseshoe coffee shop to have breakfast one morning and when I walked in there were very few people. I'm walking past this table and this guy introduces himself. "Hi, I'm Benny Binion and welcome to the place, looks like you're the only one in here, why don't you sit down with me." That's the one time alone with Benny I got. It was fantastic.

Doyle Brunson

Doyle "Texas Dolly" Brunson made tremendous contributions to poker, and in many ways, was the most prominent ambassador for the game. In January 2006, *Bluff* magazine recognized Brunson as the most influential force in the world of poker, and I concur. His was undoubtedly the most recognizable name in poker, from old-timers to newbies. The whole poker world and I were very saddened by his passing.

But Doyle Brunson didn't think I qualified for the WSOP Hall of Fame. Here's the story.

"Times have changed. Need to rewrite the criteria for the Poker HOF. Define high stakes? What is top competition? Tournament poker? Thoughts?"

—*Doyle Brunson (@TexDolly)*
October 21, 2013 (Twitter Post)

Scotty Nguyen and I were nominated and inducted into the Poker Hall of Fame in 2013, and Doyle was opposed to both of us getting in. He had his reasons, and they were not personal, as they were explained to me, not by him but by my good friend Wendeen Eolis (the "grand dame of poker," and the first woman to cash in the WSOP Main Event). From his perspective, a major prerequisite for this honor was being a high-stakes cash-game player, like the games he frequented. Scotty and I were both known more for our tournament play than cash-game play. It wasn't like he was just picking on us. He also didn't want the guy who developed the hole-card camera, Henry Orenstein, in the Hall of Fame either. Doyle lobbied for high-stakes players like Jennifer Harmon, and I feel he is a primary reason she got in. Not that she doesn't deserve it, but if I had to pick a woman to go into the Poker Hall of Fame who was more deserving, it would be Kathy Liebert. As is common with honors like this that are voted on—in this case only past Poker Hall of Famers get to vote—there is a popularity aspect involved. That doesn't work in Kathy's favor.

The reason I know 100 percent that Doyle didn't want me in the Hall of Fame is because Phil Hellmuth did. Once, when we were all three at a World Series event, Phil and I were talking, and Doyle was standing nearby. With me still standing there, Phil went up to Doyle and said, pointing to me, "This is the guy we gotta get into the Hall of Fame." Phil was singing my praises to Doyle, who then very gruffly said, "Leave me out of this," and walked off. In other words, he was telling Phil to forget it. This was right in front of me. I didn't say a word, just smiled and filed it away in my memory. Like the rest of the poker world, I admire Doyle, so it stung a bit.

Here's a Doyle Brunson/Phil Hellmuth story as told to me by my friend Dan Alspach:

> *I was at a table with Doyle one time and Phil Hellmuth was at the other end of the table and they were sitting there next to each other. It got to the break, and Phil had been doing his usual talking up a stream and Doyle hadn't said a*

word. Doyle went broke and stood up and said, "Thank God I don't have to listen to him anymore!"

T. J. Cloutier

Thomas James Cloutier is one of my closest friends. I know he feels the same way. We were among a group of friends at Linda Johnson's house once when he said, "Can you believe that this nerd over here is my best friend?" I mean, I was his polar opposite. He's a big guy with a very engaging personality. When he comes into a room, people gravitate toward him. When I come into a room, well, I don't get noticed so much.

We are opposites with a common bond—poker. He was this great athlete playing major league sports, while my athletic claim to fame was being a pretty good table tennis player. I'm sure to this day he is considered a much better poker player than me. He has won six bracelets. Two seconds, a third, and a fifth in the Main Event. The only thing I did differently was actually win it. For 20 years, T. J. to me in his heyday was the best tournament player alive, period. Especially in No-Limit Hold'em. When he won his bracelet in Razz, he complained every inch of the way how much he hated this game—all while playing the tournament and winning it. In fact, he won six different bracelets in six different events. He always said that If you know how to play tournament poker and you have a good basic knowledge of the game, even though you don't play it often, you have a chance to win it.

We were just casual friends when we started writing books to-gether. We spent a great deal of time getting down in the weeds and discussing the nuances and strategy of poker. We developed a deep-seated respect for each other based on how we viewed the game and how we viewed the world. Did we always agree? No, that's part of the beauty of having a best friend—you can express your point of view without fear of a fight. Talking poker, we put our differences of opinion in the books and let people decide for themselves. Nobody plays poker the same all the time anyway . . . there is more than one successful approach. I used to say that I taught the students, and T. J. taught the teachers.

T. J. is human. He admits he was addicted to the game of craps for a while. Used to be, he couldn't wait to go out there and play . . . even when he was in a tournament, he would go play craps during the breaks. He hasn't touched a craps table in 15 years. A lot of credit for that goes to his wife, Joy, and the empathetic support of his friends. But, like anybody who beats an addiction, most of the credit goes to the individual who emerges victorious from a difficult passage. And there is nobody stronger than T. J.

Larry Flynt

At the 1983 World Series of Poker Main Event (the event I won), Larry Flynt didn't quite make the last table. But not for lack of buying, er, trying. At the end of day two he was at the very bottom of the survivors, in last place, 69th. He barely survived day two, but he was determined. Larry Flynt made a big comeback because he bought people off. They dumped their chips to him. He tried to buy his way to poker fame. I talked with one of the guys who was in the tournament, a guy from Alaska I had never heard of before. There was a knock on his door after dark, and they gave him a big bunch of money. He was sitting at Larry Flynt's table, and he was to throw off all his chips to him. And he did—he took a bribe.

Larry made a $1,000 bet with Doyle Brunson at 1,000 to 1 odds—in other words, Doyle would have to pay him a million dollars if he won the tournament. Don't forget, they only paid the top nine spots. Larry almost got through day three. He ran his stack up to a big number of chips. He finished 11th or so. Just missed the final table (only nine went to the final table on day four). From 69th to 11th at the end of the third day. Because of the big bet, Doyle was sweating it a bit. I remember Larry Flynt as a 7-Card Stud player, and not much of a No-Limit Hold'em player, so everyone was surprised—and maybe a little suspicious—of his meteoric rise in chips.

Phil Hellmuth

I met Phil Hellmuth in Reno, where he used to come to the same poker tournaments I was playing. We played and got to know each other. He's the one who busted me on his way to victory in the 1989 Main Event, causing me to bubble the tournament. There were 40 players left, and only 36 got paid. He was at my table, super aggressive, raising a lot of hands. He raised another one when I was in the big blind with A - Q of spades. So, I called—I wanted to look at the flop. The flop comes Queen high with two spades. I was already getting short-stacked at this point, so I didn't mess around—I shoved all in. He called me with two Kings, and they held up. I had a lot of "outs"—twice. Nine flush cards, three Aces, and two Queens that could help. Fourteen outs twice, which is basically a dead-even proposition. That's my sad story. He took my chips and went on to victory. I bubbled the tournament and didn't make any money.

Here's another thing I can tell you about Phil Hellmuth. He recognized the value of bracelets way before most people. I knew winning the Main Event was more important than the money, and Phil understood that concept early on. That's why he became obsessed with winning as many bracelets as possible. He's got 17 and thinks he can get to 25 or more. That may be a little bit of a stretch, even playing small fields with big buy-ins, but I wouldn't be surprised if he won a few more, for sure. He's in his mid-fifties, still in good physical shape, and he has all the confidence in the world and the opportunity to play in a lot of events. Frankly, I would be surprised if he doesn't add to his collection. There is nobody near him in the bracelet count, and nobody likely to catch him.

Phil Ivey

Phil Ivey's is a phenomenal poker story. I don't think he ever worked a conventional job. He started playing as an underage teenager. He got a fake ID, called himself Jerome something, and used it to play poker in Atlantic City. He was one of the two people that really impressed me the first time I played with them, not knowing who they were. The first time I ever laid eyes on Phil Ivey was in a Limit Hold'em tournament I was playing at Jack Binion's casino in Tunica, Mississippi. He was positioned on my right, and he was playing hyper aggressively. Raising, raising, raising all the time. And he kept winning! I thought, how can this guy do that? My first impression was this guy's a maniac, what's going on here? He was winning and getting results. I said to myself, wait a minute, when a guy is playing like a maniac and is winning, I have to re-evaluate. This guy is either totally nuts, or he's something really special, a future superstar. I wasn't sure which at the time, and obviously he became something very special. I hadn't seen anybody play like that—successfully—since Stu Ungar.

In the 2002 World Series of Poker, I got to play heads-up against Phil. This was the WSOP tournament where I had put together the whole schedule and structure of the tournament. Among my innovative ideas that year was a new event I named the Gold Bracelet Match Play tournament. To be eligible for this $2,500 buy-in event, you had to be a WSOP bracelet winner. In this inaugural tournament, we ended up with 29 players, so three random players got byes in the first round. The field involved some of the biggest names in poker, including the Phils—Ivey and Hellmuth. And me. One of the byes was Jennifer Harman. In my first match I beat Captain

Tom Franklin. For my second round I drew Jennifer Harman, and I beat her.

Now we were down to eight players, the quarter finals. Only the top four finishers made the money, so you had to win your quarter final match in order to cash. For my quarter-final match, I drew Phil Ivey, who was considered the young superstar. Everyone saw Phil as the favorite over old McEvoy, who was over the hill at age 57 and had had his day. I privately asked Phil if he "wanted to save anything." Translation: Would he like to make a deal for the winner of our match to pay the loser his buy-in back, thus "saving" the $2,500 entry fee. Phil declined. I don't blame him. I was confident I would win, and so was he. So, we played. Phil was playing his loose aggressive game, playing a lot of hands, and raising a lot of hands. Then the big hand came. I got pocket Jacks and made a standard-size raise. It's a heads-up match, so you play a lot more hands, and he called with 9 - 7 off-suit. The flop came J - 7 - 7 or J - 9 - 9, I forget which. He flopped the magic trips, but basically, he was drawing to one out. He was not going to get away from this hand, and he didn't, and I busted him for the win. Then I got to play the other Phil, Hellmuth, who ended up finishing in second place. In our big hand Hellmuth had the pocket Jacks and he got it all in. I called with A - Q, and his Jacks held up like gold. I cashed for $8,575.

John "Austin Squatty" Jenkins

I was casual friends with John "Austin Squatty" Jenkins. We became better acquainted after he made the final table with me at the 1983 WSOP Main Event, finishing in seventh place after I busted him with 6 - 6 versus his A - K. He wasn't somebody that I regularly associated with, but we developed a low-key kind of friendship after our World Series connection. Squatty was, obviously, from Austin, Texas, a guy short in stature who got his nickname because of the way he would sit cross-legged in his chair at the poker table. He owned a rare bookstore in Austin that was lodged inside a big warehouse. He hosted some private home poker games in his warehouse once in a while. I was down in Austin visiting him and played in one or two of his games prior to his death in April 1989.

His life had started to come unraveled. He suffered a huge warehouse fire that was suspicious. As I understand it, his insurance company investigated him, but they found that his coverage was limited and the loss of the stuff that burned up was greater than what he could get from insurance. So, he took a financial hit because of the fire. Then, in 1988, Squatty was named in a scandal as one of several dealers who had sold fake copies of historic Texas documents to museums, libraries, and private collectors.

Earlier, Squatty was also involved in some shady deals, as either a crook or a hero, depending on whose story you believe. I have a copy of the book Austin Squatty himself wrote about his life and experiences, *Audubon and Other Capers: Confessions of a Texas Bookmaker*. He wrote how he became an informant and helped the FBI recover an extremely valuable portfolio of color engravings by John James Audubon, the famed naturalist. Made himself out to be a hero. Much more recently, there was a book written about Squatty that took a different viewpoint. It basically shredded him as a dishonest dealer who had sold some documents and memorabilia from the Alamo era that he presented as original, but that others claimed were not.

Maybe, just maybe, all this history led to his demise. Austin "Squatty" Jenkins was shot in the back of the head. Normally, that doesn't happen by accident. But before the incident, he had purportedly talked about how one could do that—kill yourself with a gunshot to the head while in a stream of water by tying a balloon to the gun—and the weapon would float downstream and disappear without being found. I was told he talked about that, and then it happened that way. It's all very spooky.

Squatty was shot in the back of the head close to a cemetery in Austin he was visiting, supposedly to do research for a new book. His body was hooked in the nearby river by a fisherman. After he died, the authorities thought it could be suicide, but they couldn't figure out how the gun could disappear. They couldn't find it in the water or anywhere on the property. That's why to this day they suspect murder, but they never found the weapon. The local newspaper reported this as a murder, with robbery mentioned as the motive for the grizzly killing. It is still listed as an unsolved cold case. Eerily, that's exactly what he had projected would happen. The chances of finding out what really happened are nonexistent.

They say sometimes you get really lucky right before you die. He finally won a pretty good-sized tournament—the $1,000 No-Limit Hold'em tournament of Amarillo Slim's Super Bowl of Poker at Caesars Palace a few months earlier in February 1989, for a six-figure payoff.

Personally, I liked him a lot. I don't have a strong opinion one way or other as to his guilt. Austin Squatty tried to build himself up as this great poker player, but with nonpoker media. He spent a lot of energy to present himself as something more than what he really was, in and out of the poker world. Allegedly, he also had a couple of other high-money poker finishes where he had tried to buy his opponent off to get the title for publicity purposes. Like so many poker players, he led a big life with an ego to match.

Gabe Kaplan

I had an interesting conversation with Gabe Kaplan, star of the TV show *Welcome Back, Kotter,* about a year or so after my WSOP Main Event victory over Rod Peate. A Las Vegas poker pro had said in a newspaper article that actor/comedian Gabe Kaplan had drafted a tentative agreement for a film depicting Rod Peate's rags-to-riches story, aptly named *The Rod Peate Story*. I understand Kaplan was going to play Rod Peate in this movie they had mapped out. But Peate had reportedly disagreed over what he would get out of the project, and that it was killed as far as he was concerned. I had heard through the poker grapevine that the background story was that Rod Peate tried to change the script. He wanted control over it, and that didn't go over well. I don't know any of this for sure, but that was the rumor at the time.

There were other aspects of Rod Peate's story Gabe must have found interesting. Rod was more of a blue-collar guy than me. Purportedly, Rod didn't know who his real father was until after his second-place finish in the World Series.

The funny thing is, after this mess with Rod fell apart, I happened to be on the same plane with Gabe flying from Las Vegas to L.A. We sat next to each other, and we talked. I wondered out loud that, now that the deal with Rod had fallen through, if Gabe would be interested in trying to do my story instead? I told him I would be much more cooperative. He said, "Nah, it needs too much work . . . it needs a lot of work." I knew that was the end of that. He liked Rod Peate's story better than mine. He also looked more like Rod Peate than me, so maybe that was a factor if he planned to play the title role.

Other than that one plane ride, I never really talked to Gabe Kaplan much. He was a really good poker player, but an even better talker and a funny, funny man. I wish he had won a bracelet.

Mason Malmuth

Mason Malmuth was one of my favorite critics. Well, favorite is a strong word. In 1995, we had a public disagreement on the practical way to chop a tournament. I went with the easy, understandable math, while the mathematician went with the exact numbers, which resulted in odd numbers and cents. This made no sense to me, so one of my first articles in *Card Player* was titled "Memo to Malmuth." It included this aptly worded rebuff:

> *Gosh Mason, I haven't seen your name lately on the leader boards of any major tournaments. Is that because you publicly admit in poker essays that (you) don't particularly like to play tournaments for many reasons? On the other hand (you say) because of the different gambling mathematics that tournaments offer they are fascinating to write about. Could it be writing about tournaments is easier than winning them?*
>
> *Gotta rush off now. I have to pick up my tickets for Hawaii that I won for being one of the top three most valuable players at the Queens Poker Classic Summer Edition II. See you at the final table, Mason! Oops I forgot; you don't play tournaments.*

Malmuth was very good at dishing out criticism, but he wasn't very good at taking it. Neither was his buddy, David Sklansky. Not too many people would openly challenge these two "brilliant" mathematicians, but I did.

Mason Malmuth didn't play No-Limit Hold'em; he played Limit Hold'em. He once wrote that Limit Hold'em was the more complicated of the two games, which was stupidest thing he ever wrote, and he was roundly criticized for that. There's a reason Doyle Brunson called No-Limit Hold'em the "Cadillac of all poker games." It's the most complicated game to master, way more complicated than Limit Hold'em, which is more technical because there's more math involved.

Men "The Master" Nguyen

In 1998, Men and I had an ugly incident at the Masters of Poker VI Tournament, where I was the tournament director. It made the poker press:

> *The inauspicious target of Nguyen's wrath was Tom McEvoy, who I've heard has earned favorable reviews for the manner in which he has always conducted his tournaments. Of course, McEvoy is well known for his success as a poker champion as well as for being a popular author and columnist, giving his floor judgments added integrity in his role as a "Celebrity Director." McEvoy understands first-hand the unique pressures that a professional poker player faces at the highest level. He is one of the few authorities who is able to call upon a vast reservoir of wisdom that combines the perspectives of a world-class player, an experienced tournament official and a dedicated promoter of the game.*
> —Nolan Dalla, *Card Player* magazine, July 24, 1998

Here's what happened. With four tables left in the $100 buy-in 7-Card Stud High/Low Split event, enough players were eliminated to break down the few remaining players at one table and move then to the other three tables. We were at break, and one player accidentally took another player's chips to her newly assigned table. That player returned from break to find his chips gone. I was made aware of what happened, and I got everyone who had been at table four together to get input on how many chips each of the two affected players had. After a lengthy discussion and some savvy negotiation, I ruled the two players should divide the chips based on the closest possible estimate that they both could agree on. They were good with that, but for some inexplicable reason, Nguyen wasn't.

He was seated at an adjacent table and had a fair amount of chips. When the floor decision was announced, Nguyen became outraged. He stormed over to me and, within inches of my face, began to hurl a litany of profanities at me. The players, bystanders, and I were stunned. Men kept it up, and I warned Nguyen that if the cussing didn't stop, he would be penalized. But his tirade of personal insults ratcheted up a level. So, I told him if he didn't return to his seat immediately, he would face a 20-minute time-out. The profanity did not stop. Faced with this uncalled-for disruptive behavior, I had little choice but to take action. Nguyen was penalized for 20 minutes and departed the room. Play continued.

After his penalty time was up, Nguyen returned to his table. He busted out of the tournament shortly after, the 20-minute penalty not helping his chip position. This caused another onslaught of personal insults, and I had to warn him that security would be called. That only made the situation worse, as Nguyen's swearing escalated. So, after a cease-and-desist warning and penalty, I announced that Nguyen would be banned from all subsequent events. Still, the profanity continued. In fact, Nguyen threatened to get a gun. That's when I announced that Nguyen would be banned from the Showboat Poker Spectacular in November (where I was also to serve as tournament director).

Lest anyone think that the details of the Nguyen-McEvoy controversy were exaggerated in any way, witnesses included several notable poker players and officials who are known for their objectivity. Everyone who was questioned about the spectacle described the events in much the same manner. All agreed that Nguyen was out of line and that something had to be done. Yet, no one could explain Nguyen's seemingly unknown motive for voicing such strong objection to McEvoy's ruling, and his subsequent behavior. While Nguyen and

McEvoy did exchange words back in March during the Four Queens tournament, the two have been on reasonably good terms. McEvoy has even gone so far as to praise Nguyen publicly in his column several times. So, what prompted Nguyen's outrage? That's a good question. He had no relationship to either player involved. He wasn't present at the table where the dispute occurred, and he did not even witness the initial circumstances.

—Nolan Dalla, *Card Player* magazine, July 24, 1998

Mike Matusow

I remember a poker seminar in Buffalo, New York, where I was teaching along with Mike Matusow when he just broke down and started to cry. The reason—the students who attended the seminar just weren't comprehending what he was trying so hard to convey to them. They just weren't getting it. These were not high-caliber poker players at the seminar. He just kind of came apart. Mike suffered at the time with some sort of a mood disorder, which means he wasn't always on the right medication and therefore in the moment. He's capable of brilliant poker play and is still a top player. And Mike is capable of great acts of generosity. One woman he didn't know well was crying because she didn't have the buy-in for a $5,000 World Series of Poker event, and he paid her buy-in so she could play. She didn't cash, but the point is, only a guy with a really big heart does that.

Mike spent nine months or so in jail once, and feels he was framed. An undercover policeman approached him to get him some drugs. Mike took drugs but did not sell them. This guy talked Mike into getting drugs and then arrested him for it. Entrapment, from Mike's viewpoint, and if it happened the way Mike said it did, it was. And then I guess he got in front of the judge, and they were going to let him off with a light sentence, maybe a month or so or probation.

But Mike "The Mouth"—they call him that because sometimes he just talks when silence would be better—he's before the judge and he wants to explain why he felt this whole situation was unjust. He was going to get a slap on the wrist, but he ended up doing real jail time because he shot his mouth off in front of the judge. Like so many of us poker players, you could say Mike makes his own luck.

Rod Peate

Rod Peate's friends used to needle him about how he lost the Main Event to me with the K - J of diamonds. My good friend and prankster, Albert Ethier ("Al Jay"), along with his buddy John Mattix, concocted this little gem. Al sent Rod a Christmas card with the K - J of diamonds in it and wished him a Merry Christmas. Of course, Al signed my name (as "Cowboy Tom," in reference to my Main Event outfit). Rod was the card room manager at Hollywood Park at the time, and as anticipated, when Al Jay walked into the card room, Rod said, "Come here Al Jay, I want to show you something." He took Al into his office and showed him the card . . . that *he* had sent. Rod said, "After all these years, look what he said to me, that McEvoy." Al agreed and told him, "You know what, he's a dirty louse."

I saw Rod the next month when I was running the Four Queens tournament in Vegas. He came up to me and said, "After all these flipping years." I wasn't in on the little joke and had to tell him I had no idea what he was talking about. I still don't know if Rod believed me. But *you* have to believe me when I say that both Al Jay and I have the same opinion of Rod Peate. He's a genuine nice guy.

Walter "Puggy" Pearson

Walter "Puggy" Pearson was another iconic player from the early days of the World Series of Poker, winner of the fourth Main

Event in 1973. I knew and played against Puggy, and I knew he would cheat at every opportunity, and at everything he did, if he thought he could get away with it. It wasn't necessarily malicious with guys of this era—it was considered just part of the game. Puggy had a reputation for being very abusive toward casino personnel, especially dealers. He would throw cards, berate floor persons, and was well known as a notoriously poor tipper.

I was in some games with him, and I witnessed him making negative comments to the dealers, like somehow, they influenced the cards he got. There was more 7-Card Stud played back then than Hold'em, and he was a pretty good Stud player. The Limit version is what he won his first WSOP bracelet for back in 1971. In 7-Card Stud, you had to ante every hand. Puggy would sometimes not ante and get away with it. He had a good slight-of-hand action where he made it look like he was dropping a chip in the pot, but he would actually conceal his chip in his hand. He got caught doing that more than once.

This is a true story, but one I did not witness. Puggy was abusing a woman dealer one time to the point that she couldn't take it anymore. She got out of the box (her seat), took off one of her high heels, and attacked Puggy. He had a lot of hundred-dollar chips on the table, and she took handfuls of them and tossed them to the audience, and then started tattooing his bald forehead with her shoe. She put a whole bunch of marks on his head before she was stopped. This was at the Dunes, where Johnny Moss was the card room manager. When this incident was brought to Moss's attention, he demanded to know the name of the dealer—so he could give her a raise!

This incident I did witness. Linda Johnson, the second woman inducted into the Poker Hall of Fame, ran poker cruises. Still does. Talk about a great concept, onboard a cruise ship, with tournaments and cash games between prominent ports of call. These cruises were a ball. Puggy had asked Linda if he could join this poker cruise. Linda, well aware of Puggy's reputation, agreed on the condition that he post a bail of something like $10,000 so he would behave himself. She was not going to allow him to abuse any of her poker-room staff and get away with it. Linda was the sole arbitrator of whether he would get a refund or not based on his behavior. He had to agree to that before he could go on the cruise. If he misbehaved, in her opinion—just in her opinion—she would keep the money. Linda was judge, jury, and executioner. Puggy did behave himself and got his money back. Linda did the same thing several years later with "a famous Asian player," who was also abusive at times. Knowing Linda, if she had collected, she would have donated the money to charity. They both behaved.

Interestingly, when I first started coming to Las Vegas, I broke into $10/$20 Limit Hold'em poker playing with Puggy's brother, J. C. Pearson. He was one of the regulars at the Golden Nugget casino, where the game was a crash course in survival with some of the best Limit Hold'em players around.

Amarillo Slim Preston

Amarillo Slim Preston Jr. was declared the winner of the 1972 WSOP Main Event and was inducted into the Poker Hall of Fame in 1992. He used this fame to host "Amarillo Slim's Super Bowl of Poker"—the second-biggest tournament for a number of years, second only to the World Series of Poker. The tournament was in full swing in the early 1980s, long before poker tournaments became so widespread. Amarillo Slim kept having to move his tournament from one location to another because he did things that were unacceptable to management. One casino would hire him, couldn't handle him anymore, and wouldn't renew his contract, so the tournament had to keep finding new venues, four or five times over the years.

Amarillo Slim was a womanizer. He was also a bigot. This was after the Vietnam War, and a lot of Americans didn't like Vietnamese people. At the time, there were a lot of Vietnamese playing poker, many of them risk-taking immigrants who had escaped Communism. Slim would often make racially charged remarks about other minorities, too. He was not a nice person. He actually was quite good for poker, however, because he had this line of bullshit and a gift for gab. He was colorful, and he got on the Johnny Carson TV show and talked up poker and the World Series in a way that was entertaining and intriguing to a whole country full of amateur poker players.

He did a lot of things that were good for poker, but as a person, he was a snake. I'll give you an example. A player I know, "Oklahoma" Johnny Hale, had a bet with someone else, and they had Amarillo Slim hold the stakes. When Johnny Hale won the bet, he went to get the money from Slim and discovered it was missing a hundred bucks. Even when confronted, Slim wouldn't fork it over.

I have a more personal illustration. After 1983, in one of his tournaments at Caesars Tahoe, Amarillo Slim and I got into a physical altercation where we actually shoved each other back and forth with a card room full of people watching. Here's what happened. I was friends with Paul Magriel, the 1978 World Backgammon Champion who had turned to poker. He taught me how to play backgammon (I don't know to this day if he did me a favor or not). Slim was going to announce the player seat and table assignments . . . they did it differently back then; it was not just paying for your entry and getting a seat assignment like it is now. Magriel had asked me if I could get him signed up for the tournament—he was up in his room and was going to be a little late getting down to the card room.

Back then, they didn't let you into the poker room right away, and you were supposed to be there when your name was called. I went up to Slim when he was announcing the names and told him—politely, mind you—that Paul Magriel had asked me to get him signed up for the tournament, and that he was still up in his room and would be down in a few minutes. Amarillo Slim got on his little high horse and said, "I'm not gonna hold up this tournament for some fool that can't get down here . . . " and on and on. I listened to his rant and simply told him, "You're the fool," and walked away. I had already signed myself up. I called Magriel and told him he had better get down here because Slim was being difficult and wouldn't let me sign him up.

Magriel came down and Slim let him in the tournament. Then, during the early stage of *his* tournament, Amarillo Slim came marching over to me. This was while we are playing, not during a break. He bent over and whispered in my ear, "I'm gonna kick your ass." No one heard it but me. I stood up and said, "You and who else?" The last thing he expected was this nerdy accountant type to stand up to him. There I was, in the middle of a hand, standing nose-to-nose with the tournament director. There was a little shoving, and that was that. There were no blows. That was it, and I sat back down thinking I may be getting escorted out of Amarillo Slim's tournament, but he was sensible enough not to kick me out. I wasn't an anonymous player at the time, and my status as a World Series champion probably helped. There was another long-time pro who was there, Gene Fisher (he came in third in the 1981 Main Event), who told me later, "Tom, the fight was over the minute you stood up to him."

Erik Seidel

The only other guy that impressed me the most at our first encounter was Erik Seidel. I was in a tough cash game between tournaments at the 1988 World Series. It was the same year Erik Seidel would later come in second to Johnny Chan in the Main Event. There was this tall, thin guy who was just dominating the cash game. I thought, Who the hell is this guy? I definitely felt everyone at the table was getting outplayed, including me. The guy who had built a huge stack in the cash game was Erik Seidel. I have played innumerable hands of live poker, and that kind of first impression has only happened twice.

Mike Sexton

In my early years in Vegas, Omaha was relatively new and gaining momentum. We first started playing Limit, then switched to Pot-Limit. Omaha didn't really come on the scene until 1984, the first year it became a World Series of Poker bracelet event. I came in third in that very first pot-limit World Series tournament. I put a bad beat on Mike Sexton that 20 years later he was still reminiscing about. I made an aggressive play, got lucky and hit a gut shot, and broke his heart.

After the 1983 Main Event lasted seven and a half hours, a then not-so-famous Mike Sexton told me Rod Peate and I had set poker back ten years. Television was publicity, and TV frowned on the lengthy match and the long expanses of time with no excitement. Note this was 19 years before the hole camera was first used in the World Series of Poker. Turns out Mike knew a thing or two about televising poker!

David Sklansky

David Sklansky has authored or coauthored 14 books on gaming theory and poker, including the renowned *The Theory of Poker*, and won three WSOP bracelets. With all this poker fame and contributions to the game, he should be in the Poker Hall of Fame. But he hasn't even been nominated. Why do you think this is? Well, the WSOP Poker Hall of Fame is a little bit of a popularity contest, and Sklansky isn't popular in the poker community. There are plenty of reasons, and here's one. If you ever wondered why you have to post when you join a poker game, you can thank Sklansky.

The Golden Nugget had to change their house Hold'em rules (and the other casinos followed suit) because of what came to be called the "Sklansky Rule." Here's why. When you left the table and came back, you didn't have to post back then. So, to take advantage of that, Sklansky would duck the blinds. Sometimes he would change seats, coming back in behind the blinds. Sometimes he would play an orbit, leave the table when it was his turn to ante the big blind, and come back to his seat after the blinds had passed. He did all kinds of stuff like that, which did not endear him to the players. He was really a piece of work.

Now when you enter a game, you either have to come in as the big blind, or wait and come in after the dealer button has passed your seat. Because Sklansky took advantage of the rules at the time when you didn't have to post when you sat back down, the rules were changed "in his honor."

One time, he offered me a $2 bribe at the Stardust if I would not join the $10/$20 game he was in and go play somewhere else. This was in front of the whole table, and everybody was watching us. I said alright, give me the two bucks, took his money, and I left. Talk about your backhanded compliment. He wasn't a terrible player—he wasn't that good of a no-limit player, but he played the other games reasonably well and played Limit Hold'em pretty good.

He had 5 percent of my action in the 1983 World Series of Poker Main Event. I didn't start out despising him. You know, he wrote some good books. I was impressed with the guy. I'd read his first book on Hold'em—a little pamphlet, really—and it helped me. I'm impressed with smart people. Until I realize that they are not nice people, and then I just avoid them. He was not a nice person.

Jack "Treetop" Straus

The 6-foot 6-inch Jack Straus, aptly nicknamed "Treetop," won the 1982 World Series of Poker Main Event, famously coming back from the loss of all of his chips except one, the origin of the "all it takes is a chip and a chair" legend. Straus came all the way back from the edge of disaster. In the final hand, with over a million dollars in chips, Dewey Tomko, with A - 4 of diamonds, went all-in preflop against Straus, who called the bet with an A - 10 off-suit. There was a 4 on the flop, but a 10 hit the river, giving Straus the Main Event victory. The wisdom of either player getting all the money in with well over a hundred big blinds left with those hands is a discussion for another day.

About that single solitary $500 chip Jack had left. My friend Al Jay, who is a good friend of Jack Binion, tells me that Treetop's last chip was actually under a napkin, allegedly overlooked. Straus bet all his visible chips, but he never said "all-in." After all the chips in the pot were pushed to his opponent, the hidden chip was discovered, and the tournament officials had to make a ruling. The ruling was he could keep the chip, after which he went on a winning streak.

The story goes that the chip under the napkin was there accidentally. Al said that it was Jack Binion's opinion that Jack Straus never did anything accidentally. In other words, he knew he had that chip, and he knew exactly what he was doing. So, if he lost that pot, he wouldn't be out of the tournament. That turned out to be a very savvy move. It set the stage for his legendary comeback, and a poker adage that will likely live forever.

Jack Straus and Crandell Addington

Here's another story my friend Al Jay told me about Jack Straus and his buddy, Poker Hall of Famer Crandell Addington.

Jack would gamble on anything . . . he was a great gambler who had trouble holding onto money. Jack and Crandell lived close to each other in Texas. Crandell was a first-class cowboy-type poker player that made a lot of money in oil.

One day, Crandell and Jack were talking on the phone when Crandell realizes his friend is no longer talking. Crandell says "Jack, Jack" and there is no answer. Crandell suspects foul play, so he put his gun in his pocket and drove down to Jack's house. The door was open, and he slowly inched in the house along the wall and went into the living room with his hand on his gun, expecting some trouble. He went to every room in the home, and no Jack. Totally perplexed, he walked out through the front door when he saw Jack driving up.

Jack jumps out of his car, and Crandell says, "Jack, don't ever do that to me again. What the hell is going on here? Why did you just drop the phone and leave?" Jack says, "Crandell, I just got barred from Baskin Robbins! While I was talking with you on the phone, I realized I had left a bag of money up there, $125,000, underneath the table after I finished my ice cream. I just left there. I went back to Baskin Robbins and the bag was gone. I found the manager and told him I left a bag under this table and asked if he had picked it up." The manager said, "Yeah, I picked it up. And I'm turning it over to the police." Jack said, "That's not money that belongs to the police, you know that, it's my money, now give me the bag."

The manager said, "Well, I'm going to give you the bag back with the money, but you are barred from Baskin Robbins and ever coming back in here again!

Stu Ungar

Stu Ungar launched his poker career playing high-stakes 7-Card Stud cash games at the Silver Bird casino. This funky poker icon was truly a savant. I believe he had something very close to a photographic memory. He didn't start out as a drug addict, but he became one. He was the only guy that I ever knew who would bet his entire net worth every day, regardless of whatever his net worth was that day. He was a degenerate sports better. He played and bet on every game and sport you could think of—backgammon, horses, whatever. The first time he ever picked up a golf club, he lost something like $100,000 to Jack "Treetop" Straus on the putting green. Stu was not athletic at all, so for him to be playing any kind of sports, let alone gambling on them, was a stretch, from my point of view. Even with all the handicaps they would give him, he still couldn't win very often. When he wasn't playing poker, he took the worst of it all the time in other forms of gambling, and he gambled at everything.

I was not in his little circle of friends. I played him at poker a couple of times. Jack Straus hosted a heads-up, double-elimination tournament where I had to play Stuey. And he beat me. Then he went on and won the whole tournament. I also played against Stu in the Irish Open in Dublin in 1983, and that time I won. When Stuey Ungar had a clear head—before he was all drugged up or when he came out of different rehabs clean again for a little while—there was no better poker player that ever lived. But only when his mind was not clouded with drugs. He won his third World Championship title in 1997, after everybody had written him off and thought that because of his drug habit he had lost it and just couldn't play anymore.

He had pulled himself together just enough, and he dominated a tournament table full of superstars like Doyle Brunson, Billy Baxter, Bobby Baldwin, Phil Hellmuth, and Johnny Chan. He completely crushed the tables on his way to victory at the Main Event, where the final table was played for the first and only time on the street outside the Horseshoe casino on Fremont Street. I was there watching him do it. He was just smashing everybody to pieces. All the people were talking about it right and left.

Stu had a remarkable, uncanny ability to read players, not only knowing the range of cards they played, but also kind of getting inside their head to understand the way they were thinking. He seemed to know when he could get someone to fold a slightly better hand than his, and when to back off. He was a master of the three-bet bluff. After the flop, he would make a bet and get called. Then he would fire a second barrel. But he was also very good, when, after the first two bets didn't work, he fired a third barrel. And that worked for him a lot of times. He had this super-aggressive style, and at the time he was the only player that was successful playing this way. He knew who he could intimidate and who he had to be careful of—the guy was just phenomenal as a judge of players and as a card reader. When he was drugged up, he was the loosest player at the table. People were always check-raising him and beating him when he was messed up, and he was messed up most of the time during about the last 15 years or so of his poker career.

During the 1990 WSOP Main Event tournament, Stu had built a monster lead of chips after the second or third day, and then collapsed at the tournament from a drug overdose. They had to haul him off in an ambulance. He was in the hospital, and he was leading the tournament. He was so far ahead of everybody that his empty stack made the final table. He was really sick, but he still wanted to come back and play. The doctors said if he checked himself out to play poker, he probably wouldn't survive. The net result was he stayed in the hospital, and they blinded him off. It was the only time he made the final table of the Main Event and didn't win. He, and his empty chair, finished ninth.

By the way, it's interesting that T. J. Cloutier credits Stu Ungar with coining one of the most popular phrases in sports— "threepeat"—when he was going for his third win in Amarillo Slim's Super Bowl of Poker.

But it was in gin rummy that Stu Ungar really excelled. According to Jack Binion, "There's never been a guy who could play Gin like Stuey. Not even close. Of all the players that dominated a game, there has never been a player dominate one game like Stuey did gin rummy. He was so much further ahead of anybody else. Some way or another, after seven discards, Stuey could tell almost exactly what was in your hand."

Byron "Cowboy" Wolford

The year after I won the Main Event, this charismatic character was the Main Event runner-up. He got his nickname because he was a rodeo champion, winning back-to-back championships at the Calgary Stampede. He still holds the all-time speed record for calf roping at Madison Square Garden in the 1950s (because they stopped holding it there). He wrote a book about his escapades and told this story to my good friend, Dan Alspach. Somebody said to Cowboy, okay you can rope calves, but I bet you can't rope chickens. He laughed and took the bet. He said "Dan, I was a poor kid on a farm in Texas. What do you think I learned to rope on? I roped my chickens!"

He told Dan he would marry a beautiful young girl every year when he was on the rodeo circuit, back when he was making money, and then as soon as the money ran out, they would all leave him. One year, he had a young wife, and there was a poker game near the end of the rodeo season. He said, "There's a sucker in that game I gotta go play." He lost half his bankroll, and said, "Well, he'll be there tomorrow night. I'll go back and get him." He went back and lost another half of his bankroll. He said, "Well, I've got to get him tomorrow night." He went again, but the sucker wasn't there. When he went back home, his wife had left him a note that read "I left with the sucker." Cowboy Wolford told Dan that story, and it's in his book *Cowboys, Gamblers & Hustlers: The True Adventures of a Rodeo Champion & Poker Legend* that he cowrote with my coauthor, Dana Smith.

Tom is the most honest man I have ever met, equal with my father. If Tom tells you something, it's the truth. A lot of people in the poker world are full of bullshit. Not Tom.

—T. J. Cloutier

CHAPTER 31

Who Is This Tom McEvoy Guy? Telling on Tom.

Dan Alspach (Close friend)

*T*om's a sweetheart who really cares about people. He's one of the nicest guys in poker. I'll tell you a story to prove my point. This happened when Tom was at the final two tables at a World Series tournament in 2007. At his table was Robert Paul "Eskimo" Clark.

This guy was a colorful character. He won more than a million dollars in one year, and when he was on a roll, he would play with a hundred thousand dollars on the table. But like too many poker players, he lost his money as quickly as he made it—which made it difficult to pay his taxes. When he was basically broke and living in a car with a hole in the bottom, the IRS came after him. After they jailed him, he told them he didn't want to leave. He got free food, and he won all the cigarettes. And he would smell so bad. One time, the WSOP Tournament Director Jack McCellan told Eskimo on the dinner break if he didn't go up to his room and shower and change clothes, he was out of the tournament.

So, Tom is at the World Series event table with this character when Eskimo started to have a fit. He's foaming at the mouth, his eyes roll back, and he fell over on the floor. Everybody at the table said, well, shuffle up and deal the cards. Not Tom. He stood up and made them call the paramedics and get Eskimo some help. Tom got down on the floor and helped Eskimo. The paramedics arrived, gave him oxygen, and told him they were going to take him to the hospital. Eskimo said, "Hell no, I'm in a poker tournament!" He got back up, took his seat at the table, and in the next hand he knocked Tom out of the tournament. The guy who had probably saved his life! Eskimo didn't win the tournament, he came in third or fourth, but he busted Tom with two tables left. Needless to say, there were a lot of interesting side bets as to whether Eskimo would die or win the tournament.

Another story. Many years ago, I won a satellite after I had already purchased my seat in a $5,000 tournament, so I gave the seat to Tom. And this dealer who had always been very nasty to me was suddenly very nice. He said it was because I did that—kind of a secondary effect. The dealer liked Tom. Tom was always nice to the dealers.

Buddy Ashmore (Close friend)

If Tom includes you as a friend, it's for life. He's always there for you. He's been a confidant over the years, a good listener, and just an all-around good friend. I'm lucky to have three lifetime friends, and Tom is one of them.

Tom introduced me to Oklahoma Johnny Hale years and years ago. Johnny told me that he wouldn't play in a cash game with some of the best-known players of his era, even with my money. But if it was a game Tom McEvoy was involved in, you knew it was an honest game with no shadiness going on. Tom is one of the most trusted people there is in the poker community.

Jack Binion (Legendary WSOP promoter, son of World Series of Poker originator Benny Binion)

Actually, I never knew Tom really well as much as I did some of these other guys. From my perspective, Tom wasn't a gambler like 90 percent of the poker players back in the early days. These guys were really smart about poker, but they loved to gamble and just couldn't hold onto money. Tom approached poker much more like a business and viewed the game more in an academic way. He had better discipline than most poker players because he didn't gamble away his money. Everybody speaks well of him because he is such a good fellow.

Mike Caro (Poker pro and poker author)

In one of his articles, Mike "The Mad Genius" Caro wrote, with his usual tongue in cheek delivery:

My hastily contrived scientific poll showed that of 37 players asked, all but none of them used the word "nice" in their description of Tom McEvoy. In the parlance of pollsters, "all but none" means unanimous. McEvoy is nice.

T. J. Cloutier (Poker Hall of Famer and close friend)

Let me start right off with this—Tom is the most honest man I have ever met, equal with my father. If Tom tells you something, it's the truth. A lot of people in the poker world are full of bullshit. I guess I am sometimes, too. But not Tom. He has never lied to me or embellished one thing. He's just straight down the line. And to me, that's a very honest person. You never have to worry about what he tells you because it's right on. I couldn't give him more praise than that.

Tom treated everybody really good, and his word was his bond. Excuse the card pun, but Tom called a spade a spade. No going around sideways. Never heard him say anything to try to hurt anybody. That's a pretty good compliment about a man, you know.

I have always considered Tom my best friend. He was always very loyal to his friends and would do anything for you. Here's an example. I had a lot of problems with the craps for a while. He rode me through it and he's one of the main reasons I gave it up. Used to be I couldn't wait to go out there and play . . . even when I was in a tournament, I would go play craps during the breaks. You can get addicted to many things, and I was addicted to the craps for a while. Tom, along with my wife, kept me going and I beat it. I haven't touched a craps table in 14 years.

One of the things he did for everybody probably saved my life. He was one of the main forces against smoking in the poker room. Hell, I was smoking four-and-a-half packs a day at the time when we were playing tournaments. I had one behind my ear, one in my mouth lit, and one in the ashtray waiting. I wasn't in favor of the smoking ban right off the bat, but I sure was once he started the whole thing. I wanted to quit, and that's how I finally quit. I knew I had to quit after I had two coughing jags in Las Vegas in 2000 where I passed out. One by the swimming pool, and one at the Horseshoe by the escalator going up to the poker room where I was rescued by Mike Sexton and a security guard. After over 20 years of smoking, I never touched another cigarette.

A lot of people would say Tom was like a nerd. Me, I'm the opposite of a nerd, I'm one of those outgoing types of people. But anytime you wanted to do something, Tom was ready and rarin' to go, too. I mean out to dinner and shows . . . we went to a lot of movies together. When we were in Hawaii, my wife Joy and I would take trips and take Tom with us . . . we would rent a car and drive around and stuff. Then we finally took the helicopter ride. Joy and I were in the back seat and Tom was up front with the pilot. Tom was reading a book and he fell asleep. And that was typical Tom. He would never have sat up there, but he thought it would be better for me and my wife to sit together. That's just the kind of guy he is.

Steve Diano (Professional sports gambler and poker player)

I met Tom at a WSOP satellite at Binion's Horseshoe in 2004. When we got down to heads-up, the dealer was unsure which of us would be the big blind. Tom assured us of the way this was supposed to be handled. It was the first time I had encountered this situation, so I asked for a ruling. Tom said, "Trust me, I've been around poker a long time, and I know what I'm talking about." I didn't have a clue who he was, so I said, "Yea, well who the heck are you?" Tom simply pointed to his picture on the wall.

So now, knowing this guy is a pretty good poker player, I patiently waited for the opportunity to trap him. It came with pocket Jacks. I checked and the flop was 2 - 4 - 9, with two diamonds, giving me an over pair. Tom bet and I checked again. The next card is the third Jack. Bingo! I checked a third time, and Tom fired a bet again. I had him right where I wanted him! I went all in, and he called with a 3 - 5 of diamonds, giving him a flush draw and a straight draw. Of course, he made the heartbreaking straight.

I soon learned he was one of the nicest guys on the planet. Despite his enduring personality, and all of his great accomplishments which includes his WSOP Main Event victory, I learned over the years that many people have no idea who he is. This became clear to me when one time I offered to bring him to a charity poker event, and the guy running it asked me, "Who's Tom McEvoy?"

I have a nickname for Tom; the "Bluffless Wonder." We became great friends over the years, and I played lots of poker with him, including multiple poker leagues. I made the observation one time that I had never seen him bluff, ever. I then conducted an investigation of all fellow league members, plus many other pros that have played with him. Not one person could recollect a hand where Tom had ever bluffed. I maintain that he is the one member of the Poker Hall of Fame to have never bluffed, which is reason enough for him to have been inducted.

My friend is also a little quirky. When I moved from Vegas to Grand Rapids, I needed someone to drive in the car with me. I asked Tom if he would make the drive with me to keep me company; then he could visit his family and I would fly him home. He brought reading material with him for a three-day trip. Not just a few books, but a whole box of books. He would read a chapter from one book, put it down and read a chapter from another book. Who reads like that? I yelled at him in the car. I can't take this—pick a book and read it!

Eric Drache (WSOP Tournament Director)

As quoted in the December 18, 1983, *Detroit Free Press* article by Mark Kram:

Tom is simply a better poker player than most. He has a restrained ego, is extremely calculating and is free of all the vices that invariably destroy talent.

Mori Eskandani (President of PokerGO)

Tom is an old acquaintance. He broke my heart in 1983 when he won the World Series of Poker Main Event and defeated Rod Peate, the poker hero of my hometown of Vancouver, Washington. I moved to Vegas in 1985 as a professional poker player and played with Tom in tournaments and cash games for years.

You know, you can always tell people's true character when they are losing in a poker game. It just shows up. They can't hide it. If they are angry people, you're going to see the cards and the chips flying. If they are bitter, you are going to hear some words that you're not supposed to hear. And if they are a first-class act, you're going to see that, too, and that's what we saw from Tom.

Poker is a game that you take two steps forward, three steps backward, four steps forward—it's never a straight line, it's always back and forth. So, how one takes the backwards steps, like I said, reveals true character, and which players exhibit with class. That's part of the reason nobody ever doubted Tom was a good representative of poker as a World Champion. His reputation in the poker world was definitely impeccable.

Albert J. ("Al Jay") Ethier (Poker pro and close friend)

I've known Tom since his early days in Vegas in the 1970s, and he's on the opposite spectrum of the rounders, thieves, pool and dice hustlers, and card guys who could deal from the bottom and the middle of the deck and all that. I've seen the outside life and the inside life, so to speak, so I think my judgment of people is pretty damn good. From my many years of personal experiences with Tom McEvoy and what people have said, he's extremely honorable and

everybody knows it. I've never known anybody to knock him as far as his honorability is concerned. His truthfulness. They might knock his poker play, but they won't knock him personally like some kind of scammer or teamer with somebody else. He's never been accused of anything like that and he's never done it. He's a very straightforward guy. His integrity is impeccable, trust me.

Dr. Paul Fischman (Psychiatrist, poker student, and close friend)

Tom is one of my favorite human beings on earth. I just don't know any people who are as good a person as he is. He is a 100 percent guileless human being, which I don't know too many people who fall in that category. He never will say anything bad about anybody. If he says anything about anybody that is even a little bit negative, it will be so soft-pedaled that you miss it. He's one of the good guys, I mean one of the really good guys. But he doesn't hold people accountable.

Like all of his life he has loaned money to people and only occasion-ally gotten paid back. He has let people take advantage of him on a regular basis just because he is very nonconfrontational.

To my knowledge, Tom hasn't ever told a lie to anybody on pur-pose. Now, I can't say that about anybody else I know. He's a very warm guy. He hugs people and he's glad to see them. He's a nice man, not to mention that's he's probably got one of the better minds of most of the people that I know, including some of the people I went to medical school with. I mean he's really, really smart.

Phil Hellmuth (Poker pro with the most WSOP bracelets)

Tom has perfect honor, ethics, and morals. And that's important. Not every champion in our world is pure. Staking him was easy because I always knew that every penny was spent the way it was supposed to be spent. It's just nice to be able to completely trust some-body. Tom has a perfect reputation. Would I say that's a rarity? No. But it is certainly hard won in our world.

I always liked dealing with him because of his integrity. We saw it in each other. Having perfect integrity is just a really big thing. And you see when you are gambling with people and you are at the tables with them, you do business with them, who has the perfect ethics and morals and who doesn't. Tom has earned my respect.

William "Uncle Bill" Howard (Card Player poker writer)

I have invested in Tom McEvoy tournament outcomes twice. Won once, lost once. I'm ahead of the game. The risk is only in the cards; there is no character risk with Tom McEvoy. He is a solid player without the bad habits that have been the downfall of other high-stakes players.

Linda Johnson (Poker Hall of Fame member)

Tom is a dear friend of mine. He's a genuine person. Tom has integrity, a lot of integrity, and that's what stands out. In our business, to have someone who is willing to basically lay their life on the line to do the right thing is uncommon. He would be the one to do that, always. Even if it caused him a lot of trouble, he did the right thing.

He's honest, he has a good sense of humor, and he likes to have a good time. But "honest" is one thing that really would describe Tom.

There are a lot of unsavory people in poker, and he is head and shoulders above the rest when it comes to honesty.

Alan McEvoy (Brother)

He's generous. He's kind. He's a good man. He's an honest broker. There's a lot of cheats and slime bags in this world, and he's an honorable person in this world. Always has been.

He has uncommon honesty within his chosen industry and the poker community. He will give back every cent he ever borrowed from you, right to the penny. I have an arrangement with him. I give him money sometimes to play tournaments. He keeps track of exactly how much money is left in the pot. He's done the same with other players.

The bottom line, with my brother Tom, he has given more than he has taken. He's an honest man. He's a fundamentally good human being with a moral compass. And I love him. But I still worry about him.

Marcia McEvoy Madden (Sister)

Tom left our house to go to college when I was seven or eight, so I don't have a lot of memories of him growing up. I would say from my perspective, he was a little aloof and self-absorbed, like a typical teenager. He had his own hobbies and buddies, and he wasn't too interested in a baby sister.

I have a funny story to tell about Tom. In the early 1980s, Tom gave me as a legitimate *Christmas gift, a fake gold medallion from Caesars Palace, on a long fake gold chain. This was his idea of a fine piece of jewelry. He thought I would love it. Because of his social-awareness issues, he sometimes has a hard time taking other people's perspective. He wasn't around when I opened it, and after laughing hysterically, I decided to do something interesting with it. I made that gold medallion into something our family calls "Stinky Poo." The first year of Stinky Poo, I wrote a short rhyming poem about it, wrapped it up, and gave it to my brother Steve at Christmas. Steve, in turn, had to write a rhyming poem that covered the goings-on of our extended family over the past year, wrapped it up, and gave it to my brother Alan the following year. We passed around that Stinky Poo every year, with a family poem attached, for 20 years before we let Tom in on the joke. In 2003, Tom finally received Stinky Poo for the first time. He was surprised but laughed a lot, especially as we read the poems from all the previous years. He was a really good sport about it. We still do Stinky Poo every Christmas when the family gathers, and it has now been 40 years with different siblings and now their children receiving Stinky Poo every year. We have 40 years of poems about our family that recall precious memories and a lot of laughs.*

Patrick McEvoy (Son)

Growing up in Las Vegas was great. Both of my parents worked nights, and they were both very much there, just different hours. In a way it was a blessing because my siblings and I learned to be more self-reliant.

When I was in high school, I moved in with my dad and Vicki Rose. I have fond memories of those days, living in a wild love-hate bipolar manic relationship with lots of high points and crazy fights. Vicki and I got along great. It was all very entertaining and cool for a high school senior. Dad knew the teenage propensity to find trouble, and he preferred my buddies and I would have fun at home. So, we drank beer, smoked cigars (not Dad, of course), and played poker with Dad. He let us hang out and party, so it became kind of a relaxed, fun environment.

Dad was always supportive of what I did. He was happy with my future trajectory desire, and he understood pursuing a career dream with passion. I always felt a calling to serve my country, and he and Mom gave me parental consent to join the Marine Corps after my

junior year, and I shipped off for boot camp three weeks after gradu-
ating. And I'm so glad they trusted my wishes.

Trust is an issue with my dad. He's sometimes too quick to trust
people. I remember that growing up, not so much now, but back in the
1990s and 2000s, when he was really successful at poker, he seemed to
have more friends and more wannabe friends. He was gullible when
people would ask him for money, and I appreciate that he owns it
now with no denials. It's just who he is; he loves everybody and trusts
everybody and doesn't necessarily know who to not trust. And that
has hurt him in the long run.

As a father, he had a hard time connecting with children. He was
there, he was present, he always provided for us. He's a better adult
communicator than a kid one, and my relationship with him as an
adult is a lot closer than it was as a kid. Poker and everything about it
is his driving passion, but he cares deeply for his friends and he cares
deeply for those who care about him.

Steve McEvoy (Brother)

My brother is a wonderful person, but he is oblivious to many
things. He has no clue sometimes that his behavior, in some respects, is
almost outrageous. He doesn't pay enough attention to certain small
things around him that after a while can actually become irritating.
Things like leaving the refrigerator door ajar and not even realizing
it. Sometimes I could just whack him on the side of the head because
he's so outrageous in some of his omissions rather than commissions.
None of this is malicious, it's just unconscious. He's been that way his
whole life. But you have to accept him for all of his good qualities, as
well as some of these peculiar ones.

This is how I view Tom. There's the fable of a very gentle, very large
moose that ends up giving a ride on his tall antlers to a dozen animals
in the forest because the going is so slow and tedious on the forest

floor. He's carrying them along on his antlers because he is so kind and so helpful and he's trying to rescue—emphasis on rescue—all of these animals/people. That's Tom. Tom is the moose. That's the way he's been his whole life. He has spent more time, wasted more money, made more mistakes trying to rescue people that shouldn't be rescued, especially financially. Part of the problem with Tom is that he has no respect for money. Which means he doesn't really care about it.

Antonio Pinzari (Longtime friend and poker columnist)

I don't embellish. He was friendly when we first met at a 7-Card Stud tournament 35 years ago when I introduced myself. Tom is the kindest person I have ever known. He's a true gentleman that would help anyone. There's no pretense with Tom—what you see is what you get. I have never heard him volunteer a bad word about anyone—you have to kind of force it out of him. He doesn't have a mean bone in his body. People could take a lesson from him as far as humanity goes.

Matt Savage (Executive Tour Director of the World Poker Tour)

Tom to me is a legend of the game. He definitely did a lot in his time to advance poker and make it better for all of us. He pursued

poker as a career, as a profession, and was one of the leaders in that regard. Tom had a good feel for the pulse of the industry, and if you went to him with any kind of question, you knew he would shoot straight with you.

He has a high degree of integrity. Tom was always the kind of guy you could trust. You knew if you were taking a piece of his action, he was going to come through and pay it. There were a lot of people that played in his era that you had to worry about. When they made the money, you weren't sure they would pay you what you were owed. You would never have to worry about that with Tom.

I probably wouldn't even have had the opportunity to run the World Series of Poker (2002) if it wasn't for Tom, so I definitely owe him a great debt of gratitude. My career would not be the same without that opportunity. That was the first year they had no smoking at the World Series, and I played a big part in not allowing any abuse of the dealers or other players. It was a time when players, basically, were able to do and say whatever they wanted to the dealers, and I was influential in making sure that didn't happen. I think Tom really supported that as well, because he was never a guy that would abuse a dealer or blame a dealer like so many people did back then.

Dana Smith (Coauthor of six books with Tom)

In the Poker business, reputation is everything. And McEvoy's reputation for being honest, trustworthy, and fair is sterling. Few players in the volatile, roller coaster world of high-stakes poker have earned as much respect as he has.
   —Gaming Times, December 1996

Danielle Striker (Close friend and poker grinder)

Empath. He's empathetic. Tom is always there for the underdog or undercat. If someone is bleeding, needs money, needs help—he runs to it. He's an empath to a fault who will help anybody, anywhere, anytime.

His other great quality is that he is ridiculously humble. In my opinion, he is a poker legend. But he doesn't operate like that, which is nice. That's why we love him. Because he's humble.

I think poker strips you of your confidence. When you play a lot of tournament poker, you are a loser much more often than you are a winner. It's very hard to be a consistent winner in tournaments. Tom has a very high cash percentage, but he's a rarity. The normal, average person that plays, if they are a good player, cashes about 12 percent of the time.

Tom has lots of great characteristics. He's very well read and intelligent. He's always been a gentleman. And he's such a good person, and honest. Which is also weird. He's an honest poker player. I have no idea how this man wound up in this field. It's just funny. When I first met him, he told me, "If you ever take a loan to play poker, which I don't suggest, but if you do, make sure you pay back right away. If you give your word you have to keep it. Because there are a lot of players that are unscrupulous and don't pay back their loans." That's not something a lot of people understand until they play poker, and Tom impressed on me that you have to have a lot of integrity. To yourself. You have to be able to keep promises to yourself and live with yourself.

Bill "Bulldog" Sykes (Pro player and poker columnist)

The risk is only in the cards; there is no character risk with Tom McEvoy.

Jennifer Synder (Ex-girlfriend)

Tom is a very thoughtful person. He is unbelievably kind, and he has always been that way. Honestly, I have to say he is very sweet to most people. If he gets in a heated argument about something he's very passionate about, yes, he's a different person, but for the most part Tom has always been the nice guy, the sweet guy that will always help someone. That's who he is. He's always been that way with me, and I've heard other stories. Just a good, good man.

Sam Waldner (Close friend)

Tom has a very strong code. When he committed to something, he was in. With the exception of some of the people in this book, Tom doesn't say anything bad about anybody. He doesn't do bad things and he doesn't lie. And he's not a spender—he didn't buy fancy cars and fancy houses—too often he spent his money on other people, who have taken advantage of him. Tom cares about people. If a person needs to be nurtured, that's not Tom. But he's the kind of person that if something is wrong, he will be there. I was in the hospital once and

unconscious for three days, and Tom was there every day for a minimum of three hours. He's a great guy that does stupid things. Doesn't do drugs or alcohol or anything like that, but he is self-destructive. I count him as my best friend.

Peter Victor (Close friend)

I'm from Portugal, and I came to Vegas in 2007 because poker intrigued me. I wasn't wealthy and I struggled, getting laid off several times during the recession from jobs like cab driving and construction. Then my father passed away in 2010 and left me some money I was not expecting, and suddenly I'm able not to have to work. My psychic introduced me to Bonnie Dominio, and I joined her poker league. That's how I met Tom. We've been friends for 11 years.

Tom is a person of integrity. He takes that seriously. Definitely a good man and a good friend. We live in a world where character and staying true to yourself are unfortunately not a high priority. Tom is not that kind of person. I consider myself privileged that I have his friendship and I associate with a person that has a good moral compass like he does.

We like to get together often for breakfast and conversation. The two of us often take opposing viewpoints about all kinds of subjects, including poker. He says yes, I say no, but we are best of friends. It's like verbal Ping-Pong, like two brothers who always try to get advantage over each other. We laugh a lot. Go figure.

It's the little things that count, hundreds of them.
—Cliff Shaw

CHAPTER 32

Tom McEvoy Tournament Results.

Unofficial Total Live Earnings $3,093,122

607th on the All-Time Money List (2023)

1979 - $4,136

Aug	**Silver City Casino, Las Vegas**		
	Hold'em	1st	$1,080
	Hold'em	1st	$840
Oct	**Golden Nugget Casino, Las Vegas**		
	Hold'em	1st	$600
	5-Card Stud	1st	$580
Nov	**Golden Nugget Casino, Las Vegas**		
	Hold'em	3rd	$436
Dec	**Golden Nugget Casino, Las Vegas**		
	Pineapple	1st	$600

1980 - $4,758+

May	**Aladdin Casino, Las Vegas**		
	Hold'em	1st	$1,325

June	**Aladdin Casino, Las Vegas**		
	Hold'em	1st	$1,720
Oct	**Golden Eagle Casino, Las Vegas**		
	7-Card Stud	2nd	?
Nov	**Golden Eagle Casino, Las Vegas**		
	7-Card Stud	3rd	$132
	7-Card Stud	3rd	$132
Dec	**Golden Nugget Casino, Las Vegas**		
	Limit Hold'em	2nd	$1,449
Dec	**Golden Eagle Casino, Las Vegas**		
	Hold'em	3rd	?

1981 - $7,150

Jan	**Bingo Palace Casino, Las Vegas**		
	7-Card Stud	7th	$75
Feb	**Imperial Palace Casino, Las Vegas**		
	Hold'em	1st	$2,830
June	**Golden Nugget Casino, Las Vegas**		
	Hold'em	2nd	$400
July	**Golden Nugget Casino, Las Vegas**		
	Hold'em	1st	$1,110
	Hold'em	1st	$1,075
Sept	**Bingo Palace Casino, Las Vegas**		
	Hold'em	2nd	$550
Sept	**Golden Nugget Casino, Las Vegas**		
	Limit Hold'em	1st	$1,000
Oct	**Bingo Palace Casino, Las Vegas**		
	7-Card Stud	5th	$110

1982 - $73,219

Jan	**Showboat Casino, Las Vegas**		
	Hold'em	1st	$1,255

	7-Card Stud	2nd	$725
Feb	**Amarillo Slim's Superbowl of Poker, Lake Tahoe**		
	$ 1,000 Limit Hold'em	1st	$ 57,600
Ma	**Maxim Casino, Las Vegas**		
	7-Card Stud	3rd	$10
	Hold'em	1st	$875
April	**Maxim Casino, Las Vegas**		
	7-Card Stud	3rd	$635
May	**13th World Series of Poker, Las Vegas**		
	$ 1,000 Razz	6th	$ 3,200
May	**Showboat Casino, Las Vegas**		
	7-Card Stud	3rd	$225
June	**Sahara Casino. Las Vegas**		
	7-Card Stud	2nd	$563
June	**Maxim Casino, Las Vegas**		
	7-Card Stud	3rd	$400
	7-Card Stud	2nd	$295
Aug	**Showboat Casino, Las Vegas**		
	Hold'em	1st	$905
Sept	**Maxim Casino, Las Vegas**		
	Hold'em	4th	$245
Oct	**Sahara Casino, Las Vegas**		
	7-Card Stud	1st	$905
Oct	**Showboat Casino, Las Vegas**		
	Hold'em	2nd	$650
Oct	**Sahara Casino, Las Vegas**		
	Hi-Low Split	1st	$1,035
Dec	**Golden Nugget**		
	Hold'em	3rd	$3,696

1983 - $761,110

Jan	**Sahara Casino, Las Vegas**		
	7-Card Stud	3rd	$405
Jan	**1983 Stairway to the Stars, Las Vegas**		
	$ 500 No-Limit Hold'em	3rd	$ 5,050
Feb	**Desert Inn Casino, Las Vegas**		
	7-Card Stud	1st	$535
Mar	Bingo Palace Casino, Las Vegas		
	Hold'em (WSOP Satl)	4th	$460
May	**14th World Series of Poker**		
	$ 10K Main Event	1st	$ 540,000
	$ 1K Limit Hold'em	1st	$ 117,000
Sept	**Irish Eccentric Club Intl. Poker, Dublin, Ireland**		
	No-Limit Hold'em	1st	$43,125
Dec	**Jack Straus World Match Play Championships, LV**		
	$ 2.5K No-Limit Hold'em	8th	$ 3,375
	$ 1K Razz	3rd	$ 4,950
	$ 1K Limit 7-Card Std H/L	4th	$ 2,150
	$ 1,000 No-Limit Hold'em	3rd	$ 11,550

1984 - $48,170

Mar	**Celebrity Poker Classic, Las Vegas**		
	$ 1K Limit 7-Card Stud	2nd	$ 9,600
May	**15th World Series of Poker, Las Vegas**		
	$ 1K Pot-Limit Omaha	3rd	$ 16,800
Sep	**America's Cup of Poker 1984, Las Vegas**		
	$ 200 Limit 7-Card Stud	2nd	$ 3,320
	$ 500 Limit 7-Card Stud	1st	$ 13,500
Dec	**Jack Straus World Match Play Championships, LV**		
	$ 1K No-Limit Hold'em	3rd	$ 4,950

1985 - $20,025

Jan	**1985 Stairway to the Stars, Las Vegas**		
	$ 1K Razz	4th	$ 1,800
	$ 1K Limit 7-Card Stud	2nd	$ 8,000
	$ 500 Limit Hold'em	5th	$ 5,625
	$ 5K No-Limit Hold'em	9th	$ 1,100
	$ 1K Stud/Hold'em Dbles	1st	$ 3,500

1986 - $81,949

Jan	**1986 Stairway to the Stars, Las Vegas**		
	$ 200 Limit Hold'em	2nd	$ 4,896
	$ 1K No-Limit Hold'em	7th	$ 1,800
	$ 500 No-Limit Hold'em	9th	$ 938
	$ 500 Razz	7th	$ 960
Jan	**Grand Prix of Poker 1986, Las Vegas**		
	$ 1K000 No-Limit Hold'em	6th	$ 8,050
	$ 500 Limit Omaha	17th	$ 1,425
Mar	**1986 Pot of Gold, Reno**		
	$ 200 Razz	1st	$ 7,800
	Limit Hold'em	2nd	?
May	**17th World Series of Poker, Las Vegas**		
	$ 1K 7-Card Stud Hi/Lo	8th	$ 3,680
	$ 1K 7-Card Razz	1st	$ 52,400

1987 - $70,884

Jan	**Super Stars of Poker, Tahoe**		
	No-Limit Hold'em	2nd	Ford Mustang
	$ 1K Razz	3rd	$ 4,800
Jan	**America's Cup of Poker 1987, Las Vegas**		
	$ 1.5K Pot-Limit Omaha	3rd	$ 11,250
	$ 750 Limit Hold'em	6th	$ 1,549

Feb	**Amarillo Slim's Superbowl of Poker, Las Vegas**		
	$ 1K 7-Card Stud	6th	$ 5,150
May	**18th World Series of Poker, Las Vegas**		
	$ 1.5K No-Limit Hold'em	7th	$ 17,160
	$ 1K 7-Card Stud	14th	$ 2,590
Jun	**1987 Knights of the Round Table, Atlantic City**		
	$ 500 Limit 7-Card Stud	1st	$ 24,000
Nov	**1987 Pot of Gold, Reno**		
	$ 200 Limit Hold'em	5th	$ 2,024
	$ 300 Limit A-5 Lowball	4th	$ 2,361
Nov	**3rd Annual Diamond Jim Brady, L.A. (Bell Gardens)**		
	$ 300 Limit Hold'em	16th	$ 1,250

1988 - $13,528

Jan	**Super Stars of Poker, Tahoe**		
	$ 500 Limit Hold'em	4th	$ 3,080
Apr	**1988 Pot of Gold, Reno**		
	$ 200 Limit Hold'em	2nd	$ 6,920
	$ 200 Limit Omaha Hi/Lo	5th	$ 2,028
May	**19th World Series of Poker, Las Vegas**		
	$ 1,500 Limit Hold'em	23rd	$ 1,500

1989 - $91,990+

Jan	**Super Stars of Poker, Tahoe**		
	$ 500 + 30 7-Card Stud	1st	?
May	**20th World Series of Poker, Las Vegas**		
	$ 1K Limit Hold'em	14th	$ 4,490
Jul	**7th Annual America's Cup, Las Vegas**		
	$ 1K No-Limit Hold'em	1st	$ 17,500
Dec	**Hall of Fame Poker Classic 1989, Las Vegas**		
	$ 2.5K Pot-Limit Omaha	1st	$ 70,000

1990 - $127,628

Jan	**Super Stars of Poker, Tahoe**		
	$ 2.5K No-Limit Hold'em	6th	$ 4,764
	$ 300 Pot-Limit Hold'em	1st	$ 23,625
	$ 300 Limit Hold'em	2nd	$ 13,651
Mar	**1990 Winnin' o' The Green, L.A. (Bell Gardens)**		
	$ 300 Limit Hold'em	8th	$ 2,060
May	**21st World Series of Poker, Las Vegas**		
	$ 1.5K Limit Omaha	8th	$ 5,340
Jun	**US Open, Las Vegas**		
	$ 300 Pot-Limit Omaha	8th	$ 1,818
	$ 200 Limit Omaha	2nd	$ 5,900
Aug	**6th Diamond Jim Brady, L.A. (Bell Gardens)**		
	$ 1.5K Hold'em/Lowball	3rd	$ 27,885
	$ 1.5K 7-Card Stud	2nd	$ 34,875
	$ 1K Limit Hold'em	8th	$ 3,530
Oct	**Final Four of Poker, Lake Tahoe**		
	$ 50 Hold'em	1st	$ 3,000
Nov	**National Finals, Las Vegas**		
	$ 200 7-Card Std/ Omha	7th	$ 1,180

1991 - $41,541

Jan	**King of the Hill, Lake Tahoe**		
	$ 250 Lowball / Hold'em	3rd	$ 660
Jun	**US Open, Las Vegas**		
	$ 500 Pot-Limit Omaha	4th	$ 3,800
	$ 300 + 30 P.L. Hold'em	8th	$ 1,800
Aug	**7th Diamond Jim Brady, L.A. (Bell Gardens)**		
	$ 500 NLH/ 7-Card Std	8th	$ 1,770
	$ 500 Omaha Hi/Lo	3rd	$ 9,030

Dec **National Finals, Las Vegas**
$ 300 Pot-Limit Hold'em 1st $ 24,480

1992 - $181,086

Jan **Queens Poker Classic II, Las Vegas**
$ 1K Pot-Limit Hold'em 4th $ 8,255

Apr **1992 Peppermill Spring Tournament, Reno**
$ 100 No-Limit Hold'em 4th $ 2,065

Apr **23rd World Series of Poker, Las Vegas**
$ 1.5K Omaha Limit 1st $ 79,200
$ 1.5K 7-Card Stud 2nd $ 60,300

Jun **LA Poker Classic, Los Angeles**
$ 1K 7-Card Stud 8th $ 2,010
$ 500 Hold'em/Lowball 16th $ 660

Aug **Jim Brady Tournament, L.A. (Bell Gardens)**
$ 5K No-Limit Hold'em 6th $ 12,600

Nov **Hall of Fame Poker Classic 1992, Las Vegas**
$ 1K Limit 7-Card Stud 3rd $ 10,600
$ 1.5K 7-Card Razz 8th $ 2,610

Nov **1992 Peppermill Fall Tournament, Reno**
$ 100 Omaha Hi/Lo 3rd $ 2,786

1993 - $44,735

Jan **Four Queens Poker Classic III, Las Vegas**
$ 500 Omaha Hi/Lo 4th $ 5,493
Limit Hold'em 14th $1,246

Mar **Masters of Poker Championship II, Gardena**
$ 100 Limit Hold'em 5th $ 2,940
$ 100 Lowball 6th $ 2,250

Mar **Bicycle Club March Madness, Bell Gardens**
Hold'em 1st $19,800

Apr	**Circus Circus Spring Poker Tournament, Reno**		
	$ 100 Hold'em	7th	$ 384
May	**24th World Series of Poker, Las Vegas**		
	$ 1.5K 7-Card Razz	7th	$ 5,805
Jul	**Gold Coast Open, Las Vegas**		
	$ 200 Limit Hold'em	9th	$ 1,079
Oct	**Oktober Pokerfest, Los Angeles (Bell Gardens)**		
	$ 300 Limit Hold'em	5th	$ 3,150
Nov	**1993 LA Poker Open, Gardena**		
	$ 200 Omaha Hi/Lo	9th	$ 324
	$ 200 7-Card Stud Hi/Lo	9th	$ 284
Dec	**1993 Winter Oasis, Las Vegas**		
	$ 100 Omaha	3rd	$ 1,980

1994 - $119,847

Jan	**Queens Poker Classic IV, Las Vegas**		
	$ 1K Omaha Hi/Lo	4th	$ 8,190
	$ 1K 7-Card Razz	6th	$ 3,900
	$ 500 No-Limit Hold'em	12th	$ 2,364
	$ 500 7-Card Stud	7th	$ 2,760
Feb	**U LA Poker Classic III - 1994, Los Angeles**		
	$ 300 No-Limit Hold'em	4th	$ 6,806
	$ 300 7-Card Stud	13th	$ 618
Mar	**Masters of Poker Championship III, Gardena**		
	$ 500 Limit Hold'em	1st	$ 10,200
	$ 300 No-Limit Hold'em	2nd	$ 6,969
	$ 500 1/2 NLH/ Lowball	3rd	$ 2,400
	$ 300 Omaha	1st	$ 7,320
	$ 300 Lowball	8th	$ 603
	$ 300 Limit Hold'em	14th	$ 363
May	**25th World Series of Poker, Las Vegas**		
	$ 1.5K Limit Omaha	14th	$ 2,085

	$ 1.5K Limit Hold'em	9th	$ 10,845
Jul	**1st Annual Seniors Championship of Poker, Oceanside**		
	$ 500 No-Limit Hold'em	6th	$ 1,050
Aug	**10th Annual Diamond Jim Brady, Oceanside**		
	Points championship	1st	$ 30,000 + car
	$ 1K Limit Hold'em	1st	$ 41,200
	$ 500 NLH/ 7-Card Stud	6th	$ 2,220
Sep	**Queens Poker Classic Summer Edition, Las Vegas**		
	$ 500 No-Limit Hold'em	9th	$ 1,320
Oct	**Big Poker Oktober - 1994, Los Angeles (Bell Gardens)**		
	$ 200 Limit Hold'em	7th	$ 599
	$ 200 Limit Hold'em	1st	$ 11,520
Dec	**1994 World Poker Finals, Mashantucket**		
	$ 100 Omaha	1st	$ 4,680
	$ 500 No-Limit Hold'em	1st	$ 14,800
	$ 1K Pot-Limit Hold'em	2nd	$ 8,160
Dec	**Hall of Fame Poker Classic 1994, Las Vegas**		
	$ 5K No-Limit Hold'em	9th	$ 9,200
	$ 1K No-Limit Hold'em	5th	$ 9,675

1995 - $143,509

Mar	**1995 Peppermill Spring Tournament, Reno**		
	$ 200 Limit Hold'em	2nd	$ 8,008
Apr	**Run For The Roses, Inglewood**		
	$ 200 Limit Hold'em	8th	$ 540
May	**26th World Series of Poker 1995, Las Vegas**		
	$ 1,500 PLO	3rd	$ 35,850
May	**Masters of Poker Championship III, Gardena**		
	$ 50 No-Limit Hold'em	1st	$ 4,325
Jun	**Queens Poker Classic Summer Edition, Las Vegas**		
	$ 500 Pot-Limit Omaha	1st	$ 28,400
	$ 300 Limit Hold'em	9th	$ 715

	$ 300 Pot-Limit Hold'em	4th	$ 4,053
Jun	**1995 Peppermill Summer Tournament, Reno**		
	$ 120 Limit Hold'em	4th	$ 1,376
	$ 120 No-Limit Hold'em	7th	$ 498
	$ 330 Limit Hold'em	5th	$ 1,350
Sept	**1995 Card Player Cruise, International**		
	No-Limit Hold'em	2nd	$ 2,440
Sept	**1995 Four Queens Poker Classic, Las Vegas**		
	$ 500 No-Limit Hold'em	2nd	$ 21,300
	$ 500 Limit Hold'em	4th	$ 7,737
Sept	**1995 Peppermill Fall Tournament, Reno**		
	$ 100 Limit Hold'em	3rd	$ 3,727
Oct	**LA Poker Open III, Gardena**		
	$ 300 Limit Hold'em	7th	$ 800
	$ 100 Limit Hold'em	4th	$ 750
	$ 300 No-Limit Hold'em	7th	$ 750
	$ 100 No-Limit Hold'em	2nd	$ 3,900
	$ 100 NLH/7-Card Stud	4th	$ 700
	$ 50 7-Card Stud	6th	$ 360
	$ 50 Limit Hold'em	8th	$ 450
Nov	**1995 World Championship of H.O.R.S.E, Inglewood**		
	$ 300 Razz	1st	$ 6,600
	$ 300 Omaha Hi/Lo	1st	$ 8,880

1996 - $53,495

Feb	**1996 L.A. Poker Classic, Los Angeles**		
	$ 300 7-Card Stud	2nd	$ 8,040
May	**Masters of Poker Championship IV, Gardena**		
	$ 300 No-Limit Hold'em	4th	$ 2,525
Aug	**1996 Legends of Poker, Los Angeles (Bell Gardens)**		
	$ 300 + 30 7-Card Stud	3rd	$ 6,300

Aug	**Seniors III, Oceanside**		
	$ 300 + 30 H.O.R.S.E	2nd	$ 2,500
	$ 2K No-Limit Hold'em	5th	$ 1,100
Sep	**August Sizzle, Lake Elsinore**		
	$ 500 No-Limit Hold'em	1st	$ 5,250
Sep	**1996 Four Queens Poker Classic, Las Vegas**		
	$ 535 Limit Hold'em	7th	$ 1,650
	$ 1,055 7-Card Stud	4th	$ 4,800
Oct	**LA Poker Open IV, Gardena**		
	$ 330 Limit Hold'em	8th	$ 690
	$ 220 NLH/Stud Tag Team	1st	$ 4,000
Oct	**1996 Big Poker Oktober, L.A. (Bell Gardens)**		
	$ 200 Limit Hold'em	5th	$ 2,500
Nov	**1996 U.S.Poker Championship, Atlantic City**		
	$ 7.5K No-Limit Hold'em	12th	$ 7,000
	$ 1.5K Pot-Limit Omaha	4th	$ 7,140

1997 - $211,895

Mar	**Card Player Cruises, International**		
	$ 200 Omaha Hi/Lo	7th	$ 320
Apr	**28th World Series of Poker, Las Vegas**		
	$ 3K Hold'em Pot-Limit	2nd	$ 102,000
	$ 2K Hold'em Pot-Limit	3rd	$ 46,930
	$ 1.5K 7-Card Stud	3rd	$ 36,622
Jun	**Masters of Poker Championship V, Gardena**		
	$ 100 Limit Hold'em	5th	$ 800
	$ 100 7-Card Stud	3rd	$ 825
	$ 50 7-Card Stud	6th	$ 325
	$ 50 Omaha Hi/Lo	4th	$ 1,000
Oct	**1997 Peppermill Fall Tournament, Reno**		
	$ 200 Limit Hold'em	3rd	$ 15,708

Oct **10 Days of Poker, Lake Elsinore**
   No-Limit Hold'em 1st $ 6,610
Dec **1997 World Poker Finals, Mashantucket**
   $ 500 No-Limit Hold'em 9th $ 755

1998 - $33,600

Jan **International Pot-Limit Rendezvous, Oceanside**
   $ 300 Pot-Limit Omaha 9th $ 750
   $ 500 Pot-Limit Hold'em 6th $ 1,320
Jan **Carnivale of Poker, Las Vegas**
   $ K 7-Card Stud 6th $ 4,060
Jan **Drive for Five, Lake Elsinore**
   $ 60 Limit Hold'em 4th $ 1,200
Feb **1998 L.A. Poker Classic, Los Angeles**
   $ 300 Limit Hold'em 4th $ 4,254
May **29th World Series of Poker, Las Vegas**
   $ 3K Limit Hold'em 17th $ 5,130
Aug **Poker Challenge Week, Compton**
   $ 100 No-Limit Hold'em 2nd $ 8,436
Sep **3rd Annual Ventura Poker Championships, Ventura**
   $ 100 Omaha Hi/Lo 1st $ 2,730
Nov **1998 Tom McEvoy Poker Spectacular, Compton**
   $ 100 Razz/Omaha/Stud 6th $ 1,600
Dec **$50,000 Guaranteed Ladies Challenge, Compton**
   Omaha Hi/Lo/NLH Team 1st $ 4,120

1999 - $3,480

Apr **1999 Spring Challenge, Compton**
   $ 100 No-Limit Hold'em 4th $ 1,470
Sep **1999 Fall Vacation Tournament, Lake Elsinore**
   $ 300 Limit/NLH 6th $ 1,080

Oct   **Big Poker Oktober - 1999, L.A. (Bell Gardens)**

$ 200 Limit Hold'em   6th $ 930

2000 - $35,411

Jan   **Carnivale of Poker III, Las Vegas**

$ 500 Pot-Limit Omaha   2nd $ 17,400

Jun   **2000 America's Poker Classic, L.A. (Bell Gardens)**

$ 500 Limit Hold'em   2nd $ 9,545

$ 300 Pot-Limit Hold'em   3rd $ 4,680

Jun   **2000 Card Player Cruise - Alaska, Cruise**

$ 200 Limit Hold'em   2nd $ 1,600

Jul   **2000 Orleans Open, Las Vegas**

$ 260 Limit Omaha   6th $ 2,010

Oct   **Celebrity Poker Challenge, San Jose Costa Rica**

$ 10 Omaha Hi-Lo   10th $ 176

2001 - $69,987

Jan   **1st Annual World Poker Challenge, Reno**

$ 500 No-Limit Hold'em   3rd $ 13,408

$ 500 Pot-Limit Hold'em   5th $ 4,169

Feb   **2001 L.A. Poker Classic, Los Angeles**

$ 1K Pot-Limit Hold'em   4th $ 6,370

May   **32nd World Series of Poker, Las Vegas**

$ 3K Hold'em (pot limit)   15th $ 6,575

$ 2K S.H.O.E.   3rd $ 35,115

$ 1.5K Omaha (limit)   9th $ 3,350

Nov   **2001 Tom McEvoy Poker Spectacular, Inglewood**

$ 500 No-Limit Hold'em   8th $ 650

$ 200 Omaha Hi-Lo   8th $ 350

2002 - $112,221

Jan	**2002 World Poker Challenge, Reno**		
	$ 500 No-Limit Hold'em	5th	$ 3,143
	$ 300 7-Card Stud Hi/Lo	5th	$ 2,033
Feb	**2002 L.A. Poker Classic, Los Angeles**		
	$ 7K No-Limit Hold'em	4th	$ 60,000
	$ 1K No-Limit Hold'em	17th	$ 1,720
Mar	**Casinos Europa Invitational, San Jose Costa Rica**		
	$ 100 No-Limit Hold'em	2nd	$ 12,956
Apr	**Bellagio High Buy-in Tournament Series, Las Vegas**		
	$ 3.1K No-Limit Hold'em	16th	$ 3,987
Apr	**33rd World Series of Poker, Las Vegas**		
	$ 1K Seniors NLH	32nd	$ 1,480
	$ 2.5K NLH Match Play	3rd	$ 8,575
Jun	**Linda Johnson Celebrity Challenge, Costa Rica**		
	$ 10 NLH - Scotty Nguyen	2nd	$ 9,865
Sep	**Hall of Fame Poker Classic 2002, Las Vegas**		
	$ 1.5K Razz	5th	$ 1,820
	$ 500 Omaha Hi/Lo	5th	$ 1,820
	$ 500 Limit Hold'em	5th	$ 2,350
Nov	**3rd Annual 49'er Gold Rush Bonanza, San Francisco**		
	$ 500 NLH Shootout	9th	$ 1,000
Dec	**Bellagio Five Diamond Poker Classic, Las Vegas**		
	$1K Pot-Limit Hold'em	13th	$ 1,472

2003 - $26,320

Jan	**WPT Jack Binion World Poker Open, Tunica**		
	$ 10K No-Limit Hold'em	19th	$ 9,162
Feb	**Larry Flynt's Poker Challenge Cup, Gardena**		
	$ 200 No-Limit Hold'em	8th	$ 1,185
May	**34th World Series of Poker, Las Vegas**		
	$ 1.5K No-Limit Hold'em	36th	$ 2,500

	$ 1.5K Limit Omaha	14th	$ 2,300
Aug	**BARGE 2003, Las Vegas**		
	$ 80 No-Limit Hold'em	16th	$ 100
Sep	**2003 Four Queens Poker Classic, Las Vegas**		
	$ 100 No-Limit Hold'em	1st	$ 9,959
	$ 100 Seniors NLH	5th	$ 599
	$ 100 No-Limit Hold'em	8th	$ 515

2004 - $50,750

Jan	**Jack Binion World Poker Open, Tunica**		
	$ 500 Pot-Limit Hold'em	24th	$ 1,222
Feb	**2004 L.A. Poker Classic, Los Angeles**		
	$ 300 Limit Hold'em	23rd	$ 2,470
Feb	**WPT Bay 101 Shooting Star, San Jose**		
	$ 1.5K No-Limit Hold'em	9th	$ 4,530
Mar	**7th Annual Spring Poker Roundup, Pendleton**		
	$ 150 No-Limit Hold'em	2nd	$ 12,290
	$ 150 Omaha Hi/Lo	3rd	$ 6,398
	$ 150 7-Card Stud	6th	$ 1,600
May	**35th World Series of Poker, Las Vegas**		
	$ 1.5K No-Limit Hold'em	77th	$ 1,720
Jun	**Festa al Lago II, Las Vegas**		
	$ 1K No-Limit Hold'em	27th	$ 1,727
Sep	**2004 Four Queens Poker Classic, Las Vegas**		
	$ 100 No-Limit Hold'em	2nd	$ 2,300
	$ 100 No-Limit Hold'em	3rd	$ 2,270
Sep	**WPT 2004 Ultimatebet.com Poker Classic, Aruba**		
	$ 6K No-Limit Hold'em	137th	$ 7,000
Nov	**2004 Fall Poker Round Up, Pendleton**		
	$ 150 Omaha Hi/Lo	3rd	$ 7,223

2005 - $316,802

Mar	**WPT Bay 101 Shooting Star, San Jose**		
	No-Limit Hold'em	1st	$ 225K
Mar	**Rio Las Vegas Poker Festival, Las Vegas**		
	$ 1K No-Limit Hold'em	14th	$ 2,910
	$ 2K No-Limit Hold'em	16th	$ 3,510
Apr	**WPT 3rd Annual Five-Star World Poker Classic, L.V.**		
	$ 25K NLH Main Event	74th	$ 30,000
Apr	**Plaza World Poker Classic, Las Vegas**		
	$ 1K No-Limit Hold'em	5th	$ 5,730
May	**2005 Mirage Poker Showdown, Las Vegas**		
	$ 2K Pot-Limit Hold'em	3rd	$ 20,952
Jun	**36th World Series of Poker, Las Vegas**		
	$ 1.5K Limit Hold'em	28th	$ 2,795
Oct	**Bellagio Festa Al Lago IV, Las Vegas**		
	$ 1.5K No-Limit Hold'em	10th	$ 5,370
Nov	**2005 Fall Poker Round Up, Pendleton**		
	$ 500 Main Event – NLH	4th	$ 20,130
	$ 200 Omaha Hi/Lo	12th	$ 405

2006 - $32,020

Jan	**WPT PokerStars Caribbean, Paradise Isle, Bahamas**		
	$ 7.8K NLH Main Event	95th	$ 10,700
Jan	**The Seneca World Poker Classic, Niagara Falls**		
	$ 200 No-Limit Hold'em	24th	$ 160
	$ 1.5K Can/U.S. NLH	7th	$ 4,990
	$ 300 OK Johnny Hale Evt	19th	$ 390
May	**Mandalay Bay Poker Championship, Las Vegas**		
	$ 2K No-Limit Hold'em	8th	$ 5,780
Jun	**PokerStars.com World Cup, Barcelona, Spain**		
	No-Limit Hold'em	2nd	$ 10,000

Sept	**37th World Series of Poker, Las Vegas**		
	$ 1.5 No-Limit Hold'em	11th	$ 6,306
	$ 10K NLH Main Event	371st	$ 34,636

2007 - $64,421

Feb	**The Wynn Classic, Las Vegas**		
	$ 1K No-Limit Hold'em	2nd	$ 32,786
Mar	**WPT Bay 101 Shooting Star, San Jose**		
	$ 1,920 NLH	16th	$ 4,500
Mar	**World Poker Challenge, Reno**		
	$ 2K No-Limit Hold'em	17th	$ 3,790
Apr	**WPT Poker by the Book: Chapter 2, Las Vegas**		
	No-Limit Hold'em	2nd	$0
May	**Mirage Poker Showdown, Las Vegas**		
	$ 1K No-Limit Hold'em	20th	$ 1,402
Jun	**38th World Series of Poker, Las Vegas**		
	$ 2K No-Limit Hold'em	93rd	$ 5,378
	$ K Seniors NLH	34th	$ 8,820
	$ 1.5K No-Limit Hold'em	239th	$ 2,947
	$ 1.5K No-Limit Hold'em	202nd	$ 3,408
Aug	**Oasis Open, Mesquite**		
	$ 80 No-Limit Hold'em	4th	$ 1,390

2008 - $28,947

Apr	**WPT World Championship, Las Vegas**		
	$ 2.5K Seniors NLH	14th	$ 3,375
Jun	**39th World Series of Poker, Las Vegas**		
	$ 1K Seniors NLH Event	28th	$ 7,669
	$ 1.5K Pot-Limit Hold'em	24th	$ 5,547
Jul	**Eureka Summer Open 2008, Mesquite**		
	$ 80 No-Limit Hold'em	1st	$ 1,080

Oct	**2008 Caesars Palace Classic, Las Vegas**		
	$ 500 PLH/Omaha	2nd	$ 8,924
	$ 500 Pot-Limit Omaha	7th	$ 2,352

2009 - $32,898+

Jan	**PokerStars Caribbean Adv., Paradise Isle, Bahamas**		
	$ 9.K NLH Main Event	134th	$ 12,500
Mar	**Dream Team Poker Championship, Las Vegas**		
	$ 1.5K NLH Team Event	6th	$ 3,996
Apr	**European Poker Tour, Sanremo, Italy**		
	€ 5,000 NLH - Main Event	106th	$ 7,595
May	**40th World Series of Poker, Las Vegas**		
	Champion of Champions	1st	Car
Jun	**40th World Series of Poker, Las Vegas**		
	$ 2K No-Limit Hold'em	53rd	$ 8,807

2010 - $20,221

Jan	**PokerStars Caribbean, Paradise Island Bahamas**		
	$ 500 Pot-Limit Omaha	2nd	$ 2,330
	$ 1K No-Limit Hold'em	12th	$ 3,125
Feb	**NAPT 2010 Deep Stack Extravaganza, Las Vegas**		
	$ 5K No-Limit Hold'em	101st	$ 8,839
Jun	**41st World Series of Poker, Las Vegas**		
	$ 1.5K Pot-Limit Hold'em	41st	$ 3,992
Sep	**TJ Cloutier Choctaw Poker Classic, Durant**		
	$ 120 No-Limit Hold'em	6th	$ 618
Oct	**Festa Al Lago, Las Vegas**		
	$ 500 No-Limit Hold'em	49th	$ 677
Nov	**Venetian Deep Stack Extravaganza IV, Las Vegas**		
	$ 300 No-Limit Hold'em	34th	$ 640

2011 - $20.499

Apr	**2011 Deep Stack Extravaganza II, Las Vegas**		
	$ 330 H.O.R.S.E.	3rd	$ 3,242
Apr	**2011 2011 Spring Poker Round-Up, Pendleton**		
	$ 150 Limit Hold'em	7th	$ 1,396
June/Jul	**2011 42nd World Series of Poker, Las Vegas**		
	$ 1.5K No-Limit Hold'em	302nd	$ 2,882
	$ 1K No-Limit Hold'em	177th	$ 2,628
Oct	**2011 TJ Cloutier Choctaw Poker Challenge, OK**		
	$ 400 No-Limit Hold'em	13th	$ 897
Dec	**2011 Aruba Poker Open, Palm Beach, Aruba**		
	$ 560 No-Limit Hold'em	2nd	$ 4,729
	$ 125 No-Limit Hold'em	1st	$ 1,725
	$ 235 No-Limit Hold'em	1st	$ 2,000
	$ 125 No-Limit Hold'em	3rd	$ 1,000

2012 - $19,990

Feb	**Deep Stack Extravaganza I, Las Vegas**		
	$ 340 PLO - Triple Barrel	8th	$ 822
May	**Grand Challenge Tournament Series, Las Vegas**		
	$ 200 H.O.R.S.E. Event 21	6th	$ 795
	$ 200 H.O.R.S.E. Event 10	1st	$ 2,892
May	**Chop Pot Poker Classic, Reno**		
	$ 100 H.O.R.S.E.	1st	$ 1,534
Jun	**2012 Mega Stack Series, Las Vegas**		
	$ 200 Pot-Limit Omaha	9th	$ 868
Nov	**Golden Saturday Poker Tournament, Las Vegas**		
	$ 100 No-Limit Hold'em	7th	$ 1,437

2013 - $11,642

| Jun | **Rio Daily Deepstacks, Las Vegas** | | |
| | $ 235 No Limit Hold'em | 141st | $ 366 |

	$ 235 No Limit Hold'em	111th	$ 373
Dec	**WSOP Circuit - WSOPC San Diego, San Diego**		
	$ 580 No Limit Hold'em	2nd	$ 10,903

2014 - $10,240

Jan	**Senior Poker Tour - SPT Tunica, Tunica**		
	$ 200 PLO – Turbo	2nd	$ 1,319
	$ 150 LH/Omaha Hi/Lo	1st	$ 655
Feb	**Deep Stack Extravaganza I, Las Vegas**		
	$ 300 H.O.R.S.E – Survivor	1st	$ 2,000
Mar	**2014 Wynn Classic, Las Vegas**		
	$ 500 No-Limit Hold'em	17th	$ 1,135
Mar	**Atlantis All-In Poker Series, Reno**		
	$ 200 NLH - Mega Stack	6th	$ 837
	$ 100 NLH - Survivor	5th	$ 365
	$ 300 NLH - Final Day	6th	$ 2,709
Jun	**8th Annual Binion's Poker Classic, Las Vegas**		
	$ 200 Pot-Limit Omaha	5th	$ 700
	$ 200 Pot-Limit Omaha	7th	$ 520

2015 - $13,963

Apr	**2015 Master's Series, Dover**		
	$ 150 No-Limit Hold'em	1st	$ 2,850
	$ 150 H.O.S. Event	4th	$ 1,200
May	**2015 Orleans Poker Open, Las Vegas**		
	$ 330 No-Limit Hold'em	2nd	$ 3,575
	$ 230 H.O.R.S.E.	5th	$ 2,247
Oct	**Dover Downs Masters Poker Series Fall OPEN, Dover**		
	$ 500 NLH - Sr Event	7th	$ 2,000
	$ 200 NLH - DeepStack	7th	$ 1,000
	$ 100 NLH - Meet Masters	3rd	$ 1,091

2016 - $23,175

Jun   **2016 Binion's Poker Classic, Las Vegas**

$ 240 7-Card Stud   2nd $ 2,150

Jul   **47th World Series of Poker, Las Vegas**

$ 10,000 NLH Main Event 644th $ 18,714

$ 1,500 Pot-Limit Omaha   93rd $ 2,311

2017 - $16,349

Apr   **Deepstack Extravaganza II, Las Vegas**

$ 1,600 NLH - Superstack   10th $ 8,248

Jun   **Grand Poker Series, Las Vegas**

$ 250 NLH - Super Seniors   10th $ 1,545

Nov   **DeepStack Extravaganza IV, Las Vegas**

$ 400 PLO Bounty   1st $ 4,263

Dec   **December Extravaganza, Las Vegas**

$ 400 NLH - Double Stack 8th $ 2,293

2018 - $31,613

Jan   **WPT Lucky Hearts Poker Open, Hollywood**

$ 120 No-Limit Hold'em   9th $ 723

Feb   **DeepStack Extravaganza I, Las Vegas**

$ 300 LO - Bounty   6th $ 842

Jun   **Rio Daily Deepstacks 2018, Las Vegas**

$ 250 NLH - 1PM   115th $ 423

Jul   **49th World Series of Poker, Las Vegas**

$ 10,000 NLH Main Event 430th $ 29,625

2019 - $7,763

Jun   **50th World Series of Poker, Las Vegas**

$ 400 NLH - Colossus   93rd $ 3,546

$ 1,000 NLH - Super Srs.   283rd $ 1,772

$ 500 NLH - BIG 50   2085th $ 1,220

Nov   **Aria Casino Recurring Tournaments, Las Vegas**

$ 110 No-Limit Hold'em   2nd $ 1,225

2020 - $3,340

Jul   **World Series of Poker - WSOP Online**

$ 1,000 NLH - Chmpnshp)   171st $ 2,222

$ 500 NLH - Senior's   97th $ 680

$ 100 NLH - The Opener   1454th $ 438

2021 - $7,552

May   **2021 South Point Recurring Tournaments, LV**

$ 60 NLH - 6pm   11th $ 106

Jul   **2021 Summer Poker Series, Las Vegas**

$ 150 NLH - Friday Night   19th $ 449

$ 150 NLH - Super Stack   21st $ 357

$ 150 NLH - Friday Night   16th $ 480

Oct   **52nd World Series of Poker, Las Vegas**

$ 1,000 PLO 8 Handed   67th $ 2,382

$ 1,500 7-Card Stud   29th $ 2,687

Oct   **Rio Daily Deep Stack Series 2021, Las Vegas**

$ 250 H.O.R.S.E.   18th $ 444

Nov   **Orleans Casino Recurring Tournaments, LV**

$ 130 NLH - Friday Night   13th $ 647

2022 - $4,998

Mar   **March Mania Poker Series, Las Vegas**

$ 150 NLH - Super Stack   16th $ 408

$ 150 NLH - Super Stack   10th $ 605

Aug   **Orleans Casino Recurring Tournaments, LV**

$ 150 NLH - Friday Night   6th $ 1,050

Oct   **2022 Orleans Fall Poker Open, Las Vegas**

$ 250 No-Limit Hold'em   36th $ 878

Dec   **WPT World Championship at Wynn, Las Vegas**
$ 515 + 85 H.O.R.S.E.   15th $ 2,057

Much data courtesy of the Henden Mob.

Winners in the higher echelon win roughly 1 start in 40.
                                  —Doyle Brunson

For a while there, with smaller fields, I was winning al-most 14 percent of my events. That didn't last very long. The realistic numbers are 15 percent to 20 percent of the time you will cash if you are really good. No more than 25 percent. I don't care who you are, you can't do better than that. They can keep track of your tournament wins, but not your net wins—which are substantially less. And they don't track your losses or cash games.

                                  —Tom McEvoy

ABOUT THE COAUTHOR

Life's experiences can run an unimagined path through our lives, creating memories that are ours to keep and treasure. My journey began when my advertising and public relations career took me to a trade show in Las Vegas in 1982, where I began my love affair with the city, and started my casino chip collection with a 50-cent beauty from the Riviera. I discovered other collectors and an international club, and joined the Casino Collectibles Association. As the number of my Vegas chips grew, so did my interest in learning more about the obsolete chips from long-forgotten casinos. After retirement, that fascination led me to research and write a series of articles for the club magazine titled *The Little-Known Casino Pioneers of Las Vegas*. The exposure led me to be asked to take on the PR Director position to promote the club's annual show/convention, held, of course, in Vegas. One of my PR ideas was to recruit VIPs to attend the show for a promotable meet-and-greet session, which is how I met Tom McEvoy.

I'm also a poker player, and I've cashed in three out of four WSOP tournaments so far. With history and poker in common, Tom and I hit it off immediately. He invited me to his home and started sharing his fascinating stories. I shared my Vegas articles with Tom, and the idea was born. Tom was a living example of Vegas and poker history, and we both wanted to get his poker life down on paper.

The last year and a half have been a labor of love, both for the history and for the man I've come to consider as one of my best friends. Will this book be successful? It's immaterial to me. What's driven me is the opportunity to tell Tom McEvoy's captivating story, and to document the many pioneering contributions he has made to the game we both love.

Many thanks to my life partner, Sharon, as well as all my friends (especially Gregg) and family for all of their support.

—Brad Smith